Argosy

**Junior
Certificate
ENGLISH**

Editor - J. Moriarty

© Copyright:- Mentor Publications 1991
All Rights Reserved

Text by :- Kate Keaveney
John Moriarty
Deirdre Lawrence

Edited by :- John Moriarty

Typesetting :- Jill Quinn
Maria O'Reilly
Michelle Keegan

Published by :- Mentor Publications,
43 Furze Road,
Sandyford Industrial Estate,
Dublin 18
Tel: (01) 2952112/3
Fax: (01) 2952114

ISBN:- 0 947548 08 4

5 7 9 10 8 6

The Title — ARGOSY

The word ARGOSY is a poetic reference of Greek origin meaning a large richly laden merchant ship.

The Cover

The Publishers wish to thank the National Gallery of Ireland for permission to reproduce the painting, *An emigrant ship, Dublin Bay, sunset, 1853* by Edwin Hayes (1819 - 1904).

Printed in Ireland by Colour Books Ltd., Dublin.

Contents

I - Short Stories

The Kitten	*Alexander Reid*	10
The Confessional	*Seán O Faoláin*	16
My True Kinsman	*Brian Friel*	22
The Secret Life of Walter Mitty	*James Thurber*	32
You're On Next Sunday	*John B. Keane*	39
The New Gardener	*Mary Lavin*	44
The Night the Ghost Got In	*James Thurber*	52
The Gift	*Ray Bradbury*	59
The Lumber Room	*Saki*	63
The Osage Orange Tree	*William Stafford*	70
Eveline	*James Joyce*	78
Nagasaki	*Aidan Carl Mathews*	86
The Fun They Had	*Isaac Asinov*	94
At the River-Gates	*Philippa Pearce*	98
The Diamond Maker	*H. G. Wells*	108
Flight	*Doris Lessing*	117
The Hook	*Liam O'Flaherty*	125
The Wolves of Cernogratz	*Saki*	130
The Moustache	*Robert Cormier*	135

II - Drama

The Shadow of a Gunman	*Seán O'Casey*	145
Ernie's Incredible Illucinations	*Alan Ayckbourn*	187
A Villa on Venus	*Kenneth Lillington*	201

III - Poetry

The Night Mail	*W. H. Auden*	212
Greer County	*Traditional American*	215
The Discovery	*J. C. Squire*	217
The Tigress	*Clifford Dyment*	220
Anthem for Doomed Youth	*Wilfred Owen*	221
The Road Not Taken	*Robert Frost*	223

Poetry (Continued)

The Man He Killed	*Thomas Hardy*	225
Snow in the Suburbs	*Thomas Hardy*	228
At the Railway Station, Upway	*Thomas Hardy*	230
Heredity	*Thomas Hardy*	232
Thomas MacDonagh	*Francis Ledwidge*	233
To Simon	*Patrick Devaney*	235
Basking Shark - Achill Island	*John F. Deane*	236
The Early Purges	*Seamus Heaney*	238
Interruption to a Journey	*Norman MacCaig*	241
Boy at the Window	*Richard Wilbur*	243
Harvest Hymn	*John Betjeman*	245
The Windmill	*H. W. Longfellow*	247
The Unknown Citizen	*W. H. Auden*	249
A Christmas Childhood	*Patrick Kavanagh*	251
In Memory of My Mother	*Patrick Kavanagh*	254
Epic	*Patrick Kavanagh*	256
On Raglan Road	*Patrick Kavanagh*	258
Morning Song	*Sylvia Plath*	259
Born Yesterday	*Philip Larkin*	261
My Grandmother	*Elizabeth Jennings*	263
Silver	*Walter de la Mare*	265
Snow	*Walter de la Mare*	267
The Snow	*Emily Dickinson*	269
The Fog	*W. H. Davies*	271
From Trabzon to Gumushane	*Bernard Kennedy*	273
The Tom-cat	*Don Marquis*	275
Travelling through the Dark	*William Stafford*	277
Hide and Seek	*Vernon Scannell*	279
Sea	*Brendan Kennelly*	281
The Coming of the Cold	*Theodore Roethke*	283
Uncle Jack and the Other Man	*Keith Harrison*	285
Hard Cheese	*Justin St. John*	287
Haiku	*Various*	290
Praise of a Collie	*Norman MacCaig*	291
Vegetarians	*Roger McGough*	293
Child on Top of a Greenhouse	*Theodore Roethke*	294
The Bat	*Theodore Roethke*	295
He Wishes for the Cloths of Heaven	*W. B. Yeats*	296
The Wild Swans at Coole	*W. B. Yeats*	298

IV - Media Studies

Mass Media	300
I - Making the Headlines Hit!	301
Read All About It!	302
Verbs in Headlines	305
Word Play in Headlines	307
II - Writing News Reports	312
Sentence Structure in News Reports	314
News Reports - Different Styles	316
Paragraphs in News Reports	320
III - Commenting on the News	324
Editorials	324
Letters to the Editor	331
Features	334
Writers' Workshop	339
Essay Writing	339
Keeping a Diary	341
Reviews (T.V. and Radio)	342
Book Reviews	344
Crosswords (Nos. 1-5)	348 - 352
IV - Advertising	353
Advertisements - Questions and Assignments	355 - 370

V - Novels

(Introduction and Questions on . . .)

Goodnight Mister Tom	*Michelle Magorian*	372
The Silver Sword	*Ian Serraillier*	372
The Red Pony	*John Steinbeck*	373
Going Solo	*Roald Dahl*	373
The Hobbit	*J. R. R. Tolkien*	373
The Machine-Gunners	*Robert Westall*	376
Buddy's Song	*Nigel Hinton*	376
Carrie's War	*Nina Bawden*	376
Walkabout	*James Vance Marshall*	377
Z for Zachariah	*Robert O'Brien*	380
The Ghost of Thomas Kempe	*Penelope Lively*	380
Rua, The Red Grouse	*Patrick Devaney*	380
The Twelfth Day of July	*Joan Lingard*	381
To Kill a Mockingbird	*Harper Lee*	381
General Questions on Novels		383
Index		384

Introduction

ARGOSY meets the requirements of the *Junior Certificate English* programme and is principally aimed at Second and Third Year students preparing for **Ordinary or Higher levels**.

Divided into five sections - **Short Stories, Poetry, Drama, Media Studies** and **Novels**, - it provides a wide selection of material and offers teachers much scope in devising a variety of Units to suit the needs of their particular classes. The views and advice of many experienced teachers of Junior Certificate English were taken into consideration in selecting and devising the material in this book.

Special Features

Questions and Assignments

The *Questions and Assignments* which follow all items provide opportunities for both written and oral work. Most of these *Questions and Assignments* are suitable for students of all abilities, though a proportion are clearly more suited to Higher Level students. Many of the questions and assignments are modelled on sample papers issued for the *Junior Certificate*. The written responses will provide students with a record of the literature they have studied and their responses to it. This in turn will clearly be a useful examination aid.

Points to Note

These follow most items and aim to highlight important features relating to style and technique. All relevant literary terms, including those listed in the syllabus, are clearly explained in the context of the short stories, poems, plays and media extracts in which they arise. A knowledge of these literary terms provides students with the technical language for discussing and writing about all forms of literature as well as a solid foundation for *Senior English*. An integrated approach is also adopted towards grammar and its importance, in clear and accurate writing, is stressed.

Writers' Workshop

This section offers a set of practical guidelines to develop students' writing skills. This section also reviews and develops the points already covered in *"Writing for Junior Certificate" (Odyssey)*.

Outline Short Story Ideas

These aim to help students write their own stories. With a little imagination, each idea can be developed into many of different stories.

✓ — Sample Answers

These should not be regarded as model answers but rather as guidelines for students on possible approaches to the type of questions they are likely to face in the examination. It will be clear to teachers that a number of the sample answers will be relevant to Higher Level students only. A further selection of sample answers - principally on *Media Studies* and *Novels* - is included in the Teacher's Handbook.

V Vocabulary Development

The book contains a selection of word games - anagrams, matching words to meanings, crosswords, cloze tests, proof correcting etc. - designed to improve spelling, vocabulary, syntax and other literacy skills. These word games are intentionally demanding and some pupils may encounter difficulties. Should this occur, teachers can provide additional clues, such as the initial letters of the solutions. Answers to all word games are included in the Teacher's Handbook.

The *Index* provides a quick reference guide.

A Teacher's Audio Cassette **Tape** plus **Teacher's Handbook** is available **FREE of Charge** to teachers using **ARGOSY** as a class text.

ACKNOWLEDGEMENTS

For permission to reproduce copyright material, the publishers and authors wish to thank the following :- Macmillan London Limited, for The Shadow of a Gunman by Seán O'Casey; The Abbey Theatre, Dublin and Fergus Bourke Photography for photographs of the 1990 Production of The Shadow of a Gunman; Margaret Ramsey Ltd., St. Martin's Lane, London for Ernie's Incredible Illucinations by Alan Ayckbourn. (Caution: All rights whatsoever in this play are strictly reserved and application for performance etc., should be made before rehearsal to Margaret Ramsey Ltd., 14a Goodwin's Court, St. Martin's Lane, London WC 2N 4LL. No performance may be given unless a licence has been obtained.) The National Gallery of Ireland for An Emigrant Ship, Dublin Bay, Sunset, 1853, by Edwin Hayes; the Portrait of James Joyce by Jacques Emile Blanche and the Portrait of Seán O'Casey by Harry Kernoff; Patrick Devaney for the poem "To Simon"; Father Bernard Kennedy for the poem "From Trabzon to Gumushane". For Advertisements, photographs, visual material, and permission to reproduce same - the Voluntary Health Insurance Board, Lower Abbey Street, Dublin; Super Valu Supermarkets Limited, Group Marketing Office, Dublin; the Electricity Supply Board; Commuter Advertising Network (CAN), Lower Abbey Street, Dublin; Linguaphone Institute (Ireland) Limited, Upper Abbey Street; Mr. Philip Cozens of Boyne Valley Foods Limited, Drogheda and Killeen (Steel Wool) Limited, Drogheda, for his help; also the many Advertising Agencies for their invaluable help and assistance; Mr. Brendan McNamara for his advice and assistance with Advertisements; for artwork, photographs and illustrations - Brenda Fox, Helen Maher and A. M. Walker. Irish Times Limited, Newspaper, Dublin for various extracts; Independent Newspapers Limited and the Sunday Independent, Middle Abbey Street, Dublin; Irish Press Limited and The Sunday Press, Tara Street, Dublin; Evening Press, Tara Street, Dublin; The Sunday Tribune Newspaper, Dublin; The Liffey View Sound Studios for the recording of the Teacher's Audio tape; International Newsprint Limited, Paris, for selected extracts; European Photographic Library, Bonn, West Germany; Office of the European Commission, Brussels, Belgium, American Library of Congress, Washington D.C.; Mississippi Publications Limited, Atlanta, Georgia, USA for selected extracts and use of photographic material. For the book title - Liam Moriarty and John McCormack; for their patience, understanding, encouragement and support - Margaret, Paul, Liam, Nuala, Paddy, Brian and Seán.

At the date of publication the copyright source and ownership of a small number of extracts could not be accurately established. When the ownership of these extracts is established, the publishers are willing to fulfill any outstanding obligations.

I - SHORT STORIES

The Kitten

The feet were tramping directly towards her. In the hot darkness under the tarpaulin the cat cuffed a kitten to silence and listened intently.

She could hear the scruffling and scratching of hens about the straw-littered yard; the muffled grumbling of the turning churn in the dairy; the faint clink and jangle of harness from the stable — drowsy, comfortable, reassuring noises through which the clang of the iron-shod boots on the cobbles broke ominously.

The boots ground to a halt, and three holes in the cover, brilliant, diamond-points of light, went suddenly black. Couching, the cat waited, then sneezed and drew back as the tarpaulin was thrown up and glaring white sunlight struck at her eyes.

She stood over her kittens, the fur of her back bristling and the pupils of her eyes narrowed to pin-points. A kitten mewed plaintively.

For a moment, the hired man stared stupidly at his discovery, then turned towards the stable and called harshly: "Hi, Maister! Here a wee."

A second pair of boots clattered across the yard, and the face of the farmer, elderly, dark and taciturn, turned down on the cats.

"So, that's whaur she's been," commented the newcomer slowly.

He bent down to count the kittens and the cat struck at him, scoring a red furrow across the back of his wrist. He caught her by the neck and flung her roughly aside. Mewing she came back and began to lick her kittens. The Master turned away.

"Get rid of them," he ordered. "There's ower mony cats aboot this place."

"Aye, Maister," said the hired man.

Catching the mother he carried her, struggling and swearing, to the stable, flung her in, and latched the door. From the loft he secured an old potato sack and with this in his hand returned to the kittens.

There were five, and he noticed their tigerish markings without comprehending as, one by one, he caught them and thrust them into the bag. They were old enough to struggle, spitting, clawing and biting at his fingers.

Throwing the bag over his shoulder he stumped down the hill to the burn, stopping twice on the way to wipe the sweat that trickled down his face and neck, rising in beads between the roots of his lint-white hair.

Behind him, the buildings of the farmsteading shimmered in the heat. The few trees on the slope raised dry, brittle branches towards a sky bleached almost white. The smell of the farm, mingled with peat-reek, dung, cattle, milk, and the dark tang of the soil, was strong in his nostrils, and when he halted there was no sound but his own breathing and the liquid burbling of the burn.

Throwing the sack on the bank, he stepped into the stream. The water was low, and grasping a great boulder in the bed of the burn he strained to lift it, intending to make a pool.

He felt no reluctance at performing the execution. He had no feelings about the matter. He had drowned kittens before. He would drown them again.

Panting with his exertion, the hired man cupped water between his hands and dashed it over his face and neck in a glistening shower. Then he turned to the sack and its prisoners.

He was in time to catch the second kitten as it struggled out of the bag. Thrusting it back and twisting the mouth of the sack close, he went after the other. Hurrying on

The Kitten

the sun-browned grass, treacherous as ice, he slipped and fell headlong, but grasped the runaway in his outflung hand.

It writhed round immediately and sank needle-sharp teeth into his thumb so that he grunted with pain and shook it from him. Unhurt, it fell by a clump of whins and took cover beneath them.

The hired man, his stolidity shaken by frustration, tried to follow. The whins were thick and, scratched for his pains, he drew back, swearing flatly, without colour or passion.

Stooping he could see the eyes of the kitten staring at him from the shadows under the whins. Its back was arched, its fur erect, its mouth open, and its thin lips drawn back over its tiny white teeth.

The hired man saw, again without understanding, the beginnings of tufts on the flattened ears. In his dull mind he felt a dark resentment at this creature which defied him. Rising, he passed his hand up his face in heavy thought, then slithering down to the stream, he began to gather stones. With an armful of small water-washed pebbles he returned to the whins.

First he strove to strike at the kitten from above. The roof of the whins was matted and resilient. The stones could not penetrate it. He flung straight then — to maim or kill — but the angle was difficult and only one missile reached its mark, rebounding from the ground and striking the kitten a glancing blow on the shoulder.

Kneeling, his last stone gone, the hired man watched, the red in his face deepening and thin threads of crimson rising in the whites of his eyes as the blood mounted to his head. A red glow of anger was spreading through his brain. His mouth worked and twisted to an ugly rent.

"Wait — wait," he cried hoarsely, and, turning, ran heavily up the slope to the trees. He swung his whole weight on a low-hanging branch, snapping if off with a crack like a gun-shot.

Seated on the warm, short turf, the hired

The Kitten

man prepared his weapon, paring at the end of the branch till the point was sharp as a dagger. When it was ready he knelt on his left knee and swung the branch to find the balance. The kitten was almost caught.

The savage lance-thrust would have skewered its body as a trout is spiked on the beak of a heron, but the point, slung too low, caught in a fibrous root and snapped off short. Impotently the man jabbed with his broken weapon while the kitten retreated disdainfully to the opposite fringe of the whins.

In the slow-moving mind of the hired man the need to destroy the kitten had become an obsession. Intent on this victim, he forgot the others abandoned by the burn side; forgot the passage of time, and the hard labour of the day behind him. The kitten, in his distorted mind, had grown to a monstrous thing, centring all the frustrations of a brutish existence. He craved to kill . . . .

But so far the honours lay with the antagonist.

In a sudden flash of fury the man made a second bodily assault on the whins and a second time retired defeated.

He sat down on the grass to consider the next move as the first breath of the breeze wandered up the hill. As though that were the signal, in the last moments of the sun, a lark rose, close at hand, and mounted the sky on the flood of its own melody.

The man drank in the coolness thankfully, and, taking a pipe from his pocket, lit the embers of tobacco in the bowl. He flung the match from him, still alight, and a dragon's tongue of amber flame ran over the dry grass before the breeze, reached a bare patch of sand and flickered out. Watching it, the hired man knitted his brows and remembered the heather-burning, and mountain hares that ran before the scarlet terror. And he looked at the whins.

The first match blew out in the freshening wind, but at the second the bush burst into crackling flame.

The whins were alight on the leeward side and burned slowly against the wind. Smoke rose thickly, and sparks and lighted shivers of wood sailed off on the wind to light new fires on the grass of the hillside.

Coughing as the pungent smoke entered his lungs, the man circled the clump till the fire was between him and the farm. He could see the kitten giving ground slowly before the flame. He thought for a moment of lighting this side of the clump also and trapping it between two fires; took his matches from his pocket, hesitated, and replaced them. He could wait.

Slowly, very slowly, the kitten backed towards him. The wind fought for it, delaying, almost holding the advance of the fire through the whins.

Showers of sparks leaped up from the bushes that crackled and spluttered as they burned, but louder than the crackling of the whins, from the farm on the slope of the hill, came another noise — the clamour of voices. The hired man walked clear of the smoke that obscured his view and stared up the hill.

The thatch of the farmhouse, dry as tinder, was aflare.

Gaping, he saw the flames spread to the roof of the byre, to the stables; saw the farmer running the horses to safety, and heard the thunder of hooves as the scared cattle, turned loose, rushed from the yard. He saw a roof collapse in an uprush of smoke and sparks, while a kitten, whose sire was a wild cat, passed out of the whins unnoticed and took refuge in a deserted burrow.

From there, with cold, defiant eyes, it regarded the hired man steadfastly.

— *Alexander Reid*

The Kitten

? Questions and Assignments

1. Why did the holes in the tarpaulin cover go black?
2. Did the mother cat injure the farmer? Give a reason for your answer.
3. What details are given that show the protective instinct of the mother cat?
4. (i) In what kind of weather does the story take place?
   (ii) How does the author convey the nature of the weather?
5. Outline clearly what happens when the hired man reaches the stream.
6. Comment on the character of the hired man.
7. Comment on the writer's use of the following words in the second paragraph of the story - *scruffling; scratching; clink; jangle; clang.*
8. Tell the story from the point of view of the kitten.
9. Write in dialogue form, the conversation that you imagine might have taken place between the hired man and the farmer after the event.
10. Comment briefly on
    (a) the theme of the story.
    (b) the irony in the story.
11. Imagine that the events in the story happened in your locality. Write a brief news report (150 words max.) suitable for inclusion in a news bulletin on a national radio station.

S Spelling

Below are anagrams of words that are sometimes misspelt. Rearrange the letters to find the words. All the words are in the story.

- lunggrimb
- worthing
- rmostnosu
- dethrun
- lanrilbit
- cherrouseat
- ogenut
- palsolec
- golruhy
- torasinurft
- breedmerem
- tonundice
- garinwes
- mentesrent
- pedeal
- atefind
- tarhinbeg
- ebblesp
- malcuor
- ratsed

V Vocabulary Development

Find words in the story to match each of the following meanings.

- standing up
- effort
- twisted; deformed
- sheltered side
- edge
- scornfully, contemptuously
- saying little; uncommunicative
- gliding off; oblique; not direct
- thread-like; of a strong stringy texture
- mournfully
- squirmed
- opponent
- stinging; biting; acrid
- pierced; gone through
- understanding
- pushing with force
- ascended
- hid; made invisible
- walked clumsily and noisily.
- deadened; made dull; stifled
- slowness to feel or show feeling
- firmly; constantly; unwaveringly
- unwillingness
- powerlessly
- mixed; blended

The Kitten

- dry substance readily taking fire from a spark
- small particles or pieces of fuel in a dying fire
- prophetically; showing a sign of some future event.
- glistened; wrapped in faint diffused light; gleamed tremulously.
- to bounce back to its normal shape; resume original shape after compression.

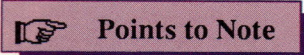 **Points to Note**

The Kitten has all the elements of a good short story.
- It is not cluttered with characters. There are two major characters, the hired man and the kitten. (In the context of this story the kitten can be regarded as a character). The farmer plays a very minor role.
- The setting and the timescale are compact and straightforward. The entire action takes place on a farm in the Scottish Highlands over the course of a hour or so.
- The story deals with a single event of importance and significance.
- The conflict is presented in a clear manner.
- The plot is straightforward, ending with a clever ironic twist.

 **Writers' Workshop**

WRITING YOUR OWN STORIES

The Kitten is a particularly suitable story to use as a model for some stories of your own. The outline idea of *The Kitten* could be summarised as follows:-

Character A (the hired man) *thoughtlessly attempts to destroy or hurt* **Character B** (the kitten). *However, as a result of his own stupidity or inefficiency he ends up destroying something of much greater value or importance. The irony is that* **Character B** *escapes.*

Throughout this section of the book a number of short story ideas are presented in this basic form. They provide foundations on which you can build your own stories and offer you scope to create your own plots, characters and settings. Each idea may be developed into dozens of different stories.
- First begin with an idea. In most cases, a story has a greater impact when the author is dealing with a topic or an incident of which he or she has first-hand experience. Try to remember an incident from your life that is somewhat similar to the *basic short story idea* on which you are working. You will probably have to change the facts a little.
- Give some thought to the point of view from which the story is to be told. You may choose to have one of the characters involved narrate the story or you can present it from the omniscient (all seeing) point of view.
- Base your characters on people you know — friends, neighbours, relatives, teachers etc. However, in your stories, you can give them different roles from their real roles in life.
- You need not confine your stories to your own experience. With your knowledge of History and Geography (and a little imagination) the incidents in your story can happen to anybody, anywhere and at anytime.
- In your story make your point gently but effectively. Don't hammer the point home for the reader; let him or her figure it out for themselves.

The Kitten

- Keep descriptive passages to a minimum — just long enough to set the scene or make a point. For example, a single sentence, such as "The river glinted in the moonlight" will probably be more effective than a long poetic paragraph describing a moonlit night.
- Pay attention to dialogue. Good, natural-sounding dialogue usually grabs the attention of the reader.
- Your characters should not only speak; they should also do things. You can show the reader the kind of people that your characters are by the way they respond and act.

Outline Short Story Ideas

- **Character A** is presented to the reader as an unpleasant person engaged in some irritating activity. In the closing stages of the story he/she is revealed as a good person pursuing an admirable purpose - e.g. **A** a rather untalented busker on a street corner, at a crisis point, turns out to be an undercover garda. The narrator could be a bank manager.

- The reverse of the first idea - **A** is a pleasant person engaged in some kind of admirable activity. In the closing stages he/she is revealed in an opposite light - e.g. **A** calls on householders collecting for a 'good' cause. However, he/she proves to be a thief.

- Two characters **A** and **B** are presented in such a way that the reader (and the narrator perhaps) assumes a certain relationship between them - e.g. father/son, employer/employee, garda/tramp. In the end, appearances prove to be deceptive. This idea will require a fair degree of ingenuity and imagination on your part.

✓ Q. 6 — Sample Answer

When the hired man discovered the kittens he called 'harshly'. Most people would react in a gentle and affectionate manner to a batch of kittens. The hired man obviously has no feelings for animals.

He is not very intelligent. The author describes him as 'staring stupidly' and talks about his 'slow-moving mind'. He notices the 'tigerish markings' and the little tufts on the ears - but doesn't understand what they mean. A man who lived and worked in the countryside would normally understand such things. His stupidity is obvious also at the end of the story as he is not able to work out the possible effects of setting fire to the bush.

Is he cruel? At the start he is not. We are told that he had 'no feelings' about the matter of drowning the kittens. It is only when the kitten escapes that the cruel streak in him comes out. He tries to stab the kitten with a stick and, when he fails, he tries to burn the animal alive.

The Confessional

In the wide nave the wintry evening light was faint as gloom and in the shadows of the aisle it was like early night. There was no sound in the chapel but the wind blowing up from the river valley, or an occasional tiny noise when a brass socket creaked under the great heat of a dying flame. To the three small boys crouched together on a bench in the farther aisle, holding each other's hands, listening timidly to the crying wind, staring wide-eyed at the candles, it seemed odd that in such a storm the bright flames never moved.

Suddenly the eldest of the three, a redheaded little ruffian, whispered loudly; but the other two, staring at the distant face of the statue, silenced him with a great hiss like a breaking wave. In another moment the lad in the centre, crouching down in fear and gripping the hand on each side of him, whispered so quietly that they barely heard, "She's moving."

For a second or two they did not even breathe. Then all three expelled a deep sigh of disappointment.

It was Monday afternoon, and every Monday, as they had each heard tell over and over again in their homes, Father Hanafin spoke with the Blessed Virgin in the grotto. Some said she came late at night; some said in the early morning before the chapel was opened; some said it was at the time when the sun goes down; but until now nobody had dared to watch. To be sure, Father Hanafin was not in the chapel now, but for all that the three little spies had come filled with high hope. The eldest spoke their bitter disappointment aloud.

"It's all my eye," he said angrily. The other two felt that what he said was true, but they pretended to be deeply shocked.

"That's an awful thing you said, Foxer," whispered the boy in the middle.

"Go away, you, Philpot!" said Foxer.

"Got! I think it's a cause for confession, Foxer!" whispered Philpot again.

"It's a mortal sin, Foxer!" said the third, leaning over to say it.

"Don't you try to cod me, Cooney, or I'll burst yer jaw!" cried Foxer angrily.

Philpot hushed them sternly and swiftly, but the spell was broken. They all leaned back in the bench.

Beside them was Father Hanafin's confession box, its worn purple curtains partly drawn back, his worn purple stole hanging on a crook on the wall inside, and as Foxer gazed into the box with curiosity the Adversary tempted him in his heart.

"Come on, Cooney!" he invited at last. "Come on, and I'll hear yer confession."

"Got! Come on," said Cooney, rising.

"That's a sin," said Philpot, though secretly eager to sit in the priest's chair.

"You're an awful ould Aunt Mary!" jeered Foxer, whereupon all Philpot's scruples vanished and the three scrambled for the confessor's seat.

But Foxer was there before either of them, and at once he swished the curtains together as he had seen Father Hanafin do, and put the long stole about his neck. It was so nice in there in the dark that he forgot his two penitents waiting beyond the closed grilles on either side, and he was putting imaginary snuff into his nostrils and flicking imaginary specks of snuff from his chest when Cooney's angry face appeared between the curtains.

"Are yeh going to hear me confession, Foxer, or are yeh not?" he cried in rage, eager for his turn to be priest.

"Go back, my child," said Foxer crossly, and he swished the curtains together again.

The Confessional

Then, as if in spite, he leaned over to the opposite grille and slowly and solemnly he drew the slide and peered into the frightened eyes of Philpot.

"Tell me how long since your last confession, my child," he said gravely.

"Twenty years," whispered Philpot in awe.

"What have you done since then?" intoned Foxer sadly.

"I stole sweets, Father. And I forgot my prayers. And I cursed, Father."

"You cursed!" thundered Foxer. "What curse did you say?"

"I said that our master was an ould sod, Father," murmured Philpot timidly.

"So he is, my child. Is there anything else?"

"No, Father."

"For your penance say two hundred and forty-nine Rosaries, and four hundred and seventy Our Fathers, and three hundred and thirty-two Hail Marys. And now be a good, obedient boy. And pray for me, won't you? Gawd bless you, my child."

And with that Foxer drew the slide slowly before the small astonished face.

As he turned to the other side his hand fell on a little box — it was Father Hanafin's consolation during the long hours spent in that stuffy confessional listening to the sins and sorrows of his parishioners. Foxer's awkward fingers lifted the cover and the sweet scent rose powerfully through the darkness as he coaxed the loose snuff down from the cover. Then drawing the slide on Cooney, he gravely inhaled a pinch and leaned his ear to the cool iron of the grille.

Outside a footstep sounded on the marble floor, and peering out Foxer saw the priest walk slowly up the farther aisle, turn and walk slowly down again, his breviary held high to the slanting radiance of the Virgin's alter.

"It's Father Hanafin," whispered Foxer to Cooney; and to Philpot. "Keep quiet or we're all ruined."

Up and down the solemn footsteps went, and high above their heads in the windows of the clerestory* and along the lath and plaster of the roof the wind moaned and fingered the loose slates, and now and again they heard the priest murmur aloud the deep, open vowels of his prayer, Gaudeamus Domine, or Domine, Domine meo, in a long breathing sigh.

"He's talking to the Virgin," breathed Cooney to Foxer.

"He's talking to the Virgin," breathed Foxer in turn to Philpot.

"Amen," sighed the priest, and went on his knees before the candles that shone steadily and were reflected brilliantly in the burnished brass.

The three spies had begun to peep from their hiding place when the snuff fell on Foxer's lap and the grains began to titillate his nose. In agony he held his mouth for a full minute and then burst into a furious sneeze. In astonishment the priest gazed about him and once again Foxer held his breath and once again he sneezed. At the third sneeze the priest gazed straight at the box.

"Come out!" he said in a loud voice. "Come out of that box!"

And as the three guilty forms crept from the three portals he commanded "Come here!"

Awkwardly they stumbled forward through the seats, trying to hide behind one another until they stood before him.

"What were you doing in there?" he asked Foxer.

"I was hearing their confession, Father," trembled Foxer, and half raised his arm as if to ward off a blow.

For a moment the priest glared at him and he asked, "And what penance did you

17

give?"

"I — I gave three hundred and thirty-two Hail Marys, Father, and I think four hundred Our Fathers, Father, and two hundred and forty-nine Rosaries, Father."

"Well!" pronounced the priest in a solemn voice. "Go home and let each one of ye say that penance three times over before nine o'clock tomorrow morning."

Stumbling over one another's heels the three crept down the dark aisle and crushed out through the green baize door and into the falling night that was torn by the storm. The street lamps were lit and under one of these they halted and looked at each other, angry and crestfallen.

"Nine hundred and ninety Hail Marys!" wailed Philpot, and Cooney squared up to Foxer with clenched fists.

"Yerrah!" said Foxer. "It's all a cod!"

And he raced suddenly away to his supper, followed by the the shouts and feet of the other two.

— *Seán Ó'Faoláin*

clerestory* : the upper part of a church with its own row of windows.

The Confessional

? Questions and Assignments

1. Why were the three boys waiting in the chapel?
2. What did the boys do while they waited?
3. (a) Describe each of the three boys.
   (b) Who would you consider was the leader? Explain your answer.
4. What are your impressions of Fr. Hanafin
   (a) before he enters the story and
   (b) at the end of the story?
5. Select three good descriptive phrases from the story and say why each of them appeals to you.
6. Make out a story board for a television version of this story. What three scenes do you think would be the funniest? Explain why.
7. Had you been in Foxer's place when Fr. Hanafin's foot sounded on the marble floor, what would you have done?
8. The snuff box plays a crucial role in the development of the plot. Write another version of the story omitting any reference to the snuff box. Imagine the boys see and hear Fr. Hanafin talking to the statue. The boys escape unnoticed from the chapel and tell the first person they meet about what they saw. Continue the story.
9. Write your own short story entitled, "Caught in the Act".
10. Retell the story from
    (a) the point of view of one of the boys
              or
    (b) the point of view of the priest.

$ Spelling

Below are anagrams of words that are sometimes misspelt. Rearrange the letters to find the words. All the words are in the story.

- alancocois
- nigdy
- tutase
- rabely
- threabe
- toppadisinment
- grilany
- dezag
- rosicuity
- dredthune
- muredrum
- druhned
- wardawk
- lantlilyirb
- rasqued

V Vocabulary Development

Find words in the story to match each of the following meanings.

- stooped
- comfort
- polished
- rough lawless fellow
- strictly; severely
- keen; anxious
- breathed in
- brightness; splendour
- thin strip of wood
- tickle
- recited; said with a certain tone
- formal; impressive
- feelings of doubt about proposed action
- swung with hissing sound; pulled over with hissing sound
- an upper storey or part of a church with its own row of windows

19

The Confessional

- reproaching; giving out to; scolding
- the main part of a church
- passageway between pews or seats
- made a harsh grating noise
- faint-heartedly; in a manner showing some fear

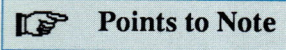 **Points to Note**

POINTS OF VIEW

In *The Confessional* neither the priest nor any of the boys is **narrating** (telling) the story. We do not learn about the incident from the priest's *point of view* or any of the boys' *points of view*. Instead, the author has opted for the *omniscient* point of view to tell the story. 'Omniscient' means 'all seeing'. When a story is narrated (told) from the omniscient point of view, the narrator is almost a god-like figure who is looking down on the event. He is not involved in the action. He can see separate events as they occur simultaneously and knows the inner thoughts and feelings of all the characters in the story. However, the narrator must be careful to reveal just enough information to hold the interest of the reader.

 **Writers' Workshop**

SETTING THE SCENE

Frequently, in your writing, you will need to describe the setting of an event or story. This involves describing *when* and *where* the action took place. Your description must help your reader to visualise (see in his/her imagination) the setting. Your description need not be lengthy. A vivid picture can be painted in a sentence or two. Examine the second sentence of *The Confessional* — "There was no sound . . . . a dying flame." The sentence only mentions a few details but these are enough for the reader to picture the entire scene in his/her imagination. Now, using a similar structure to the above sentence, describe the following settings :-

(i) An empty classroom.
(ii) An empty football stadium.
(iii) A farmyard in early morning.
(iv) A street at night.
(v) The principal's office.

e.g. — "There was no sound in the classroom . . . ." (i)

SIMILES AND CLICHES

To help a reader visualise something more clearly — writers use **similes** — i.e. "a great hiss like a breaking wave". Note the simile in the first sentence of the second paragraph of the story. It is an example of a fresh and original simile.

However, in everyday speech we frequently use expressions, including similes, that have become stale and colourless through constant use. These are called **cliches**. Examples of these are — *"as black as coal", "as cold as ice", "slept like a log".*

Make a list of as many of these as you can think of and compose fresh ones — e.g. "as cold as death . . . ."

The Confessional

IRONIC SIMILES
Writers sometimes use ironic similes — usually to give a touch of humour to their writing e.g. *"as exciting as watching paint dry"*, *"like being attacked by a dead sheep"*.

Can you explain why these are *ironic*? Compose some of your own.

DIALOGUE
Note how the dialogue is laid out in the story. When does the author begin a new paragraph when writing dialogue? Note also how capitals, full stops, commas and quotation marks are used. We can tell a good deal about a character, not only from the things he/she says, but also from the way it is said.

VERBS AND ADVERBS
When you are writing dialogue, try to avoid repeating the verb *"said"*. There are many other *verbs* that can be used to describe more accurately how a character spoke.

Make a list of those used in *The Confessional* and other stories. Keep a list for reference. Sometimes you will not be able to think of a suitable verb in order to describe accurately a particular tone of voice.

In this case, you should try and think of a suitable *adverb* to qualify the verb
— e.g. He roared angrily.   He roared happily.

Make a list of the verbs/adverbs used in this way in *The Confessional*. Add to this list from your other reading and keep the list for reference.

📖 Outline Short Story Ideas

- Character **A** makes his/her dislike and contempt for a person or organisation very obvious. The surprise is that the subject of **A**'s dislike turns out to be a source of invaluable help and support to **A**.
- Character **A** is described following a course of action that is obviously dangerous. When this is completed you reveal that the danger was much greater than the reader supposed or a far more important task was accomplished than appeared to be.

✓ Q. 10 — Sample Answer

In attempting this question, you could begin as follows :-

(a) It was all Philpot's idea. He had heard his aunt, who was a very religious woman, telling his mother about Father Hanafin. She said that he used to chat with the Virgin Mary in the chapel every Monday evening. According to her, they used to have long talks, mainly about religion. So Philpot and myself decided to go and see for ourselves. We shouldn't have asked Foxer though . . . .

(b) I thought that I was the only person in the church so you can imagine my shock and surprise when I heard a loud sneeze coming from inside the confession box . . . .

My True Kinsman

When we were children, one of our favourite games was playing "grandfather." I had the title role and my two sisters played supporting parts. We made-believe that the lane down to the spring well was the main street of the nearest village of Mullaghduff and my sisters would walk along it, looking from side to side as if they were window shopping. Then suddenly I would jump up from behind the hawthorn hedge and with the deepest voice I could produce for my eight or nine years, I would say, "Ah! If it's not my daughter-in-law and her careful brood! Good day to you, madam. A very good day to you."

That was enough to send the three of us into fits of laughing. Indeed, many a time I did not get finished my speech. Even though they knew I was going to pop up somewhere along that hedge, sometimes I was able to give them a genuine surprise; or perhaps my imitation of Grandfather would be more lifelike. Then my sisters would squeal with genuine shock, their fright would spread to me and, forgetting we had created the myth ourselves, the three of us would take to our heels and race to the far end of the well field where we would laugh ourselves sore with near hysteria. Sometimes Father found us playing this game. A strange look would come into his eyes and he would walk quickly away, not saying a word. It was his father we were playing and he knew that but what he did not understand was that we meant no harm. I suppose he thought we were mocking the old man.

But when Mother caught us playing Grandfather, she skelped us round the legs with her bare hand, called us bold, disobedient children and said that all her rearing and good example was for nothing, that we seemed determined to come to a bad end despite her efforts. That would stop the game for a couple of weeks — until we would find ourselves out of earshot of the house and bored and in a rebellious mood and I would creep up behind the girls and intone the forbidden words again.

The real grandfather could never have been as awesome as the invented one but we never got the chance of learning that by experience. Mother took every care to keep us apart. From the day she married, she never allowed him to visit our house nor did we ever see the inside of his house. Indeed, if she could have hidden his existence from us altogether, she would have. But that was impossible because every Saturday evening when she dressed us up and brought us into the village for confession, invariably we got a quick nervous glimpse of him either going into or coming out of a public house. But only a glimpse because as soon as he appeared, Mother would be fussing about us: "Have you got your rosary beads? Do you know all your sins? How long is it since your last confession?" — she must have known it could never have been more than a week — "Stop gawking about. Keep your eyes on the footpath." But we would have seen him and I remember the peculiar thrill of forbidden delight at watching him from the corner of my eye: tall, straight-backed, heavily built, his huge red face framed between a wild crop of white hair and side whiskers and a full-length beard. And we would have heard him, because whenever he saw us — and I remember few Saturdays when he did not — he gave us a grand, regal salute and called to us in his deep, resonant voice, even though we would be twenty yards past him. His greeting varied but he always addressed

Mother as "daughter-in-law" and us as "the brood". Sometimes he would say, in his faintly mocking way, "Ah! the Burkes! How do you do? Not off to confession, again, daughter-in-law? Heavens, woman, but you must lead a profligate life!" at which Mother's face would tighten and she would say under her breath, "The scourge! The scourge!" and drag us roughly towards the chapel gate. Or he might call, "Well, well, well. Mrs. Burke and her brood! Anxious as ever in the services of the Lord. Will you join me in some refreshment? No? Some other time." We never, never answered him and if, on the way home after confession, we brought up his name, Mother seldom said more than, "He's just a man, God forgive him. He can't help himself because he's a man."

But even then we had pieced together a sketchy picture of the man from what Mother let drop occasionally and from what we had learned from the other children in the school. Father was his only child and his wife, our grandmother, died the same year that father got married to Mary Neeson, the eldest of a cautious, well-to-do family from County Louth. The old man was then close on seventy himself but within one month of his wife's death, he got married again, this time to a flighty woman of forty-five from the village of Mullaghduff. On marrying for the second time — "God forgive him," Mother used to say, "may God in His mercy forgive him. Aw, the dirty thing! The dirty thing! — he sold his home and bit of a farm and went into the village to his new wife's place. But he had not spent a summer when she died too — "Would you blame her?" — and from then on, he took to the wild living: point-to-point meetings, drinking, every fair within forty miles, wakes, weddings, and christenings. He became unkempt. He had tussles with the police on fair days.

And it was whispered by the older children in school that he took whiskey for his breakfast, gin for his dinner, and rum for his supper. I remember grouping him mentally with the unfamiliar and terrifying things which I encountered in the world beyond my immediate home area: the haunted house in the school field; old, demented Lizzy Quinn who used to come rushing out of her one-roomed house at the roadside, catch me by the lapels, and ask, with limp intensity, "Are the boys back from the front yet?"; Jack Taylor's cross terrier bitch. Grandfather was one of these; but his menace was greater because I always knew that one day, one day of doom, he would get me and, I honestly believed it, devour me.

He got me on my tenth birthday. Birthdays in our house were celebrated with the same formal, ceremonious jubilation as major feast days of the Church. We did not actually prepare for them by fasting but Mother did attempt to heighten the enjoyment of the event itself by imposing petty restrictions on us for a week beforehand. We would have no sweets, no playing after supper time, no visiting our school friends or having them call on us, "not until your birthday." The result was that we moped about the house and quarrelled with one another and when the birthday or feast day would arrive and we were dressed up in our Sunday clothes and Father, with a bad grace, would agree to do no work around the farm and when the good things of this world would be arranged generously before us, we would then be in no form for celebrating anything and the occasion frequently fizzled out with further squabbling and very often in tears. Anyhow, my tenth birthday was a failure like so many of the others before. It was the month of May and the day had been warm and heavy and thick with threatened thunder. I had fought with one of my sisters during the celebration meal over the sugar-coated elf that decorated the cake and the other sister was sulking because Mother had called her obstinate and mulish when she refused to sing as we sat round the table after eating. Father had ambled off in his usual fashion, his hands in his pockets, looking vaguely at the apple trees or at the roof of the byre or out towards the Gortin Mountains where the thunder growled. Only Mother was brisk and purposeful. She had arranged family games for us for the afternoon and she was determined that we would enjoy them.

The accident occurred when she was tying a piece of string with an apple at the other end of it to the drawing-room ceiling. The steps on which she was standing overturned and she fell to the ground, cutting her forehead on the brass fender. The cut was long and deep and she lay full length on the carpet with her head propped up on a cushion. Had Father been an efficient man, she would have allowed herself to faint but she had to think and act for the two of them.

"Get a basin of warm water and a clean handkerchief and bring them here beside me," she directed. "Then go to my bedroom and in the bottom left-hand corner of the wardrobe, you will find a bottle of iodine. Bring it too."

My sisters and I stood gaping down at her, each of us feeling responsible for this mishap because we had been difficult all day. Father came running back with the water and the cloth. But there was no iodine.

"I told you," said Mother. "It's in the wardrobe. In the bottom left-hand corner."
"I looked," said Father. "This is the bottle. But it's empty."

Mother hesitated momentarily. "Yes, Tom. You're a big man now. You can go to the village for some," she said to me. "It won't take you more than half an hour to run in and back again." She turned to Father. "You'll find a ten-shilling note in my purse under the stairs. Give it to Tom." She turned to me again. "And if the chemist asks you any questions just say . . . . just say it's for dressing a slight wound. That'll satisfy him."

I must have kept staring down at her because she added, "Well, you know the way, don't you? What sort of baby are you? Run both ways and be careful. Get the money and off you go. Run!"

Of course I knew the way, every inch of it. But today the journey was different: the road was narrower and more tortuous and the high, full-leafed hedges concealed vague enemies who would try to prevent me from saving my mother's life. The countryside had fallen quiet, waiting for the thunder to spill over it. I steeled myself for the dangers I knew — the haunted house in the school field; old, demented Lizzy Quinn; Taylor's cross terrier bitch — and successfully negotiated each one as it came. But it was only when I came to the outskirts of Mullaghduff that I remembered Grandfather and panic suddenly flooded me. It was one thing to steal sly glances at him from behind my mother's elbow but quite another thing to meet him in all his grizzly strength with my two arms the one length. I stood at the mouth of the main street and looked up it. The chemist's shop was near the top, on the right hand side. My best plan was to run like a hare along the houses, dart into the shop, get the iodine, and dart out again. I clutched the note in my fist and ran. I never got the length of the shop. I did not get even halfway. Just as I was passing the post office, the giant's voice boomed out.

"Well, if it isn't the grandchild, eh? Who have we got here? Which of them is it?"

So intent had I been on reaching my goal that I had no eyes for anything else. Now the huge, terrifying figure towered over me and, afraid to look up, my face looked into a spherical stomach.

"It is a Burke, isn't it? Well, speak up. Isn't it?"

I said I was.

"This is an occasion! An unescorted Burke roaming the big, bad world all alone! Look up at me, man! Look up at me!"

He put a hand the size of a plate under my chin and tilted my head back and I saw the big, hairy face and the red, hungry mouth; and since our bodies were so close that they touched one another, I became aware of something that was completely new to me: there was a smell off this mountain of a man. It was not an unpleasant smell but it was very strong and very heavy, as heavy as the smell of poppies or of cows on a frosty night, and it lay stagnant all around him, like an aura on this sultry day. Even as I looked into his face, my only thoughts were that I was breathing this smell into me and that it was making me drowsy.

"You're the boy," said Grandfather.

"You're Tom, are you not? My own name, lad, and a good name. Carry it with dignity, always." His hand moved from my chin to my cheeks and over my hair. "Yes. A Burke all right — a Burke to the backbone. But there's something about the mouth, lad, something that's not ours. Aye, it's small and watchful — a Neeson mouth that, I'm afraid. But no matter. No matter." He rumpled my hair. "Have you a tongue, lad?"

I said I had. "And do you know who I am?"

I said I did. "Tell me, then."

"You're my grandfather."

"Aye," he said slowly. "Your grandfather." Then he suddenly burst out laughing so that his swollen belly shook before my nose.

"Dammit, that's a good one, eh? Tom Burke and Tom Burke. I'll tell you what, lad." His voice sank to a whisper. "We'll make a day of it, the two of us. Eh? What about it? We'll do a tour of the ancient settlement of Mullaghduff, a tour of inspection by the Burkes, grandfather and grandson. What do you say."

I began to explain about my mother but he broke in on my excuse. "All in due course," he said. "But our tour first. You're a straight-backed lad and well shaped and I want the whole town to see us parading together. You wouldn't deny an old man that pleasure, would you?"

He gripped my elbow and turned me back towards the direction I had come from. "We'll inspect the south side first before the sun begins to drop." And he marched me off with him.

I was too afraid to resist and fell in along with him, taking three or four steps to every one of his. From the moment we set off he never ceased talking, and for the first while, I was too scared to listen to what he was saying. But gradually my fear scattered and in its place came a mixture of awe and curiosity, a real passion of curiosity about his age and his height and the texture of his beard and his crosses with the police and his travels and his escapades. But when I was on the point of asking the first question, my tongue stalled on me and I let him talk on and on. He spoke like a grand judge with wonderful words flowing out of him and he made the one main street that was Mullaghduff into the most romantic place in the whole of Ireland. He showed me the ruins of the home of Golden Gallagher, the man who discovered a Spanish galleon on the bed of Donegal Bay and who employed every boy for miles around — Grandfather included — to dive down into the black hulk to bring up the doubloons and moidores and sapphires and bijoux by the handful and in their mouths and between their toes. And he pointed out the spot where Cromwell's troops had been ambushed and everyman of them torn asunder by bare hands. And we stood on the ground where the Druid temple had once been; and here Grandfather got down on his knees on the ground to demonstrate how those holy men worshipped the sun. And he brought me to the edge of the town to a field under which flowed a silver river whose singing could be heard on Midsummer night only and along to a tinker's caravan close by wherein, he told me, lived the only man in the whole of Ireland who could claim direct relationship back to Cathal Mór, King of Leinster. We saw the second-oldest goat in Europe and a calf that had been born with two heads (one had been removed the week before we saw it). We looked over the wall at the workhouse where, in the old days, young orphan boys had been beaten to death by a savage workhouse master called Bloody Baldrick who himself had been kicked to death by a savage, one-eyed horse. And we went to the harbour and looked across the Atlantic at New York where a hundred million lights burned day and night and where volcanoes threw whole streets sky high.

I had forgotten completely about my mother. Indeed, had Grandfather kept on talking, I might never have remembered her. But when we arrived back at the place where he had got me, he came to a halt and said, "Well, now. What do you think of Mullaghduff, eh?"

He caught a fistful of his beard and eyed me roguishly, "One other place I forgot," he said. "The chapel. But I think you have been there once or twice before."

"Mother . . . ."

"Yes. She cut herself, didn't she? Never worry, lad, never worry. The Neesons are seldom taken in the prime of life. The Lord gives them a long span in this valley of tears before He calls them. And now, lad, after all that talking, I'm thirsty. You'll join me in some refreshment, won't you?"

I got no chance to consider the proposal because he had me by the elbow again and brought me into a nearby public house. The place was empty except for a boy of about my own age who stood behind the counter. As soon as he saw us, he disappeared into the kitchen through a door at the back of the shop. We waited for him to return. Grandfather's fingers drummed impatiently on the brass rail and he called, "Shop! Shop! Hello! Hello!" No one came to attend us. Then, after a long delay, the door opened again and the boy reappeared. He stood at the far end of the counter and addressed us from there. "My da says that you're to get no more drink here, Burke. He says no more tick for you."

To this day, I have never been certain about what happened then: I have never been able to distinguish between what I felt and knew then and what I think now I must have felt and known then. But of this much I am sure. I could see Grandfather's face in the mirror behind the bar and the face I saw was old and lined and weary and I had instinctive sympathy for him. Nor can I remember now how exactly the hot ten-shilling note which I had been clutching all afternoon slipped from my hand into his. I know nothing was said. I know there cannot have been a second's hesitation. I know that when our fingers fumbled below the counter, I was not aware of being reckless or generous or patronising or foolhardy. At that time, it seemed the only thing to do: money was needed and I had some. That was all.

"Tick? Who wants tick?" Grandfather demanded. "Don't you recognise money

My True Kinsman

when you see it?" He banged the note on the counter and grunted his contempt. "Here, lad, quickly! The usual for myself and a soft beverage for my grandson, Tom Burke . . . ." — he hesitated momentarily — ". . . . my true kinsman. Hurry up, lad! Hurry up! Don't stand there gawking at us! Hurry up."

The skies opened on us as soon as we came out into the street again, straight sheets of rain that soaked into me in seconds. We lowered our heads and ran into it. At the end of the street, Grandfather stopped as if he had come to the boundary of his terrain and could go no further. Then he took off his jacket and draped it over my head and shoulders.

"You're a good lad. Tom Burke," he said quietly. "A good lad. We'll have another day together soon again. Go on, now. Off home with you." He pushed me gently from behind to start me on my way. I moved off a few paces and turned around. He was running through the downfall in his shirt sleeves, his huge head down on his chest, his back hunched. I watched him until he was out of sight but he did not look back.

I was in no hurry home. I dawdled along the road, deliberately walking into the puddles of water that had gathered on it. Grandfather's jacket was a huge tent from under which I could see the lines of rain driving down in front of me. Inside my tent, it was warm and damp and comfortable. And then as I ambled along, I became aware again of the smell, the smell of Grandfather. It filled my cavern and floated around my nose and eyes. I raised my arm and smelt it. Now my arm was permeated with it and my chest and my whole body. The smell was through me and all about me. And I knew that as long as it lasted, I would have the courage to meet my mother and tell her the terrible news — that I had no iodine and no money and that Grandfather had got me.

— *Brian Friel*

? Questions and Assignments

1. Describe the game of "Grandfather" that the children played. How did their parents react when they caught the children playing that game?
2. The fourth paragraph of the story provides us with an impression of both the mother and the grandfather. Referring only to the fourth paragraph, outline briefly your impressions of each of these people. Describe also their feelings towards each other.
3. We learn, in the fifth paragraph, of the narrator's feelings towards his grandfather. Describe these feelings briefly. Refer to the fifth paragraph *only*, to support the points you make.
4. Explain how the narrator's tenth birthday was a failure. Who do you blame for this? Give one or more reasons.
5. Why was the narrator afraid when going alone to the village?
6. (i) Would you agree that the tone of the passage ("Birthdays in our house . . . . for a week beforehand") is sarcastic? Give reasons for your answer.
   (ii) Comment on the comparison used by the writer in the passage.
7. ". . . . and he made the one main street that was Mullaghduff into the most romantic place in the whole of Ireland . . . ." Explain clearly how Grandfather made Mullaghduff a 'romantic' place.
8. What made the narrator slip the ten shilling note to his Grandfather?

My True Kinsman

9. The events in the story happened when Tom was ten. Is the story told from the point of view of a ten-year-old boy? Explain your answer.

10. What are your impressions of
    (a) Mother
    (b) Grandfather?
    Refer to the story to support your points.

11. Write the dialogue that you imagine takes place when Tom arrives home.

12. Grandfather tells his grandson a number of stories as they toured Mullaghduff together. Using your imagination, write one of the stories as Grandfather might have told it or write a similar type of story set in your own neighbourhood.
    (Bear in mind that your reader is a ten-year old.)

S Spelling

Below are anagrams of words that are sometimes misspelt. Rearrange the letters to find the words. All the words are in the story.

- degeh
- ninugee
- dostibdenie
- tughorb
- alipruce
- usotauic
- nelceadoc
- ugeav
- gulhagin
- tugone
- ruborah
- ulasu
- tashetied
- kagwing
- elirbeldatey

V Vocabulary Development

Find words in the story to match each of the following meanings.

- hit
- threat
- rejoicing
- disrespect
- drink
- winding
- grey-haired
- unaccompanied
- not moving
- ship of war
- best part
- hearing-distance
- scuffles; fights
- faced; met
- failed feebly
- saturated with
- tract of country; his territory
- walked in a leisurely fashion.
- attacked by people lying in wait
- resounding; continuing to sound
- sweltering; close; oppressively hot
- difficult; unmanageable
- tossed; crumpled
- dealt successfully with
- mimicking; ridiculing
- untrue or fictitious thing
- inspiring awe or wonder
- always; without change
- body of a dismantled ship
- uncontrollable excitement
- untidy; neglected-looking
- treating a person in a condescending manner
- acts of irresponsible conduct; mischievous adventures
- a curse, nuisance; a person regarded as an instrument of divine vengeance
- subtle emanation; an air that gives a person a distinctive character.

My True Kinsman

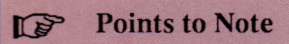 **Points to Note**

CONFLICT
The word *'conflict'* means a struggle or a contest. All stories have some conflict in them. It may be between two characters; a character and an organisation; a character and a natural obstacle; a character and his/her beliefs or principles. Of course it can occur in many other forms. Many stories have more than one situation of conflict in them. Indeed, the plots of most novels are built on a complex network of conflicts. In *My True Kinsman* there is conflict between the mother and the grandfather. Can you suggest why?

Internal Conflict
The narrator also experienced conflict. He makes a sudden, yet brave (or foolish?) decision to pay for Grandfather's drink with Mother's money. When a character faces a decision between two conflicting situations this is known as *internal conflict*.

Resolving Conflict
In all situations of conflict, one side eventually wins out. When this occurs we say that the conflict is *resolved*.

CLIMAX
The *climax* of a story is the point in the story where the reader's interest and excitement is at its highest pitch. The climax of the story nearly always occurs close to the end. This generally occurs around the point in the story where the main conflict is resolved.

Occasionally a writer may put a 'false' climax into a story, so that the reader will be doubly surprised when the real climax is reached. It may be helpful in identifying the climax of a story to imagine a film of the story. Then ask yourself which scene, incident or piece of dialogue would be the most dramatic and exciting part of the film.

CHARACTER DEVELOPMENT
Character development occurs when, over the course of a story, something happens which brings about a change in one of the leading characters. This change or 'development' usually takes the form of overcoming some fear, learning something new of themselves or gaining a more valuable insight into a situation. In general, characters develop for the better. They may become more tolerant, patient, mature or brave. This change is the result of the character having to face and overcome a crisis or problem. He/She usually emerges as a more admirable and likeable character in the eyes of the readers.

Explain how the character of the narrator developed over the course of the story.

 **Writers' Workshop**

YOU NEED NOT BE YOURSELF
It is important to remember that the ***narrator*** (Tom Burke) and the ***author*** (Brian Friel) of *My True Kinsman* are two different people. Tom Burke is a piece of fiction, created by Brian Friel. It would be incorrect to assume that Brian Friel's family and childhood in any way resembled Tom Burke's.

My True Kinsman

One of the advantages of writing fiction is that the author need not be himself or herself. They can be anybody — a girl across the road, the parish priest, the school bully. The possibilities are endless. Brian Friel has frequently used this technique in his stories. Rather than describe an incident as an onlooker or from the omniscient point of view, Friel gets the person who was involved to tell it himself. This technique offers great scope in approaching all types of writing — even essays whose titles seem to require that you tell the truth. Examples of these kinds of titles could include "My neighbourhood", "My favourite relative" or "A family outing you did not enjoy" etc.

 Outline Short Story Ideas

- Two friends or a couple have fallen out and are not on speaking terms. One sends a message or gives some indication to the other which cleverly but indirectly signals that he/she wishes to renew the friendship. The significance of the message is understood and the friendship is renewed — e.g. this could be used in a school situation or neighbourhood. The nature of the message will require a little imagination. One of those involved could be the narrator.

- This is a slight variation on the idea above. This time the friendship is renewed when one of those involved is facing some problem or some danger and the other impulsively comes to his/her assistance.

✓ Q. 10(a) — Sample Answer

The narrator's mother is simply an obnoxious person. As the story opens, we glimpse her hitting her children for playing an innocent game. Obviously the game makes her feel uncomfortable. This harsh, cruel streak in her is always there. She is clearly a hypocrite, regularly running to the church and nagging the children about sins and confession. Yet when it came to 'loving her neighbour' (her father-in-law), her 'christianity' is hard to see. Even though he is a fearsome man in the eyes of the children, he is really a poor, lonely old man.

Her comments on him are harsh and unsympathetic. She regards him almost as an animal when she calls him 'a dirty thing'.

She is unjust both to Grandfather and the children. She should not be keeping them apart. Grandparents and grandchildren have a right to be friends.

Her method of running birthday parties is warped. The narrator's sarcasm and bitterness gives us a very grim picture of his mother.

We don't learn much of what the mother looked like but Grandfather's words sum her up well — "the mouth . . . small and watchful . . . a Neeson mouth."

One small thing that might be said in her favour is that she tried to do what she thought was best for her children — even if it wasn't.

The Secret Life of Walter Mitty

"We're going through!" The Commander's voice was like thin ice breaking. He wore his full-dress uniform, with the heavily braided white cap pulled down rakishly over one cold grey eye. "We can't make it, sir. It's spoiling for a hurricane, if you ask me." "I'm not asking you, Lieutenant Berg," said the Commander. "Throw on the power lights! Rev her up to 8,500. We're going through!" The pounding of the cylinders increased: ta-pocketa-pocketa-pocketa-*pocketa-pocketa*. The Commander stared at the ice forming on the pilot window. He walked over and twisted a row of complicated dials. "Switch on No. 8 auxiliary!" he shouted. "Switch on No. 8 auxiliary!" repeated Lieutenant Berg. "Full strength in No. 3 turret!" shouted the Commander. "Full strength in No. 3 turret!" The crew, bending to their various tasks in the huge, hurtling eight-engined Navy hydroplane, looked at each other and grinned. "The Old Man'll get us through," they said to one another. "The Old Man ain't afraid of Hell!". . . .

"Not so fast! You're driving too fast!" said Mrs. Mitty. "What are you driving so fast for?"

"Hmm?" said Walter Mitty. He looked at his wife, in the seat beside him, with shocked astonishment. She seemed grossly unfamiliar, like a strange woman who had yelled at him in a crowd. "You were up to fifty-five," she said. "You know I don't like to go more than forty. You were up to fifty-five." Walter Mitty drove on toward Waterbury in silence, the roaring of the SN202 through the worst storm in twenty years of Navy flying fading in the remote, intimate airways of his mind. "You're tensed up again," said Mrs. Mitty. "It's one of your days. I wish you'd let Dr. Renshaw look you over."

Walter Mitty stopped the car in front of the building where his wife went to have her hair done. "Remember to get those overshoes while I'm having my hair done," she said. "I don't need overshoes," said Mitty. She put her mirror back into her bag. "We've been all through that," she said, getting out of the car. "You're not a young man any longer." He raced the engine a little. "Why don't you wear your gloves? Have you lost your gloves?" Walter Mitty reached in a pocket and brought out the gloves. He put them on, but after she had turned and gone into the building and he had driven on to a red light, he took them off again. "Pick it up, brother!" snapped a cop as the lights changed, and Mitty hastily pulled on his gloves and lurched ahead. He drove around the streets aimlessly for a time, and then he drove past the hospital on his way to the parking lot.

. . . . "It's the millionaire banker, Wellington McMillan," said the pretty nurse. "Yes?" said Walter Mitty, removing his gloves slowly. "Who has the case?" "Dr. Renshaw and Dr. Benbow, but there are two specialists here, Dr. Remington from New York and Mr. Pritchard-Mitford from London. He flew over." A door opened down a long, cool corridor and Dr. Renshaw came out. He looked distraught and haggard. "Hello, Mitty," he said. "We're having the devil's own time with McMillan, the millionaire banker and close personal friend of Roosevelt. Obstreosis of the ductal tract. Tertiary. Wish you'd take a look at him." "Glad to," said Mitty.

In the operating room there were whispered introductions: "Dr. Remington, Dr. Mitty, Mr. Pritchard-Mitford, Dr. Mitty." "I've read your book on streptothricosis," said Pritchard-Mitford,

The Secret Life of Walter Mitty

shaking hands. "A brilliant performance, sir." "Thank you," said Walter Mitty. "Didn't know you were in the States, Mitty," grumbled Remington. "Coals to Newcastle, bringing Mitford and me up here for a tertiary." "You are very kind," said Mitty. A huge, complicated machine, connected to the operating table, with many tubes and wires, began at this moment to go pocketa-pocketa-pocketa. "The new anaesthetiser is giving way!" shouted an interne. "There is no one in the East who knows how to fix it!" "Quiet, man!" said Mitty, in a low, cool voice. He sprang to the machine, which was now going pocketa-pocketa-queep-pocketa-queep. He began fingering delicately a row of glistening dials. "Give me a fountain pen!" he snapped. Someone handed him a fountain pen. He pulled a faulty piston out of the machine and inserted the pen in its place. "That will hold for ten minutes," he said. "Get on with the operation." A nurse hurried over and whispered to Renshaw, and Mitty saw the man turn pale. "Coreopsis has set in," said Renshaw nervously. "If you would take over, Mitty?" Mitty looked at him and at the craven figure of Benbow, who drank, and at the grave, uncertain faces of the two great specialists. "If you wish," he said. They slipped a white gown on him; he adjusted a mask and drew on thin gloves; nurses handed him shining . . . .

"Back it up, Mac! Look out for that Buick!" Walter Mitty jammed on the

The Secret Life of Walter Mitty

brakes. "Wrong lane, Mac," said the parking-lot attendant, looking at Mitty closely. "Gee. Yeh," muttered Mitty. He began cautiously to back out of the lane marked "Exit Only." "Leave her sit there," said the attendant. "I'll put her away." Mitty got out of the car. "Hey, better leave the key." "Oh," said Mitty, handing the man the ignition key. The attendant vaulted into the car, backed it up with insolent skill, and put it where it belonged.

They're so damn cocky, thought Walter Mitty, walking along Main Street; they think they know everything. Once he had tried to take his chains off, outside New Milford, and he had got them wound around the axles. A man had had to come out in a wrecking car and unwind them, a young, grinning garageman. Since then Mrs. Mitty always made him drive to a garage to have the chains taken off. The next time, he thought, I'll wear my right arm in a sling; they won't grin at me then. I'll have my right arm in a sling and they'll see I couldn't possibly take the chains off myself. He kicked at the slush on the sidewalk. "Overshoes," he said to himself, and he began looking for a shoe store.

When he came out into the street again, with the overshoes in a box under his arm, Walter Mitty began to wonder what the other thing was his wife had told him to get. She had told him, twice, before they set out from their house for Waterbury. In a way he hated these weekly trips to town - he was always getting something wrong. Kleenex, he thought, Squibb's, razor blades? No. Toothpaste, toothbrush, bicarbonate, carborundum, initiative and referendum? He gave it up. But she would remember it. "Where's the what's-its-name?" she would ask. "Don't tell me you forgot the what's-its-name." A newsboy went by shouting something about the Waterbury trial.

. . . . "Perhaps this will refresh your memory." The District Attorney suddenly thrust a heavy automatic at the quiet figure on the witness stand. "Have you ever seen this before?" Walter Mitty took the gun and examined it expertly. "This is my Webley-Vickers 50.80," he said calmly. An excited buzz ran around the courtroom. The Judge rapped for order. "You are a crack shot with any sort of firearms, I believe?" said the District Attorney, insinuatingly. "Objection!" shouted Mitty's attorney. "We have shown that the defendant could not have fired the shot. We have shown that he wore his right arm in a sling on the night of the fourteenth of July." Walter Mitty raised his hand briefly and the bickering attorneys were stilled. "With any known make of gun," he said evenly, "I could have killed Gregory Fitzhurst at three hundred feet *with my left hand.*" Pandemonium broke loose in the courtroom. A woman's scream rose above the bedlam and suddenly a lovely, dark-haired girl was in Walter Mitty's arms. The District Attorney struck at her savagely. Without rising from his chair, Mitty let the man have it on the point of the chin. "You miserable cur!". . . .

"Puppy biscuit," said Walter Mitty. He stopped walking and the buildings of Waterbury rose up out of the misty courtroom and surrounded him again. A woman who was passing laughed. "He said 'Puppy Biscuit,'" she said to her companion. "That man said 'Puppy biscuit' to himself." Walter Mitty hurried on. He went into an A. & P., not the first one he came to but a smaller one farther up the street. "I want some biscuit for small, young dogs," he said to the clerk. "Any special brand, sir?" The greatest pistol shot in the world thought a moment. "It says 'Puppies Bark for It' on the box," said Walter Mitty.

The Secret Life of Walter Mitty

His wife would be through at the hairdresser's in fifteen minutes, Mitty saw in looking at his watch, unless they had trouble drying it; sometimes they had trouble drying it. She didn't like to get to the hotel first; she would want him to be there waiting for her as usual. He found a big leather chair in the lobby, facing a window, and he put the overshoes and the puppy biscuit on the floor beside it. He picked up an old copy of *Liberty* and sank down into the chair. "Can Germany Conquer the World Through the Air?" Walter Mitty looked at the pictures of bombing planes and of ruined streets.

. . . . "The cannonading has got the wind up in young Raleigh, sir," said the sergeant. Captain Mitty looked up at him through tousled hair. "Get him to bed," he said wearily. "With the others, I'll fly alone." "But you can't, sir," said the sergeant anxiously. "It takes two men to handle that bomber and the Archies are pounding hell out of the air. Von Richtman's circus is between here and Saulier." "Somebody's got to get that ammunition dump," said Mitty. "I'm going over. Spot of brandy?" He poured a drink for the sergeant and one for himself. War thundered and whined around the dugout and battered at the door. There was a rending of wood and splinters flew through the room. "A bit of a near thing," said Captain Mitty carelessly. "The box barrage is closing in," said the sergeant. "We only live once, Sergeant," said Mitty, with his faint, fleeting smile. "Or do we?" He poured another brandy and tossed it off. "I never see a man could hold his brandy like you, sir," said the sergeant. "Begging your pardon, sir." Captain Mitty stood up and strapped on his huge Webley-Vickers automatic. "It's forty kilometres through hell, sir," said the sergeant. Mitty finished one last brandy. "After all," he said softly. "what isn't?" The pounding of the cannon increased; there was the rat-tat-tatting of machine guns, and from somewhere came the menacing pocketa-pocketa-pocketa of the new flame-throwers. Walter Mitty walked to the door of the dugout humming 'Auprès de Ma Blonde.' He turned and waved to the sergeant. "Cheerio!" he said . . . .

Something struck his shoulder. "I've been looking all over this hotel for you," said Mrs. Mitty. "Why do you have to hide in this old chair? How did you expect me to find you?" "Things close in," said Walter Mitty vaguely. "What?" Mrs. Mitty said. "Did you get the what's-its-name? The puppy biscuit? What's in that box?" "Overshoes," said Mitty. "Couldn't you have put them on in the store?" "I was thinking," said Walter Mitty. "Does it ever occur to you that I am sometimes thinking?" She looked at him. "I'm going to take your temperature when I get you home," she said.

They went out through the revolving doors that made a faintly derisive whistling sound when you pushed them. It was two blocks to the parking lot. At the drugstore on the corner she said, "Wait here for me. I forgot something. I won't be a minute." She was more than a minute. Walter Mitty lighted a cigarette. It began to rain, rain with sleet in it. He stood up against the wall of the drugstore, smoking . . . . He put his shoulders back and his heels together. "To hell with the handkerchief," said Walter Mitty scornfully. He took one last drag on his cigarette and snapped it away. Then, with that faint, fleeting smile playing about his lips, he faced the firing squad; erect and motionless, proud and disdainful, Walter Mitty the Undefeated, inscrutable to the last.

—James Thurber

The Secret Life of Walter Mitty

? Questions and Assignments

1. The story describes an afternoon in Walter Mitty's life. Write what you imagine would be his own diary account of the day. (Limit your answer to around 150 words and refer briefly to each of the daydreams.)
2. Write a character sketch of Walter Mitty from the point of view of his wife.
3. Describe the daydream that you found most interesting or amusing and comment very briefly on the characters and events.
4. Do you regard Walter Mitty as a sane person? Give reasons for your answer.
5. What are your impressions of Mitty's wife?
6. What evidence is there in the story to show that it is set in America?
7. Explain briefly how the author provides links or 'bridges' between the real world and Mitty's fantasy world.
8. Do you consider the story to be sad or humorous? In relation to this question you should carefully consider the final daydream. Has it a deeper significance than the others?
9. Does the story offer an important comment on modern life? Explain your answer.
10. (i) Imagine that an advertising agency discovered that a large proportion of adults indulged in fantasies similar to those of Walter Mitty. Describe the type of television advertisement they would produce, aimed at that group of adults, to sell
    (a) a car, (b) an aftershave lotion, (c) any other product of your choice.
    (ii) Describe some advertisements that seem to play on people's fantasies.
11. As Walter Mitty returns home, a police car speeds by with its siren blaring. Describe the daydream that follows.

S Spelling

Below are anagrams of words that are sometimes misspelt. Rearrange the letters to find the words. All the words are in the story.

- umornif
- uraylixia
- gorhuth
- arolliminie
- sistelciap
- defrin
- heminac
- inotigin
- ocatitaum
- fandented
- nargeset
- youlixsan
- rutapmerete
- etigatcer
- droulshes

V Vocabulary Development

Find words in the story to match each of the following meanings.

- shining
- splitting
- far away; distant
- threatening; dangerous
- mysterious; impenetrable
- scene of confusion or uproar
- much agitated in mind; distracted; perplexed
- totally
- mocking
- overbearing; insulting
- scornful; feeling superior
- more than ripe or ready for
- abject; degrading; cowardly; spiritless
- leapt
- spoke sharply
- quarrelling; wrangling
- untidy

The Secret Life of Walter Mitty

- moving swiftly, especially with clattering sound
- suddenly moved or plunged ahead; pitched suddenly forward.
- contemptuous; in a manner showing that he thought it beneath him.

☞ **Points to Note**

THEMES

The Secret Life of Walter Mitty is a very famous short story. It explores many themes that are very relevant in today's world. It highlights :-
- the difference between the real world and the world portrayed in many films, television dramas, comics and popular fiction.
- the need people have for some respect, admiration and sense of achievement to make life bearable.
- how the 'popular' media encourage people to escape into the world of dreams and fantasies and to shut out the real world.

Discuss in greater detail how the story deals with each of these themes. Can you suggest some other themes explored in the story?

REALISM IN LITERATURE

We all know what people mean when we hear them using expressions like *"the real world"* or *"be realistic"*. The word 'real' refers to situations as they are, rather than situations as we would wish them to be.

When a story, a play, a novel or a poem portrays the 'real' world with its hardships, injustices, disappointments and its other imperfections we would describe that literature as 'realistic'. We could say that it contains *'realism'*.

Sentimentality and *fantasy* are opposites to 'realism'. Stories, in which the wicked characters eventually suffer while the good ones find happiness, could be described as having elements of 'sentimentalism' in them. Much popular literature, such as 'love' stories and 'romances' rely on a large element of 'sentimentalism' for their popularity. Can you suggest why?

When a writer creates characters and events that are completely exaggerated and unreal, such writing is called 'fantasy'. Most stories tend to have elements of both 'realism' and 'sentimentalism' in them to varying degrees.

In *The Secret Life of Walter Mitty* we encounter *'realism'*. Mitty is a sad figure, living a life that seems to be completely devoid of excitement or fun. His wife seems to be a lady with a very unattractive personality, always nagging her husband and reminding him of his many faults. The people he encounters in his day-to-day activities regard him with either insolence, contempt or amusement.

In order to escape from this *'reality'* Walter Mitty uses his imagination to create a *'fantasy'* world. The characters and events of these fantasies are inspired by those of second-rate films and popular fiction.

CONTRAST

In order to give an extra impact to a particular theme or character a writer may set them off against one that is strikingly different. This is called *'contrast'*. In his portrayal of Walter Mitty, the author uses contrast. There is a striking difference between Walter Mitty in the real

The Secret Life of Walter Mitty

world and Walter Mitty in the fantasy world.

In the latter, Mitty is a truly admirable figure. He is calm in danger; a courageous and respected leader; a technical genius; modest about his talents and a heroic figure loved by a beautiful woman. In the real world he possesses none of these characteristics.

Outline Short Story Ideas

Attempt your own 'Walter Mitty' story set in Ireland of the nineties. Bear the following points in mind :-
- set the action over a short period.
- write from the omniscient point of view — i.e. you see and report the details of every fantasy.
- base the 'fantasy' episodes on people and scenarios that are frequently in the limelight such as people from the world of sport, music, business, politics etc.
- remember that your 'Walter Mitty' can be anybody — young, old, male, female — even yourself.

✓ Q. 3 — Sample Answer

The episode that I thought was very amusing was the one that takes place in the court room. Mitty is being charged with murder. He is relaxed and calm. The District Attorney is trying to pin the murder on Mitty. Mitty comes across as being an expert on guns and, according to the District Attorney, 'a crack shot with any sort of firearm'. His own lawyer claims that Mitty could not have fired the shot. The lawyers are bickering over this. Then Mitty 'stills' them with a 'brief' wave of his hand. At this point Mitty is noble, brave and honourable (and of course, foolish). "I could have killed Gregory Fitzhurst at three hundred feet *with my left hand*," he says. Uproar follows; a beautiful woman dives into his arms and he hits the District Attorney. When he calls him a 'miserable cur' Walter remembers the dog biscuits.

This fantasy is an over-the-top version of some of the court-room drama series that are often seen on television.

You're On Next Sunday

On the left the crosses and tombstones of Gale Churchyard stood pale and grey in the drenching moonlight. The pony stood rooted to the roadway, head bent, his whole frame taut and tense. There was white foam at the corners of his mouth and a look of abject terror, terrible to behold, in his bloodshot eyes.

"I don't like the look of things," my grand-uncle whispered.

"A rattling damn I don't give," Dowd shouted, "I'm getting out of here to see what the matter is."

"Stay as you are," my grand-uncle counselled but there was no stopping the headstrong Dowd. He jumped on to the roadway and walked round trap and pony several times.

"There's nothing here," he called out. He then proceeded towards the river thinking that some calamity might have overtaken the bridge and that the pony, with its animal instinct, might have sensed this. The bridge was in perfect order. Dowd looked over its twin parapets into the shallow, warbling water. He could see nothing unusual.

He retraced his steps and with a scornful toss of his grey head went towards the graveyard of Gale. As soon as he entered the little by-road which led to the gateway the pony lifted its head and followed slowly. It is well to remember that at no time did my grand-uncle leave the trap. He sat stiffly, holding the reins, carefully following his friend's every move.

When Dowd leaned across the gate of the graveyard he emitted a loud yell of genuine surprise. There before him were two hurling teams dressed in togs, jerseys and slippers. Every hurler had a hurley in his hand and at one side sitting on a low tombstone sat a small inoffensive-looking, bald-headed man. He wore a white jersey as distinct from the two teams who wore red and green respectively. He had a sliotar or hurley ball in one hand and in the other he held an ancient, burnished, copper hunting horn.

The pony had stopped dead a second time opposite the gateway over which Dowd was leaning.

"Come away out of that," my grand-uncle called out, "and leave the dead to themselves."

"What's the use?" Dowd called back, "the pony won't budge till it suits these people."

"What's the matter?" he called out to the hurlers who stood about as if they were waiting for something special to happen. At first no one heeded him but when he called out belligerently a second time a tall player with a face the colour of limestone approached the gate. He explained to Dowd that he was the captain of the red-jerseyed hurlers but that the game could not start because his team was short a man.

"Who are these teams anyway?" Dowd asked cheekily. The captain explained that his team was Ballyduff and the other team Ballybawn.

"Ho-ho," cried Dowd exultantly. "I'm your man. My mother, God be good to her, was a Ballyduff woman. If you have no objection I will play with your team."

The captain nodded silently and when my grand-uncle called to Dowd to abandon his arrant foolishness the captain turned and addressed him where he sat in the trap.

"Not an inch will you or your pony move," said he in a hollow, haunted voice, "until the final horn is sounded in this game of hurling." My grand-uncle said no more. The pony stood now like a statue and the sounds of the river were no longer to be heard. Overhead the moon shone brightly and the pitch, which was the length and breadth of the graveyard, was illuminated as though it was floodlit. Forms appeared from the ground and sat themselves on the graveyard wall. The referee looked upwards at the moon and after a few moments wait blew upon the hunting horn. Then he threw in the ball.

The exchanges started slowly enough with Dowd's team, Ballyduff, getting the worst of it from a faster Ballybawn side. The first score came when the referee awarded a free puck to Ballybawn. He also cautioned a number of the Ballyduff players, notably Dowd and the captain, for abusive language towards himself and for dirty play in general.

The Ballybawn skipper drove the ball straight between the uprights. On the graveyard walls the partisans went wild and a fist fight broke out near the gate. Somebody flung an empty cocoa cannister at the referee and he threatened to call off the game if the crowd did not behave themselves. There were a number of fistic exchanges on the field of play but by and large the standard of hurling was as good as my grand-uncle had seen for many a day. There were many fluent movements and excellent long-range scores. The wrist work and pulling left little to be desired. Half time came and went and now the two teams were playing for all they were worth. Time was slipping away and with five minutes to go the sides were level.

Neither would yield an inch. Every player strove manfully to register the single score that would put his own team ahead of the other. The ghostly forms jumped up and down on the walls egging the players on to greater deeds.

It seemed as if the game must end in a draw and the grand-uncle noted that from time to time the referee looked nervously at the full moon and feverishly fingered his hunting horn, anxious for full time to roll round so that he might wash his hands of the whole affair. There is nothing a referee loves so dearly as a drawn game. The hopes of both sides are kept alive and it is unlikely that he will be assaulted as he leaves the pitch. With less than a minute remaining there was a mêlée at midfield in which Dowd was involved. Fists flew and hurleys were raised. More than once could be heard the clash of ash against doughty skulls.

The referee intervened and taking a scroll from his togs pocket he commenced the business of taking names. It was during this lull that Dowd sat on a convenient tombstone to savour a richly-merited breather. He withdrew the half pint bottle from his trousers pocket and dolefully surveyed the remnants of his whiskey. The bottle was still quarter full. He raised it to his lips and without once taking it from his head swallowed the contents. Almost immediately he heaved a great sigh which could be heard all over the graveyard. Then he tightened his trousers belt and waited for play to resume.

With seconds remaining the hunting horn was sounded yet again and the ball was thrown in. Dowd it was who won possession. With a fierce and drunken yell he cut through his opponents like a scythe through switch-grass with the ball poised on the base of his hurley. There were times when he darted like a trout and times when he bounded like a stag. He leaped over gravemounds and skirted crosses and tombstones at breakneck speed. All the time he edged his way nearer the opposing goal line.

Seeing an opening on the left wing he seized his chance and headed straight for the goal with the entire Ballybawn team on his heels like a pack of hungry hounds. Thirty yards out he stopped dead and took a shot. The ball went away to the right but if it did it passed through the eye of a Celtic cross and rebounded off the head of a plaster angel. The rebound was deflected towards the goal by the extended hand of the figure of Michael the Archangel. It skeeved the left upright and found its way to the back of the net. Need I mention that while the ball was travelling so was the empty whiskey bottle which Dowd, with sound foresight, had flung at the Ballybawn goal-keeper as soon as the referee's back was turned. The crowd went wild. The Ballyduff team and supporters milled around Dowd and embraced him. Then they lifted him aloft and trotted round the graveyard on a lap of victory. Finishing the lap the Ballyduff captain called for three cheers for their visitor. Three eerie ullagones went heavenwards and died slowly till the muted river sounds took over once more. The teams had suddenly vanished save for the tall, ghostly presence of the Ballyduff captain. For the first time in over an hour the pony stirred. He pawed the dirt roadway, anxious for the high road.

"Come on at once," my grand-uncle called. Dowd, escorted by the captain, made his way towards the gate where the pony was now prancing and difficult to restrain. Dowd shook hands with the captain and was about to depart when a ghostly hand was laid firmly on his right shoulder. The captain leaned forward and whispered into Dowd's ear. Whatever it was he said Dowd's face underwent a terrible change. The glowing red nose was now puce-coloured and the rosy, whiskey-tinted cheeks were ashen grey. Slowly, almost painfully he climbed across the gate while the captain faded like a breeze-driven mist behind him.

In the trap Dowd was silent and thoughtful. On his face was a woebegone look that struck a chill in my grand-uncle's heart. The pony highstepped his way homewards, his dark mane flowing loosely behind him, his firm rump bobbing up and down as the miles passed by.

Finally my grand-uncle popped the question.

"What in heaven's name did he say to you?" he asked. Dowd shook his head sadly before he replied. Then he spoke slowly and deliberately with a crack in his voice.

"He informed me," Dowd announced, "that because of the way I played tonight I would be on for good next Sunday."

—*John B. Keane*

You're On Next Sunday

❓ Questions and Assignments

1. What is the first sign the two men get that there is something wrong?
2. (a) How does (i) Dowd and (ii) the writer's grand-uncle react on the two occasions when the pony stops dead?
   (b) What traits of character do their reactions reveal about each of them?
3. What does Dowd see when he leans across the gates of the graveyard?
4. Why, according to the captain of the red-jerseyed hurlers, can the game not go ahead?
5. (a) The writer sets an eerie scene before the match commences. What details does he use to build up this eerie atmosphere?
   (b) Comment on the two details you find most striking.
6. Why does the referee look at the moon a number of times?
7. Why does the referee like a drawn game?
8. What does Dowd do as the referee takes the names of a number of players?
9. The writer uses three similes to describe Dowd's speed and skill as he goes to score the winning goal : "he cut through his opponents like a scythe through switch-grass", "he darted like a trout", "he bounded like a stag". Comment on the aptness of each of these comparisons.
10. Why is Dowd "silent and thoughtful" on the way home?
11. What impressed you about the story?

Ⓢ Spelling

Below are anagrams of words that are sometimes misspelt. Rearrange the letters to find the words. All the words are in the story.

- amof
- hoprapcade
- hostgly
- tenighted
- cedellnous
- anipcat
- sauxion
- dezies
- srine
- tusate
- cemonemcd
- decblim
- sopotipe
- thadbre
- sinesubs
- nadounnce
- gudbe
- efreere
- voncentine

Ⓥ Vocabulary Development

Find words in the story to match each of the following meanings.

- fixed
- grave disaster
- triumphantly
- of the fists
- strange; weird
- singing in a sweet gentle manner
- gave out, sent forth
- a fight in which everything is confused
- cowardly; craven
- went back over
- warned
- tried
- sadly; drearily; painfully
- obstinate; self-willed
- in a fighting manner
- insulting
- appreciate
- downright
- low walls at the side of a bridge
- supporters of the teams

42

You're On Next Sunday

✓ Q. 11 — Sample Answer

What impressed me about this story is that it is a successful ghost story and yet a funny story. Parts of the story are very funny and yet I found it a little eerie and scary.

The comic description of the game of hurling really appealed to me. The details of the match — the "floodlit" pitch in the middle of the graveyard; the referee sitting on a low tombstone holding an ancient, burnished copper hunting horn; the two ghostly teams playing for their townlands; the forms that appear from the ground to support the teams — were hilarious and very original.

The description of play is at times very true to life. It is not unusual to find cautions given, fist fights breaking out or a row in the middle of the field at a local game.

As well as these realistic details, the writer adds some bizarre touches that I really liked — the referee taking a "scroll" from his pocket to take names while Dowd sits down to swallow the last quarter of his bottle of whiskey, the ball passing through the eye of a Celtic cross, rebounding off the head of a plaster angel, the rebound being deflected towards the goal by the extended hand of the figure of Michael the Archangel and finally the empty whiskey bottle travelling as well as the ball in the direction of the Ballybawn goal-keeper.

The punchline at the end gives the story a clever and original twist.

THE NEW GARDENER

Clem was the man for us. "No matter. I'll get it to rights," he said blithely, when he saw the state of the garden. Five weeks of early spring with no man in it, and a wet season at that, it was a fright. "And now where's the cottage?" he asked.

He had crossed over from Holyhead on the night boat, come down to Bective on the bus and walked up from the crossroads. "I left the family in Dublin," he said. "I want to get the cottage fixed up before they see it. It was a rough crossing, and Pearl got a little sick."

Which was Pearl? The snapshots he'd sent in lieu of an interview had shown him surrounded by a nice-sized family for so young a man. Holding on to one arm was a woman, presumably his wife, but she must have stirred as the snap was being taken, because she was a bit blurred. Her dark hair was cloudy anyway and it partly hid her face. In spite of the blurring, her features looked sharp though, but this was of small moment as long as she could take care of the small children that clung about Clem, especially the baby girl, who snuggled in his arms.

"They're coming down on the evening bus," he explained. "Where can I get a horse and cart? I want to pick up a few sticks of furniture for the place. I suppose I'll get one in the farmyard?"

In a few minutes he was rattling off in the farm cart, standing with his legs apart, his yellow hair lifting in the breeze of his departure, and the white tennis shoes — which he had worn also in the snap — looking, to the last glimpse, magnificently unsuitable. In less than an hour he was back with a load of fat mattresses, bulging pillows and bedding, the lot barricaded into the cart by a palisade of table legs and up-ended chairs.

"Another run and the job is done," he cried, as he toppled it all out on the grass patch in front of the cottage, and galloped off to town once more.

The second time he could be heard coming a mile away with a load of ewers and basins, pots and several pans, wash-hand stands, an oil cooker and tin cans, that clattered together on the cart behind him.

"These must be got into the house at once," he said solicitously to a young lad sent up from the yard to help him. "There's damp in the air, and I don't want them rusted. Don't stand there gawking, boy," he added, as Jimmy stared at the bedding already beaded with mist. "Bedding is easy aired. Rust is a serious matter. Learn to distinguish!" Then there began such a fury of lifting and carrying, pushing and pulling, such banging of nails and bringing down of plaster but, above all, such running in and out of the cottage that Clem's shoes came at last into their own. They were so apt for the job on foot.

By evening every picture was hung, every plate in place, the tables and chairs were right side up and the oil cooker lit and giving off its perfume. The bedding was still outdoors.

"No matter. Food comes first. Learn to distinguish!" cried Clem again, as he held a plate under a brown-paper bag and let plop out a mess of cream buns. "They'll be starving," he said. "Pearl isn't much of a feeder," he added sadly, "but the others have powerful appetites."

He still hadn't said which was Pearl, but it wasn't the wife anyway, because when Jimmy saw them trudging up the drive a while later, there was no wife, there was only Clem with the two small boys, the bigger girl, and the little one in his arms snuggled close to him, just as in the snap, with only her curls to be seen. Yet when Clem let down the child, Jimmy wondered no more, for she was the dead spit of a pearl.

"Did you ever see the like of her?" cried Clem delightedly, as he saw Jimmy looking at her. "She puts me in mind of apple blossom! That's what I should have called her — Blossom," he said sadly, "but no matter. I don't like fancy names anyway. Come now, Moll!" he said, turning to the bigger girl, "let's get her to bed. She's dog-tired." Planting Pearl in Moll's arms, he ran out and pulled in one of the mattresses. "It's a bit damp all right," he said, in surprise. But undismayed, he dashed into the garden and came back with three large rhubarb leaves. "Put them under the sheet," he said. "Leaves are waterproof. Trust nature every time." Then as Moll was about to stagger away with Pearl in her arms, he ran after them and gave Moll a hug. "She's the best little mother in the world," he said. "I don't know what I'd do without her."

It was the first and last reference, oblique as it was, to the absence of Mrs. Clem.

As the days went on, however, the absence of Mrs. Clem was seldom felt, for if Clem was a good father, he was a still better mother. True, he sometimes had to knock off work in the garden to cook a hot meal for them all, to fetch them from school, or oftenest of all to wash Pearl's hair, but he still did more work in one day than another man would in six. And it wasn't just hard work: Clem had a green hand if ever man had.

On the first morning of all, he made his only complaint. "There isn't enough shelter in this garden," he said. "Living things are very tender." And disregarding the fact that

The New Gardener

he'd just whitened his tennis shoes, he leapt into the soft black clay of the border and broke off branches recklessly from syringa, philadelphus and daphne. Then he rushed around sticking the twigs into the ground, here, there and everywhere.

He must be marking the places where he's going to plant, thought Jimmy. But before a week was out, the twigs that at first had wilted and lost their leaves stiffened into life again and put forth new shoots. A green hand? When Clem struck a spade into the ground at the end of a day, Jimmy half-expected to see it sprouting leaves by morning. There was nothing Clem couldn't do with a plant. In any weather he'd put down a seed. In any weather he'd take up a seedling. "It'll be all right if you handle it lightly," he'd say smiling, planting seeds gaily, with rain falling so heavily on the wet clay that it splashed back into his face and spattered it all over. And when the sun did shine, as often as not he'd be down on his knees with his box of seedlings, pricking them out.

"Won't they die in the sun?" asked Jimmy.

"Why would they die?" cried Clem. "Like all living things, they only ask to be handled gently."

To see Clem handle a young plant, you'd think it was some small animal that he held in his hands. Even the seeds got their full share of his love and care, every single one, no matter how many to a packet. Once he nearly made Jimmy scratch up a whole cement floor in the potting shed where he'd let one seed fall.

"We can't leave it there with no food and no drink and no light and no covering," he cried, as he lit a match to help in the search.

Jimmy felt a bit put upon. "What about all the packets of seeds that are up there on the shelf?" he protested. "The last fellow forgot to sow them until it was too late!"

"But it's never too late!" cried Clem. "Where are they?" And the next minute he had rummaged out the old seeds with their discoloured paper-packets and their faded flower prints. "Everything should get its chance," he cried, and he gathered up every flower pot in sight and, filling them with the finest of sieved clay, he poked a seed into each one. "If there's life in those seeds, they'll take flight before the end of the week!" he told Jimmy. And in less than a week, over each pot there hovered two frail green wings. Yet, for all the energy he spent on plants and chores, Clem still had energy to spare.

"How is the fishing around here?" he asked one evening, a few weeks after his arrival. "I'd like to take the children fishing. Wouldn't you like to go fishing, Pearl?" he asked, turning to her. She was a good little thing, and she never gave any trouble. All the minding she got was following Clem around the place. Now and again he'd tell her to get off a cold stone, or to mind would a wasp sting her. There was one thing he was very particular about though, and that was she should not take off the little woolly coat she always wore.

"Pearly hot!" Pearl would say. No matter! He made her keep the coat on. It was, however, very hot indeed that afternoon in May, and when Clem bent down to dibble in a few colchicums for the autumn, Pearl stamped her foot.

"Pearly hot," she said, defiantly, and off she took the yellow woolly coat and down she threw it on the ground. Jimmy bent down to pick it up. When he looked up, he was astonished to see Clem's eyes filled with tears. "I hate anyone to see it," said Clem. "I can't bear to look at it myself! But I knew it couldn't be covered forever!"

<u>On the inner, softer side of Pearl's arm was a long sickle-shaped scar.</u> It was healed. It wasn't really very noticeable.

The New Gardener

Many a child had a scar twice as big on its knee, or on its elbow, or even its nose! But all the same, Pearl's scar made Jimmy shudder. Perhaps because it was on the soft underflesh, perhaps because of the look it had brought to Clem's eyes, this scar of Pearl's seemed to have a terrible importance.

"Was it an accident, Clem?"

"No," said Clem shortly.

Could Clem . . .? But no, no! <u>She was his seedling, his fledgling, his little plant that, if he could, he would cup between his hands, and breathe upon, press close and hold</u> against himself forever. As it was, he put his arms around her. "Wouldn't you like to catch a little fish, Pearl?" he was asking her. "I'll get a sally wand for you, and I'll peel it white! You'll catch a great big salmon maybe!"

His own ambition was more humble. He turned abruptly to Jimmy. "I suppose there's plenty of pike?" he asked. "Can we get a frog, do you think? Frogs are the only bait for pike. Get hold of a good frog, Jimmy, and we'll meet you down at Cletty Bridge in ten minutes."

To get a frog on a May evening in Meath! On a wet day, yes — the roads were plastered with them, sprawled out where cars had gone over them. But this evening Clem and the children must have been a full hour down by Cletty pool before Jimmy came running to them, his hand over his pocket.

The children were all calling to each other and laughing, and Clem was shouting excitedly, but it was Pearl's small voice that caught the ear, <u>babbling as joyously to Clem as the pebbles to the stream.</u> There was joy and excitement in the air, and joy welled up in Jimmy's heart too, as he scrambled over the wall and tumbled happily down the bank, filling the air with the bittersweet smell of elder leaves as he caught at a branch to save himself from falling.

"Good man! You've got the bait!" cried Clem, his expert eye picking out the bulge in Jimmy's pocket. He was helping Pearl to cast her line. It was a peeled willow wand and dangling from it was a big black hairpin bent into a hook. As Jimmy took the frog out of his pocket, however, Clem reached for his own rod which, to have out of harm's way, he had placed crosswise in the cleft of an elder bush that hung over the stream. As he took it down, the taut gut slashed through tender young leaves and, once again, their bitter scent was let out upon the air.

"Here, Jimmy! Here's the hook!" he cried. "Put on the frog!" Taking a tobacco tin out of his pocket, Clem selected a hook and, fingering it gently free of the other hooks and flies, he laid it in Jimmy's palm. Then he began to unwind his reel. For a few minutes the sound of the winding reel asserted itself over all the other sounds in the glade, until gradually it was absorbed into the general pattern of sound.

Suddenly there was another sound; a horrible sound. It was a screech. And it split the air. It turned every other sound into silence. It was the frog. There was nothing human in that screech, but every human ear in the green place knew what the screech held — it held pain — and pain as humans know it.

"What did you do to him?" yelled Clem, and <u>his face went black with rage.</u> Throwing down the line, he caught hold of the screeching frog. Quick as thought, he pulled out the hook that had only gone a small way into the bulging belly, but had brought out a bubble of its bile-like blood. Then, throwing down the hook and stamping on it, he held the little slimy creature between his two hands.

"You are all right now," he told it,

The New Gardener

looking into its bulbous eyes, as if to cast out its fear. Then he turned to Jimmy again. "You didn't know any better," he said sadly. "You're only a child yourself. But let this be a lesson to you. Never in your life hurt or harm a defenceless thing! Or if you do, than don't let me see you do it! Because I could not stand it. I could not stand it," he repeated, less gently. "I never did a cruel thing in my life. I couldn't do one if I tried and — by God's blood — I could not see one done either! I only saw a cruel deed done in my presence once." Then he lowered his voice so only Jimmy could hear, "and once was enough! I couldn't stand it." And he closed his eyes and pressed his hands over them as if he saw it all again. When he took down his hands after a minute, and opened his eyes again, he had a dazed look. It was as if he was astonished to find himself here, where he was, on the sunlit bank. More than that — he looked amazed that the sun could shine, amazed that the birds could sing.

"Are you feeling all right?" asked Jimmy.

Clem looked at him dazedly. Then it was as if he took a plunge back into the happiness around him.

"Here, give me a hook!" he cried, rooting around in the box. "This is the way it's done!" Deftly tucking up the legs of the frog so it fitted snugly into one hand, he nicked its back with the point of the barb, and then swiftly he passed the hook under the skin and brought it out again as if it were a needle and thread and he had just taken a long leisurely stitch. "There! You see! It didn't feel a thing," he said, and hastily fixing the hook to the end of the line he reeled out a few yards of it and let the frog hang down.

Delightedly he gazed at it for a minute, as it moved its legs rhythmically outward and inward in a swimming motion. "Wait till we let him into the water!" he cried then, and he ran to the edge of the pool, scattering the children to either side and throwing the line out over the pool. Suspended in the air the frog hung down, as still as the lead on the end of a plumb line, its image given back by the clear water that gave back also the blue sky and the white clouds as if they were under, not over, the pebbles and stones. Then Clem began to unwind the reel, and the frog in the air and the frog in the pool began to draw close to each other, till the real frog hit the water with a smack. Once there, its legs began to work again.

"Swim away, Son," said Clem indulgently, and he unwound more of the line.

"You'd think it was taking swimming lessons, wouldn't you?" he said, watching it amiably.

"But won't the pike eat him?" said Jimmy. "Isn't that worse than getting the hook stuck in him?"

Clem turned around. "Nonsense!" he cried. "Death and pain are two different things. Learn to distinguish, boy!" And he called to Pearl "Would you like to hold the line for a while, Pearl?"

But Pearl was not looking at the frog. Something behind them had caught her attention.

"Who are those men, Daddy?" she asked, as two big men in dust-coats, who had been watching the scene for some time from the causeway, began to get over the wall and slide down the bank towards them.

Clem looked back. "Here, Jimmy," he said. That was all and he handed him the line.

"You know why we're here?" asked one of the detectives. Clem simply answered their question with a question of his own. "What about the children?" he asked.

The New Gardener

Never would Jimmy have thought that detectives could be so gentle-like and kind. "The children will be well treated, Clem," said one. The other addressed Jimmy. "Stay here with them you, Jimmy, and keep them amused. We've got a policewoman in the car up on the drive, and she'll come down to you in a minute and see what's to be done." They turned to Clem. "We'll have to ask you to come with us, I'm afraid."

Clem nodded briefly. Then he turned to Jimmy. "Here, give me the line again for a minute," he said, and as Pearl had snuggled close to him, her two arms around one leg as if it was a pillar, he freed her grasp and put the rod into her hand.

"You can have the first turn, Pearly," he said. "Then Moll. Then the others. After that it will be turn and turn about for you all!" His voice was authoritative, even stern. Then he nodded to the men, and finding it slippery to walk in the dirty tennis shoes, he caught at some of the elder branches, and by their help scrambled up the bank alongside the men.

— *Mary Lavin*

Questions and Assignments

1. A good deal of background information is implied in the opening two paragraphs of the story. State clearly what we learn from these *two paragraphs only*.
2. Comment on the narrator's response to the snapshot of Clem's family.
3. What features of his character does Clem reveal during his first evening in Bective?
4. Outline Clem's attitude towards his work.
5. Describe the kind of father that Clem was. Refer to the story to support your answer.
6. (i) Describe Clem's reaction when the frog screeched.
   (ii) What aspect of Clem's character is revealed by such a reaction?
7. Comment on the way Clem is treated by the detectives.
8. (i) Each of the underlined sections contains a comparison. Identify the comparison, in each case, and suggest its purpose.
   (ii) Which of the comparisons is a metaphor. Explain your choice.
9. The story builds up to the arrest of Clem. Comment on how the writer prepares us for this. Were you surprised at his arrest?
10. Read carefully the paragraph - "Delightedly he gazed at it . . . . began to work again" - which is near the end of the story? Now consider if this paragraph has any particular significance in relation to Clem's plight.
11. Write an alternative ending for the story.

Spelling

Below are anagrams of words that are sometimes misspelt. Rearrange the letters to find the words. All the words are in the story.

- tinreviwe
- drousrunde
- rifturune
- testapipe
- ripplesy
- uitroatvathie
- eblitanceo
- ledigledthy
- ralpil
- ulsreiley
- hisdonates
- recenerfe
- duglaraly
- tasresde
- latfenidy
- niclagtemfiny
- cotacob
- inobtaim
- evides
- drulber

The New Gardener

V Vocabulary Development

Find words in the story to match each of the following meanings.

- skilfully
- shivered
- blocked
- indirect
- ignoring
- spoke to
- instead of
- held; hung up
- drooped; faded
- held; hung up
- swallowed up; merged with
- lay close up to for warmth
- shaped like a bulb
- hanging loosely
- young dependant
- clear space in forest
- water-jugs; pitchers
- ransacked or searched
- bewildered; puzzled
- young plant raised from seed
- in the carefree manner; casually
- in a shape or manner of a cross
- anxiously; in a concerned manner
- fence of pointed stakes
- not feeling disappointed or discouraged
- plant by making holes to receive bulbs
- walking laboriously or heavily
- showing a friendly and pleasant attitude
- raised road/footway across low or wet ground
- fell with sound like a smooth object dropping into water
- made his way by clambering; made his way with disorderly struggling haste

Writers' Workshop

CREATING CHARACTERS

Short stories may occasionally have no *plots* or only the barest of settings, but they all have at least one *character* who is well drawn. each of the following points should be considered in relation to the manner in which Clem's character is drawn in *The New Gardener*.

In most stories the reader will either develop a liking for a certain character and will want him or her to succeed or else will dislike a character and will feel satisfied if that character is defeated. A story in which the reader does not care what will happen to a character will not be a successful story. However, such stories rarely succeed in getting published.

In a small proportion of stories, the author will provide the reader with a complete portrait of a character at the beginning of the story. The majority of writers, however, prefer to reveal their characters gradually and to allow the reader to make up his or her own mind about a character.

In drawing life-like characters, writers use all or most of the following techniques :-
- *Appearance:* details of a character's appearance help a reader to visualise the character. Appearance frequently provides insight into a person's character. Sometimes first impressions and appearances can deceive.
- *Actions:* the things a character does, or fails to do, can tell a good deal about the kind of person that character is.
- *Words:* the things a person says (and how he or she speaks) can reveal much about their personality. In their words they may often reveal things which they did not intend to reveal.
- *Other characters' attitudes*: the views and attitudes of other characters can be important in making an assessment of a certain character.
- *Motivation:* All characters want to achieve some goal or other. The nature of that goal (selfish, generous, noble, etc.) can be very revealing.

The New Gardener

- *Facing a crisis:* The manner in which a character acts when faced with a sudden and unexpected decision or crisis often shows a side of somebody that may never have otherwise been revealed.

Most of the short story assignments in this book offer scope for creating and developing your own fictitious characters. In doing so you should bear the above points in mind.

These points will also be useful when you are writing descriptions of characters from short stories, novels and plays that you have studied.

📖 Outline Short Story Ideas

Character A is faced with a decision. He/She must choose between private personal gain or the public good. Most of the story outlines and dramatises this situation. In the closing paragraph we see **A** making the choice. Two points worth noting: (i) you must decide whether A's choice is in keeping with his/her character or not. (ii) you will give the story a further dramatic edge by revealing that **A** will not be publicly linked to the consequences of his/her decision. This idea has many possibilities. Here are just two suggestions:-

(a) Somebody whom you dislike is accused in the wrong. You know that your best friend/son/father is guilty . . . . (b) **A** who is a wealthy industrialist has an opportunity to use a new manufacturing process that will boost profits. However, he/she also knows that the new process will have serious long-term effects on the environment . . . .

✓ Q. 9 — Sample Answer

From almost the beginning of the story the narrator creates a sense of mystery around Clem's wife. She is first referred to when the family photograph is described. In it, the children all bunch close to Clem and the wife's features looked 'sharp'. The narrator is clearly hinting that the wife is not a likeable lady.

When the rest of the family arrive, Clem describes his older daughter as "the best little mother in the world". The narrator tells us that this was Clem's only reference to his absent wife. He gives no explanation and he is not asked for one by his new employers. I find this hard to believe.

When Pearl takes off her coat and Jimmy sees the scar, Clem's response is a little too dramatic to be believable. When he admits that the scar wasn't accidental, it is fairly obvious that Clem's wife was responsible.

Clem's behaviour, when Jimmy hurts the frog, is very extreme. He goes into a black rage and then talks about 'cruel deeds'. It is very obvious from his words what deed he meant. Shortly afterwards he comments on the difference between pain and death. At this point it is clear he killed his wife and his arrest came as no surprise to me.

The Night the Ghost Got In

The ghost that got into our house on the night of November 17, 1915, raised such a hullabaloo of misunderstanding that I am sorry I didn't just let it keep on walking, and go to bed. Its advent caused my mother to throw a shoe through a window of the house next door and ended up with my grandfather shooting a patrolman. I am sorry, therefore, as I have said, that I ever paid any attention to the footsteps.

They began about a quarter past one o'clock in the morning, a rhythmic quick-cadenced walking around the dining-room table. My mother was asleep in one room upstairs, my brother Herman in another; grandfather was in the attic, in the old walnut bed which, as you will remember, once fell on my father. I had just stepped out of the bathtub and was busily rubbing myself with a towel when I heard the steps. They were the steps of a man walking rapidly round the dining-room table downstairs. The light from the bathroom shone down the back steps, which dropped directly into the dining-room; I could see the faint shine of plates on the plate-rail; I couldn't see the table. The steps kept going round and round the table; at regular intervals a board creaked, when it was trod upon. I supposed at first that it was my father or my brother Roy, who had gone to Indianapolis but were expected home at any time. I suspected next that it was a burglar. It did not enter my mind until later that it was a ghost.

After the walking had gone on for perhaps three minutes, I tiptoed to Herman's room. "Psst!" I hissed, in the dark, shaking him. "Awp," he said, in the low hopeless tone of a despondent beagle — he always half suspected that something would 'get him' in the night. I told him who I was. "There's something downstairs!" I said. He got up and followed me to the head of the back staircase. We listened together. There was no sound. The steps had ceased. Herman looked at me in alarm: I had only the bath towel around my waist. He wanted to go back to bed, but I gripped his arm. "There's something down there!" I said. Instantly the steps began again, circled the dining-room table like a man running, and started up the stairs toward us, heavily, two at a time. The light still shone palely down the stairs; we saw nothing coming; we only heard the steps. Herman rushed to his room and slammed the door. I slammed shut the door at the stairs top and held my knee against it. After a long minute, I slowly opened it again. There was nothing there. There was no sound. None of us ever heard the ghost again.

The slamming of the doors had aroused mother: she peered out of her room. "What on earth are you boys doing?" she demanded. Herman ventured out of his room. "Nothing," he said, gruffly, but he was, in colour, a light green. "What was all that running down-stairs?" said mother. So she had heard the steps too! We just looked at her. "Burglars!" she shouted, intuitively. I tried to quiet her by starting lightly downstairs.

"Come on, Herman," I said.

"I'll stay with mother," he said. "She's all excited."

I stepped back on to the landing.

"Don't either of you go a step," said mother. "We'll call the police." Since the phone was downstairs, I didn't see how we were going to call the police — nor did I want the police — but mother made one of her quick, incomparable decisions. She flung up the window of her bedroom which faced the bedroom windows of the house of a neighbour, picked up a shoe, and

The Night the Ghost Got In

whammed it through a pane of glass across the narrow space that separated the two houses. Glass tinkled into the bedroom occupied by a retired engraver named Bodwell and his wife. Bodwell had been for some years in rather a bad way and was subject to mild 'attacks'. Most everybody we knew or lived near had *some* kind of attacks.

It was now about two o'clock of a moonless night; clouds hung black and low. Bodwell was at the window in a minute, shouting, frothing a little, shaking his fist. "We'll sell the house and go back to Peoria," we could hear Mrs. Bodwell saying. It was some time before mother 'got through' to Bodwell. "Burglars!" she shouted. "Burglars in the house!" Herman and I hadn't dared to tell her that it was not burglars but ghosts, for she was even more afraid of ghosts than of burglars. Bodwell at first thought that she meant there were burglars in his house, but finally he quietened down and called the police for us

The Night the Ghost Got In

over an extension phone by his bed. After he had disappeared from the window, mother suddenly made as if to throw another shoe, not because there was further need of it but, as she later explained, because the thrill of heaving a shoe through a window glass had enormously taken her fancy. I prevented her.

The police were on hand in a commendably short time: a Ford sedan full of them, two on motorcycles, and a patrol wagon with about eight in it and a few reporters. They began banging at our front door. Flashlights shot streaks of gleam up and down the walls, across the yard, down the walk between our house and Bodwell's. "Open up!" cried a hoarse voice. "We're men from Headquarters!" I wanted to go down and let them in, since there they were, but mother wouldn't hear of it. "You haven't a stitch on," she pointed out. "You'd catch your death." I wound the towel around me again. Finally the cops put their shoulders to our big heavy front door with its thick bevelled glass and broke it in: I could hear a rending of wood and a splash of glass on the floor of the hall. Their lights played all over the living room and crisscrossed nervously in the dining room, stabbed into hallways, shot up the front stairs and finally up the back. They caught me standing in my towel at the top. A heavy policeman bounded up the steps. "Who are you?" he demanded. "I live here," I said. "Well, whattsa matta, ya hot?" he asked. It was, as a matter of fact, cold; I went to my room and pulled on some trousers. On my way out, a cop stuck a gun in my ribs. "Whatta you doin' here?" he demanded. "I live here," I said.

The officer in charge reported to mother. "No sign of nobody, lady," he said. "Musta got away — whatt'd he look like?" "There were two or three of them," mother said, "whooping and carrying on and slamming doors." "Funny," said the cop. "All ya windows and doors was locked on the inside tight as a tick."

Downstairs, we could hear the tromping of the other police. Police were all over the place; doors were yanked open, drawers were yanked open, windows were shot up and pulled down, furniture fell with dull thumps. A half-dozen policemen emerged out of the darkness of the front hallway upstairs. They began to ransack the floor; pulled beds away from walls, tore clothes off hooks in the closets, pulled suitcases and boxes off shelves. One of them found an old zither that Roy had won in a pool tournament. "Looky here, Joe," he said, strumming it with a big paw. The cop named Joe took it and turned it over. "What is it?" he asked me. "It's an old zither our guinea pig used to sleep on," I said. It was true that a pet guinea pig we once had would never sleep anywhere except on the zither, but I should never have said so. Joe and the other cop looked at me a long time. They put the zither back on a shelf.

"No sign o' nuthin'," said the cop who had first spoken to mother. "This guy," he explained to the others, jerking a thumb at me, "was nekked. The lady seems historical." They all nodded, but said nothing; just looked at me. In the small silence we all heard a creaking in the attic. Grandfather was turning over in bed. "What's 'at?" snapped Joe. Five or six cops sprang for the attic door before I could intervene or explain. I realised that it would be bad if they burst in on grandfather unannounced, or even announced. He was going through a phase in which he believed that General Meade's men, under steady hammering by Stonewall Jackson, were beginning to retreat and even desert.

When I got to the attic, things were pretty confused. Grandfather had evidently jumped to the conclusion that the police

The Night the Ghost Got In

were deserters from Meade's army, trying to hide away in his attic. He bounded out of bed wearing a long flannel nightgown over long woollen underwear, a nightcap, and a leather jacket around his chest. The cops must have realised at once that the indignant white-haired old man belonged in the house, but they had no chance to say so. "Back, ye cowardly dogs!" roared grandfather. "Back t' the lines, ye goddam lily-livered cattle!" With that, he fetched the officer who found the zither a flat-handed smack alongside his head that sent him sprawling. The others beat a retreat, but not fast enough; grandfather grabbed Zither's gun from its holster and let fly. The report seemed to crack the rafters; smoke filled the attic. A cop cursed and shot his hand to his shoulder. Somehow, we all finally got downstairs again and locked the door against the old gentleman. He fired once or twice more in the darkness and then went back to bed. "That was grandfather," I explained to Joe, out of breath. "He thinks you're deserters." "I'll say he does," said Joe.

The cops were reluctant to leave without getting their hands on somebody besides grandfather; the night had been distinctly a defeat for them. Furthermore, they obviously didn't like the 'lay-out'; something looked — and I can see their viewpoint — phoney. They began to poke into things again. A reporter, a thin-faced, wispy man, came up to me. I had put on one of mother's blouses, not being able to find anything else. The reporter looked at me with mingled suspicion and interest. "Just what the hell is the real lowdown here, Bud?" he asked. I decided to be frank with him. "We had ghosts," I said. He gazed at me a long time as if I were a slot machine in which he had, without results, dropped a nickel. Then he walked away. The cops followed him, the one grandfather shot holding his now-bandaged arm, cursing and blaspheming. "I'm gonna get my gun back from that old bird," said the zither cop. "Yeh," said Joe. "You — and who else?" I told them I would bring it to the station house the next day.

"What was the matter with that one policeman?" mother asked, after they had gone. "Grandfather shot him," I said. "What for?" she demanded. I told her he was a deserter. "Of all things!" said mother. "He was such a nice-looking young man."

Grandfather was fresh as a daisy and full of jokes at breakfast next morning. We thought at first he had forgotten all about what had happened, but he hadn't. Over his third cup of coffee, he glared at Herman and me. "What was the idee of all them cops tarryhootin' round the house last night?" he demanded.

He had us there.

—*James Thurber*

? Questions and Assignments

1. Who were the occupants of the house?
2. Describe briefly the noises made by the 'ghost'. Does the writer reveal if there really was a ghost? Explain.
3. What features of the story did you find particularly funny?
4. Was the mother a 'normal' person? Give reasons for your answer.
5. How did Herman respond to the crisis?
6. Why did the police break down the door?

The Night the Ghost Got In

7. Were you impressed with the manner in which the police handled the crisis?
8. "Joe and the other cop looked at me for a long time". Comment on the significance of this sentence.
9. Police are regularly required to write reports on situations they encounter in the course of duty. Imagine that you were one of the policemen in the story. Write a report on the incident. Your report should not be longer than 250 words.
10. Imagine a reporter from *The Sun* arriving at the scene when all the excitement is over. The police and the reporters have gone. All in the narrator's house are asleep. The only people awake are the Bodwells and they are very confused and in a state of shock. The reporter conducts a brief interview with the couple and then writes a report of the event, based on the interview. Compose a suitable headline to accompany your story.
    Suggestion: **Poltergeist in Shoot-out Drama**

Spelling

Below are anagrams of words that are sometimes misspelt. Rearrange the letters to find the words. All the words are in the story.

- thogs
- supraits
- cedidde
- neciham
- gingebnin
- iposcunis
- largrub
- catit
- lisuby
- nufruiter
- sonciside
- naplexied
- vayhe
- seadec
- lugrare
- arpedseat
- poccudie
- leaply
- counanunned

Vocabulary Development

Find words in the story to match each of the following meanings.

- dared to go
- dim
- uproar
- swearing
- throwing
- leaped, sprung
- angry, scornful
- shut with a bang
- without an equal
- pulled with a jerk
- with sloping edge
- looked searchingly
- woven woollen cloth
- a backward movement
- in a praiseworthy manner
- in a rough or abrupt manner
- made sound as of a small bell
- regularly occurring; with a regular beat
- sloping beams forming framework of roof

Points to Note

NARRATOR AND POINT OF VIEW

The Night the Ghost Got In is narrated (told from the point of view of the principal character in the story. Almost from the beginning he strikes us as a rather odd individual. He is a somewhat naive and eccentric character. At times he appears stupid and unable to understand or control the events that he has set in motion. He seems blind to the fact that other members of his family are also somewhat crazy. He speaks about them as if they were well-balanced

The Night the Ghost Got In

and sane people. He describes the events of the night in a serious and deadpan manner, as if other households suffered similar mishaps. He is completely unaware that the police and the reports regard him as being an odd-ball.

By giving this type of personality to the narrator the author allows much of the humour to occur at the expense of the narrator.

Humour in Stories - Principal Elements

"One man's meat is another man's poison" is a proverb that readily applies to humour. Not everybody finds the same situation funny. Therefore attempts to define or explain humour are, to an extent, futile. However, the humorous elements in *The Night the Ghost Got In* provide useful examples of the basics of much successful humorous writing. In the story we find examples of:-

Situation Comedy

This type of comedy arises from a series of misunderstandings and mis-ups, leading to characters ending up in odd or ridiculous situation.

Odd Characters

People with an eccentric or an odd side to their personality are a source of humour, especially in their efforts to carry out everyday tasks or deal with minor problems.

Humorous Dialogue

The two elements above - situation comedy and odd characters invariably result in humorous exchanges of words. All comic drama on film and stage is largely made up of these three elements above. However, the writer who is aiming for a humourous effect has some further scope.

The Way It's Told

The writer can use phrases and expressions that are funny in themselves.

Let The Joke Be On You

Also, the writer can choose to become the main source of the humour, by directing the laughter at herself or himself.

Writers' Workshop

HUMOROUS WRITING - ONE APPROACH

Humorous writing primarily aims to make readers smile and even laugh a little. On that topic, Casanova, an Italian writer had this to say:

"If you want to make people weep you must weep yourself. If you want to make people laugh, your face must remain serious."

Thurber's technique in *The Night The Ghost Got In* largely reflects these words. Much can be learned about humorous writing by looking closely at this technique. Much of the humour is allowed to occur at the narrator's expense. (Don't confuse the narrator and the author). To attempt a short humorous story that loosely follows Thurber's technique you should find it useful to bear the following suggestions in mind.

The Night the Ghost Got In

- Begin by adopting an odd or eccentric personality. You can be anybody - young, old, rich, poor, male, female. Establish your new 'identity' early in your story.
- Next become entangled in a situation (or a series of situations) which will appear ridiculous and comical to all except you. Try to keep these just within the bounds of possibility.
- Avoid pointing out the funny side of things to your readers. Let them spot them for themselves.
- Television situation comedies and books such as the William series will provide you with plenty of ideas. Below are a few outline ideas, some of which you may like to develop.

📖 Outline Short Story Ideas

Now attempt a humorous story, applying the techniques outlined above. You may get some inspiration from one of the extracts that follow.

- Let me make it plain from the beginning: training guinea-pigs to play snooker is not an easy task. Some people would laugh at the idea. Yet I felt it had potential. Just look at the size of the horse racing business, I said to myself.
- 'A clean home is a happy home' - that's my motto . . . .
- The thing about insects is that they make very loyal pets. Not many people realise this.
- What made me realise that people are afraid of me happened last week. When I walked up to this man to ask him the time, he shoved his watch and his wallet into my hand and ran off. Maybe it's the way I dress. Or then again my hairstyle?
- Being a poet can be a very dangerous and exciting occupation. I should know . . . .
- When you consider that it's a historical fact that Sir Edmund Hannibal climbed Mount Everest on an elephant it makes you realise just how much animals can do - with a little training.
- As a hobby, tight-rope walking has its ups and downs . . . .

✓ Q. 3 — Sample Answer

There are some very funny touches in the story *The Night the Ghost Got In* (by James Thurber).

One example is when the narrator's mother throws a shoe through the neighbour's bedroom window. She does this to wake them up and to get them to call the police. If there had been any burglars in the house the racket the mother made would surely have frightened them away. To add insult to injury she wants to throw another shoe at another window because she enjoyed the first effort so much!

Another funny touch is the way some of the characters were dressed. The narrator starts out in a bath-towel and ends up wearing a trousers and one of his mother's blouses. The grandfather also had odd tastes when it came to dressing for bed.

Another example of humour is the behaviour of the police, not to mention the large number of them that turned up to arrest the burglars - who were never there in the first place.

These are just some examples of humour in the story. There are many more to be found in this story which tells about a very odd family in a very odd situation. It would make a hilarious film.

The Gift

Tomorrow would be Christmas and even while the three of them rode to the rocket port, the mother and father were worried. It was the boy's first flight into space, his very first time in a rocket, and they wanted everything to be perfect. So when, at the customs table, they were forced to leave behind his gift which exceeded the weight limit by no more than a few ounces and the little tree with the lovely white candles, they felt themselves deprived of the season and their love.

The boy was waiting for them in the Terminal room. Walking towards him, after their unsuccessful clash with the Interplanetary officials, the mother and father whispered to each other.

"What shall we do?"

"Nothing, nothing. What *can* we do?"

"Silly rules!"

"And he so wanted the tree!"

The siren gave a great howl and people pressed forward into the Mars Rocket. The mother and father walked at the very last, their small pale son between them, silent.

"I'll think of something," said the father.

"What . . . ?" asked the boy.

And the rocket took off and they were flung headlong into dark space.

The rocket moved and left fire behind and left Earth behind on which the date was December 24th, 2052, heading out into a place where there was no time at all, no month, no year, no hour. They slept away the rest of the first 'day'. Near midnight, by their Earth-time New York watches, the boy awoke and said, "I want to go look out the porthole."

There was only one port, a 'window' of immensely thick glass, of some size, up on the next deck.

"Not quite yet," said the father. "I'll take you up later."

"I want to see where we are and where we are going."

"I want you to wait, for a reason," said the father.

He had been lying awake, turning this way and that, thinking of the abandoned gift, the problem of the season, the lost tree and the white candles. And at last, sitting up, no more than five minutes ago, he believed he had found a plan. He need only carry it out and this journey would be fine and joyous indeed.

"Son," he said, "in exactly one half-hour it will be Christmas."

"Oh," said the mother, dismayed that he had mentioned it. Somehow she had rather hoped the boy would forget.

The boy's face grew feverish and his lips trembled. "I know, I know. Will I get a present, will I? Will I have a tree? You promised —"

"Yes, yes, all that, and more," said the father.

The mother started. "But —"

"I mean it," said the father. "I really mean it. All and more, much more. Excuse me, now. I'll be back."

He left them for about twenty minutes. When he came back he was smiling. "Almost time."

"Can I hold your watch?" asked the boy, and the watch was handed over and he held it ticking in his fingers as the rest of the hour drifted by in fire and silence and unfelt motion.

"It's Christmas *now*! Christmas! Where's my present?"

"Here we go," said the father, and took his boy by the shoulder and led him from the room, down the hall, up a rampway, his wife following.

"I don't understand," she kept saying.

"You will. Here we are," said the father.

59

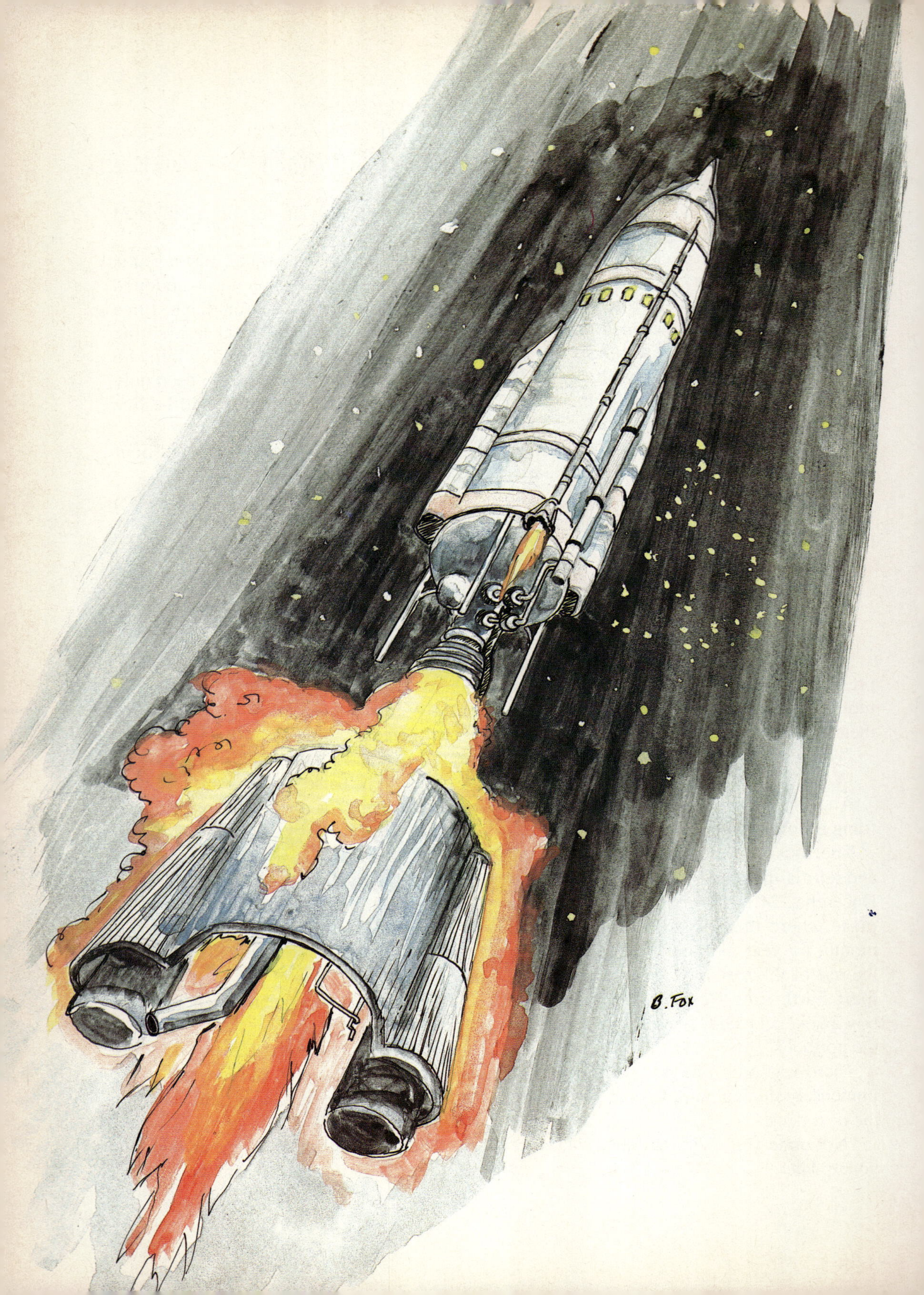
B. Fox

The Gift

They had stopped at the closed door of a large cabin. The father tapped three times and then twice, in a code. The door opened and the light in the cabin went out and there was a whisper of voices.

"Go on in, son," said the father.

"It's dark."

"I'll hold your hand. Come on, mama."

They stepped into the room and the door shut, and the room was very dark indeed. And before them loomed a great glass eye, the porthole, a window four feet high and six feet wide, from which they could look out into space.

The boy gasped.

Behind him, the father and the mother gasped with him, and then in the dark room some people began to sing.

"Merry Christmas, son," said the father.

And the voices in the room sang the old, the familiar carols, and the boy moved forward slowly until his face was pressed against the cool glass of the port. And he stood there for a long long time, just looking and looking out into space and the deep night at the burning and the burning of ten billion white and lovely candles . . . .

— *Ray Bradbury*

? Questions and Assignments

1. Why were the parents worried on their way to the rocket station?
2. Explain why the parents were forced to leave their son's gift behind.
3. What do you think the boy's thoughts were as he waited for his parents in the Terminal room?
4. The father had been lying awake. What was troubling him?
5. Write a brief description of the father in the story.
6. What is the significance of the playing of the carols?
7. In the last sentence of the story a number of words are repeated. What effect does this have?
8. What did the parents learn from their experience?
9. Is "The Gift" a suitable title for this story? Explain your answer.
10. Tell the story of "The Gift" as the boy might tell it to his own child in the year 2072.
11. Describe a rocket port at rush hour. Include in your description details of the equipment and facilities of the port itself and details of the passengers, their destinations and their luggage.

S Spelling

Below are anagrams of words that are sometimes misspelt. Rearrange the letters to find the words. All the words are in the story.

- dirwore
- hewtig
- mostcus
- fessculsucun
- ledvibee
- drephiswe
- odentmien
- lowh
- tinumes
- smelnimye

The Gift

V Vocabulary Development

Find words in the story to match each of the following meanings.

- moved aimlessly
- small opening or window
- given up altogether, left behind
- disheartened, horrified, upset
- dispossessed
- quivered, shook
- appeared dimly
- caught breath with open mouth, in surprise
- conflict, row
- was more than

Outline Short Story Ideas

- **Character A** is weak and defenceless. **B** a powerful character wants to own an object that is of great sentimental value to **A**. **B** puts great pressure on **A** to part with the object. **A** finally destroys the object rather than let another person possess it.

- **Character A** owns an object that is of immense value but is totally unaware of its value. **B** spots the object and knows its value. She fakes a casual interest in the object and indicates that is without value, hoping eventually to gain possession of it.
  Meanwhile **A,** as a result of **B's** comments, destroys the object or sells it for a fraction of its value to another.

✓ Q. 9 — Sample Answer

'The Gift' is a Christmas story and Christmas is a time for giving and receiving gifts. The story tells of a father and mother finding themselves unable to give a gift to their son. It was to be a simple gift.

However, the father hits on a idea and, with the help of the crew of the space-ship, gives his son a really fantastic gift. The boy was given a view of the heavens from the port-hole of a space-ship speeding towards Mars.

The word 'gift' makes us think of objects - toys, sweets and so on. Yet the gift that made the boy so happy was not an object but an experience. This gives a wider meaning to the idea of a gift.

The gift brought joy not only to the boy, but to all those involved in giving it. That is the way it should be for all worthwhile gifts.

I think therefore that the title is a good one because the story gives the reader the idea of the full meaning of a gift.

THE LUMBER ROOM

The children were to be driven, as a special treat, to the sands at Jagborough. Nicholas was not to be of the party; he was in disgrace. Only that morning he had refused to eat his wholesome bread-and-milk on the seemingly frivolous ground that there was a frog in it. Older and wiser and better people had told him that there could not possibly be a frog in his bread-and-milk and he was not to talk nonsense; he continued, nevertheless, to talk what seemed the veriest nonsense, and described with much detail the colouration and markings of the alleged frog. The dramatic part of the incident was that there really was a frog in Nicholas' basin of bread-and-milk; he had put it there himself, so he felt entitled to know something about it. The sin of taking a frog from the garden and putting it into a bowl of wholesome bread-and-milk was enlarged on at great length, but the fact that stood out clearest in the whole affair, as it presented itself to the mind of Nicholas, was that the older, wiser, and better people had been proved to be profoundly in error in matters about which they had expressed the utmost assurance.

"You said there couldn't possibly be a frog in my bread-and-milk; there *was* a frog in my bread-and-milk," he repeated, with the insistence of a skilled tactician who does not intend to shift from favourable ground.

So his boy-cousin and girl-cousin and his quite uninteresting younger brother were to be taken to Jagborough sands that afternoon and he was to stay at home. His cousins' aunt, who insisted, by an unwarranted stretch of imagination, in styling herself his aunt also, had hastily invented the Jagborough expedition in order to impress on Nicholas the delights that he had justly forfeited by his disgraceful conduct at the breakfast table. It was her habit, whenever one of the children fell from grace, to improvise something of a festival nature from which the offender would be rigorously debarred; if all the children sinned collectively they were suddenly informed of a circus in a neighbouring town, a circus of unrivalled merit and uncounted elephants, to which, but for their depravity, they would have been taken that very day.

A few decent tears were looked for on the part of Nicholas when the moment for the departure of the expedition arrived. As a matter of fact, however, all the crying was done by his girl-cousin, who scraped her knee rather painfully against the step of the carriage as she was scrambling in.

"How she did howl!" said Nicholas cheerfully, as the party drove off without any of the elation of high spirits that should have characterised it.

"She'll soon get over that," said the *soi-disant** aunt; "it will be a glorious afternoon for racing about over those beautiful sands. How they will enjoy themselves!"

"Bobby won't enjoy himself much, and he won't race much either," said Nicholas with a grim chuckle; "his boots are hurting him. They're too tight."

"Why didn't he tell me they were hurting?" asking the aunt with some asperity.

"He told you twice, but you weren't listening. You often don't listen when we tell you important things."

"You are not to go into the gooseberry garden," said the aunt, changing the subject.

"Why not?" demanded Nicholas.

"Because you are in disgrace," said the aunt loftily.

Nicholas did not admit the flawlessness of the reasoning; he felt perfectly capable of being in disgrace and in a gooseberry garden at the same moment. His face took on an expression of considerable obstinacy. It was clear to his aunt that he was determined to get into the gooseberry garden, "only," as she remarked to herself, "because I have told him he is not to."

Now the gooseberry garden had two doors by which it might be entered, and once a small person like Nicholas could slip in there he could effectually disappear from view amid the masking growth of artichokes, raspberry canes, and fruit bushes. The aunt had many other things to do that afternoon, but she spent an hour or two in trivial gardening operations among flower beds and shrubberies, whence she could keep a watchful eye on the two doors that led to the forbidden paradise. She was a woman of few ideas, with immense powers of concentration.

Nicholas made one or two sorties into the front garden, wriggling his way with obvious stealth of purpose towards one or other of the doors, but never able for a moment to evade the aunt's watchful eye. As a matter of fact, he had no intention of trying to get into the gooseberry garden, but it was extremely convenient for him that his aunt should believe that he had; it was a belief that would keep her on self-imposed sentry-duty for the greater part of the afternoon. Having thoroughly confirmed and fortified her suspicions, Nicholas slipped back into the house and rapidly put into execution a plan of action that had long germinated in his brain. By standing on a chair in the library, one could reach a shelf on which reposed a fat, important-looking key. The key was as important as it looked; it was the instrument which kept the mysteries of the lumber-room secure from unauthorised intrusion, which opened a way only for aunts and suchlike privileged persons. Nicholas had not had much experience of the art of fitting keys into keyholes and turning locks, but for some days past he had practised with the key of the schoolroom door; he did not believe in trusting too much to luck and accident. The key turned stiffly in the lock, but it turned. The door opened, and Nicholas was in an unknown land, compared with which the gooseberry garden was a stale delight, a mere material pleasure.

The Lumber Room

📖 Outline Short Story Ideas

- **Character(s) A** and **1B** boast of their high or low standards or express certain opinions or beliefs. However, when they are faced with a problem or when action is called for, we see them in their true colours - exactly opposite to what they claimed to be.

✓ Q. 11 — Sample Answer

(a)   The story opens at breakfast with the information that the children, except for Nicholas, are to get a special treat - a day at the seaside. The 'treat' was thought up to punish Nicholas for his behaviour at breakfast when he put a frog in his bread-and-milk.

   The result is that he is left alone with his Aunt, who forbids him to go into the gooseberry garden. He puts on a face which indicates to her that he will try to disobey her. This causes her to take up position in the gooseberry garden and do a few gardening chores, simply to make sure that Nicholas doesn't disobey her. He pretends to attempt to get in but his real aim is to explore the lumber room. With the other children away and the Aunt busy elsewhere, he is now free to visit the lumber room. A further twist is added to the plot when the Aunt falls into a tank in the gooseberry garden. She calls for Nicholas to help her out. Playing at being the innocent, Nicholas tells her that he is forbidden to go into the gooseberry garden. He adds that she may be the Evil One tempting him and 'proves' this by questioning her about the strawberry jam. She is eventually rescued by a kitchen maid and the evening meal is a silent affair.

(b)   The feature of the plot that impressed me most was its final twist. Nicholas wanted to get into the lumber room and he finally succeeds in this. His aunt wished to punish him and she fails in this.

   However, the writer is not content to let her potter around the garden, while Nicholas enjoys the lumber room. He could have ended the story at that point. Instead he allows the aunt to go through a very embarrassing experience. This gives Nicholas the chance to punish his aunt by using her own words against her. This extra twist to the plot made the ending of the story very funny.

THE OSAGE ORANGE TREE

On that first day of high school in the prairie town where the tree was, I stood in the sun by the flagpole and watched, but pretended not to watch, the others. They stood in groups and talked and knew each other, all except one - a girl though - in a faded blue dress, carrying a sack lunch and standing near the corner looking everywhere but at the crowd.

I might talk to her, I thought. But of course it was out of the question.

That first day was easier when the classes started. Some of the teachers were kind; some were frightening. Some of the students didn't care, but I listened and waited; and at the end of the day I was relieved, less conspicuous from then on.

But that day was not really over. As I hurried to carry my new paper route, I was thinking about how in a strange town, if you are quiet, no one notices, and some may like you, later. I was thinking about this when I reached the north edge of town where the scattering houses dwindle. Beyond them to the north lay just openness, the plains, a big swoop of nothing. There, at the last house, just as I cut across a lot and threw to the last customer, I saw the girl in the blue dress coming along the street, heading on out of town, carrying books. And she saw me.

"Hello."

"Hello."

And because we stopped we were friends. I didn't know how I could stop, but I didn't hurry on. I stood.

There was nothing to do but to act as if I were walking on out too. I had three papers left in the bag, and I frantically began to fold them - box them, as we called it - for throwing. We had begun to walk and talk. The girl was timid; I became more bold. Not much, but a little.

"Have you gone to school here before?" I asked.

"Yes, I went here last year."

A long pause. A meadowlark sitting on a fencepost hunched his wings and flew. I kicked through the dust of the road.

I began to look ahead. Where could we possibly be walking to? I couldn't be walking just because I wanted to be with her.

Fortunately, there was one more house, a gray house by a sagging barn, set two hundred yards from the road.

"I thought I'd see if I could get a customer here," I said, waving toward the house.

"That's where I live."

"Oh."

We were at the dusty car tracks that turned off the road to the house. The girl stopped. There was a tree at that corner, a straight but little tree with slim branches and shiny dark leaves.

"I could take a paper tonight to see if my father wants to buy it."

A great relief, this. What could I have said to her parents? I held out a paper, dropped it, picked it up, brushing off the dust. 'No, here's a new one' - a great action, putting the dusty paper in the bag over my shoulder and pulling out a fresh one. When she took the paper we stood there a minute. The wind was coming in over the grass. She looked out with a tranquil expression.

She walked away past the tree, and I hurried quickly back toward town. Could anyone in the houses have been watching? I looked back once. The girl was standing on the small bridge halfway in to her house. I hurried on.

The next day at school I didn't ask her whether her father wanted to take the paper. When the others were there I wouldn't say anything. I stood with the boys. In American history the students could choose their seats, and I saw that she was too quiet and plainly dressed for many to notice her. But I crowded in with the boys, pushing one aside, scrambling for a seat by the window.

That night I came to the edge of town.

The Osage Orange Tree

Two papers were left, and I walked on out. The meadowlark was there. By some reeds in a ditch by the road a dragonfly - snake feeders, we called them - glinted. The sun was going down, and the plains were stretched out and lifted, some way, to the horizon. Could I go on up to the house? I didn't think so, but I walked on. Then, by the tree where her road turned off, she was standing. She was holding her books. More confused than ever, I stopped.

"My father will take the paper," she said.

She told me always to leave the paper at the foot of the tree. She insisted on that, saying their house was too far; and it is true that I was far off my route, a long way, a half-mile out of my territory. But I didn't think of that.

And so we were acquainted. What I remember best in that town is those evening walks to the tree. Every night - or almost every night - the girl was there. Evangeline was her name. We didn't say much. On Friday night of the first week she gave me a dime, the cost of the paper. It was a poor newspaper, by the way, cheap, sensational, unreliable. I never went up to her house. We never talked together at school. But all the time we knew each other; we just happened to meet. Every evening.

There was a low place in the meadow by that corner. The fall rains made a pond there, and in the evenings sometimes ducks would be coming in - a long line with set wings down the wind, and then a turn, and a skimming glide to the water. The wind would be blowing and the grass bent down. The evenings got colder and colder. The wind was cold. As winter came on the time at the tree was dimmer, but not dark. In the winter there was snow. The pond was frozen over; all the plains were white. I had to walk down the ruts of the road and leave the paper in the crotch of the tree, sometimes, when it was cold. The wind made a sound through the black branches. But usually, even on cold evenings, Evangeline was there.

At school we played ball at noon - the boys did. And I got acquainted. I learned that Evangeline's brother was janitor at the school. A big dark boy he was - a man, middle-aged I thought at the time. He didn't every let on that he knew me. I would see him sweeping the halls, bent down, slow. I would see him and Evangeline take their sack lunches over to the south side of the building. Once I slipped away from the ball game and went over there, but he looked at me so steadily, without moving, that I pretended to be looking for a book, and quickly went back, and got in the game and struck out.

You don't know about those winters, and especially that winter. Those were the dust years. Wheat was away down in price. Everyone was poor - poor in a way that you can't understand. I made two dollars a week, or something like that, on my paper route. I could tell about working for ten cents an hour - and then not getting paid; about families that ate wheat, boiled, for their main food, and burned wheat for fuel. You don't know how it would be. All through that hard winter I carried a paper to the tree by the pond, in the evening, and gave it to Evangeline.

In the cold weather Evangeline wore a heavier dress, a dark, straight, heavy dress, under a thick black coat. Outdoors she wore a knitted cap that fastened under her chin. She was dressed this way when we met and she took the paper. The reeds were broken now. The meadowlark was gone.

And then came the spring. I have forgotten to tell just how Evangeline looked. She was of medium height, and slim. Her face was long, her forehead high, her eyes blue. Her tranquil face I remember

The Osage Orange Tree

well. I remember her watching the wind come in over the grass. Her dress was long, her feet small. I can remember her by the tree, with her books, or walking on up the road toward her house and stopping on the bridge halfway up there, but she didn't wave, and I couldn't tell whether she was watching me or not. I always looked back as I went over the rise toward town.

And I can remember her in the room at school. She came into American history one spring day, the first really warm day. She had changed from the dark heavy dress to the dull blue one of the last fall; and she had on a new belt, a gray belt, with blue stitching along the edges. As she passed in front of Jane Wright, a girl who sat on the front row, I heard Jane say to the girl beside her, 'Why look at Evangeline - that old dress of hers has a new belt!'

"Stop a minute, Evangeline," Jane said, "let me see your new dress."

Evangeline stopped and looked uncertainly at Jane and blushed. "It's just made over,' she said, "it's just . . . "

"It's cute, Dear,' Jane said; and as Evangeline went on Jane nudged her friend in the ribs and the friend smothered a giggle.

Well that was a good year. Commencement time came, and - along with the newspaper job - I had the task of preparing for finals and all. One thing, I wasn't a student who took part in the class play or anything like that. I was just one of the boys - twenty-fourth in line to get my diploma.

And graduation was bringing an end to my paper-carrying. My father covered a big territory in our part of the state, selling farm equipment; and we were going to move at once to a town seventy miles south. Only because of my finishing the school year had we stayed till graduation.

I had taught another boy my route, always leaving him at the end and walking on out, by myself, to the tree. I didn't really have to go around with him that last day, the day of graduation, but I was going anyway.

At the graduation exercises, held that May afternoon, I wore my brown Sunday suit. My mother was in the audience. It was a heavy day. The girls had on new dresses. But I didn't see her.

I suppose that I did deserve old man Sutton's 'Shhh!' as we lined up to march across the stage, but I for the first time in the year forgot my caution, and asked Jane where Evangeline was. She shrugged, and I could see for myself that she was not there.

We marched across the stage; our diplomas were ours; our parents filed out; to the strains of a march on the school organ we trailed to the hall. I unbuttoned my brown suit coat, stuffed the diploma in my pocket, and sidled out of the group and upstairs.

Evangeline's brother was emptying wastebaskets at the far end of the hall. I sauntered toward him and stopped. I didn't know what I wanted to say. Unexpectedly, he solved my problem. Stopping in his work, holding a partly empty wastebasket over the canvas sack he wore over his shoulder, he stared at me, as if almost to say something.

"I noticed that your sister wasn't here," I said. The noise below was dwindling. The hall was a quiet, and echoey place; my voice sounded terribly loud. He emptied the rest of the wastebasket and shifted easily. He was a man, in big overalls. He stared at me.

"Evangeline couldn't come," he said. He stopped, looked at me again, and said, "She stole."

"Stole?" I said. "Stole what?"

He shrugged and went toward the next wastebasket, but I followed him.

73

The Osage Orange Tree

"She stole the money from her bank - the money she was to use for her graduation dress," he said. He walked stolidly on, and I stopped. He deliberately turned away as he picked up the next wastebasket. But he said something else, half to himself. "You knew her. You talked to her . . . . I know." He walked away.

I hurried downstairs and outside. The new carrier would have the papers almost delivered by now; so I ran up the street toward the north. I took a paper from him at the end of the street and told him to go back. I didn't pay any more attention to him.

No one was at the tree, and I turned, for the first time, up the road to the house. I walked over the bridge and on up the narrow, rutty tracks. The house was gray and lopsided. The ground of the yard was packed; nothing grew there. By the back door, the door to which the road led, there was a grayish-white place on the ground where the dishwater have been thrown. A gaunt shepherd dog trotted out growling.

And the door opened suddenly, as if someone had been watching me come up the track. A woman came out - a woman stern-faced, with a shawl over her head and a dark lumpy dress on - came out on the back porch and shouted, 'Go 'way, go 'way! We don't want no papers!' She waved violently with one hand, holding the other on her shawl, at her throat. She coughed so hard that she leaned over and put her hand against one of the uprights of the porch. Her face was red. She glanced toward the barn and leaned toward me. 'Go 'way!'

Behind me a meadowlark sang. Over all the plains swooped the sky. The land was drawn up somehow toward the horizon.

I stood there, half-defiant, half-ashamed. The dog continued to growl and to pace around me, stiff-legged, his tail down. The windows of the house were all blank, with blinds drawn. I couldn't say anything.

I stood a long time and then, lowering the newspaper I had held out, I stood longer, waiting, without thinking of what to do. The meadowlark bubbled over again, but I turned and walked away, looking back once or twice. The old woman continued to stand, leaning forward, her head out. She glanced at the barn, but didn't call out any more.

My heels dug into the grayish place where the dishwater had been thrown; the dog skulked along behind.

At the bridge, halfway to the road, I stopped and looked back. The dog was lying down again; the porch was empty; and the door was closed. Turning the other way, I looked toward town. Near me stood our ragged little tree - an Osage orange tree* it was. It was feebly coming into leaf, green all over the branches, among the sharp thorns. I hadn't wondered before how it grew there, all alone, in the plains country, neglected. Over our pond some ducks came slicing in.

Standing there on the bridge, still holding the folded-boxed-newspaper, that worthless paper, I could see everything. I looked out along the road to town. From the bridge you would see the road going away, to where it went over the rise.

Glancing around I flipped that last newspaper under the bridge and then bent far over and looked where it had gone. There they were - a pile of boxed newspapers, thrown in a heap, some new, some worn and weathered, by rain, by snow.

— *William Stafford*

* *Osage Orange Tree* - a hedge-tree of the mulberry family with orange-like inedible fruit.

The Osage Orange Tree

? Questions and Assignments

1. (a) Why did the narrator first notice Evangeline?
   (b) Describe their second meeting.

2. On the narrator's first day in the school, how did the other students behave towards him and how did he behave towards them?

3. What details in the story give us an insight into how the girls in Evangeline's class feel about her?

4. What impression do you get of Evangeline's home life?

5. How do you think the boy felt when (a) Evangeline's brother said "You knew her. You talked to her .... I know" and (b) when the woman on the balcony shouted "go 'way, go 'way! We don't want no papers."

6. Outline how the friendship developed between the narrator and Evangeline and comment briefly on the nature of their friendship.

7. What traits of character does Evangeline reveal? Support your answer by reference to the story.

8. Tell the story from Evangeline's point of view.

9. (a) Over what period of time does the story take place?
   (b) What details in the story make us aware that it takes place over this period of time.

10. Comment on the use of the underlined verbs in the following excerpt :-
    "We <u>marched</u> across the stage; our diplomas were ours; our parents <u>filed</u> out; to the strains of a march on the school organ we <u>trailed</u> to the hall. I unbuttoned my brown suit coat, stuffed the diploma in my pocket, and <u>sidled</u> out of the group and upstairs. Evangeline's brother was emptying wastebaskets at the far end of the hall. I <u>sauntered</u> toward."

11. From what viewpoint is the story written? Explain your answer.

12. Write the letter Evangeline might have received from the boy some days after his discovery of the dumped newspapers.

13. Write Evangeline's entry in her diary for the graduation day.

$ Spelling

Below are anagrams of words that are sometimes misspelt. Rearrange the letters to find the words. All the words are in the story.

- oture
- bissoply
- felire
- zonhoir
- retroitry
- ebelrunial
- tredpened
- pellaicsey
- mudime
- thingcist

The Osage Orange Tree

V Vocabulary Development

Find words in the story to match each of the following meanings.

- caretaker
- serene; calm
- starting
- lean; thin
- known to each other
- sneaked; moved; stealthily
- visible; noticeable; obvious
- struggling; competing with others
- large treeless tract of grassland in North America
- glittered; flashed
- worn by the weather
- becoming gradually less
- passing over lightly and quickly, making very slight contact
- a hedge-tree of the mulberry family with orange-like inedible fruit
- intended to cause a wild reaction; causing or intended to cause excited or violent feeling in the community

☞ Points to Note

THEME
This story explores the strange relationship that develops between two young people during their final year at school. The narrator is unaware of the value the girl placed on his friendship. She is afraid to confide in him about her home or her feelings. Her inability to confide in him leads ultimately to a very unhappy situation for her.

SETTING
The story takes place in the past, probably in the first half of this century. It spans a school year through the seasons of Autumn, Winter, Spring to Summer. The events occur in a town in the flat North American grasslands, commonly known as "the prairies". The story opens in the yard of a high school. It moves from the school to the outskirts of the town, along the boy's paper route. The countryside that surrounds the town is flat, open and almost treeless. The boy eventually goes up to Evangeline's home on the edge of the town. It is a dismal, dreary place that provides little relief from the level monotonous landscape in which it is situated.

The flat featureless landscape in which this story is set leads the reader to focus more sharply on the characters themselves, their actions and their interaction.

CHARACTERS
The main characters in the story are Evangeline and the boy. We are given only brief glimpses of the two minor characters, Evangeline's brother and the old woman at Evangeline's house.

We can assess the two main characters mainly by their actions and behaviour towards each other. Evangeline's brother merely implies his disapproval of his sister's behaviour. The woman doesn't even mention her. Their association with their classmates tells only a little about them.

The writer refers to Evangeline's brother on just two occasions in the story. We are given a brief description of him when he first meets the boy. The second time we meet him he is being questioned by the boy about Evangeline's absence from the graduation ceremony.

The author gives a brief description of the old woman. We can also judge her character from her reaction to the boy's visit.

The Osage Orange Tree

📖 Outline Short Story Ideas

- **Character A** regards herself as being an outsider in a group (family, community, class etc.). She doesn't conform. However, a problem or some danger threatens the group. Impulsively, **A** lends her help towards solving the problem. At the end she no longer feels an outsider.

- This is a slight variation on the above. The group rejects **A**. However, when she faces a problem they become helpful and supportive. At the end **A** is accepted by the group.

✓ Q. 10 — Sample Answer

Each of the five underlined verbs describe a particular way of walking.

The use of the word "march" gets across the formal and solemn nature of the graduation ceremony. The students behaved almost like soldiers on parade. They "filed" out when the conferring ceremony was over. Together the use of the words "marched" and "filed" conveys the idea that there was nothing haphazard and unplanned about the event. Everything was organised and nobody stood out of line.

The use of the word "trailed" tells as much about the attitude of the students as it does about their movement. The word "trailed" here implies that there was no great enthusiasm on the part of the students who had graduated. They had probably found the ceremony too long and very boring.

The boy "sidled" out of the room because he did not want to be noticed by anyone. We can picture his quiet smooth movement as he left the room.

The use of the verb "sauntered" gives the impression that the boy approached Evangeline's brother in a slow casual manner. He was giving himself time to think of what to say. He didn't want to make an over-enthusiastic approach which might have caused the brother to become wary of him.

EVELINE

She sat at the window watching the evening invade the avenue. Her head was leaned against the window curtains and in her nostrils was the odour of dusty cretonne. She was tired.

Few people passed. The man out of the last house passed on his way home; she heard his footsteps clacking along the concrete pavement and afterwards crunching on the cinder path before the new red houses. One time there used to be a field in which they used to play every evening with other people's children. Then a man from Belfast bought the field and built houses in it — not like their little brown houses, but bright brick houses with shining roofs. The children of the avenue used to play together in that field — the Devines, the Waters, the Dunns, little Keogh the cripple, she and her brothers and sisters. Ernest, however, never played: he was too grown up. Her father used often to hunt them in out of the field with his blackthorn stick; but usually little Keogh used to keep *nix* and call out when he saw her father coming. Still they seemed to have been rather happy then. Her father was not so bad then; and besides; her mother was alive. That was a long time ago; she and her brothers and sisters were all grown up; her mother was dead. Tizzie Dunn was dead, too, and the Waters had gone back to England. Everything changes. Now she was going to go away like the others, to leave her home.

Home! She looked round the room, reviewing all its familiar objects which she had dusted once a week for so many years, wondering where on earth all the dust came from. Perhaps she would never see again those familiar objects from which she had never dreamed of being divided. And yet during all those years she had never found out the name of the priest whose yellowing photograph hung on the wall above the broken harmonium beside the coloured print of the promises made to Blessed Margaret Mary Alacoque. He had been a school friend of her father. Whenever he showed the photograph to a visitor her father used to pass it with a casual word:

"He is in Melbourne now."

She had consented to go away, to leave her home. Was that wise? She tried to weigh each side of the question. In her home anyway she had shelter and food; she had those whom she had known all her life about her. Of course she had to work hard, both in the house and at business. What would they say of her in the Stores when they found out that she had run away with a fellow? Say she was a fool, perhaps; and her place would be filled up by advertisement. Miss Gavan would be glad. She had always had an edge on her, especially whenever there were people listening.

"Miss Hill, don't you see these ladies are waiting?"

"Look lively, Miss Hill, please."

She would not cry many tears at leaving the Stores.

But in her new home, in a distant unknown country, it would not be like that. Then she would be married — she, Eveline. People would treat her with respect then. She would not be treated as her mother had been. Even now, though she was over nineteen, she sometimes felt herself in danger of her father's violence. She knew it was that that had given her the palpitations. When they were growing up he had never gone for her, like he used to go for Harry and Ernest, because she was a girl; but latterly he had begun to threaten her and say what he would do to her only

Eveline

for her dead mother's sake. And now she had nobody to protect her. Ernest was dead and Harry, who was in the church decorating business, was nearly always down somewhere in the country. Besides, the invariable squabble for money on Saturday nights had begun to weary her unspeakably. She always gave her entire wages — seven shillings — and Harry always sent up what he could but the trouble was to get any money from her father. He said she used to squander the money, that she had no head, that he wasn't going to give her his hard-earned money to throw about the streets, and much more, for he was fairly bad of a Saturday night. In the end he would give her the money and ask her had she any intention of buying Sunday's dinner. Then she had to rush out as quickly as she could and do her marketing, holding her black leather purse tightly in her hand as she elbowed her way through the crowds and returning home late under her load of provisions. She had hard work to keep the house together and to see that the two young children who had been left to her charge went to school regularly and got their meals regularly. It was hard work — a hard life — but now that she was about to leave it she did not find it a wholly undesirable life.

She was about to explore another life with Frank. Frank was very kind, manly, open-hearted. She was to go away with him by the night-boat to be his wife and to live with him in Buenos Ayres where he had a home waiting for her. How well she remembered the first time she had seen him; he was lodging in a house on the main road where she used to visit. It seemed a few weeks ago. He was standing at the gate, his peaked cap pushed back on his head and his hair tumbled forward over a face of bronze. Then they had come to know each other. He used to meet her outside the Stores every evening and see her home. He took her to see *The Bohemian Girl* and she felt elated as she sat in an unaccustomed part of the theatre with him. He was awfully fond of music and sang a little. People knew that they were courting and, when he sang about the lass that loves a sailor, she always felt pleasantly confused. He used to call her Poppens out of fun. First of all it had been an excitement for her to have a fellow and then she had begun to like him. He had tales of distant countries. He had started as a deck boy at a pound a month on a ship of the Allan Line going out to Canada. He told her the names of the ships he had been on and the names of the different services. He had sailed through the Straits of Magellan and he told her stories of the terrible Patagonians. He had fallen on his feet in Buenos Ayres, he said, and had come over to the old country, just for a holiday. Of course, her father had found out the affair and had forbidden her to have anything to say to him.

"I know these sailor chaps," he said.

One day he had quarrelled with Frank and after that she had to meet her lover secretly.

The evening deepened in the avenue. The white of two letters in her lap grew indistinct. One was to Harry; the other was to her father. Ernest had been her favourite but she liked Harry too. Her father was becoming old lately, she noticed; he would miss her. Sometimes he could be very nice. Not long before, when she had been laid up for a day, he had read her out a ghost story and made toast for her at the fire. Another day, when their mother was alive, they had all gone for a picnic to the Hill of Howth. She remembered her father putting on her mother's bonnet to make the children laugh.

Her time was running out but she continued to sit by the window, leaning her head against the window curtain, inhaling the odour of dusty cretonne. Down far in the avenue she could hear a street organ playing. She knew the air. Strange that it should come that very night to remind her of the promise to her mother, her promise to keep the home together as long as she could. She remembered the last night of her mother's illness; she was again in the close dark room at the other side of the hall and outside she heard a melancholy air of Italy. The organ-player had been ordered to go away and given sixpence. She remembered her father strutting back into the sickroom saying:

"Damned Italians! Coming over here!"

As she mused the pitiful vision of her mother's life laid its spell on the very quick of her being — that life of commonplace sacrifices closing in final craziness. She trembled as she heard again her mother's voice saying constantly with foolish insistence:

"Derevaun Seraun! Derevaun Seraun!"

She stood up in a sudden impulse of terror. Escape! She must escape! Frank would save her. He would give her life, perhaps love, too. But she wanted to live. Why should she be unhappy? She had a right to happiness. Frank would take her in his arms, fold her in his arms. He would save her.

She stood among the swaying crowd in the station at the North Wall. He held her hand and she knew that he was speaking to her, saying something about the passage over and over again. The station was full of soldiers with brown baggages. Through the wide doors of the sheds she caught a glimpse of the black mass of the boat, lying in beside the quay wall, with illumined portholes. She answered nothing. She felt her cheek pale and cold and, out of a maze of distress, she prayed to God to direct her,

Eveline

to show her what was her duty. The boat blew a long mournful whistle into the mist. If she went, to-morrow she would be on the sea with Frank, steaming towards Buenos Ayres. Their passage had been booked. Could she still draw back after all he had done for her? Her distress awoke a nausea in her body and she kept moving her lips in silent fervent prayer.

A bell clanged upon her heart. She felt him seize her hand:

"Come!"

All the seas of the world tumbled about her heart. He was drawing her into them: he would drown her. She gripped with both hands at the iron railing.

"Come!"

No! No! No! It was impossible. Her hands clutched the iron in frenzy. Amid the seas she sent a cry of anguish!

"Eveline! Evvy!"

He rushed beyond the barrier and called to her to follow. He was shouted at to go on but he still called to her. She set her white face to him, passive, like a helpless animal. Her eyes gave him no sign of love or farewell or recognition.

— *James Joyce*

James Joyce (1882 - 1941)

James Joyce was born in Dublin in 1882. You can read about his schooldays in Clongowes Wood College and Belvedere College in his autobiographical novel *Portrait of the Artist as a Young Man.*

His most famous novel, *Ulysses,* was first published in 1922. Its style and technique were very original and it is still regarded as one of the greatest novels of all by most critics. The book outlines in great detail the character, relationships and world of Leopold Bloom. It achieves this by conveying his thoughts and experiences over a single day, the 16th June 1904, in Dublin.

Joyce's final novel *Finnegan's Wake*, published in 1939, has been described as the most original experiment ever undertaken in the novel form. It is based on the dreams of H. C. Earwicker, a Dublin publican, over a single night. It is an extremely difficult read, partly because Joyce combines words from foreign languages with English words. This, according to critics, gives the book "a European dimension."

Eveline is from *Dubliners* a collection of short stories by Joyce published in 1914. The stories are based on the theory that deep insights can be gained into the character of the city and its people by circumstances and incidents which seem outwardly insignificant. Some of the stories have a humorous edge, while others are poignant and sensitive. The final story in the collection, *The Dead,* is regarded as a masterpiece. A filmed version of *The Dead* is available on video.

Eveline

? Questions and Assignments

1. In the second paragraph Eveline reflects on the changes that have taken place in her neighbourhood. List these changes.
2. What do we learn about Eveline's job?
3. What sentence first tells of the circumstances under which Eveline was leaving home?
4. What specific details of Frank did Eveline notice when she first saw him? How, in your opinion, might these details distinguish Frank from other young men that Eveline might have known?
5. Is there any evidence in the story to suggest that Frank was from Ireland? Explain.
6. What details are revealed about the ship? Explain the effect achieved by these details.
7. Joyce uses the phrase *"familiar objects"* twice in paragraph three and then later uses the phrase *"distant unknown country"*. Would you agree that these two phrases focus on the central theme or idea of the story? Explain your answer.
8. What impression do you get of Eveline's family life from the story?
9. What kind of a man was Eveline's father?
10. What is the significance of the street organ in the story? (see **Points to Note**).
11. Explain the sentence — "As she mused the pitiful vision of her mother's life laid its spell on the very quick of her being — that life of commonplace sacrifices closing in final craziness."
12. In the fourth paragraph Eveline is described as trying to "weigh each side of the question". List the factors that were (i) holding her back and (ii) luring her away.
13. Write the story from Frank's point of view.
14. Compose a letter that Eveline might write to Frank a year after that fateful evening.

S Spelling

Below are anagrams of words that are sometimes misspelt. Rearrange the letters to find the words. All the words are in the story.

- ulalsuy
- afrilaim
- dedivid
- hopgrotaph
- dentonces
- treathe
- olecvine
- threenat
- elreath
- ginglod
- nefridtef
- tellay
- miglesp
- cifrascies
- etixnecemt
- asaltenply
- nibredfod
- arelledqur
- cunomacduste
- emertvadenist

V Vocabulary Development

Find words in the story to match each of the following meanings.

- food
- sad
- pain
- grasp
- constant
- in high spirits
- unclear; faint
- journey; voyage
- spend wastefully
- consider; examine
- sickness
- pondered; thought
- take over; come into
- walking pompously
- making a sharp sound
- inactive; expressionless
- moving from side to side

82

Eveline

- the part of the body sensitive to pain
- violent, irregular beating of the heart
- curtain material; unglazed cotton cloth printed in coloured patterns

☞ **Points to Note**

SETTING

The setting of this story is very simple. The action takes place over a single evening and takes place in two locations — Eveline's home and the departure station at the North Wall docks. Yet, through Eveline's thoughts and memories, Joyce skilfully reveals the important details of her life. These details enable us to understand how difficult a decision she faces.

While the story is told in the third person, it is told from Eveline's point of view. Joyce uses many phrases and expressions that a girl like Eveline would use if, for example, she were to relate her entire experience to a friend. His technique here is to give voice to Eveline's thoughts over a crucial evening in her life.

CHARACTER

While the principal subject of the story is the character of Eveline, you should note how Joyce succeeds in bringing minor characters to life. For example, it is easy to imagine the kind of person Miss Gavan is although she is only referred to in four sentences.

PLOT

What makes this story effective is the vivid portrayal of Eveline and her world. It has no plot, as such, in that it does not set out to make an impact with a series of logically linked incidents, leading to a surprise twist at the end. As evening descends, Eveline considers her past and her future. She is faced with an important choice. At the last moment she makes her decision. Would you agree that her earlier decision to leave is as logical — or illogical — as a decision to remain?

UNDERSTANDING SYMBOLS

This is one of the more difficult literary terms to understand. A symbol can be defined as an object that has further significance or meaning beyond the obvious. For example, a harp is obviously a musical instrument — yet, for many people, it *symbolises* Ireland and Irishness. In a piece of literature a symbol is something that evokes (brings to mind) a deeper awareness of a situation. Consider the significance of the sound of the street organ in the story *Eveline*. What memory does it evoke for Eveline? Why can the sound of the street organ be regarded as a symbol?

CHOOSING VERBS

Note the author's choice of verbs in the opening lines of the story to describe the sound of footsteps. In order to write a vivid description of an event or a place you should take care to choose verbs that best describe the sounds associated with the topic.

Eveline

📝 Writers' Workshop

The writing technique used in *Eveline* is a particularly effective one for bringing a single character and his or her world to life. It can be used also to present a character's own view of an event.

This technique is occasionally used in magazines or newspapers in profiles of people in the public eye.

Method
- Get into the mind of the character — be clear on his/her attitudes, feelings, fears, hopes etc. These must come across clearly.
- Use a number of phrases or expressions which the character would use in speech — e.g. *"She would not cry many tears at leaving the store."*
- Write in the third person — e.g. *She* was tired; *She* knew . . . .
- When describing settings use a more ornate or imaginative style but limit it to a few sentences — e.g. ". . . . watching the evening invade the avenue." "The boat blew a long mournful whistle into the mist."
- You can achieve an ironic and often funny effect when profiling a character that both you and your readers would obviously dislike.

📖 Outline Short Story Ideas

None of the short story ideas below depend on an ingenious plot for effect. All can be modelled, to some extent, on *Eveline*.
- A young person reconsiders a course of action that he has planned — e.g. leaving school; getting a weekend job; confronting a classmate etc. Again he weighs up the factors for and against. His final choice is not revealed until the end. Perhaps some symbolic object or event influences his final choice.
- A child observes a group of neighbours or relatives at a gathering at which a disagreement or an unpleasant incident develops.
- An elderly person reflects on his past — and future — as he prepares to leave his home, perhaps for the last time.
- A parent reflects on his or her relationship with a son or daughter on the night before the son/daughter is going to make the final break with home. The parent may have regrets that he/she didn't always do his/her best for the child.
- Reflections of a character who is shortly emigrating from Ireland for good.
- A character who lives by crime reflects on what promises to be an eventful night or day as it approaches.
- At a crucial point in his life, a vain celebrity contemplates on how fame has affected him. You should get inspiration for this by reading a few celebrity interviews in newspapers or magazines.

Eveline

✓ Q. 7 — Sample Answer

The central theme of *Eveline* can be summed up in the proverb — "The devil you know is better than the devil you don't know!" In the story, Eveline is faced with a choice. Also, once she makes that choice, there will be no going back.

She can remain in Dublin, putting up with the nasty Miss Gavan in her job and putting up with her father when she comes home. He is abusive and an alcoholic and he makes home life extremely unpleasant. Yet she sees that her life has some advantages — she has food and shelter and she is "among those she has known all her life." Also, her father has a kind side to him on rare occasions.

Eveline, on the other hand, can elope with Frank. In Buenos Ayres she would find respect and happiness — or would she? She wanted to escape from her life in Dublin, but she was escaping to a "distant unknown country". She would be leaving a world that was familiar to her with its "familiar objects" and familiar faces. It was only when she faced the boat on the quay blowing "a long mournful whistle into the mist" that her courage and determination left her. She chooses to stay among the "familiar objects" rather than take her chances in a "distant unknown country". This choice is the central theme of the story.

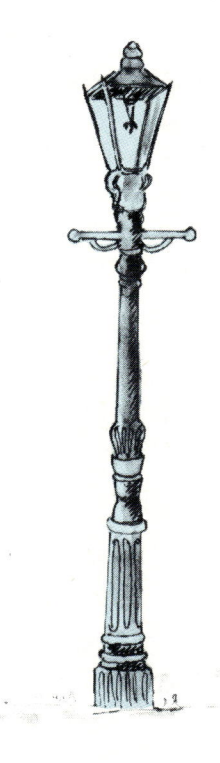

NAGASAKI

It is early in the morning of the ninth of August, 1945, and the clouds have parted over the city of Nagasaki to let the sun in. The horns and hooters of the distant shipyard are in full throat, a dawn chorus of screams and screeches that ricochet among the roof-slates of the houses by the harbour. They shriek so piercingly that Mrs. Kawabata abandons her mangle and walks across her living-room to close the yellow shutters of her home in Natsue Street, while her husband, stone deaf since the death of their second son in Singapore three years ago, smiles at her amiably, and wipes his reading glasses with a piece of newsprint. He is deaf to the cries of this world, and has never looked younger.

On the other side of the city, where the sounds of the shipyard hooters die away, the noise of the coal tenders starts up. The length and breadth of the depot reverberate with the banging of engines, the incensed hiss of the iron wheels as they cool under the hoses, and the noise of the slow goods stopping with the sharp cry of pain that always reminds Mr. Toraiwa of a dying pig as the knife sinks deeper. It reminds him of that now as he stands to remove his cap and fan his forehead. His face is flushed with the effort of loading coal, and a red wedge runs across his temples where the rim of the hat is too tight, and bites into the skin. But he can't rub his face with the back of his hand as he wants to, because they're both so dirty from hauling sacks that not even a pumice stone would ever make them clean. So he leans against the fender where the carriages are coupled, and he thinks of pigs strung tightly between the shafts of a cart, and he thinks of the farmyard where he grew up in the country near Nagoya. And that gives him the strength to resume the loading when the breeze has dried his neck.

But let's leave Mr. Toraiwa to his memories and Mrs. Kawabata to her mutterings. After all, they are only two persons out of how many who woke that morning of August the ninth to squint up at the sunlight, and wash their bodies in clear, cool water. Life had not singled them out in any strange or special way, and were it not that each had a daughter attending the German Convent near the Ministry of Finance, it is altogether likely that the only thing they would have had in common is the death they shared in a single instant. And to tell you that at the start is not to spoil the story. The story itself is thoroughly spoiled to begin with, and it has gone on to spoil everything else as well. For as Mr. Toraiwa pulls his shirt collar this way and that to cool his throat, and as Mrs. Kawabata folds clean linen in a walnut box, an American plane has taken off shakily from a crowded airstrip on a small Pacific island. It is flying straight towards the rising sun, and the people who try to make it out as it disappears into the distance have to shield their eyes against the fierce glare of the new day. Even the priest who blessed the plane and who is wearing very dark glasses has to strain so much that his eyes are beginning to stream.

Miss Yoshiyuki is busy preparing her class for confirmation. She has good reason to be pleased with their progress; they have covered great ground in a matter of weeks.

"What is grace?" she says to the twenty-eight girls who are seated at their desks in front of her.

And the twenty-eight girls respond: "Grace is a supernatural gift bestowed upon us by our loving Creator."

"How may we receive grace?"

"We receive grace through the

Nagasaki

Sacraments instituted by Christ."

"Well," says Miss Yoshiyuki, "That's quite an improvement on last week's effort. Fr. Dietrich will be very proud of you. He'll have to ask you the hardest questions at the very end of the Catechism, and leave the simpler one at the start for the weaker class. So perhaps we ought to look again at four hundred to four-eighty."

The twenty-eight girls make various faces. They are too young to care greatly about such abstruse subjects as Extreme Unction or the Last Judgement.

"Repetition," says Miss Yoshiyuki. "Repetition is the key to success. How often must I say it? Now let's begin with the questions about the rewards of the blessed and the punishment of the damned; then we'll revise the three questions about the Apocalypse and the Elect. Fr. Dietrich tells me the Bishop has a bee in his bonnet about those ones."

The class titters, and Miss Yoshiyuki lets them. How could anyone fail to be in wonderful form on such a splendid day? Especially Miss Yoshiyuki, who is wearing an orchid given her by a secret admirer whom the class is determined to identify as Saburo Tanikazi, the gym instructor with the gammy leg.

When the tittering has stopped, Miss Yoshiyuki resumes.

"Close your Catechisms, please, and turn them face downward on the desks. Yumiko, I can't imagine why you're still grinning, but I can guess. Now sit straight and face front. Miyako, I think you could open the window. It's very warm today. Just a little."

And the lavish sounds of the late summer, deft and delicate, circulate in the classroom: insects and birdsong, the light scuff of sandals on gravel, the low patter of a watering-can as it shifts among the rose-beds.

"That's perfect," says Miss Yoshiyuki. "Good girls. All together now — that is, as soon as Maki has returned to us from dreamland. Good. So. How are the blessed rewarded in Heaven?"

"The blessed in Heaven shall see God face to face."

"Good. Though I'm not sure I saw your lips moving, Komako. Don't be shy or I may make the mistake of thinking that you don't know."

And there are more titters, the lovely sanity of laughter.

"Quiet please. Now. A simple one. What are angels?"

It is her favourite question; she was asked it herself at her own confirmation fifteen years before, and her heart had hammered as she stuttered the answer.

But the twenty-eight students have it off pat.

"Angels are pure spirits created by God to love and worship Him."

The schoolroom where Miss Yoshiyuki is teaching her pupils is part of the German Convent in the city of Nagasaki. It is a spacious, intimate room overlooking a park where no leaves have yet fallen, and the park-keeper passes his time by raking the gravel in subtle, concentric circles that are beautiful to examine from the height of three storeys. Otherwise, the poor man sits without moving among the maple trees, and lets his cigarette burn down to the butt before lifting it from his lips with his good arm. The girls at the Catholic convent school think he is mad; Miss Yoshiyuki knows he was driven there. Only a good man could cast such a clean, definite shadow whether he stands or sits. So she shares her egg ration with him each week; in return, he gives her a portion of his sugar allowance. They are the best of friends.

The plane is approaching.
It is twelve noon.

The children you heard being called by name are Yumiko, Maki, Komako and Miyako. They are twelve years of age, the daughters of Christian converts. Of the four, three have brothers who went to the war; of the three, two have a brother who cannot come home. When the news was brought to them, each was made to feel quite special in school, and the teachers spoke differently as they passed in the corridor. Even when they idle in the library now, months later, reading a romance instead of reference works, Miss Yoshiyuki strokes the tops of their heads although once she would have tweaked their pigtails sharply. But none of this is of any help at all when they go home again in the late afternoon to find that every room in their respective houses is awash with their brothers' absence, and the tiniest details, like hairs in the soap or a stain in the carpet, can summon them up and in.

I would prefer to have them speak to you in their own voices about these matters and about much else besides, but the dead make a habit of silence, though I think that they listen intently. Were those twenty-eight students to have listened as hard after their lunch-break on August the ninth, they might hear an airplane approaching. They might hear the water tremble in the glass on the stone sill of the classroom window, or the leaves of the geranium quiver minutely under that ugly portrait of the tight-lipped Italian foundress.

But they are occupied, and preoccupied. In a little while, they are to be confirmed. The heavens will open above them, Fr. Dietrich has said, and the gifts of the Holy Spirit will rain down upon them in the form of tongues of fire. They must brace themselves for that moment.

"And you will be soldiers of Christ! Or perhaps not soldiers, hmmm?" Fr. Dietrich chuckles, and the whole class chuckles with him. This is not because they see the point of the joke, but because they are each and every one of them so fond of this big and bearlike priest whose stomach rumbles at morning mass and whose soutane has a shiny bottom from the saddle of the bicycle he rides to and fro among his parishioners. "No, not soldiers," Fr. Dietrich muses. "Perhaps we have too many of them already, no? Well, if not soldiers, ambulance drivers. Or stretcher-bearers, yes? The stretcher-bearers of the Lord. How about that? Orderlies, nurses, attendants. Noble work."

The girls are grinning openly. Miss Yoshiyuki is afraid she may be losing control; and she prides herself on her discipline.

"Miyako," she calls, in that curious habit we have of singling out one where all are at fault. "Miyako, will you please pay attention to what Fr. Dietrich is saying? And leave the wasp alone. If you don't bother it, it won't bother you."

Fr. Dietrich is undecided about this.

"I wonder is that wise?"

"What, Father?"

"The wasp. I will happily turn my cheek to a human hostile, but wasps are, if you will pardon the eccentricity of the expression, a horse of a different colour."

"I don't follow you, Father."

"I can hardly follow myself. Mixed metaphors have always been my forte. I mean perhaps that Miyako can pummel the wasp with my priestly approval. The last time I got bitten on my hand, I couldn't type for two days."

Miss Yoshiyuki hides her impatience. Fr. Dietrich is, after all, a special case. In the early spring of that same year, he had left his bedroom and slept in the corridor so that sparrows could nest above his curtain rail. Allowance had to be made.

"But I must go," says the burly priest. "I must try to ring Fr. Kleinsorge; I've been trying to get through for two days now. You'd think that Hiroshima had vanished off the face of the earth."

"And are you happy with them?" asks Miss Yoshiyuki anxiously. "With the girls, I mean? With their knowledge of the Catechism?"

"They are word perfect. They have all the answers off to a T. Now the only question which remains is one for which no answer exists. A reply perhaps, but no answer."

Miss Yoshiyuki is puzzled.

"Is it a question of doctrine?"

"No," says Fr. Dietrich. "It is a question of love."

The plane is nearer still, almost on target. It is early afternoon.

It is nearly time to leave you but before I do, in the minutes that remain to us, I want to tell you what little I know of the last moments of our Confirmation class. Where to begin is a problem; where to end, especially with an ending such as this, is a mystery.

Maki was at the dentist this morning. She tried very hard not to whimper as he shook the fragments of tooth back and forth until they broke free separately from her swollen gum. The side of her mouth is still numb from the anaesthetic. It feels strange. When she speaks, she slurs. When she bends down, her jaw aches. So she sits bolt upright and holds a damp napkin against her cheek. When the wound throbs, she offers it up for her brother aboard an aircraft carrier a thousand miles south of Japan.

Komako is thinking about her father, Mr. Toraiwa. He works too hard and has difficulty breathing when he gets out of bed or when he laughs too much. She wishes he could find another job away from the depot. Only last night she crept out from between the sheets and walked on tip-toe to his bedroom to listen at the door and make sure he was sleeping and not staring up at the ceiling as if it were the sea or a fire.

Nagasaki

Perhaps it is best that he never speaks of his wife and his son; on the other hand, perhaps it would be good to do so. Perhaps it would ease his grief. Komako thinks she will talk to Fr. Dietrich about this the next time he sees him. He had a way with him; he would understand.

Yumiko and Miyako sit together. Yumiko is colouring an atlas with a pretend empire which stretches from Rangoon to Adelaide. She is about to conquer Indonesia with the colour purple. Then she plans to annex Mexico in a lightning strike.

Miyako scarcely notices her friend. She is in another world, thinking about her boyfriend Yasunari who brought her powdered chocolates two days before. These are pleasant thoughts, and the only thing that disturbs them is her worry over the violin lesson that same morning. The teacher had left her alone for a time, and Miyako had tired of the instrument's weight within minutes. So she laid the violin down on the desk and practised by sawing it like a joint of meat. But the teacher caught her and threatened to inform her parents that their hard-earned supplementary fees were wasted on a most ungrateful girl. Now Miyako is not afraid of her father, Mr. Kawabata, because he is deaf in both ears and cares about little other than his budgie but her mother is another matter, with cross lips and a bony hand.

The plane is overhead.
It is the fulness of time.

We covered those questions last week. And we revised them several times. I sometimes think that whatever I say to you goes up in smoke, goes in one ear and out the other. Try to remember — if not for my sake for Fr. Dietrich's. What is forgiveness? And what is meant by the sacrament of penance? How did sin enter the world, and how is the world restored to grace again? What happened to the apostles at Pentecost when flame descended upon them? Can none of you tell me? Have none of you a word to say? Are your lips sealed?
Miyako?
Yumiko?
Maki?
Komako?
Sometimes I think I might as well be speaking to the dead.

— Aidan Carl Mathews

? Questions and Assignments

1. What do we learn about the Kawabata family from (a) paragraph one of the story and (b) from the entire story?
2. Having read the whole story, give your impressions of Mr. Toriawa.
3. (a) In his description of early morning in Nagasaki, the author focuses particularly on one aspect. What is this?
   (b) Can you suggest why he did so, having considered the same scene a day later?
4. Which of the following words best describes the atmosphere of the classroom — lazy; gloomy; pleasant; easygoing? Give reasons for your answer.
5. What details of the character of the teacher, Miss Yoshiyuki, reveal her as a sensitive and caring person?
6. "The story is rich in irony." Do you agree? Refer to the story to support your answer. (See **Points to Note**).

Nagasaki

7. Comment on the writer's style in the following passages. (a) "The horns .... by the harbour" (Parag. 1), (b) "The length .... sinks deeper" (Parag. 2), (c) "And the lavish sounds .... among the rose-beds." (d) "But they are occupied .... for the moment."
8. To what extent does the war affect the lives of the young people that we meet in the story?
9. Could the theme of *Nagasaki* be regarded as being broadly similar to the theme of *Guests of the Nation* (by Frank O'Connor)? Give reasons to support your answer.
10. Read *The Shatterer of Worlds* (by Kildare Dobbs). As a "war" story, do you find it more impressive than *Nagasaki*?
11. Write a brief letter to the author of *Nagasaki*, outlining to him why you did *or* did not find his story impressive.
12. Continue the story for another two paragraphs from the point where the author stops.

S Spelling

Below are anagrams of words that are sometimes misspelt. Rearrange the letters to find the words. All the words are in the story.

- rathot
- aborhur
- hikres
- thelng
- thabred
- ulorhotghy
- aparpedsis
- iverece
- niterdeemd
- etifdine
- anallcowe
- gonetus
- redilsos
- matchos
- tantsendat
- cislindpie
- paprolav
- kewoldeng
- lespaleciy
- edsecdend

V Vocabulary Development

Find words in the story to match each of the following meanings.

- rebound
- tremble
- unfriendly
- giggles
- skilful
- crippled
- repeating
- storehouse
- additional
- roomy; large
- fine; delicate
- oddness; strangeness
- having the same centre
- of stout sturdy build; big and strong
- individual share or allowance of provisions
- flooded by; filled with
- pulled with sudden jerks
- in a pleasant/friendly manner
- hard to understand; profound
- take possession of; take over
- conferred as gift; given as a gift
- strike repeatedly; pound or beat especially with fist
- trucks attached to a steam locomotive and carrying fuel
- machine with rollers for pressing water out of washed clothes
- a piece of light porous lava used as an abrasive to clean or smooth the skin

Nagasaki

> **Points to Note**

PLOT
The story is virtually without a plot. Instead the author focuses on characters and setting. He sets out to provide a sketch of everyday life in Nagasaki on the ninth of August, 1945.

The fact that the story lacks a plot adds, in a sense, to its impact. It presents a haphazard series of loosely connected events, somewhat like the events of the real world, which very rarely follow the pattern of a neat plot.

IRONY
Nagasaki is rich in irony. The basis of the irony is that the writer and reader share knowledge at the expense of the characters in the story. Consequently, for example, the words the characters speak have different significance for the reader, who is aware of what lies in store for the girls, their parents and their teacher.

There is irony also in the situations of the characters. Little do they realise that, in a short while, their worries and fears, hopes and dreams, pain and suffering will be no more.

Select five examples of irony from the story and, in each case, explain your choice.

> **Writers' Workshop**

FINDING A THEME
The backbone of every short story is its theme. The theme of a story is the idea or viewpoint illustrated by the events of the story. Authors rarely spell out the themes of their works. To do so would be too much like preaching. Instead the author leaves it to the reader to discover it for themselves. **The theme** and **subject matter** should not be confused. The subject matter of *Nagasaki* is the description of a number of events in the city on the day it was bombed. The theme of the story, however, could be stated as follows :- *In all wars, the 'enemy' are human beings like ourselves. Like us, they have ambitions and worries; illness and pain; friends and families and they feel the same kind of grief and love as we do.* If you read **Guests of the Nation** you will find that it has a similar theme.

'War', 'Revenge', 'Emigration' are not themes — they are subjects. However, each of them could form the basis of many themes. In *Nagasaki* we have seen a theme developed on the subject of war. Arising from the subject of 'Revenge' would be themes like 'Revenge is sweet' or, conversely, 'Revenge brings no satisfaction'. 'Far away hills are not always greener' is a theme that ties up with the subject of 'Emigration'.

PROVERBS
In two of the examples above a theme has been expressed in the form of a proverb. Proverbs provide us with a rich collection of ready-made themes. Furthermore, each proverb can be developed into dozens of short stories. Below are some proverbs with which you may not be familiar. Now try writing a story, inspired by one of these proverbs :-

Nagasaki

- A bad workman always blames his tools.
- A cat may look at a king.
- We never miss the water till the well runs dry.
- Grasp all lose all.
- A hungry man is an angry man.
- A small leak will sink a great ship.
- Faint heart never won fair lady.
- Great oaks from little acorns grow.
- Set a thief to catch a thief.
- Fine words butter no parsnips.
- Anytime means no time.
- New brooms sweep clean.

✓ Q. 7 (a) — Sample Answer

The sentence describes the sounds coming from the shipyard. The writer states that the horns and hooters are in "full throat" — as if they are singing like birds.

The songs of the birds at dawn in the countryside is known as the "dawn chorus". For the people of Nagasaki though, these shipyard hooters were the only "dawn chorus" that could be heard. The sound of the birds could not be heard above the din.

He describes "screams" and "screeches". Neither of these words describe pleasant sounds. Both words together form a harsh sounding alliteration. We can almost hear their unmusical din. He ends the sentence by saying that the sounds "ricochet" off the roofs. This is a metaphor. It compares the sounds to stray bullets bouncing off things.

The entire sentence describes the sounds of the city in an imaginative way. I think, though, that two metaphors (dawn chorus; ricochet) make it difficult to understand. It needs to be read a few times to get its full meaning.

THE FUN THEY HAD

Margie even wrote about it that night in her diary. On the page headed May 17, 2157, she wrote, "Today Tommy found a real book!"

It was a very old book. Margie's grandfather once said that when he was a little boy his grandfather told him that there was a time when all stories were printed on paper.

They turned the pages, which were yellow and crinkly, and it was awfully funny to read words that stood still instead of moving the way they were supposed to — on a screen, you know. And then, when they turned back to the page before, it had the same words on it that it had had when they read it the first time.

"Gee," said Tommy, "what a waste. When you're through with the book, you just throw it away, I guess. Our television screen must have had a million books on it and it's good for plenty more. I wouldn't throw it away."

"Same with mine," said Margie. She was eleven and hadn't seen as many telebooks as Tommy had. He was thirteen.

She said, "Where did you find it?"

"In my house." He pointed without looking, because he was busy reading. "In the attic."

"What's it about?"

"School."

Margie was scornful. "School? What's there to write about school? I hate school."

Margie always hated school, but now she hated it more than ever. The mechanical teacher had been giving her test after test in geography and she had been doing worse and worse until her mother had shaken her head sorrowfully and sent for the County Inspector.

He was a round little man with a red face and a whole box of tools with dials and wires. He smiled at Margie and gave her an apple, then took the teacher apart. Margie had hoped that he wouldn't know how to put it together again, but he knew how all right, and, after an hour or so, there it was again, large and black and ugly, with a big screen on which all the lessons were shown and the questions were asked. That wasn't so bad. The part Margie hated most was the slot where she had to put homework and test papers. She always had to write them out in a punch code they made her learn when she was six years old, and the mechanical teacher calculated the mark in no time.

The Inspector had smiled after he was finished and patted Margie's head. He said to her mother, "It's not the little girl's fault, Mrs. Jones. I think the geography sector was geared a little too quick. Those things happen sometimes. I've slowed it up to an average ten-year level. Actually, the overall pattern of her progress is quite satisfactory." And he patted Margie's head again.

Margie was disappointed. She had been hoping they would take the teacher away altogether. They had once taken Tommy's teacher away for nearly a month because the history sector had blanked out completely.

So she said to Tommy, "Why would anyone write about school?"

Tommy looked at her with very superior eyes. "Because it's not our kind of school, stupid. This is the old kind of school that they had hundreds and hundreds of years ago." He added loftily, pronouncing the word carefully, "Centuries ago."

Margie was hurt. "Well, I don't know the kind of school they had all that time ago." She read the book over his shoulder for a while, then said, "Anyway, they had a

The Fun They Had

teacher."

"Sure they had a teacher, but it wasn't a regular teacher. It was a man."

"A man? How could a man be a teacher?"

"Well, he just told the boys and girls things and gave them homework and asked them questions."

"A man isn't smart enough."

"Sure he is. My father knows as much as my teacher."

"He can't. A man can't know as much as a teacher."

"He knows almost as much, I betcha."

Margie wasn't prepared to dispute that. She said, "I wouldn't want a strange man in my house to teach me."

Tommy screamed with laughter. "You don't know much, Margie. The teachers didn't live in the house. They had a special building and all the kids went there."

"And all the kids learned the same thing?"

"Sure, if they were the same age."

"But my mother says a teacher has to be adjusted to fit the mind of each boy and girl it teaches and that each kid has to be taught differently."

"Just the same they didn't do it that way then. If you don't like it, you don't have to read the book."

"I didn't say I didn't like it," Margie said quickly. She wanted to read about those funny schools.

They weren't even half-finished when Margie's mother called, "Margie! School!"

Margie looked up. "Not yet, Mamma."

"Now!" said Mrs. Jones. "And it's probably time for Tommy too."

Margie said to Tommy, "Can I read the book some more with you after school?"

"Maybe," he said nonchalantly. He walked away whistling, the dusty old book tucked beneath his arm.

Margie went into the schoolroom. It was right next to her bedroom and the

The Fun They Had

mechanical teacher was on and waiting for her. It was always on at the same time every day except Saturday and Sunday, because her mother said little girls learned better if they learned at regular hours.

The screen was lit up, and it said : "Today's arithmetic lesson is on the addition of proper fractions. Please insert yesterday's homework in the proper slot."

Margie did so with a sigh. She was thinking about the old schools they had when her grandfather's grandfather was a little boy. All the kids from the whole neighbourhood came, laughing and shouting in the schoolyard, sitting together in the schoolroom, going home together at the end of the day. They learned the same things, so they could help one another on the homework and talk about it.

And the teachers were people . . . .

The mechanical teacher was flashing on the screen : "When we add the fractions $1/2$ and $1/4$ —"

Margie was thinking about how the kids must have loved it in the old days. She was thinking about the fun they had.

— *Isaac Asimov*

? Questions and Assignments

1. (a) What does Tommy discover on May 17th, 2157?
   (b) Describe his find.
2. What is Margie's attitude to her school?
3. Describe Margie's teacher.
4. What is the inspector's verdict on Margie's progress?
5. (a) What do you learn about the relationship between Margie and Tommy from the dialogue between them?
   (b) What contribution does this dialogue make to the story as a whole?
6. Imagine you could move to the year 2157. Write the conversation you might have with Margie and Tommy in a discussion about your school and their school.
7. Describe what you think schools will be like in a hundred years hence. As well as the physical aspects include in your description comments on attitudes to others, successes and problems and social changes which will have occurred.
8. Make a short list of the advantages books have over telebooks.
9. Compose a letter to Mr. Asimov telling him what you think of the story.

S Spelling

Below are anagrams of words that are sometimes misspelt. Rearrange the letters to find the words. All the words are in the story.

- rayid
- nersec
- hetgoter
- trapnet
- glistwhin
- lulfawy
- furoslorwly
- delatlucac
- pinadotdiesp
- hinlamecac

The Fun They Had

V Vocabulary Development

Find words in the story to match each of the following meanings.

- altered slightly
- creased; wrinkled
- contemptuous; derisive
- indifferently; coolly; showing he could not care less
- proudly; haughtily, arrogantly, in a manner showing he is superior

☞ Points to Note

THEME

"It could be worse" is the message we get from this story. The subject is school and what it might be like in the future when teachers and schools are to be replaced by teaching machines in the home and learning becomes an isolated and solitary experience.

✓ Q. 5 — Sample Answer

(a) From the dialogue between Margie and Tommy we learn that Margie has to make a great effort to get information from Tommy. He is very absorbed in the book and so gives her very short answers. He talks down to Margie. At one point he actually addresses her as "stupid". He tries to impress her by speaking in a lofty tone and by using a word like "centuries". At another point in the conversation when they discuss the teacher, he says to her "You don't know much Margie". He doesn't encourage her to read the book: "If you don't like it you don't have to read the book". When she asks him to read it with her after school, he shows little enthusiasm in his reply.

From their conversation it would seem that Tommy and Margie needed each other's company. Tommy considered himself to be the superior one in the relationship and Margie was probably resigned to this because she did not react to his terrible attitude to her.

(b) Margie and Tommy's conversation consists mainly of a series of questions and answers. This type of conversation helps to maintain the reader's interest in the story. We are interested in the questions that Margie asks and we are anxious to hear Tommy's answers. The dialogue also helps to link the different threads of the story together. For example, when the writer describes Margie's experience of school in some detail, he returns to the topic of school as we know it by having Margie and Tommy resume their conversation.

The overall effect of the use of dialogue in the story is that it brings the story together and makes it more interesting. It is mainly the conversation between Margie and Tommy that brings this story to life.

At The River-Gates

Lots of sisters I had (said the old man), good girls, too; and one elder brother. Just the one. We were at either end of the family: the eldest, my brother John — we always called him Beany, for some reason; then the girls, four of them; then me. I was Tiddler, and the reason for that was plain.

Our father was a flour miller, and we lived just beside the mill. It was a water-mill, built right over the river, with the mill-wheel underneath. To understand what happened that wild night, all those years ago, you have to understand a bit about the working of the mill-stream. About a hundred yards before the river reached the mill, it divided: the upper river flowed on to power the mill, as I've said; the lower river, leaving the upper river through sluice-gates, flowed to one side of the mill and past it; and then the upper and lower rivers joined up again well below the mill. The sluice-gates could be opened or shut by the miller to let more or less water through from the upper to the lower river. You can see the use of that: the miller controlled the flow of water to power his mill; he could also draw off any floodwaters that came down.

Being a miller's son, I can never remember not understanding that. I was a little tiddler, still at school, when my brother, Beany, began helping my father in the mill. He was as good as a man, my father said. He was strong, and he learnt the feel of the grain, and he was clever with the mill machinery, and he got on with the other men in the mill — there were only ten of them, counting two carters. He understood the gates, of course, and how to get just the right head of water for the mill. And he liked it all: he liked the work he did, and the life; he liked the mill, and the river, and the long river-bank. One day he'd be the miller after my father, everyone said.

I was too young to feel jealousy about that; but I would never have felt jealous of Beany, because Beany was the best brother you could have had. I loved and admired him more than anyone I knew or could imagine knowing. He was very good to me. He used to take me with him when you might have thought a little boy would have been in the way. He took me with him when he went fishing, and he taught me to fish. I learnt patience, then, from Beany. There were plenty of roach and dace in the river; and sometimes we caught trout or pike; and once we caught an eel, and I was first of all terrified and then screaming with excitement at the way it whipped about on the bank, but Beany held it and killed it, and my mother made it into eel-pie. He knew about the fish in the river, and the little creatures, too. He showed me fresh-water shrimps, and leeches — "Look, Tiddler, they make themselves into croquet-hoops when they want to go anywhere!" and he showed me the little underwater cottages of caddis-worms. He knew where to get good watercress for Sunday tea — you could eat watercress from our river, in those days.

We had an old boat on the river, and Beany would take it upstream to inspect the banks for my father. The banks had to be kept sound: if there was a breach, it would let the water escape and reduce the water-power for the mill. Beany took Jess, our dog, with him in the boat, and he often took me. Beany was the only person I've ever known who could point out a kingfisher's nest in the river-bank. He knew about birds. He once showed me a flycatcher's nest in the brickwork below the sluice-gates, just above where the water dashed and roared at its highest. Once, when we

At The River-Gates

were in the boat, he pointed ahead to an otter in the water. I held on to Jess's collar then.

It was Beany who taught me to swim. One summer it was hotter than anyone remembered, and Beany was going from the mill up to the gates to shut in more water. Jess was following him, and as he went he gave me a wink, so I followed too, although I didn't know why. As usual, he opened the gates with the great iron spanner, almost as long in the handle as he was tall. Then he went down to the pool in the lower river, as if to see the water-level there. But as he went he was unbuttoning his flour-whitened waistcoat; by the time he reached the pool he was naked, and he dived straight in. He came up with his hair plastered over his eyes, and he called to

At The River-Gates

me: "Come on, Tiddler! Just time for a swimming lesson!" Jess sat on the bank and watched us.

Jess was really my father's dog, but she attached herself to Beany. She loved Beany. Everyone loved Beany, and he was good to everyone. Especially, as I've said, to me. Just sometimes he'd say, "I'm off on my own now, Tiddler," and then I knew better than to ask to go with him. He'd go sauntering up the river-bank by himself, except for Jess at his heels. I don't think he did anything very particular when he went off on his own. Just the river and the river-bank were happiness enough for him.

He was still not old enough to have got himself a girl, which might have changed things a bit; but he wasn't too young to go to the War. The War broke out in 1914, when I was still a boy, and Beany went.

It was sad without Beany; but it was worse than that. I was too young to understand then; but, looking back, I realise what was wrong. There was fear in the house. My parents became gloomy and somehow secret. So many young men were being killed at the Front. Other families in the village had had word of a son's death. The news came in a telegram. I overheard my parents talking of those deaths, those telegrams, although not in front of the girls or me. I saw my mother once, in the middle of the morning, kneeling by Beany's bed, praying.

So every time Beany came home on leave, alive, we were lucky.

But when Beany came, he was different. He loved us as much, but he was different. He didn't play with me as he used to do; he would sometimes stare at me as though he didn't see me. When I shouted "Beany!" and rushed at him, he would start as if he'd woken up. Then he'd smile, and be good to me, almost as he used to be. But, more often than he used to, he'd be off all by himself up the river-bank, with Jess at his heels. My mother, who longed to have him within her sight for every minute of his leave, used to watch him go, and sigh. Once I heard her say to my father that the river-bank did Beany good, as if he were sickening for some strange disease. Once one of the girls was asking Beany about the Front and the trenches, and he was telling her this and that, and we were all interested, and suddenly he stopped and said, "No. It's hell." And walked away alone, up the green, quiet river-bank. I suppose if one place was hell, then the other was heaven to him.

After Beany's leaves were over, the mill-house was gloomy again; and my father had to work harder, without Beany's help in the mill. Nowadays he had to work the gates all by himself, a thing that Beany had been taking over from him. If the gates needed working at night, my father and Beany had always gone there together. My mother hated it nowadays when my father had to go to the gates alone at night: she was afraid he'd slip and fall in the water, and, although he could swim, accidents could happen to a man alone in the dark. But, of course, my father wouldn't let her come with him, or any of my sisters, and I was still considered much too young. That irked me.

Well, one season had been very dry and the river level had dropped. The gates were kept shut to get up a head of water for the mill. Then clouds began to build up heavily on the horizon, and my father said he was sure it was going to rain; but it didn't. All day storms rumbled in the distance. In the evening the rain began. It rained steadily: my father had already been once to the gates to open the flashes. He was back at home, drying off in front of the fire. The rain still drove against the windows. My mother said, "It can't come down worse

At The River-Gates

than this." She and my sisters were still up with my father. Even I wasn't in bed, although I was supposed to have been. No one could have slept for the noise of the rain.

Suddenly the storm grew worse — much worse. It seemed to explode over our heads. We heard a pane of glass in the skylight over the stairs shatter with the force of it, and my sisters ran with buckets to catch the water pouring through. Oddly, my mother didn't go to see the damage: she stayed with my father, watching him like a lynx. He was fidgeting up and down, paying no attention to the skylight either, and suddenly he said he'd have to go up to the gates again and open everything to carry all possible floodwater into the lower river. This was what my mother had been dreading. She made a great outcry, but she knew it was no use. My father put on his tarpaulin jacket again and took his oil lamp and a thick stick — I don't know why, nor did he, I think. Jess always hated being out in the rain, but she followed him. My mother watched him from the back door, lamenting, and urging him to be careful. A few steps from the doorway and you couldn't see him any longer for the driving rain.

My mother's lingering at the back door gave me my chance. I got my boots on and an oilskin cape I had (I wasn't a fool, even if I was little) and I whipped out of the front door and worked my way round in the shelter of the house to the back and then took the path my father had taken to the river, and made a dash for it, and caught up with my father and Jess, just as they were turning up the way towards the gates. I held on to Jess's tail for quite a bit before my father noticed me. He was terribly angry, of course, but he didn't want to turn back with me, and he didn't like to send me back alone, and perhaps in his heart of hearts he was glad of a little human company on such a night. So we all three struggled up to the gates together. Just by the gates my father found me some shelter between a tree-trunk and a stack of drift-wood. There I crouched, with Jess to keep me company.

I was too small to help my father with the gates, but there was one thing I could do. He told me to hold his lamp so that the light shone on the gates and what he was doing. The illumination was very poor, partly because of the driving rain, but at least it was better than nothing, and anyway my father knew those gates by heart. Perhaps he gave me the job of holding the light so that I had something to occupy my mind and keep me from being afraid.

There was plenty to be afraid of on that night of storm.

Directing what light I could on to my father also directed and concentrated my attention on him. I could see his laborious motions as he heaved the great spanner into place. Then he began to try to rack up with it, but the wind and the rain were so strong that I could see he was having the greatest difficulty. Once I saw him stagger sideways nearly into the blackness of the river. Then I wanted to run out from my shelter and try to help him, but he had strictly forbidden me to do any such thing, and I knew he was right.

Young as I was, I knew — it came to me as I watched him — that he couldn't manage the gates alone in that storm. I suppose he was a man already just past the prime of his strength: the wind and the rain were beating him; the river would beat him.

I shone the light as steadily as I could, and gripped Jess by the collar, and I think I prayed.

I was so frightened then that, afterwards, when I wasn't frightened, I could never be sure of what I had seen, or what I thought I had seen, or what I imagined I had seen.

101

At The River-Gates

Through the confusion of the storm I saw my father struggling and staggering, and, as I peered and peered, my vision seemed to blur and to double, so that I began sometimes to see one man, sometimes two. My father seemed to have a shadow-self besides himself, who steadied him, heaved with him, worked with him, and at last together they had opened the sluice-gates and let the flood through.

When it was done, my father came back to where Jess and I were, and leant against the tree. He was gasping for breath and exhausted, and had a look on his face that I cannot describe. From his expression I knew that he had felt the shadow with him, just as I had seen it. And Jess was agitated too, straining against my hold, whining.

I looked past my father, and I could still see something by the sluice-gates: a shadow that had separated itself from my father, and lingered there. I don't know how I could have seen it in the darkness. I don't know. My father slowly turned and looked in the direction that he saw me looking. The shadow began to move away from the gates, away from us; it began to go up the long river-bank beyond the gates, into the darkness there. It seemed to me that the rain and the wind stilled a little as it went.

Jess wriggled from my grasp and was across the gates and up the river-bank, following the vanished shadow. I had made no move, uttered no word, but my father said to me, "Let them go!" I looked up at him, and his face was streaming with tears as well as with rain.

He took my hand as we fought our way back to the house. The whole house was lit up, to light us home, and my mother stood at the open back door, waiting. She gave a cry of horror when she saw me with my father; and then she saw his face, and her own went quite white. He stumbled into her arms, and he sobbed and sobbed. I didn't know until that night that grown men could cry. My mother led my father indoors, and I don't know what talk they had together. My sisters looked after me, dried me, scolded me, put me to bed.

The next day the telegram came to say that Beany had been killed in action in Flanders.

It was some time after that that Jess came home. She was wet through, and my mother thought she was ill, for she sat shivering by the fire, and for two days would neither eat nor drink. My father said: "Let her be."

I'm an old man: it all happened so many years ago, but I've never forgotten my brother Beany. He was so good to us all.

— *Philippa Pearce*

? Questions and Assignments

1. Describe clearly and in your own words, how the river gates worked.
   (In order to illustrate your answer, you may draw a simple sketch based on the information in the story).
2. What kind of an attitude did Beany have towards his work?
3. Explain why Tiddler admired Beany so much?
4. How did home life change for Tiddler's family when Beany left for war?
5. Describe how Beany had changed when he returned on leave from the war.
6. (a) From what point of view is the story told?
   (b) Comment on the character of the narrator.

At The River-Gates

7. "This was what my mother had been dreading". What do you think was the author's purpose in this sentence?
8. What features of the author's description of the storm did you find impressive?
9. "It's hell" was Beany's comment on the Front. In relation to this comment, discuss the significance of the river-bank in the story. (Note the narrator's description of the river-bank).
10. Discuss the role of the dog in the story.
11. Imagine that an elderly and very honest friend of yours had told you this story. How would it affect your belief in ghosts?
12. Write a brief letter to the author of this story telling her what aspects of the story impressed you.
13. Suggest an alternative - and a happy - ending to the story. Begin at the point where the father is struggling with the sluice-gates.

S Spelling

Below are anagrams of words that are sometimes misspelt. Rearrange the letters to find the words. All the words are in the story.

- vedidid
- lontrocdel
- youjesal
- catpenie
- guthac
- hagothul
- aritrulpac
- asedies
- cupcoy
- tardapees

V Vocabulary Development

Find words in the story to match each of the following meanings.

- gap
- crying with grief
- animal of cat family
- dallying; staying
- told off severely
- break suddenly into many pieces
- annoyed
- depressed, unhappy
- disturbed
- amount of light
- lifted
- stood with legs bent close to body
- waterproof cloth
- make smaller, lessen
- tool for turning nut or bolt
- walking in a leisurely way
- made a continuous deep sound
- strongly requesting; earnestly begging; entreating; exhorting

☞ Points to Note

SUSPENSE AND TENSION

An important element in stories is *suspense* or *tension*. Broadly speaking, both terms refer to the same thing - i.e. the excitement experienced by us, the readers, as we wait for some important event that seems to be about to occur. Note how the suspense is powerfully built up in the story *At The River-Gates*. From an early stage in the story the reader is made to feel doubts and fears that things may go wrong. It is not clear how events will unfold. We are given the first hint that things may be about to go wrong when Beany is called up to fight in the war. From this point onwards the suspense is gradually increased.

At The River-Gates

Writers' Workshop

WRITING GHOST STORIES

At The River-Gates is a ghost story. The technique used by the writer is very effective for the **ghost story genre** and is worth noting.

Firstly, she selects as *narrator* a character who was involved in and witnessed the events of the story - i.e. Tiddler.

The narrator strikes us as a sincere and reliable person. Although the opening paragraphs of the story are chiefly concerned with Beany, Tiddler reveals **his own** character by the way he describes his older brother.

The events of the story are described in a straight-forward, matter-of-fact style. The tone is calm and relaxed - i.e. we can imagine the old man speaking in a relaxed and calm way.

He doesn't claim that a ghost was involved. He merely tells what he saw and allows us to decide for ourselves if a ghost was involved.

However, his account of the event contains at least one incident that cannot be explained logically. This technique, with slight variations, is frequently used both by ghost story writers and also science fiction writers. A narrator who seems reliable and level-headed helps to give extra credibility to strange and, often, unexplainable events. Bram Stoker, the author of *Dracula*, which is probably one of the best known of all stories of the supernatural, uses such an approach. The story of Dracula is told in diary form by an English solicitor and a few of the solicitor's acquaintances.

Outline Short Story Ideas

- **Character A** is in trouble, facing danger or is unaware of a danger that lies ahead. He encounters **B**, a stranger, who assists **A** or warns of the danger ahead. When **A** has solved his/her problem or avoided the danger he/she sets out to identify **B** only to discover he/she had been dead for many years. Furthermore, the 'ghost' (**B**) will have some link with **A**. Perhaps **B** met his/her death in circumstances similar to those that **A** faced or perhaps **B** is a relative of **A**.

- This story may involve **Character A** and/or **B**. **A** (and **B**) find themselves in an old building with a reputation for being haunted. **A** is sceptical (and **B** is afraid). The building might be an old house, hotel or hostel. There they meet **Character C** who puts them at their ease and chats about the place, its history, legends etc. As they prepare to retire for the night it becomes apparent to **A** that **C** is a ghost. Use your imagination to outline how this is revealed.

- This short story idea can be approached from a variety of viewpoints. It can be written from the objective (omniscient) viewpoint or from that of any of the characters. If approached from the viewpoint of **Character C** the effect would likely be humorous.

✓ Q. 7 — Sample Answer

The author's purpose in writing this sentence is to increase the suspense at that point in the story. When we, the readers, learn that the mother was afraid of something happening to her husband at the sluice-gates we also share her dread. As we watch him head out into the storm, we wonder whether he will complete his task safely - or will he not? It is sentences such as this one that make us want to read on to find out what will happen.

Improve Your Handwriting

Clear legible handwriting, laid out neatly, gives all written work extra impact. Note the contrast between the handwriting sample in the box below and the story that follows :-

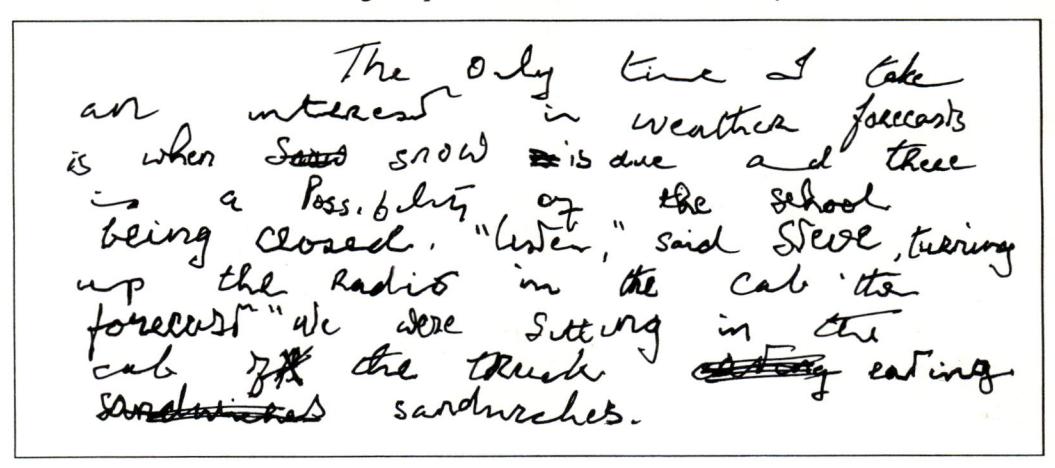

> *The only time I take an interest in weather forecasts is when ~~snow~~ snow ~~is~~ is due and there is a possibility of the school being closed. "Listen," said Steve, turning up the radio in the cab 'the forecast." We were sitting in the cab ~~of~~ the truck ~~eating~~ eating ~~sandwiches~~ sandwiches.*

The most common faults in handwriting are :-
- Individual letters badly formed.
- Letters bunched too closely together.
- Letters which are the wrong size or height in relation to other letters.
- Letters that are not on the line.
- Many words and letters crossed out.

POOR HANDWRITING USUALLY CONSISTS OF A COMBINATION OF THESE FAULTS

Improve your handwriting by avoiding these faults.

This handwritten story below is based on the outline short story idea that follows **At The River-Gates**, providing you with an example of how the outline short story ideas can be used. However, the story requires another paragraph or so to complete it. Write an ending for the story and identify and correct any punctuation or spelling errors that you find.

> *The only time I take an interest in weather forecasts is when snow is due and there is the possibility of the school being closed.*
>
> *"Listen", said Steve, turning up the radio, "the forecast".*
>
> *Steve and I were sitting in the cab of our truck, eating sandwiches and chatting about fishing. We had just made our last delivery of the*

105

day and we were about to set off home to Athlone. Steve was the driver and I was his helper. It was my first summer job and I loved it.

"..... the met. office has issued a weather alert .... the present hot humid spell is to end .... thunder storms, accompanied by gale force winds and heavy rain are moving in from the Atlantic .... will affect most areas by midnight ..... drivers of high vehicles should take extra care ..... ". Steve switched off the radio, cutting short the rest of the news.

"High vehicles," that's us", said Steve, starting the engine, "if 'we're lucky' we'll beat the storm home".

Our luck ran out twenty miles from home. When the storm broke, or rather exploded, on the countryside darkness had fallen and the rain battered against the sides of the truck and hit the windscreen in sheets. The wipers were no match for it and the headlight beams were swallowed up after a few yards by the darkness and downpour.

We had almost passed him when I spotted him. He was on the ditch on my side, waving frantically. I caught a glimpse of him in a long coat, a white beard and a cap with a shiny peak.

"There's an ol' fellow on the ditch back there," I shouted at Steve, "He was waving. Did you see him?"

"I didn't" he replied but he pulled up. My friend on the ditch didn't show up though and Steve was about to start the truck again when we heard it — the horn of a train, but hooting like an angry motorist, and then a crashing sound just up ahead.

Steve moved forward cautiously. I didn't know what to expect but I felt nervous. A quarter of a mile on the road, illuminated in the truck's headlights, were the splintered remains of a level-crossing barrier. The train had disappeared into the distance.

After a few moments Steve spoke.

"I don't know who or what you saw back the road, son, but if we hadn't stopped for him we would have likely copped it here. Obviously the storm affected the signals. We better move on and find a phone. Then we'll go home".

Three weeks later I called to Steve's house to return a fishing reel. When a photograph on the wall caught my eye.

THE DIAMOND MAKER

Some business had detained me in Chancery Lane until nine in the evening, and thereafter, having some inkling of a headache, I was disinclined either for entertainment or further work. So much of the sky as the high cliffs of that narrow cañon of traffic left visible spoke of a serene night, and I determined to make my way down to the Embankment, and rest my eyes and cool my head by watching the variegated lights upon the river. Beyond comparison the night is the best time for this place; a merciful darkness hides the dirt of the waters, and the lights of this transition age, red, glaring orange, gas-yellow, and electric white, are set in shadowy outlines of every possible shade between grey and deep purple. Through the arches of Waterloo Bridge a hundred points of light mark the sweep of the Embankment, and above its parapet rise the towers of Westminster, warm grey against the starlight. The black river goes by with only a rare ripple breaking its silence, and disturbing the reflections of the lights that swim upon its surface.

"A warm night," said a voice at my side.

I turned my head, and saw the profile of a man who was leaning over the parapet beside me. It was a refined face, not unhandsome though pinched and pale enough, and the coat collar turned up and pinned round the throat marked his status in life as sharply as a uniform. I felt I was committed to the price of a bed and breakfast if I answered him.

I looked at him curiously. Would he have anything to tell me worth the money, or was he the common incapable — incapable even of telling his own story? There was a quality of intelligence in his forehead and eyes, and a certain tremulousness in his nether lip that decided me.

"Very warm," said I; "but not too warm for us here."

"No," he said, still looking across the water, "it is pleasant enough here . . . just now."

"It is good," he continued after a pause, "to find anything so restful as this in London. After one has been fretting about business all day, about getting on, meeting obligations, and parrying dangers, I do not know what one would do if it were not for such pacific corners." He spoke with long pauses between the sentences. "You must know a little of the irksome labour of the world, or you would not be here. But I doubt if you can be so brain-weary and footsore as I am . . . . Bah! Sometimes I doubt if the game is worth the candle. I feel inclined to throw the whole thing over — name, wealth, and position — and take to some modest trade. But I know if I abandoned my ambition — hardly as she uses me — I should have nothing but remorse left for the rest of my days."

He became silent. I looked at him in astonishment. If ever I saw a man hopelessly hard-up it was the man in front of me. He was ragged and he was dirty, unshaven and unkempt; he looked as though he had been left in a dust-bin for a week. And he was talking to me of the irksome worries of a large business. I almost laughed outright. Either he was mad or playing a sorry jest on his own poverty.

"If high aims and high positions," said I, "have their drawbacks of hard work and anxiety, they have their compensations. Influence, the power of doing good, of assisting those weaker and poorer than ourselves; and there is even a certain gratification in display . . . ."

My banter under the circumstances was

in very vile taste. I spoke on the spur of the contrast of his appearance and speech. I was sorry even while I was speaking.

He turned a haggard but very composed face upon me. Said he: "I forget myself. Of course you would not understand."

He measured me for a moment. "No doubt it is very absurd. You will not believe me even when I tell you, so that it is fairly safe to tell you. And it will be a comfort to tell someone. I really have a big business in hand, a very big business. But there are troubles just now. The fact is .... I make diamonds."

"I suppose," said I, "you are out of work just at present?"

"I am sick of being disbelieved," he said impatiently, and suddenly unbuttoning his wretched coat he pulled out a little canvas bag that was hanging by a cord round his neck. From this he produced a brown pebble. "I wonder if you know enough to know what that is?" He handed it to me.

Now, a year or so ago, I had occupied my leisure in taking a London science degree, so that I have a smattering of physics and mineralogy. The thing was not unlike an uncut diamond of the darker sort, though far too large, being almost as big as the top of my thumb. I took it, and saw it had the form of a regular octahedron, with the carved faces peculiar to the most precious of minerals. I took out my penknife and tried to scratch it — vainly. Leaning forward towards the gas-lamp, I tried the thing on my watch-glass, and scored a white line across that with the greatest ease.

I looked at my interlocutor with rising curiosity. "It certainly is rather like a diamond. But, if so, it is a Behemoth of diamonds. Where did you get it?"

"I tell you I made it," he said. "Give it back to me."

He replaced it hastily and buttoned his jacket. "I will sell it to you for one hundred pounds," he suddenly whispered eagerly. With that my suspicions returned. The thing might, after all, be merely a lump of that almost equally hard substance, corundum, with an accidental resemblance in shape to the diamond. Or if it was a diamond, how came he by it, and why should he offer it at a hundred pounds?

We looked into one another's eyes. He seemed eager, but honestly eager. At that moment I believed it was a diamond he was trying to sell. Yet I am a poor man, a hundred pounds would leave a visible gap in my fortunes and no sane man would buy a diamond by gaslight from a ragged tramp on his personal warranty only. Still, a diamond that size conjured up a vision of many thousands of pounds. Then, thought I, such a stone could scarcely exist without being mentioned in every book of gems, and again I called to mind the stories of contraband and light-fingered Kaffirs at the Cape. I put the question of purchase on one side.

"How did you get it?" said I.

"I made it."

I had heard something of Moissan, but I knew his artificial diamonds were very small. I shook my head.

"You seem to know something of this kind of thing. I will tell you a little about myself. Perhaps then you may think better of the purchase." He turned round with his back to the river, and put his hands in his pockets. He sighed. "I know you will not believe me."

"Diamonds," he began — and as he spoke his voice lost its faint flavour of the tramp and assumed something of the easy tone of an educated man — "are to be made by throwing carbon out of combination in a suitable flux and under a suitable pressure; the carbon crystallises out, not as black-lead or charcoal-powder, but as small diamonds. So much has been known to chemists for years, but no one yet has hit upon exactly the right flux in which to melt up the carbon, or exactly the right pressure for the best results. Consequently the diamonds made by chemists are small and dark, and worthless as jewels. Now I, you know, have given up my life to this problem — given my life to it.

"I began to work at the conditions of diamond making when I was seventeen, and now I am thirty-two. It seemed to me that it might take all the thought and energies of a man for ten years, or twenty years, but, even if it did, the game was still worth the candle. Suppose one to have at last just hit the right trick, before the secret got out and diamonds became as common as coal, one might realise millions. Millions!"

He paused and looked for my sympathy. His eyes shone hungrily. "To think," said he, "that I am on the verge of it all, and here!"

"I had," he proceeded, "about a thousand pounds when I was twenty-one, and this, I thought, eked out by a little teaching, would keep my researches going. A year or two was spent in study, at Berlin chiefly, and then I continued on my own account. The trouble was the secrecy. You see, if once I had let out what I was doing, other men might have been spurred on by my belief in the practicability of the idea; and I do not pretend to be such a genius as to have been sure of coming in first, in the case of a race for the discovery. And you see it was important that if I really meant to make a pile, people should not know it was an artificial process and capable of turning out diamonds by the ton. So I had to work all alone. At first I had a little laboratory, but as my resources began to run out I had to conduct my experiments in a wretched unfurnished room in Kentish Town, where I slept at last on a straw mattress on the floor among all my apparatus. The money simply flowed away. I grudged myself everything except scientific appliances. I tried to keep things going by a little teaching, but I am not a very good teacher, and I have no university degree, not very much education except in chemistry, and I found I had to give a lot of time and labour for precious little money. But I got nearer and nearer the thing. Three years ago I settled the problem of the composition of the flux, and got near the pressure by putting this flux of mine and a certain carbon composition into a closed-up gunbarrel, filling up with water, sealing tightly, and heating."

He paused.

"Rather risky," said I.

"Yes. It burst, and smashed all my windows and a lot of my apparatus; but I got a kind of diamond powder nevertheless. Following out the problem of getting a big pressure upon the molten mixture from which the things were to crystallise, I hit upon some researches of Daubrée's at the Paris Laboratoire des Poudres et Salpêtres. He exploded dynamite in a tightly screwed steel cylinder, too strong to burst, and I found he could crush rocks into a muck not unlike the South African bed in which diamonds are found. It was a tremendous strain on my resources, but I got a steel cylinder made for my purpose after his pattern. I put in all my stuff and my explosives, built up a fire in my furnace, put the whole concern in, and - went out for a walk."

I could not help laughing at his matter-of-fact manner. "Did you not think it would blow up the house? Were there other people in the place?"

"It was in the interest of science," he said ultimately. "There was a costermonger family on the floor below, a begging-letter writer in the room behind mine, and two flower-women were upstairs. Perhaps it was a bit thoughtless. But possibly some of them were out."

"When I came back the thing was just where I left it, among the white-hot coals. The explosive hadn't burst the case. And then I had a problem to face. You know time is an important element in crystallisation. If you hurry the process the crystals are small - it is only by prolonged standing that they grow to any size. I resolved to let this apparatus cool for two years, letting the temperature go down slowly during that time. And I was now quite out of money; and with a big fire and the rent of my room, as well as my hunger to satisfy, I had scarcely a penny in the world.

"I can hardly tell you all the shifts I was put to while I was making the diamonds. I have sold newspapers, held horses, opened cab-doors. For many weeks I addressed envelopes. I had a place as assistant to a man who owned a barrow, and used to call down one side of the road while he called down the other. Once for a week I had absolutely nothing to do, and I begged. What a week that was! One day the fire was going out and I had eaten nothing all day, and a little chap taking his girl out, gave me sixpence — to show-off. Thank heaven for vanity! How the fish-shops smelt! But I went and spent it all on coals, and had the furnace bright red again, and then — Well, hunger makes a fool of a man.

"At last, three weeks ago, I let the fire out. I took my cylinder and unscrewed it while it was still so hot that it punished my hands, and I scraped out the crumbling lava-like mass with a chisel, and hammered it into a powder upon an iron plate. And I found three big diamonds and five small ones. As I sat on the floor hammering, my door opened, and my neighbour, the begging-letter writer, came in. He was drunk — as he usually is. ' 'Nerchist,' said

111

he. 'You're drunk,' said I. ' 'Structive scoundrel,' said he. 'Go to your father,' said I, meaning the Father of Lies. 'Never you mind,' said he, and gave me a cunning wink, and hiccupped, and leaning up against the door, with his other eye against the door-post, began to babble of how he had been prying in my room, and how he had gone to the police that morning, and how they had taken down everything he had to say — ' 'siffiwas a ge'm,' said he. Then I suddenly realised I was in a hole. Either I should have to tell these police my little secret, and get the whole thing blown upon, or be lagged as an anarchist. So I went up to my neighbour and took him by the collar, and rolled him about a bit, and then I gathered up my diamonds and cleared out. The evening newspapers called my den the Kentish-Town Bomb Factory. And now I cannot part with the things for love or money.

"If I go into a respectable jewellers they ask me to wait, and go and whisper to a clerk to fetch a policeman, and then I say I cannot wait. And I found out a receiver of stolen goods, and he simply stuck to the one I gave him and told me to prosecute if I wanted it back. I am going about now with several hundred thousand pounds-worth of diamonds round my neck, and without either food or shelter. You are the first person I have taken into my confidence. But I like your face and I am hard-driven."

He looked into my eyes.

"It would be madness," said I, "for me to buy a diamond under the circumstances. Besides, I do not carry hundreds of pounds about in my pocket. Yet I more than half believe your story. I will, if you like, do this: come to my office tomorrow . . . ."

"You think I am a thief!" said he keenly. "You will tell the police. I am not coming into a trap."

"Somehow I am assured you are no thief. Here is my card. Take that, anyhow. You need not come to any appointment. Come when you will."

He took the card, and an earnest of my good-will.

"Think better of it and come," said I.

He shook his head doubtfully. "I will pay you back your half-crown with interest some day — such interest as will amaze you," said he. "Anyhow, you will keep the secret? . . . . Don't follow me."

He crossed the road and went into the darkness towards the little steps under the archway leading into Essex Street, and I let him go. And that was the last I ever saw of him.

Afterwards I had two letters from him asking me to send bank-notes — not cheques — to certain addresses. I weighed the matter over, and took what I conceived to be the wisest course. Once he called upon me when I was out. My urchin described him as a very thin, dirty, and ragged man, with a dreadful cough. He left no message. That was the finish of him so far as my story goes. I wonder sometimes what has become of him. Was he an ingenious monomaniac, or a fraudulent dealer in pebbles, or has he really made diamonds as he asserted? The latter is just sufficiently credible to make me think at times that I have missed the most brilliant opportunity of my life. He may of course be dead, and his diamonds carelessly thrown aside — one, I repeat, was almost as big as my thumb. Or he may be still wandering about trying to sell the things. It is just possible he may yet emerge upon society, and, passing athwart my heavens in the serene altitude sacred to the wealthy and the well-advertised, reproach me silently for my want of enterprise. I sometimes think I might at least have risked five pounds.

—*H. G. Wells*

The Diamond Maker

? Questions and Assignments

1. (a) Why did the narrator go to the Embankment?
   (b) Why was the night 'the best time' to be there?
2. Was the narrator determined not to give the man the price of bed and breakfast? Give a reason for your answer.
3. Shortly after the diamond maker spoke the narrator looked at him "in astonishment". Explain why.
4. Why does the diamond maker decide to tell the narrator his story?
5. How did the narrator test the so-called diamond?
6. (a) Why did he not buy the diamond?
   (b) Do you think he made a correct decision. Why?
7. (a) What do each of the following sections reveal about the narrator? (i) the first sentence (ii) "Now, a year . . . mineralogy." (iii) "no sane man . . . warranty only." (iv) "I weighed . . . wisest course." (v) the last sentence.
   (b) Give your own impressions of him in a short paragraph.
8. The diamond maker claimed that his work was 'in the interest of science'. Do you agree? Refer to the story to support your answer.
9. Write a brief note on one feature of the writer's style in the story.
10. "Sometimes I doubt if the game is worth the candle", the diamond maker declares at an early stage in the story. Could you suggest the meaning and possible origin of the expression.
11. Outline briefly what you consider to be the main theme of the story. (Consider how the story focuses on different aspects of risk-taking and wealth).
12. Imagine that the narrator buys the large diamond from the diamond maker. Write the dialogue that later takes place between him and a diamond dealer, when he attempts to sell the stone.

S Spelling

Below are anagrams of words that are sometimes misspelt. Rearrange the letters to find the words. All the words are in the story.

- daaehehc
- elevibe
- tidenomen
- pasutarpa
- eagartvide
- eusriel
- fitarlicia
- pelnesove
- timcedmot
- cispuroe
- tallyescriss
- veericre
- ehafrode
- utisriyco
- ymathpsy
- onitropupyt
- otisglibaon
- odadnim
- corpdeede
- litenimpyat

V Vocabulary Development

Find words in the story to match each of the following meanings.

- low wall at the edge of a bridge
- slight trembling, quivering
- ruffling of water's surface, a little wave
- keeping off, warding off, averting

The Diamond Maker

- guarantee of quality
- feeling of satisfaction or delight
- careworn
- gentle ridicule, jesting
- supplemented by, made last
- desire for admiration
- crafty
- speak foolishly or incoherently
- clever at contriving
- one who believes that government and law should be abolished
- untidy-looking, dishevelled
- person who takes part in a conversation
- solid figure contained by eight plane faces
- smuggled goods
- the biting or gnawing pain of conscience
- looking inquisitively
- one whose mind is obsessed by one idea or interest
- give out to, rebuke, upbraid, censure severely
- worrying
- peaceful

☞ Points to Note

H. G. Wells was one of the inventors of the Science Fiction genre. Born in England in 1866, Herbert George Wells lived through a time when a great number of spectacular advances were made in all branches of science and technology. He studied science at the University of London.

The potential, for both good and evil, that scientific discoveries offered mankind interested Wells greatly. This interest is reflected in much of his writing, including *The Diamond Maker*. His novels include *The Time Machine*, *The Invisible Man*, *The War of the Worlds* and *The First Men on the Moon*.

Two Narrators - Two Stories

- *The Diamond Maker* consists of two distinct stories that are loosely linked. Furthermore both stories are narrated by two very different individuals.

The 'outer' story outlines a night in the life of the narrator and his chance meeting with a stranger. In the 'inner' story, the stranger outlines the main events of his life to the principal narrator. At the time when the story was first published it was all but impossible to make diamonds by artificial means. Anybody who discovered such a method could become extremely wealthy. Instead of just telling the story of the Diamond Maker, the author allows us to hear it from the lips of a somewhat suspicious but curious narrator who actually meets the Diamond Maker and inspects his goods. They, in turn, seem genuine.

This method of narrating the story gives the reader a feeling of being close to the events in it.

Writers' Workshop

WRITING SCIENCE FICTION STORIES

While the genres of Science Fiction and the Ghost Story have much in common, there is a basic difference between these two genres. Many people believe that ghosts exist. The events outlined in stories such as *At The River Gates*, *The Wolves of Cernogratz* and *The Monkey's Paw* are all somewhat eerie and frightening. Yet, some people believe that such events could happen.

However, very few people - if any - would accept that people could be made invisible or could travel backwards or forwards in time - nor is it the task of the science fiction writer to convince the reader that these things are possible. Instead, science fiction explores the question **'what would happen if ...?'**

The Diamond Maker

The reader suspends belief in order to find out *what would happen if* a person could become invisible; *if* a person could travel back in time; *if* a person could make diamonds. Nevertheless a dramatic and imaginative account, based on fictitious 'scientific' principles - *how* the diamonds were made; *how* the secret of becoming invisible was discovered; *how* the time machine was invented - adds an interesting element to a story.

Therefore one approach to writing a science fiction story is the *'what would happen if ...?'* approach. This approach allows you to avoid the very difficult task of creating a vivid and convincing setting on some imaginary and distant planet and describing its inhabitants and their lives. Instead, by adopting the *'what would happen if...'* approach, you can concentrate on your own familiar world. **What would happen** to your world (i.e. home, friends, relatives, school, neighbourhood, town etc.) *if....? ? ?*

Here are some broad suggestions from which short stories could be created using the **what would happen if** approach.

If this goes on . . .
- August comes to an end but temperatures continue to increase. By late September the heat is unbearable. By Hallowe'en most reservoirs have dried up...
- Spring comes but temperatures do not rise. Snow falls in Dublin in May. The Shannon freezes over in July.
- The public's appetite for television quiz shows continues to increase at an alarming rate...

If they landed in your garden . . .
- Aliens arrive and you are their only contact... no-one believes your story?... they give you strange powers?... they take on the form of some familiar objects such as supermarkets trollies? daffodils? ... or people? Are they friendly? Hostile? ... People only begin to believe you when..."

If you invented a machine to . . . ?
- We all like to imagine devices that would change the world and make our lives easier or more interesting. Invent your own device that will... make you invisible *or* allow you to float in air *or* make people like each other *or* make people burst into song *or* produce all the food the world needs *or* make people do some very silly things.
- If you invented a time-machine? In dealing with this type of story you should be clear on whether you will tamper with past or future events or whether you will simply observe them.

The Diamond Maker

✓ Q. 7 — Sample Answer

(a) From the first section we see that the narrator is an educated man. His use of words such as 'detained', 'thereafter' and 'disinclined' give this impression. We also get the impression that he was his own boss - he stopped working because he had a headache.

In the second section he comes across as a serious person; a person who chose to study physics and mineralogy to occupy his leisure time. This would show him also to be an intelligent man. The remaining sections show him to be a very solid and cautious person, who wouldn't risk buying a diamond from a tramp. He was not a gambler or a risk-taker.

(b) My impression of the narrator is that he is a middle-aged man. He could be a lawyer from the way he speaks. He comes across as a man who could be trusted to make a sensible decision. He was not the kind of person who acted on impulse. He didn't buy the diamond on the spot. Yet he doesn't rule out the possibility of buying it at a later stage when he checked things out further. He is probably a shrewd business-man, but a little too careful and cautious to ever make a fortune.

Flight

Above the old man's head was the dovecote, a tall wire-netted shelf on stilts, full of strutting, preening birds. The sunlight broke on their grey breasts into small rainbows. His ears were lulled by their crooning, his hands stretched up towards his favourite, a homing pigeon, a young plump-bodied bird which stood still when it saw him and cocked a shrewd bright eye.

"Pretty, pretty, pretty," he said, as he grasped the bird and drew it down, feeling the cold coral claws tighten around his finger. Content, he rested the bird lightly on his chest, and leaned against a tree, gazing out beyond the dovecote into the landscape of a late afternoon. In folds and hollows of sunlight and shade, the dark red soil, which was broken into great dusty clods, stretched wide to a tall horizon. Trees marked the course of the valley; a stream of rich green grass the road.

His eyes travelled homewards along this road until he saw his grand-daughter swinging on the gate underneath a frangipani tree. Her hair fell down her back in a wave of sunlight, and her long bare legs repeated the angles of the frangipani stems, bare, shining-brown stems among patterns of pale blossoms.

She was gazing past the pink flowers, past the railway cottage where they lived, along the road to the village.

His mood shifted. He deliberately held out his wrist for the bird to take flight, and caught it again at the moment it spread its wings. He felt the plump shape strive and strain under his fingers, and, in a sudden access of troubled spite, shut the bird into a small box and fastened the bolt. "Now you stay there," he muttered; and turned his back on the shelf of birds. He moved warily along the hedge, stalking his grand-daughter, who was now looped over the gate, her head loose on her arms, singing. The light happy sound mingled with the crooning of the birds, and his anger mounted.

"Hey!" he shouted; saw her jump, look back, and abandon the gate. Her eyes veiled themselves, and she said in a pert neutral voice: "Hullo, Grandad." Politely she moved towards him, after a lingering backward glance at the road.

"Waiting for Steven, hey?" he said, his fingers curling like claws into his palm.

"Any objection?" she asked lightly, refusing to look at him.

He confronted her, his eyes narrowed, shoulders hunched, tight in a hard knot of pain which included the preening birds, the sunlight, the flowers. He said: "Think you're old enough to go courting, hey?"

The girl tossed her head at the old-fashioned phrase and sulked,

"Oh Grandad!"

"Think you want to leave home, hey? Think you can go running around the fields at night?"

Her smile made him see her, as he had every evening of this warm end-of-summer month, swinging hand in hand along the road to the village with that red-handed, red-throated, violent-bodied youth, the son of the postmaster. Misery went to his head and he shouted angrily: "I'll tell your mother!"

"Tell away!" she said, laughing, and went back to the gate. He heard her singing, for him to hear:

"I've got you under my skin,
 I've got you deep in the heart..."

"Rubbish," he shouted. "Rubbish. Impudent little bit of rubbish!"

Growling under his breath he turned towards the dovecote, which was his refuge

Flight

from the house he shared with his daughter and her husband and their children. But now the house would be empty. Gone all the young girls with their laughter and their squabbling and their teasing. He would be left, uncherished and alone, with that square-fronted, calm-eyed woman, his daughter.

He stooped, muttering, before the dovecote, resenting the absorbed cooing birds.

From the gate the girl shouted: "Go and tell! Go on, what are you waiting for?"

Obstinately he made his way to the house, with quick, pathetic persistent glances of appeal back at her. But she never looked around. Her defiant but anxious young body stung him into love and repentance. He stopped. "But I never meant . . ." he muttered, waiting for her to turn and run to him. "I didn't mean . . ."

She did not turn. She had forgotten him. Along the road came the young man Steven, with something in his hand. A present for her? The old man stiffened as he watched the gate swing back, and the couple embrace. In the brittle shadows of the frangipani tree his grand-daughter, his darling, lay in the arms of the postmaster's son, and her hair flowed back over his shoulder.

"I see you!" shouted the old man spitefully. They did not move. He stumped into the little whitewashed house, hearing the wooden veranda creak angrily under his feet. His daughter was sewing in the front room, threading a needle held to the light.

He stopped again, looking back into the garden. The couple were now sauntering among the bushes, laughing. As he watched he saw the girl escape from the youth with a sudden mischievous movement and run off through the flowers with him in pursuit. He heard shouts, laughter, a scream, silence.

"But it's not like that at all," he muttered miserably. "It's not like that. Why can't you see? Running and giggling and kissing and kissing. You'll come to something quite different."

He looked at his daughter with sardonic hatred, hating himself. They were caught and finished, both of them, but the girl was still running free.

Flight

"Can't you *see*?" he demanded of his invisible grand-daughter, who was at that moment lying in thick green grass with the postmaster's son.

His daughter looked at him and her eyebrows went up in tired forbearance.

"Put your birds to bed?" she asked, humouring him.

"Lucy," he said urgently. "Lucy . . ."

"Well what is it now?"

"She's in the garden with Steven."

"Now you just sit down and have your tea."

He stumped his feet alternatively, thump, thump on the hollow wooden floor and shouted: "She'll marry him. I'm telling you, she'll be marrying him next!"

His daughter rose swiftly, brought him a cup, set him a plate.

"I don't want any tea. I don't want it, I tell you."

"Now, now," she crooned. "What's wrong with it? Why not?"

"She's eighteen, Eighteen!"

"I was married at seventeen and I never regretted it."

"Liar," he said. "Liar. Then you should regret it. Why do you make your girls marry? It's you who do it. What do you do it for? Why?"

"The other three have done fine. They've three fine husbands. Why not Alice?"

"She's the last," he mourned. "Can't we keep her a bit longer?"

"Come, now, dad. She'll be down the road, that's all. She'll be here everyday to see you."

"But it's not the same." He thought of the other three girls, transformed inside a few months from charming petulant spoiled children into serious young matrons.

"You never did like it when we married!" she said. "Why not? Every time, it's the same. When I got married you made me feel like it was something wrong. And my girls the same. You get them all crying and miserable the way you go on. Leave Alice alone. She's happy." She sighed, letting her eyes linger on the sun-lit garden. "She'll marry next month. There's no reason to wait."

"You've said they can marry?" he said incredulously.

"Yes, dad, why not?" she said coldly,

Flight

and took up her sewing.

His eyes stung, and he went out on to the veranda. Wet spread down over his chin and he took out a handkerchief and mopped his whole face. The garden was empty.

From around a corner came the young couple; but their faces were no longer set against him. On the wrist of the postmaster's son balanced a young pigeon, the light gleaming on its breast.

"For me?" said the old man, letting the drops shake off his chin. "For me?"

"Do you like it?" The girl grabbed his hand and swung on it. "It's for you, Grandad. Steven brought it for you." They hung about him, affectionate, concerned, trying to charm away his wet eyes and his misery. They took his arms and directed him to the shelf of birds, one on each side, enclosing him, petting him, saying wordlessly that nothing would change, and that they would be with him always. The bird was proof of it, they said, from their lying happy eyes, as they thrust it on him. "There, Grandad, it's yours. It's for you."

They watched him as he held it on his wrist, stroking its soft, sun-warmed back, watching the wings lift and balance.

"You must shut it up for a bit," said the girl intimately. "Until it knows this is its home."

"Teach your grandmother to suck eggs," growled the old man.

Released by his half-deliberate anger, they fell back, laughing at him. "We're glad you like it." They moved off, now serious and full of purpose, to the gate, where they hung, backs to him, talking quietly. More than anything could, their grown-up seriousness shut him out, making him alone; also it quietened him, took the sting out of their tumbling like puppies on the grass. They had forgotten him again. Well, so they should, the old man reassured himself, feeling his throat clotted with tears, his lips trembling. He held the new bird to his face, for the caress of its silken feathers. Then he shut it in a box and took out his favourite.

"*Now* you can go," he said aloud. He held it poised, ready for flight, while he looked down the garden towards the boy and the girl. Then, clenched in the pain of loss, he lifted the bird on his wrist, and watched it soar. A whirr and a spatter of wings, and a cloud of birds rose into the evening from the dovecote.

At the gate Alice and Steven forgot their talk and watched the birds.

On the veranda, that woman, his daughter, stood gazing, her eyes shaded with a hand that still held her sewing.

It seemed to the old man that the whole afternoon had stilled to watch his gesture of self-command, that even the leaves of the trees had stopped shaking.

Dry-eyed and calm, he let his hands fall to his sides and stood erect, staring up into the sky.

The cloud of shining silver birds flew up and up, with a shrill cleaving of wings, over the dark ploughed land and the darker belts of trees and the brighter folds of grass, until they floated high in the sunlight, like a cloud of motes of dust.

They wheeled in a wide circle, tilting their wings so there was flash after flash of light, and one after another they dropped from the sunshine of the upper sky to shadow, one after another, returning to the valley and the shelter of night.

The old man turned, slowly, taking his time; he lifted his eyes to smile proudly down the garden at his grand-daughter. She was staring at him. She did not smile. She was wide-eyed, and pale in the cold shadow, and he saw the tears run shivering off her face.

—Doris Lessing

Flight

? Questions and Assignments

1. The old man strongly disapproves of his grand-daughter's association with Steven. How does she react to her grandfather's interference?
2. Write a brief comment or explanatory note on each of the following sections (towards the end of the story) and describe how each of them relates to the theme of the story.
   (i) "His eyes stung ... was empty." (ii) "*Now* you can go ... the girl."
3. (a) What are the old man's views on marriage?
   (b) Why do you think he holds these views?
   (c) Are there other views on marriage expressed in the story? Explain.
4. Do you think that Alice and Steven believe that nothing will change after they are married? Explain your answer.
5. Describe the change of heart that takes place in the old man as the story develops.
6. What impression do you get of Alice from the story as a whole?
7. (a) Study the references to the pigeons. Why did the author include them in the story?
   (b) Could they be regarded as symbols? Explain (see **Points to Note**).
8. In what way is the situation at the end of the story a reversal of the way the story begins?
9. Write a conversation between Alice and her mother which takes place after the events in the story. Their discussion should include their concern for the old man and his feelings.
10. Write (a) the grandfather's diary (b) Alice's diary - for the day described in the story.

S Spelling

Below are anagrams of words that are sometimes misspelt. Rearrange the letters to find the words. All the words are in the story.

- vatrioufe
- biteleardely
- leapap
- chiessimouv
- tefactafione
- thentig
- ugatch
- ousixan
- rabilsemy
- hignugal
- dellvater
- lirway
- pancenteer
- binivlise
- russareed
- natperts
- pimudten
- fitlyspule
- rousise
- atroth
- slobmoss
- pirenttess
- greathind
- mypet
- gluphode

V Vocabulary Development

Find words in the story to match each of the following meanings.

- walking in stiff pompous way
- walked noisily and clumsily
- pursuing somebody quietly
- shelter from trouble
- full of bitter mockery
- trimming and cleaning feathers with beak
- singing/humming in a low subdued voice
- concealed, hidden, covered
- grieved; lamented
- saucy, almost cheeky
- unloved, not held dear
- changed considerably
- open roofed platform along side of house
- blended
- stubbornly
- unbelieving
- exciting pity

Flight

> **Points to Note**

THEME

This story concentrates on a single area of emotional conflict between the generations. It highlights the pain and sorrow involved both for the young person who is leaving home and the old person who feels abandoned and unloved. By the end of the story there is a certain acceptance by both the grandfather and the grand-daughter that the inevitable must happen and that relationships must change.

SYMBOL

The symbol of the pigeons recurs throughout the story, helping us to develop a greater awareness of the theme of the story.

A young girl is about to marry and leave home or, as would be said of birds, about to fly the nest. Her grandfather who keeps pigeons is deeply upset because she is growing up and growing away from him.

The strutting and preening of the birds in the dovecote reminds the old man that his grand-daughter is on the threshold of adulthood. Just as he cannot allow his favourite pigeon her freedom neither can he break the emotional bond with his favourite grand-daughter. He tries to exert the same control over his grand-daughter as he does over his pigeons.

Towards the end of the story the young couple return with a gift of a young pigeon for the old man. The gift seems to be intended as a peace offering or an expression of understanding by the grand-daughter of her grandfather's feelings. As the old man strokes this pigeon, watching its wings lift and balance, his grand-daughter's flight is always on his mind. When he realises that he cannot prevent his grand-daughter's leaving he replaces his favourite bird with the new pigeon and allows his favourite bird to fly away with all the others. This is an outward sign that he has accepted that the old regime must change and be replaced by a new one and that a new type of relationship must replace the old one. The fact that the writer mentions that all the birds return to the shelter at night may indicate that peace and harmony are restored to some degree in the lives of all.

STYLE

This story is rich in well-chosen descriptive words which help the reader create images that bring the story to life.
Examples
- **"The sunlight broke on their grey breasts into small rainbows"** (**metaphor**). In this description we can see the colours created by the sun's rays as they are deflected off the breasts of the pigeons.
- "He felt the plump shape strive and strain." (**alliteration**). Because of the choice of verbs "strive" and "strain" one can almost tangibly feel the force of the bird moving against the old man's hand.
- When the old man is angry, "his fingers are curling like claws into his palms" (**simile** and **alliteration**) because the words "curling" and "claws" are of a very concrete nature we are made keenly aware of the extent of the old man's anger.
- "A whirr and a spatter of wings, and a cloud of birds rose into the evening from the dovecote" (**onomatopoeia**). In this sentence we find the words "whirr" and "spatter" convey the sounds made by the flight of birds, whilst the word "cloud" is a **metaphor** which helps us

Flight

to picture the birds in flight. The fact that the birds rose into the "evening" rather than the "sky" conveys the idea of the flight of birds having taken over everything.
- "He *stumped* into the little whitewashed house, hearing the wooden veranda creak *angrily* under his feet." Here the use of the verb 'stumped" and the adverb "angrily" makes the reader react either sympathetically or unsympathetically to the emotion the old man is feeling.
- Another feature of language use to note in this story is the writer's use of **adjectives**. Sometimes the writer employs two or three adjectives in succession e.g. "The old man gave quick, pathetic, sudden glances." Alice made a "sudden, mischievous movement." Alice's three sisters were transformed from "charming, petulant, spoiled children into serious young matrons." **Compound adjectives** are also used effectively in describing Lucy and Steven. Steven is described as a "red-headed, red-throated, violent-bodied youth". Lucy is described as "square-fronted and calm-eyed".

Outline Short Story Ideas

- **Character A** has decided on a certain course of action concerning a problem. The reader sees that the decision is not a wise one. **A** is then approached by **B** who is looking for advice on a similar problem. Together they discuss **B's** problem and **A** offers **B** good advice. This discussion helps **A** to see his/her problem in a new light and (s)he now makes a wise decision about his/her own affair. The nature of the problem could be a family row, a disagreement with a friend etc.

- This is a slight variation on the above. **Character A** is a person in authority. A young person in his/her care is determined to take a course of action that **A** disapproves of. However, a remark by the young person reminds **A** of a time in his/her own youth when his/her plans were opposed by somebody in authority. **A** also recalls how (s)he did his/her own thing and it worked out well. **A** now changes his/her mind and does not stand in the young person's way.

    (One approach here is to have the young person determined to pursue a career in which success is very hard to achieve - e.g. rock music, sport, etc.)

Flight

✓ Q. 5 — Sample Answer

We first meet the grandfather as a content and happy man. He loves the company of his birds.

When he sees his grand-daughter, Alice, at the gate, waiting for her boyfriend, Steven, he becomes angry. Out of spite he locks up the pigeon that was resting on his hand. He goes over to Alice and questions her about what she is doing. As he does this his fingers are "curling like claws into his palm" with anger. He wants to stop her going out with Steven, the postmaster's son. He says he will tell her mother on her. He is afraid that Alice will leave him and that he will be lonely and have no one to love him. Though he is thinking mainly about himself, he also cares a great deal about Alice. He is sorry he has threatened to tell her mother and he tries to persuade her to come back to him. When Alice ignores him spite gets the better of him again. He becomes stiff with anger when he sees Alice and Steven embrace. He wants to protect Alice. He does not want her to marry while young like her sisters did. He thinks marriage made them old. He believes that it took away their freedom and their sense of fun. He depends very much on Alice for company and love and is determined to hold on to her.

Two things seem to bring about a change of heart in the old man. The first of these is his discovering that Alice has her mother's permission to marry Steven. This is a severe blow to him. He cries bitterly. While he is still crying Alice and Steven come back with a gift of a young pigeon for him. The gift appears to be a kind of peace offering to soften the hurt. This is the second thing which greatly affects the old man's attitude. He now realises that Alice is aware of his feelings. From this point in the story he seems to accept that his grand-daughter must grow up and leave him. When Alice and Steven talk seriously to each other and ignore him, he realises that they are entitled to do this. To show everyone that he has changed he releases his favourite pigeon. He smiles proudly at Alice to let her know that he has accepted her flight like he has accepted the flight of his favourite pigeon.

THE HOOK

The seagull was very hungry. He was soaring above the fishing village with his legs hanging down, his wings perfectly still, his head turned to one side and his sharp little eyes blinking. Above him and a little to the right, a large white flock of seagulls was cackling and diving about furiously. He alone was sailing on his own, very near the ground and perfectly silent. He saw something that he didn't want the other seagulls to see until he should get an opportunity of securing it for himself.

There it was, perched enticingly on a low stone fence, the fat red liver of a fish, about three inches long and as thick as it was long. The seagull ravened for it. He would swoop down immediately and bite at it, but he wanted to bring a share to his mate that was sitting on the eggs, on the ledge of the cliff. So he was waiting for an opportunity to rest for a moment on the fence, eat his own share and take the rest between his beak northwards to the cliff.

But he could not get an opportunity. The fence on which the liver rested bordered the lane that led from the well to the wide flat crag where the village women were washing and cleaning and salting the fish that had been caught the previous night. Young girls continually passed along the lane carrying buckets of water to their mothers. And the seagull was slightly bewildered by all the noise and bustle on the crag, with the women in their red petticoats and little black shawls around their heads squatted on their heels, and their sharp knives making the white scales fly in little flaky showers from the fishes' backs. Their harsh cries, the flashing of the knives in the bright morning sun, the glittering piles of fish slipping about, all made the seagull's head swim with excitement and hunger and desire and fear.

At last he heard a hoarse 'ga-ga-ga' close by him and another seagull swooped past the fence where the liver rested and then, banking a little farther on, doubled back, cackling aggressively as he came. The first seagull knew that the liver was discovered. He must wait no longer. He swooped upwards slightly, flapped his wings twice and then came straight down with a tearing sound. He landed lightly on the fence, took fright suddenly and looked about him, uttered a queer faint shriek and was going to spread his wings to fly again when he heard a swish and the other seagull landed beside him. The first seagull lost all fear, grabbed at the liver and tried to swallow the whole piece. He got it into his mouth in two gobbles, while the other seagull picked at its end and screamed. Then with a wild yell a number of small boys who had been hiding under the fence a few yards to the right, jumped up and began to wave their arms. The second seagull screamed and darted away. The first seagull made a last violent gobble at the liver and got it completely in his mouth and then with a fierce swing of his wings he rose sideways.

But he did not rise far. With a smothered scream he came tumbling backwards. A hook had been hidden in the liver. Its barb was sticking through the seagull's mouth, in the soft part behind the lower bill, and a piece of string protruded from his mouth and was tied to a stone in the fence. The seagull was trapped.

He fell with wings outstretched inside the fence. He lay dumbfounded for two seconds, lying on his side, his little eyes motionless with fear and pain. Then a boy leaned over the fence and tried to grab at him. He fluttered away a yard or so to the full reach of the string and then when the hook jerked him back again, he uttered a

The Hook

fierce cry as if spurred to madness by the renewal of pain. Bending his head he rose with the graceful and powerful movement of an advancing wave. He rose in a twirling curve. There was a slight snap, a downward jerking of his beak, then he uttered a joyful scream like a loud sigh and he flew upwards with a curling piece of string hanging from his beak. He had burst the string and left the small boys staring after him and cursing the weak string that had robbed them of their prey.

Higher and higher he whirled, upwards from the village and northward towards his ledge on the cliff and his mate. As he whirled and banked and plunged forward the string kept dangling and going through funny little convolutions, as if it were a long worm being carried off and trying to wriggle its way out of the seagull's mouth. And the whole flock of seagulls followed the hooked one, making a tremendous noise, screaming at one another and blinking their little eyes in amazement at the hook sticking from the trapped one's bill and the string dangling.

At last the seagull reached his ledge midway down a precipitous cliff. The sea grumbled far away beneath, and as his mate sat on her eggs her bill protruded over the sea, the ledge was so narrow. The trapped seagull landed beside his mate. She wearily stretched out her beak for food and then uttered a wild scream as she saw the hook. And breasting the ledge the whole flock soared about cackling. The trapped one, stupefied by all the cackling, hid one leg under his wing and let his head fall until the tip of his bill touched the ground. A little drop of blood trickled along the bill and fell on the rock.

Then the female bird seized the string in her beak and, without rising from her eggs, she began to tear at it furiously, cackling

The Hook

shrilly the while, like a virago of a woman reviling a neighbour. The wounded bird sank down on his breast and let his head go limp, while the whole flock of birds hovered nearer and became more subdued with their cries. Some landed on neighbouring ledges and craned their necks to watch the female bird's furious pecking.

Soon the string was cut. Then she seized the hook by the barb that protruded from beneath the bill. She pulled. The male bird spluttered a cry and flapped his wings, but the female bird arched her neck and wrenched again. The hook came with her almost. But its circular end with the string tied to it remained in the male's beak. A little stream of blood ran out. Then the male bird, unable to endure the pain any longer, tried to wrench himself clear. He pulled backwards fiercely and left the hook in his mate's bill. There was wild and victorious cackling as the freed bird staggered to his feet, shook his beak, and uttering a weak, plaintive, surprised scream, dipped it into a little pool of water on the edge.

His mate lay back on her eggs, smoothed her feathers with a shrug and closed her eyes in a bored fashion.

—Liam O'Flaherty

The Hook

❓ Questions and Assignments

1. In the first paragraph the behaviour of the seagulls is described. How does the behaviour of the lone seagull differ from the behaviour of the flock?
2. What did the seagull see?
3. (a) What had the first seagull intended to do with the piece of liver?
   (b) Why did he try to swallow the whole piece?
4. Describe what was happening at the flat crag while the first seagull awaited his opportunity to get the liver?
5. How did the small boys react (a) when the seagull got the liver completely in his mouth (b) when he broke the string?
6. Why do you think the writer gives such a graphic description of the hook catching in the seagull's mouth?
7. How did (a) the other seagulls and (b) his mate react to the seagull's plight?
8. Describe the "personality" of the seagull's mate.
9. Where would you consider the climax of the story occurs? Explain your answer.
10. Tell the story from the seagull's point of view.
11. (a) "With a smothered scream"
    (b) "As he whirled and banked and plunged forward the string kept dangling and going through funny little convolutions, as if it were a long worm being carried off and trying to wriggle its way out of the seagull's mouth."
    (c) "The sea grumbled far away beneath"
    (d) "Like a virago of a woman reviling a neighbour".
    Examine the writer's use of each of the above expressions and explain the idea you think each is meant to convey.
12. Write the conversation the female seagull might have had with a friend the day following her mate's mishap.

💲 Spelling

Below are anagrams of words that are sometimes misspelt. Rearrange the letters to find the words. All the words are in the story.

- ilyurfous
- punpoirtoty
- mimedtailey
- veripous
- linlutnocay
- mitenexcet
- dracseme
- thomsered
- lawenre
- riwlting
- sourmendet
- fiedputse
- roubenigh
- edizse
- lerciefy

Ⅴ Vocabulary Development

Find words in the story to match each of the following meanings.

- sought after it, longed to devour
- perplexed, confused, puzzled
- eat hurriedly and noisily
- pulled sharply
- incited, driven
- rugged rock
- came down with a rush
- back-curved point of a hook
- made rumbling sound
- a fierce or abusive woman
- sat
- stuck out
- twists
- steep
- stretched

The Hook

- remained in one place in the air
- criticising abusively
- softer, toned down
- pulled violently
- moved with sudden rapid movement
- sad or mournful-sounding
- descended suddenly
- hanging loosely
- nonplussed, made silent with surprise
- inclining or leaning sideways for turning in flight
- flying high, flying without flapping of wings
- in a manner that would draw him to it
- bear
- triumphant
- drawing up of shoulders momentarily, sign of not caring, gesture of indifference

☞ **Points to Note**

THEME
The message we get from this story is that things are not always as they seem. What appears to be attractive and enjoyable on the outside may often conceal something that can harm us.

SETTING
This story is set by the sea - close to a fishing village that is bordered by steep cliffs. The entire story takes place within a short space of time.

SYMBOL
In this story the hook is a symbol. It stands for the hidden danger that is contained in so many of life's attractions. Because the danger is so well hidden, we tend, like the seagull, to forget that it is there and as a result, walk straight into it.

✓ **Q. 11 — Sample Answer**

(a) The use of the word 'smothered' here conveys the sharp and piercing nature of the pain felt by the bird when the hook stuck in his mouth. His whole body was so overcome by the pain he was unable to give a loud scream. ("Smothered scream" is an example of **alliteration**.)

(b) This comparison is very good because the writer compares two things that are very alike. The image of the seagull with the twisting string dangling from his mouth is very similar to the image of a wriggling worm being carried in a seagull's mouth. The movements of the string reflect the desperate and painful attempts of the seagull to fly home to his mate. (This comparison is an example of **simile**).

(c) 'Grumbled' describes the distant rumbling sound of the sea. However, 'grumble' also means to complain. Its use here gives us an impression of the sea as a person complaining about the treatment the boys gave to one of its creatures. This is an example of the use of **personification.**

(d) The sounds made by the female seagull are certainly captured by the author comparing her with a virago of a woman reviling her neighbour. A fierce or abusive woman would speak with great passion when criticising her neighbour. The female seagull also expressed great passion in her shrill cackling. She was likely to be very annoyed with her mate for his foolishness and with the boys for their deliberate cruelty in setting the trap for him. (This is another example of the use of **simile**).

The Wolves of Cernogratz

"Are there any old legends attached to the castle?" asked Conrad of his sister. Conrad was a prosperous Hamburg merchant, but he was the one poetically-dispositioned member of an eminently practical family.

The Baroness Gruebel shrugged her plump shoulders.

"There are always legends hanging about these old places. They are not difficult to invent and they cost nothing. In this case there is a story that when any one dies in the castle all the dogs in the village and the wild beasts in the forest howl the night long. It would not be pleasant to listen to, would it?"

"It would be weird and romantic," said the Hamburg merchant.

"Anyhow, it isn't true," said the Baroness complacently; "since we bought the place we have had proof that nothing of the sort happens. When the old mother-in-law died last springtime we all listened, but there was no howling. It is just a story that lends dignity to the place without costing anything."

"The story is not as you have told it," said Amalie, the grey old governess. Every one turned and looked at her in astonishment. She was wont to sit silent and prim and faded in her place at table, never speaking unless some one spoke to her, and there were few who troubled themselves to make conversation with her. Today, a sudden volubility had descended on her; she continued to talk, rapidly and nervously, looking straight in front of her and seeming to address no one in particular.

"It is not when *any one* dies in the castle that the howling is heard. It was when one of the Cernogratz family died here that the wolves came from far and near and howled at the edge of the forest just before the death hour. There were only a few couple of wolves that had their lairs in this part of the forest, but at such a time, the keepers say, there would be scores of them, gliding about in the shadows and howling in chorus, and the dogs of the castle and the village and all the farms round would bay and howl in fear and anger at the wolf chorus, and as the soul of the dying one left its body a tree would crash down in the park. That is what happened when a Cernogratz died in his family castle. But for a stranger dying here, of course no wolf would howl and no tree would fall. Oh, no."

There was a note of defiance, almost of contempt, in her voice as she said the last words. The well-fed, much-too-well dressed Baroness stared angrily at the dowdy old woman who had come forth from her usual and seemly position of effacement to speak so disrespectfully.

"You seem to know quite a lot about the von Cernogratz legends, Fräulein Schmidt," she said sharply; "I did not know that family histories were among the subjects you are supposed to be proficient in."

The answer to her taunt was even more unexpected and astonishing than the conversational outbreak which had provoked it.

"I am a von Cernogratz myself," said the old woman, "that is why I know the family history."

"You a von Cernogratz? You!" came in an incredulous chorus.

"When we became very poor," she explained, "and I had to go out and give teaching lessons, I took another name; I thought it would be more in keeping. But my grandfather spent much of his time as a

130

The Wolves of Cernogratz

boy in this castle, and my father used to tell me many stories about it, and, of course, I knew all the family legends and stories. When one has nothing left to one but memories, one guards and dusts them with especial care. I little thought when I took service with you that I should one day come with you to the old home of my family. I could wish it had been anywhere else."

There was a silence when she finished speaking, and then the Baroness turned the conversation to a less embarrassing topic than family histories. But afterwards, when the old governess had slipped away quietly to her duties, there arose a clamour of derision and disbelief.

"It was impertinence," snapped out the Baron, his protruding eyes taking on a scandalised expression; "fancy the woman talking like that at our table. She almost told us we were nobodies, and I don't believe a word of it. She is just Schmidt and nothing more. She has been talking to some of the peasants about the old Cernogratz family, and raked up their history and their stories."

"She wants to make herself out of some consequence," said the Baroness; "she knows she will soon be past work and she wants to appeal to our sympathies. Her grandfather, indeed!"

The Baroness had the usual number of grandfathers, but she never, never boasted about them.

"I dare say her grandfather was a pantry boy or something of the sort in the castle," sniggered the Baron; "that part of the story may be true."

The merchant from Hamburg said nothing; he had seen tears in the old woman's eyes when she spoke of guarding her memories — or, being of an imaginative disposition, he thought he had.

"I shall give her notice to go as soon as the New Year festivities are over," said the Baroness; "till then I shall be too busy to manage without her."

The Wolves of Cernogratz

But she had to manage without her all the same, for in the cold biting weather after Christmas, the old governess fell ill and kept to her room.

"It is most provoking," said the Baroness, as her guests sat round the fire on one of the last evenings of the dying year; "all the time that she has been with us I cannot remember that she was ever seriously ill, too ill to go about and do her work, I mean. And now, when I have the house full, and she could be useful in so many ways, she goes and breaks down. One is sorry for her, of course, she looks so withered and shrunken, but it is intensely annoying all the same."

"Most annoying," agreed the banker's wife, sympathetically; "it is the intense cold, I expect, it breaks the old people up. It has been unusually cold this year."

"The frost is the sharpest that has been known in December for many years," said the Baron.

"And, of course, she is quite old," said the Baroness; "I wish I had given her notice some weeks ago, then she would have left before this happened to her. Why, Wappi, what is the matter with you?"

The small, woolly lapdog had leapt suddenly down from its cushion and crept shivering under the sofa. At the same moment an outburst of angry barking came from the dogs in the castle-yard, and other dogs could be heard yapping and barking in the distance.

"What is disturbing the animals?" asked the Baron.

And then the humans, listening intently, heard the sound that had roused the dogs to their demonstrations of fear and rage; heard a long-drawn whining howl, rising and falling, seeming at one moment leagues away, at others sweeping across the snow until it appeared to come from the foot of the castle walls, All the starved, cold misery of a frozen world, all the relentless hunger-fury of the wild, blended with other forlorn and haunting melodies to which one could give no name, seemed concentrated in that wailing cry.

"Wolves!" cried the Baron.

Their music broke forth in one raging burst, seeming to come from everywhere.

"Hundreds of wolves," said the Hamburg merchant, who was a man of strong imagination.

Moved by some impulse which she could not have explained, the Baroness left her guests and made her way to the narrow cheerless room where the old governess lay watching the hours of the dying year slip by. In spite of the biting cold of the winter night, the window stood open. With a scandalised exclamation on her lips, the Baroness rushed forward to close it.

"Leave it open," said the old woman in a voice that for all its weakness carried an air of command such as the Baroness had never heard before from her lips.

"But you will die of cold!" she expostulated.

"I am dying in any case," said the voice, "and I want to hear their music. They have come from far and wide to sing the death-music of my family. It is beautiful that they have come; I am the last von Cernogratz that will die in our old castle, and they have come to sing to me. Hark, how loud they are calling!"

The cry of the wolves rose on the still winter air and floated round the castle walls in long-drawn piercing wails; the old woman lay back on her couch with a look of long-delayed happiness on her face.

"Go away," she said to the Baroness; "I am not lonely any more. I am one of a great old family . . . ."

"I think she is dying," said the Baroness when she had rejoined her guests; "I suppose we must send for a doctor. And

The Wolves of Cernogratz

that terrible howling! Not for much money would I have such death-music."

"That music is not to be bought for any amount of money," said Conrad.

"Hark! What is that other sound?" asked the Baron, as a noise of splitting and crashing was heard.

It was a tree falling in the park.

There was a moment of constrained silence, and then the banker's wife spoke.

"It is the intense cold that is splitting the trees. It is also the cold that brought the wolves out in such numbers. It is many years since we have had such a cold winter."

The Baroness eagerly agreed that the cold was responsible for these things. It was the cold of the open window, too, which caused the heart failure that made the doctor's ministrations unnecessary for the old Fräulein. But the notice in the newspapers looked very well —

"On December 29th, at Schloss Cernogratz, Amalie von Cernogratz, for many years the valued friend of Baron and Baroness Gruebel."

— *Saki*

? Questions and Assignments

1. Outline (a) the differences in Baroness Gruebel's and Amalie's version of the legend and (b) the differences in their attitudes towards the legend.
2. Comment briefly on the phrase "The well-fed, much-too-well dressed Baroness".
3. What characteristics of the Baron and Baroness are revealed in the story? Refer to the story to support your points.
4. When the old governess had finished speaking "the Baroness turned the conversation to a less embarrassing topic than family histories..." Can you suggest why the author used the adjective 'embarrassing' here.
5. Outline your impression of when and where the story is set.
6. Identify one feature of the writer's style that you found interesting in his description of the howls of the wolves.
7. (a) How did the Baroness respond when the wolves were heard?
   (b) Did some wolves actually arrive outside the castle? Refer to the story to support your answer.
8. The old governess ordered the Baroness to leave the window open in "a voice that for all its weakness carried an air of command such as the Baroness had never heard before from her lips". What, in your opinion, is the significance of this phrase?
9. "That music is not to be bought for any money," said Conrad. Explain the irony in Conrad's words.
10. Did the banker's wife understand the significance of the tree falling? Explain your answer.
11. From what viewpoint is the story told?
12. Why does the writer say that the notice in the newspapers "looked very well"?
13. Write a letter that you imagine the Baroness would have written to her sister outlining the events of the evening.

The Wolves of Cernogratz

S Spelling

Below are anagrams of words that are sometimes misspelt. Rearrange the letters to find the words. All the words are in the story.

- cadathet
- glowhin
- shinetasmont
- taghirst
- urgads
- santpeas
- nanygoin
- osured
- mocdamn
- ribsopnesel

V Vocabulary Development

Find words in the story to match each of the following meanings.

- rich, wealthy
- in a self-satisfied manner
- lacking smartness, shabbily dressed
- insulting or provoking jibe
- importance
- measures of travelling distance usually about 3 miles
- moving by smooth continuous movement
- high rank or position, an air of grandeur
- particularly, notably
- stiffly formal, distant
- state of not being noticed
- bulging, sticking out
- protested, remonstrated
- talkativeness
- expert
- unbelieving
- insolence
- celebrations
- forced

Outline Short Story Ideas

- **Character A**, without knowing the real plans or purpose of a villain, follows a course of action that brings about the defeat of the villain. (The 'villain' is a term used to describe a character who is up to something which the reader would disapprove of.)
- This is a slight variation on the above. This time **A** is the villain who follows a course of action that results in some happiness or success for **B**, a likeable person.

✓ Q. 6 — Sample Answer

In his description, the writer compares the howls of the wolves to sad music. This comparison makes the wolves appear unreal and magical rather than savage and dangerous. The first sentence describes how the 'music' seems to fill the whole countryside. At times the sound seems 'leagues away'; Then it sweeps across the snow until it sounds to be just outside the castle walls. The second sentence conveys how sad and lonely the howls of the wolves were. 'The starved, cold misery of the frozen world', 'the hunger-fury of the wild' are two phrases used to describe the mood of the music of the wolves. The writer refers also the the 'forlorn and haunting melodies' that seemed to be part of the cry of the wolves. This phrase 'forlorn and haunting melodies' is a very simple and yet a very poetic phrase. The feature of the writer's style that I found interesting was the comparison between music and the wailing cries of the wolves.

The Moustache

At the last minute Annie couldn't go. She was invaded by one of those twenty-four-hour flu bugs that sent her to bed with a fever, moaning about the fact that she'd also have to break her date with Handsome Harry Arnold that night. We call him Handsome Harry because he's actually handsome, but he's also a nice guy, cool, and he doesn't treat me like Annie's kid brother, which I am, but like a regular person. Anyway, I had to go to Lawnrest alone that afternoon. But first of all I had to stand inspection. My mother lined me up against the wall. She stood there like a one-man firing squad, which is kind of funny because she's not like a man at all, she's very feminine, and we have this great relationship — I mean, I feel as if she really likes me. I realise that sounds strange, but I know guys whose mothers love them and cook special stuff for them and worry about them and all but there's something missing in their relationship.

Anyway. She frowned and started the routine.

"That hair," she said. Then admitted: "Well, at least you combed it."

I sighed. I have discovered that it's better to sigh than argue.

"And that moustache." She shook her head. "I still say a seventeen-year-old has no business wearing a moustache."

"It's an experiment," I said. "I just wanted to see if I could grow one." To tell the truth, I had proved my point about being able to grow a decent moustache, but I also had learned to like it.

"It's costing you money, Mike," she said.

"I know, I know."

The money was a reference to the movies. The Downtown Cinema has a special Friday night offer — half-price admission for high school couples, seventeen or younger. But the woman in the box office took one look at my moustache and charged me full price. Even when I showed her my driver's licence. She charged full admission for Cindy's ticket, too, which left me practically broke and unable to take Cindy out for a hamburger with the crowd afterwards. That didn't help matters, because Cindy has been getting impatient recently about things like the fact that I don't own my own car and have to concentrate on my studies if I want to win that college scholarship, for instance. Cindy wasn't exactly crazy about the moustache, either.

Now it was my mother's turn to sigh.

"Look," I said, to cheer her up. "I'm thinking about shaving it off." Even though I wasn't. Another discovery: You can build a way of life on postponement.

"Your grandmother probably won't even recognise you," she said. And I saw the shadow fall across her face.

Let me tell you what the visit to Lawnrest was all about. My grandmother is seventy-three years old. She is a resident — which is supposed to be a better word than *patient* — at the Lawnrest Nursing Home. She used to make the greatest turkey dressing in the world and was a nut about baseball and could even quote batting averages, for crying out loud. She always rooted for the losers. She was in love with the Mets until they started to win. Now she has arteriosclerosis, which the dictionary says is 'a chronic disease characterised by abnormal thickening and hardening of the arterial walls.' Which really means that she can't live at home any more or even with us, and her memory has betrayed her as well as her body. She used to wander off and sometimes didn't recognise people. My mother visits her all the time, driving the thirty miles to Lawnrest almost every day. Because Annie was home for a semester break from college, we have decided to make a special Saturday visit. Now Annie was in bed, groaning theatrically — she's a drama major — but I told my mother I'd go, anyway. I hadn't seen my grandmother since she'd been admitted to Lawnrest. Besides, the place is located on the Southwest Turnpike, which meant I could barrel along in my father's new LeMans. My ambition was to see the speedometer hit seventy-five. Ordinarily, I used the old station wagon, which can barely stagger up to fifty.

Frankly, I wasn't too crazy about visiting a nursing home. They reminded me of hospitals and hospitals turn me off. I mean, the smell of ether makes me nauseous, and I feel faint at the sight of blood. And as I approached Lawnrest — which is a terrible cemetery kind of name, to begin with — I was sorry I hadn't avoided the trip. Then I felt guilty about it. I'm loaded with guilt complexes. Like driving like a madman after promising my father to be careful. Like sitting in the parking lot, looking at the nursing home with dread and thinking how I'd rather be with Cindy. Then I thought of all the Christmas and birthday gifts my grandmother had given me and I got out of the car, guilty, as usual.

Inside, I was surprised by the lack of hospital smell, although there was another odour of maybe the absence of an odour. The air was antiseptic, sterile. As if there was no atmosphere at all or I'd caught a cold suddenly and couldn't taste or smell.

A nurse at the reception desk gave me directions — my grandmother was in East Three. I made my way down the tiled corridor and was glad to see that the walls were painted with cheerful colours like yellow and pink. A wheelchair suddenly shot around the corner, self-propelled by an old man, white-haired and toothless, who cackled merrily as he barely missed me. I jumped aside — here I was, almost getting wiped out by a two-mile-an-hour wheelchair after doing seventy-five on the pike. As I walked through the corridor seeking East Three, I couldn't help glancing into the rooms, and it was like some kind of wax museum — all these figures in various stances and attitudes, sitting in beds or chairs, standing at windows, as if they were frozen forever in these postures. To tell the truth, I began to hurry because I was getting depressed. Finally, I saw a beautiful girl approaching, dressed in white, a nurse or an attendant, and I was so happy to see someone young, someone walking and acting normally, that I gave her a wide smile and a big hello and I must have looked like a kind of nut. Anyway, she looked right through me as if I were a window, which is about par for the course whenever I meet beautiful girls.

I finally found the room and saw my grandmother in bed. My grandmother looks like Ethel Barrymore. I never knew who Ethel Barrymore was until I saw a terrific movie, *None But the Lonely Heart,* on TV, starring Ethel Barrymore and Cary Grant. Both my grandmother and Ethel Barrymore have these great craggy faces like the side of a mountain and wonderful voices like syrup being poured. Slowly. She was propped up in bed, pillows puffed behind her. Her hair had been combed out and fell upon her shoulders. For some reason, this flowing hair gave her an almost girlish appearance, despite its whiteness.

She saw me and smiled. Her eyes lit up and her eyebrows arched and she reached out her hands to me in greeting. "Mike, Mike," she said. And I breathed a sigh of relief. This was one of her good days. My mother had warned me that she might not know who I was at first.

The Moustache

I took her hands in mine. They were fragile. I could actually feel her bones, and it seemed as if they would break if I pressed too hard. Her skin was smooth, almost slippery, as if the years had worn away all the roughness the way the wind wears away the surfaces of stones.

"Mike, Mike, I didn't think you'd come," she said, so happy, and she was still Ethel Barrymore, that voice like a caress. "I've been waiting all this time." Before I could reply, she looked away, out the window. "See the birds? I've been watching them at the feeder. I love to see them come. Even the blue jays. The blue jays are like hawks — they take the food that the small birds should have. But the small birds, the chickadees, watch the blue jays and at least learn where the feeder is."

She lapsed into silence, and I looked out the window. There was no feeder. No birds. There was only the parking lot and the sun glinting on car windshields.

She turned to me again, eyes bright. Radiant, really. Or was it a medicine brightness? "Ah, Mike. You look so grand, so grand. Is that a new coat?"

"Not really," I said. I'd been wearing my Uncle Jerry's old army-fatigue jacket for months, practically living in it, my mother said. But she insisted that I wear my raincoat for the visit. It was about a year old but looked new because I didn't wear it much. Nobody was wearing raincoats lately.

"You always loved clothes, didn't you, Mike?" she said.

I was beginning to feel uneasy because she regarded me with such intensity. Those bright eyes. I wondered — are old people in places like this so lonesome, so abandoned that they go wild when someone visits? Or was she so happy because she was suddenly lucid and everything was sharp and clear? My mother had described those moments when my grandmother suddenly emerged from the fog that so often obscured her mind. I didn't know the answer, but it felt kind of spooky, getting such an emotional welcome from her.

"I remember the time you bought the new coat — the Chesterfield," she said, looking away again, as if watching the birds that weren't there. "That lovely coat with the velvet collar. Black, it was. Stylish. Remember that, Mike? It was hard times, but you could never resist the glitter."

I was about to protest — I had never heard of a Chesterfield, for crying out loud. But I stopped. Be patient with her, my mother had said. Humour her. Be gentle.

We were interrupted by an attendant who pushed a wheeled cart into the room. "Time for juices, dear," the woman said. She was the standard forty- or fifty-year-old woman: glasses, nothing hair, plump cheeks. Her manner was cheerful but a businesslike kind of cheerfulness. I'd hate to be called 'dear' by someone getting paid to do it. "Orange or grape or cranberry, dear? Cranberry is good for the bones, you know."

My grandmother ignored the interruption. She didn't even bother to answer, having turned away at the woman's arrival, as if angry about her appearance.

The woman looked at me and winked. A conspiratorial kind of wink. It was kind of horrible. I didn't think people winked like that anymore. In fact, I hadn't seen a wink in years.

"She doesn't care much for juices," the woman said, talking to me as if my grandmother weren't even there. "But she loves her coffee. With lots of cream and two lumps of sugar. But this is juice time, not coffee time." Addressing my grandmother again, she said, "Orange or grape or cranberry, dear?"

"Tell her I want no juices, Mike," my grandmother commanded regally, her eyes still watching invisible birds.

The woman smiled, patience like a label on her face. "That's all right, dear. I'll just leave some cranberry for you. Drink it at your leisure. It's good for the bones."

She wheeled herself out of the room. My grandmother was still absorbed in the view. Somewhere a toilet flushed. A wheelchair passed the doorway — probably that same old driver fleeing a hit-and-run accident. A television set exploded with sound somewhere, soap-opera voices filling the air. You can always tell soap-opera voices.

I turned back to find my grandmother staring at me. Her hands cupped her face, her index fingers curled around her cheeks like parenthesis marks.

"But you know, Mike, looking back, I think you were right," she said, continuing our conversation as if there had been no interruption. "You always said, 'It's the things of the spirit that count, Meg.' The spirit! And so you bought the baby-grand piano - a baby grand in the middle of the Depression. A knock came on the door and it was the delivery man. It took five of them to get it into the house." She leaned back, closing her eyes. "How I loved that piano, Mike. I was never that fine a player, but you loved to sit there in the parlour, on Sunday evenings. Ellie on your lap, listening to me play and sing." She hummed a bit, a fragment of melody I didn't recognise. Then she drifted into silence. Maybe she'd fallen asleep. My mother's name is Ellen, but everyone always calls her Ellie. "Take my hand, Mike," my grandmother said suddenly. Then I remembered — my grandfather's name was Michael. I had been named after him.

"Ah, Mike," she said, pressing my hands with all her feeble strength. "I thought I'd lost you forever. And here you are, back with me again . . . ."

Her expression scared me. I don't mean scared as if I were in danger but scared because of what could happen to her when she realised the mistake she had made. My mother always said I favoured her side of the family. Thinking back to the pictures in the old family albums, I recalled my grandfather as tall and thin. Like me. But the resemblance ended there. He was thirty-five when he died, almost forty years ago. And he wore a moustache. I brought my hand to my face. I also wore a moustache now, of course.

"I sit here these days, Mike," she said, her voice a lullaby, her hand still holding mine, "and I drift and dream. The days are fuzzy sometimes, merging together. Sometimes it's like I'm not here at all but somewhere else altogether. And I always think of you. Those years we had. Not enough years, Mike, not enough . . . ."

Her voice was so sad, so mournful that I made sounds of sympathy, not words exactly but the kind of soothings that mothers murmur to their children when they awaken from bad dreams.

"And I think of that terrible night, Mike, that terrible night. Have you ever forgiven me for that night?"

"Listen . . . ." I began. I wanted to say: "Nana, this is Mike your grandson, not Mike your husband."

"Sh . . . . sh . . . ." she whispered, placing a finger as long and cold as a candle against my lips. "Don't say anything. I've waited so long for this moment. To be here. With you. I wondered what I would say if suddenly you walked in that door like other people have done. I've thought and thought about it. And I finally made up my mind — I'd ask you to forgive me. I was too proud to ask before." Her fingers tried to mask

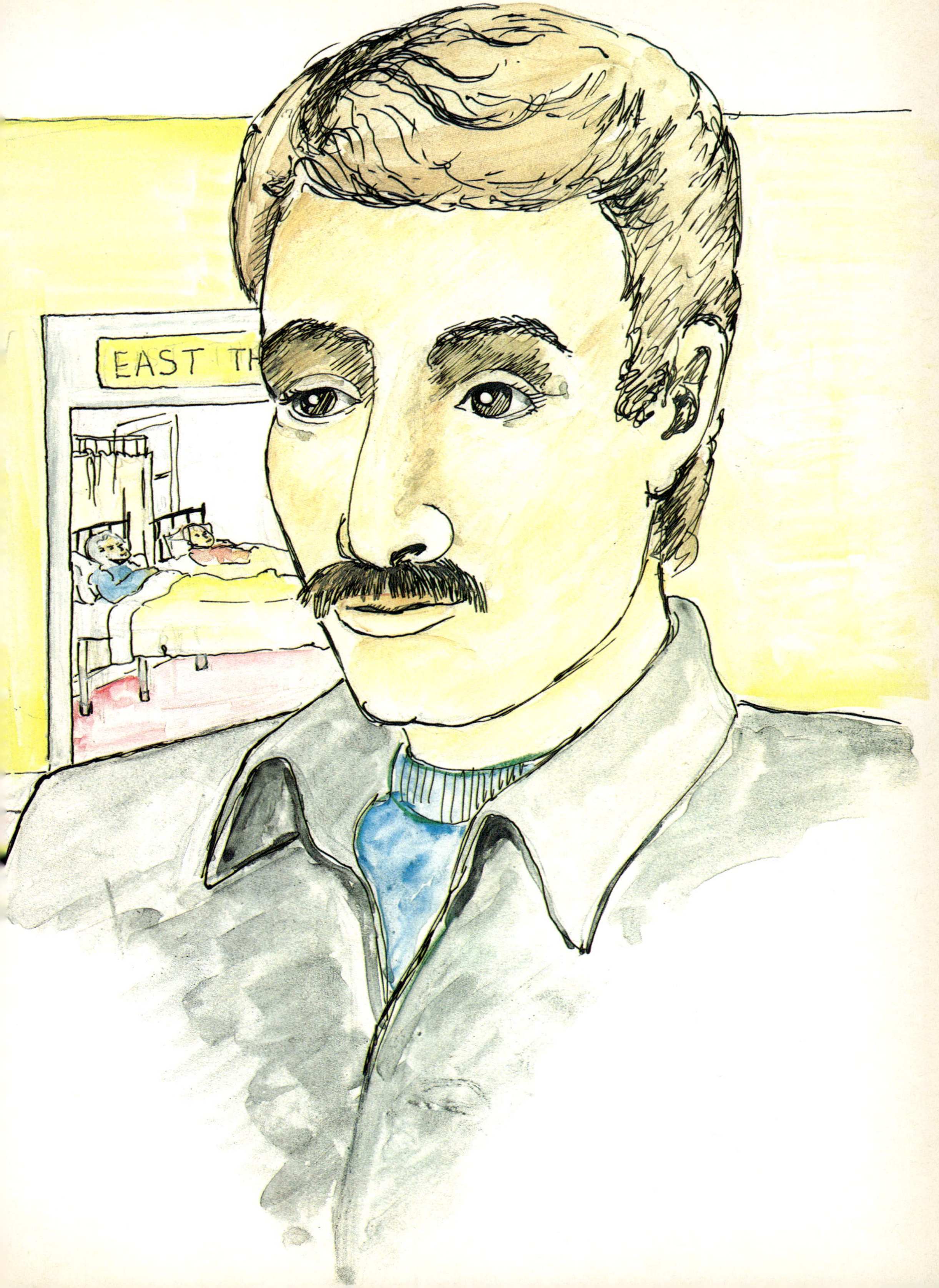
EAST TH

her face. "But I'm not proud any more, Mike." That great voice quivered and then grew strong again. "I hate you to see me this way — you always said I was beautiful. I didn't believe it. The Charity Ball when we led the grand march and you said I was the most beautiful girl there . . . "

"Nana," I said. I couldn't keep up the pretence any longer, adding one more burden to my load of guilt, leading her on this way, playing a pathetic game of make-believe with an old woman clinging to memories. She didn't seem to hear me.

"But that other night, Mike. The terrible one. The terrible accusations I made. Even Ellie woke up and began to cry. I went to her and rocked her in my arms and you came into the room and said I was wrong. You were whispering, an awful whisper, not wanting to upset little Ellie but wanting to make me see the truth. And I didn't answer you, Mike, I was too proud. I've even forgotten the name of the girl. I sit here, wondering now — was it Laura or Evelyn? I can't remember. Later, I learned that you were telling the truth all the time, Mike. That I'd been wrong . . . ." Her eyes were brighter than ever as she looked at me now, but tear-bright, the tears gathering. "It was never the same after that night, was it, Mike? The glitter was gone. From you. From us. And then the accident . . . and I never had the chance to ask you to forgive me . . . ."

My grandmother. My poor, poor grandmother. Old people aren't supposed to have those kinds of memories. You see their pictures in the family albums and that's what they are: pictures. They're not supposed to come to life. You drive out in you father's LeMans doing seventy-five on the pike and all you're doing is visiting an old lady in a nursing home. A duty call. And then you find out that she's a person. She's *somebody*. She's my grandmother, all right, but she's also herself. Like my own mother and father. They exist outside of their relationship to me. I was scared again. I wanted to get out of there.

"Mike, Mike," my grandmother said. "Say it, Mike."

I felt as if my cheeks would crack if I uttered a word.

"Say you forgive me, Mike. I've waited all these year . . . ."

I was surprised at how strong her fingers were.

"Say *'I forgive you, Meg'*."

I said it. My voice sounded funny, as if I were talking in a huge tunnel. "I forgive you, Meg."

Her eyes studied me. Her hands pressed mine. For the first time in my life, I saw love at work. Not movie love. Not Cindy's sparkling eyes when I tell her that we're going to the beach on a Sunday afternoon. But love like something alive and tender, asking nothing in return. She raised her face, and I knew what she wanted me to do. I bent and brushed my lips against her cheek. Her flesh was like a leaf in autumn, crisp and dry.

She closed her eyes and I stood up. The sun wasn't glinting on the cars any longer. Somebody had turned on another television set, and the voices were the show-off voices of the panel shows. At the time you could still hear the soap-opera dialogue on the other television set.

I waited awhile. She seemed to be sleeping, her breathing serene and regular. I buttoned my raincoat. Suddenly she opened her eyes and looked at me. Her eyes were still bright, but they merely stared at me. Without recognition or curiosity. Empty eyes. I smiled at her, but she didn't smile back. She made a kind of moaning sound and turned away on the bed, pulling the blankets around her.

I counted to twenty-five and then to fifty

The Moustache

and did it all over again. I cleared my throat and coughed tentatively. She didn't move; she didn't respond. I wanted to say, "Nana, it's me." But I didn't. I thought of saying, "Meg, it's me." But I couldn't.

Finally I left. Just like that. I didn't say goodbye or anything. I stalked through the corridors, looking neither to the right nor the left, not caring whether the wild old man with the wheelchair ran me down or not.

On the Southwest Turnpike I did seventy-five — no, eighty — most of the way. I turned the radio up as loud as it could go. Rock music — anything to fill the air. When I got home, my mother was vacuuming the living-room rug. She shut off the cleaner, and the silence was deafening. "Well, how was your grandmother?" she asked.

I told her she was fine. I told her a lot of things. How great Nana looked and how she seemed happy and had called me Mike. I wanted to ask her — hey, Mom, you and Dad really love each other, don't you? I mean — there's nothing to forgive between you, is there? But I didn't.

Instead I went upstairs and took out the electric razor Annie had given me for Christmas and shaved off my moustache.

— *Robert Cormier*

? Questions and Assignments

1. Why had Mike to go to Lawnrest alone?
2. In what way did having a moustache prove disadvantageous to Mike in his social life?
3. Describe the relationship Mike had with his mother.
4. How does Mike feel about visiting his grandmother?
5. The writer selects a number of details to give the reader an impression of life in the nursing home. Choose the two you find most striking and explain your choice.
6. Very often the short story provides us with new insights into a situation. Does this story provide you with any new insight?
7. Mike's grandmother mistakes him for her late husband. What impression do you get of her late husband from her conversation with Mike?
8. State briefly what you consider to be the theme of this story.
9. Comment briefly on the point of view from which the story is told.
10. This story is narrated in the first person. Continue Mike's story, beginning with what he is thinking as he shaves off his moustache.

S Spelling

Below are anagrams of words that are sometimes misspelt. Rearrange the letters to find the words. All the words are in the story.

- domeshan
- soupcle
- harpishlosc
- rodricor
- erusile
- dettidam
- silcene
- ensauous
- pachingroap
- blesranceme
- bomced
- sinodsaim
- meretcey
- pinturderte
- caussaconit
- hatcousme
- nitpimate
- rooud
- damndocme
- aigloude
- cednet
- cratentcone
- phemosreat
- viblinsie
- enotlisive

The Moustache

V Vocabulary Development

Find words in the story to match each of the following meanings.
- womanly, like a woman
- free from living germs
- one living in a place
- done by way of trial
- normal, usual
- feelings
- positions, poses
- delicate
- clear of mind
- like a queen
- fading into each other
- exciting pity or sadness
- trembled, vibrated or moved with slight rapid motion
- regular procedure
- putting things off until later
- supported
- half year term
- sick
- words marked off with brackets or commas
- darkened, made indistinct, made unclear
- free from infection
- allusion, mention
- has let her down
- dramatically, in a manner that got her attention
- vehemence, with deep feeling

☞ Points to Note

SETTING

The story opens in Mike's home. After a brief period the action moves to the nursing home where most of the story is based. The ending involves a brief return to Mike's home. The entire story takes place within one day.

The writer concentrates on conveying a picture of life in the nursing home. The backdrop of the nursing home. contrasts sharply with the grandmother's lapse into her lively past. The details of the nursing home - the sterile atmosphere, old men on wheelchairs, white-haired and toothless, people in rooms resembling figures in a wax museum, the robot-like attendant with her business-like cheerfulness - combine to give an impression of a place where life is fading and where things are dull, depressing and routine.

LANGUAGE

As Robert Cormier is an American writer we can expect to find American terms in the story like "rooting", "semester", "barrel along".

The story has some very vivid descriptions. The comparison of the nursing home and its residents to a wax museum makes a very strong impact on the reader. The description of the grandmother's hands is especially effective: "They were fragile. I could actually feel her bones, and it seemed as if they would break if I pressed too hard. Her skin was smooth, almost slippery, as if the years had worn away all the roughness the way the wind wears away the surfaces of stones."

The writer also uses figurative language in a very effective manner to describe the grandmother and the old man in the wheelchair e.g. "Her flesh was like a leaf in Autumn crisp and dry" **(Simile)**. "Her voice like a caress" **(Simile)**. "Her voice a lullaby" **(Metaphor)**. Mike's grandmother tells him how she sits there some days and "drifts and dreams" **(Alliteration)**. The old man in the wheelchair "cackles" **(Onomatopoeia)**.

The Moustache

> 📖 **Outline Short Story Ideas**

- **Character A** has lost all confidence and self-esteem. (S)he feels that (s)he is not able to do the tasks that (s)he was once good at. A crisis faces his/her community that only the skill of **A** can solve successfully. S(he) faces the situation without a thought and takes care of it perfectly. This restores **A's** confidence and purpose in life.

- **Character A** follows a course of action that requires great courage or self-sacrifice, regarding it as a normal response or his/her simple duty. The reader is aware and impressed with the extraordinary courage/generosity of **A's** action.

- **Character A** forces himself/herself to do something although he/she is afraid, in order to hold the respect and admiration of another character. The surprise is that his/her fear evaporates as soon as (s)he starts on the task which (s)he feared.

- **Character A** again finds the courage (s)he once had, by performing a difficult or a dangerous act - an act that was in some way similar to that which first resulted in the loss of courage.

✓ Q. 6 — Sample Answer

The story "The Moustache" makes one look at old people with new eyes. It makes one realise that every grandparent was once young. For most of us it is difficult to picture our grandparents other than the way we have always known them.

Mike's conversation with his grandmother in the nursing home makes him aware that his grandmother was once young and attractive. Until then he had thought of her only as his grandmother, someone who was old, feeble and not too clear of mind. Now he sees her and her husband as young lively people who were interested in clothes, music and romance. They were people who showed love and affection for each other. The grandmother has regrets about some things in her past. His grandfather was a romantic person who bought a baby grand-piano for his wife in the middle of the Depression.

Having read this story, we can now picture our grandparents and other elderly people as once being young, lively, and fun-loving.

This story is narrated from Mike's point of view in the first person. Because the writer has Mike tell the story we see the entire world of the story through Mike's eyes.

II - DRAMA

THE SHADOW OF A GUNMAN
— Seán O'Casey

ERNIE'S INCREDIBLE ILLUCINATIONS
— Alan Ayckbourn

A VILLA ON VENUS
— Kenneth Lillington

THE SHADOW OF A GUNMAN
— Seán O'Casey

INTRODUCTION

- The first performance of *The Shadow of a Gunman* took place on April 12th 1923 in the Abbey Theatre. The action of the play takes place in May 1920 against the background of the Black and Tan war. The play provides us with a view of a small but vivid segment of this guerrilla war and how it affected the lives of the occupants of a Dublin tenement house.
- The people and events of the play are based on O'Casey's personal experiences. There are strong similarities between the events of the play and a chapter - 'The Raid' - in a volume of his autobiography *Inishfallen, Fare Thee Well*. The play is set in the room of a home in Hilljoy Square, reflecting the fact that O'Casey shared a room for a time in 35 Mountjoy Square. Donal Davoren, the principal character in the play is, to an extent, a self-portrait of O'Casey. These details, however, are of no great importance in understanding and appreciating the play.
- O'Casey provides us with very detailed stage directions. These include, not only details of the appearance of the characters, but also comments on the personalities of many of the characters. These comments are particularly useful from the point of view of somebody reading the play as they help the reader to picture the characters more clearly.
- O'Casey does not take sides in the play. He approaches the historical issue of the play in an impartial manner. He doesn't set out to make a case for or against the Republican cause.
- This historical aspect of the setting of the play is not of major importance. In fact, we learn little or no details of the history of the time from the play itself. What we do see is a nation in turmoil - a native revolutionary force in conflict with what was generally regarded as an occupying force and the effects of this conflict on the lives of ordinary uncommitted people. It is the type of situation that has recurred worldwide again and again throughout the twentieth century. With some slight changes, the characters and events of the play could reflect those of other countries which have undergone similar periods of insurrection and rebellion. In the play, O'Casey aims to examine how a group of individuals behave when their everyday lives are complicated by the turmoil and instability of the times.

DRAMATIC IRONY

- The play is rich in examples of *dramatic irony*. In simple terms, *dramatic irony* occurs in a play when the audience can see the real significance and meaning of the words or actions of a character and not merely what the character wants his/her words or actions to convey. The main element of dramatic irony is ***contrast***; contrast between appearance and reality; between pretensions and achievements; contrast between lies and truths. These contrasts are revealed with differing results; at times high comedy and rich humour but also bitterness, shame and, ultimately, tragedy.
- The strength of the play is not an ingenious plot or a complex and weighty theme but the rich life-like qualities of its characters. It is important to note that, while such characters would not make ideal

The Shadow of a Gunman

neighbours or friends, they are excellent *dramatic creations*. (In fact ideal neighbours or friends are unlikely to form interesting dramatic creations). Practically all the characters of the play are striking because of the discrepancy between their actions and their words; between what they really are and what they pretend they are. As stated already, it is these discrepancies that provide us with a rich succession of humorous situations, though ultimately with a tragic one.

SEAN O'CASEY (1880-1964)

Seán O'Casey (1880-1964)

Seán O'Casey is one of Ireland's most famous playwrights. He is renowned worldwide for his realistic dramas of life in Dublin's tenement slums in times of revolution.

O'Casey was born the youngest of thirteen children, five of whom survived childhood. From an early age, he knew hunger, poverty and ill-health and he saw fear, disease, squalor and drunkenness about him. While he had only three years of formal schooling, he was an avid reader who educated himself. He began work at fourteen as a labourer and spent ten years working for the Northern Railway as well as a spell working as a shop assistant.

For a while O'Casey became involved with the Nationalist cause. However, he became disillusioned and turned his energies to the labour movement. He joined the Irish Citizen Army, formed to protect striking workers and he wrote articles for *The Irish Worker*. He became secretary of the Irish Citizen Army but eventually resigned as he felt the Irish Citizen Army was becoming involved in the Nationalist struggle rather than devoting its energies to the plight of the workers.

O'Casey, at this stage, turned his attention from politics to drama. A number of his early efforts were rejected by the Abbey Theatre which had been founded to promote Irish drama. However, he was encouraged to continue and in 1923 **The Shadow of a Gunman** was first produced by the Abbey Theatre. It was followed by **Juno and the Paycock** in 1924 and **The Plough and the Stars** in 1925. These three plays are known as his *Abbey plays* and are generally regarded as his greatest works. Each of the plays had an explosive effect on the Abbey audiences. In all three plays he placed comedy side by side with tragedy - an innovation in drama at that time. They contain many memorable character creations and, in his portrayal of the tragic world of the Dublin slums in the shadow of rebellion and civil war, O'Casey wrote some of the funniest scenes in modern drama.

His next play - *The Silver Tassie* - was rejected by the Abbey in 1926 but produced in Britain in 1928. Angered by the rejection, O'Casey settled in Britain. His later plays never achieved the same popularity as the Abbey plays.

The Shadow of a Gunman

Characters

Donal Davoren
Seumas Shields, *a pedlar*
Tommy Owens
Adolphus Grigson
Mrs. Grigson
Minnie Powell
} *Residents in the Tenement*

Mr. Mulligan, *the landlord*
Mr. Maguire, *soldier of the I.R.A.*

Mrs. Henderson
Mr. Gallogher
} *Residents of an adjoining Tenement*

An Auxiliary

The Shadow of a Gunman

Scene

A room in a tenement in Hilljoy Square, Dublin. Some hours elapse between the two acts. The period of the Play is May 1920.

Act I

A Return Room in a tenement house in Hilljoy Square. At the back two large windows looking out into the yard; they occupy practically the whole of the back wall space. Between the windows is a cupboard, on the top of which is a pile of books. The doors are open, and on these are hanging a number of collars and ties. Running parallel with the windows is a stretcher bed; another runs at right angles along the wall at right. At the head of this bed is a door leading to the rest of the house. The wall on the left runs diagonally, so that the fireplace - which is in the centre - is plainly visible. On the mantelshelf to the right is a statue of the Virgin, to the left a statue of the Sacred Heart, and in the centre a crucifix. Around the fireplace are a few common cooking utensils. In the centre of the room is a table, on which are a typewriter, a candle and candlestick, a bunch of wild flowers in a vase, writing materials and a number of books. There are two chairs, one near the fireplace and one at the table. The aspect of the place is one of absolute untidiness, engendered on the one hand by the congenital slovenliness of Seumas Shields, *and on the other by the temperament of* Donal Davoren, *making it appear impossible to effect an improvement in such a place.*

Davoren *is sitting at the table typing. He is about thirty. There is in his face an expression that seems to indicate an eternal war between weakness and strength; there is in the lines of the brow and chin an indication of a desire for activity, while in his eyes there is visible an unquenchable tendency towards rest. His struggle through life has been a hard one, and his efforts have been handicapped by an inherited and self-developed devotion to 'the might of design, the mystery of colour, and the belief in the redemption of all things by beauty everlasting'. His life would drive him mad were it not for the fact that he never knew any other. He bears upon his body the marks of the struggle for existence and the efforts towards self-expression.*

Seumas Shields, *who is in the bed next the wall to the right, is a heavily built man of thirty-five; he is dark-haired and sallow-complexioned. In him is frequently manifested the superstition, the fear and the malignity of primitive man.*

Davoren *(lilting an air as he composes)* :
   Or when sweet Summer's ardent arms
      outspread,
   Entwined with flowers,
   Enfold us, like two lovers newly wed,
   Thro' ravish'd hours -
   Then sorrow, woe and pain lose all their
      powers,
   For each is dead, and life is only ours.

[*A woman's figure appears at the window and taps loudly on one of the panes; at the same moment there is loud knocking at the door.*

Voice of Woman at Window Are you awake, Mr. Shields - Mr. Shields, are you awake? Are you goin' to get up today at all, at all?

Voice at the Door Mr. Shields, is there any use of callin' you at all? This is a nice nine o'clock: do you know what time it is, Mr. Shields?

Seumas *(loudly)* Yes.

Voice at the Door Why don't you get up, then, an' not have the house turned into a bedlam tryin' to waken you?

Seumas (*shouting*) All right, all right, all right! The way these oul' ones bawl at a body! Upon my soul! I'm beginnin' to believe that the Irish People are still in the stone age. If they could they'd throw a bomb at you.

Davoren A land mine exploding under the bed is the only thing that would lift you out of it.

Seumas (*stretching himself*) Oh-h-h. I was fast in the arms of Morpheus - he was one of the infernal deities, son of Somnus, wasn't he.

Davoren I think so.

Seumas The poppy was his emblem, wasn't it?

Davoren Ah, I don't know.

Seumas It's a bit cold this morning, I think, isn't it?

Davoren It's quite plain I'm not going to get much quietness in this house.

Seumas (*after a pause*) I wonder what time it is?

Davoren The Angelus went some time ago.

Seumas (*sitting up in bed suddenly*) The Angelus! It couldn't be that late, could it? I asked them to call me at nine so that I could get Mass before I went on my rounds. Why didn't you give us a rap?

Davoren Give you a rap! Why, man, they've been thundering at the door and hammering at the window for the past two hours, till the house shook to its very foundations, but you took less notice of the infernal din than I would take of the strumming of a grasshopper.

Seumas There's no fear of you thinking of any one else when you're at your poetry. The land of Saints and Scholars 'ill shortly be a land of bloody poets. (*Anxiously*) I suppose Maguire has come and gone.

Davoren Maguire? No, he hasn't been here - why, did you expect him?

Seumas (*in a burst of indignation*) He said

he'd be here at nine. "Before the last chime has struck," says he, "I'll be coming in on the door," and it must be - what time is it now?

Davoren Oh, it must be half-past twelve.

Seumas Did anybody ever see the like of the Irish People? <u>Is there any use of tryin' to do anything in this country?</u> Have everything packed and ready, have everything packed and ready, have . . . .

Davoren And have you everything packed and ready?

Seumas What's the use of having anything packed and ready when he didn't come? *(He rises and dresses himself.)* No wonder this unfortunate country is as it is, for you can't depend upon the word of a single individual in it. I suppose he was too damn lazy to get up; he wanted the streets to be well aired first. - Oh, Kathleen ní Houlihan, your way's a thorny way.

Davoren Ah me! alas, pain, pain ever, for ever!

Seumas That's from Shelley's *Prometheus Unbound*. I could never agree with Shelley, not that there's anything to be said against him as a poet - as a poet - but . . . .

Davoren He flung a few stones through stained-glass windows.

Seumas He wasn't the first nor he won't be the last to do that, but the stained-glass windows - more than ever of them - are here still, and Shelley is doing a jazz dance down below.

[*He gives a snarling laugh of pleasure.*]

Davoren *(shocked)* And you actually rejoice and are exceedingly glad that, as you believe, Shelley, the sensitive, high-minded, noble-hearted Shelley, is suffering the tortures of the damned.

Seumas I rejoice in the vindication of the Church and Truth.

Davoren <u>Bah. You know as little about truth as anybody else,</u> and you care as little about the Church as the least of those that profess her faith; your religion is simply the state of being afraid that God will torture your soul in the next world as you are afraid the Black and Tans will torture your body in this.

Seumas <u>Go on, me boy; I'll have a right laugh at you when both of us are dead.</u>

Davoren You're welcome to laugh as much as you like at me when both of us are dead.

Seumas *(as he is about to put on his collar and tie).* I don't think I need to wash meself this morning; do I look all right?

Davoren Oh, you're all right; it's too late now to start washing yourself. Didn't you wash yourself yesterday morning?

Seumas I gave meself a great rub yesterday. *(He proceeds to pack various articles into an attaché case - spoons, forks, laces, thread etc.)* I think I'll bring out a few of the braces too; damn it; they're well worth sixpence each; there's great stuff in them - did you see them?

Davoren Yes, you showed them to me before.

Seumas They're great value; I only hope I'll be able to get enough o' them. I'm wearing a pair of them meself - they'd do Cuchullain, they're so strong. *(Counting the spoons)* There's a dozen in each of these parcels - three, six, nine - damn it, there's only eleven in this one. I better try another. Three, six, nine - my God, there's only eleven in this one too, and one of them bent! Now I suppose I'll have to go through the whole bloody lot of them, for I'd never be easy in me mind thinkin' there'd be more than a dozen in some o' them. And still we're looking for freedom - ye, gods, it's a glorious country! *(He lets one fall, which he*

The Shadow of a Gunman

stoops to pick up.) Oh, my God, there's the braces after breakin'.

Davoren That doesn't look as if they were strong enough for Cuchullain.

Seumas I put a heavy strain on them too sudden. There's that fellow Maguire never turned up, either; he's almost too lazy to wash himself. *(As he is struggling with the braces the door is hastily shoved in and Maguire rushes in with a handbag.)* This is a nice nine o'clock. What's the use of you coming at this hour o' the day? Do you think we're going to work be moonlight? If you weren't goin' to come at nine couldn't you say you weren't . . . .

Maguire Keep your hair on; I just blew in to tell you that I couldn't go to-day at all. I have to go to Knocksedan.

Seumas Knocksedan! An' what, in the name o' God, is bringin' you to Knocksedan?

Maguire Business, business. I'm going out to catch butterflies.

Seumas If you want to make a cod of anybody, make a cod of somebody else, an' don't be tryin' to make a cod o' me. Here I've had everything packed an' ready for hours; you were to be here at nine, an' you wait till just one o'clock to come rushin' in like a mad bull to say you've got to go to Knocksedan! Can't you leave Knocksedan till tomorrow?

Maguire Can't be did, can't be did, Seumas; if I waited till tomorrow all the butterflies might be dead. I'll leave this bag here till this evening. *(He puts the bag in a corner of the room)* Good-bye. . . . ee.

[*He is gone before Seumas is aware of it.*

Seumas *(with a gesture of despair).* Oh, this is a hopeless country! There's a fellow that thinks that the four cardinal virtues are not to be found outside an Irish Republic. I don't want to boast about myself - I don't want to boast about myself, and I suppose I could call meself as good a Gael as some of those that are knocking about now - knocking about now - as good a Gael as some of those that are knocking about now, - but I remember the time when I taught Irish six nights a week, when in the Irish Republican Brotherhood. I paid me rifle levy like a man, an' when the Church refused to have anything to do with James Stephens, I tarred a prayer for the repose of his soul on the steps of the Pro-Cathedral. Now after all me work for Dark Rosaleen, the only answer you can get from a roarin' Republican to a simple question is "good-bye . . . . ee". What, in the name o' God, can be bringin' him to Knocksedan?

Davoren Hadn't you better run out and ask him?

Seumas That's right, that's right - make a joke about it! That's the Irish People all over - they treat a joke as a serious thing and a serious thing as a joke. Upon me soul, I'm beginning to believe that the Irish People aren't, never were, an' never will be fit for self-government. They made Balor of the Evil Eye King of Ireland, an' so signs on it there's neither conscience nor honesty from one end of the country to the other. Well, I hope he'll have a happy day in Knocksedan. *(A knock at the door)* Who's that?

[*Another knock.*

Seumas *(irritably).* Who's that; who's there?

Davoren *(more irritably).* Halt and give the countersign — damn it, man, can't you go and see?

[*Seumas goes over and opens the door. A man of about sixty is revealed, dressed in a*

The Shadow of a Gunman

faded blue serge suit; a half tall hat is on his head. It is evident that he has no love for Seumas, who denies him the deference he believes is due from a tenant to a landlord. He carries some papers in his hand.

The Landlord *(ironically).* Good-day, Mr. Shields; it's meself that hopes you're feelin' well - you're lookin' well anyhow - though you can't always go be looks nowadays.

Seumas It doesn't matter whether I'm lookin' well or feelin' well; I'm all right, thanks be to God.

The Landlord I'm very glad to hear it.

Seumas It doesn't matter whether you're glad to hear it or not, Mr. Mulligan.

The Landlord You're not inclined to be very civil, Mr. Shields.

Seumas Look here, Mr. Mulligan, if you come here to raise an argument, I've something to do - let me tell you that.

The Landlord I don't come here to raise no argument; a person ud have small gains argufyin' with you - let me tell you that.

Seumas I've no time to be standin' here gostherin' with you - let me shut the door, Mr. Mulligan.

The Landlord You'll not shut no door till you've heard what I've got to say.

Seumas Well, say it then, an' go about your business.

The Landlord You're very high an' mighty, but take care you're not goin' to get a drop. What a baby you are not to know what brings me here! Maybe you thought I was goin' to ask you to come to tea.

Davoren Ah me! alas, pain, pain ever, for ever!

Seumas Are you goin' to let me shut the door, Mr. Mulligan?

The Landlord I'm here for me rent; you don't like the idea of bein' asked to pay your just an' lawful debts.

Seumas You'll get your rent when you learn to keep your rent-book in a proper way.

The Landlord I'm not goin' to take any lessons from you, anyhow.

Seumas I want to have no more talk with you, Mr. Mulligan.

The Landlord Talk or no talk, you owe me eleven weeks' rent, an' it's marked down again' you in black an' white.

Seumas I don't care a damn if it was marked down in green, white, an' yellow.

The Landlord You're a terribly independent fellow, an' it ud be fitter for you to be less funny an' stop tryin' to be billickin' honest an' respectable people.

Seumas Just you be careful what you're sayin'; Mr. Mulligan. There's law in the land still.

The Landlord Be me sowl there is, an' you're goin' to get a little of it now. *(He offers the papers to* Seumas*)* Them's for you.

Seumas *(hesitating to take them).* I want to have nothing to do with you, Mr. Mulligan.

The Landlord *(throwing the papers in the centre of the room).* What am I better? It was the sorry day I ever let you come into this house. Maybe them notices to quit will stop your writin' letters to the papers about me an' me house.

Davoren For goodness' sake, bring the man in, and don't be discussing the situation like a pair of primitive troglodytes.

Seumas *(taking no notice).* Writing letters to the papers is my business, an' I'll write as often as I like, when I like, an' how I like.

The Landlord You'll not write about this house at all events. You can blow about

The Shadow of a Gunman

the state of the yard, but you took care to say nothin' about payin' rent: oh no, that's not in your line. But since you're not satisfied with the house, you can pack up an' go to another.

Seumas I'll go, Mr. Mulligan, when I think fit, an' no sooner.

The Landlord Not content with keeping the rent, you're startin' to bring in lodgers - *(to* Davoren*)* not that I'm sayin' anythin' again' you, sir. Bringin' in lodgers without as much as be your leave - what's the world comin' to at all that a man's house isn't his own? But I'll soon put a stop to your gallop, for on the twenty-eight of the next month out you go, an' there'll be few sorry to see your back.

Seumas I'll go when I like!

The Landlord I'll let you see whether you own the house or no.

Seumas I'll go when I like!

The Landlord We'll see about that.

Seumas We'll see.

The Landlord Ay, we'll see.

[*The* Landlord *goes out and* Seumas *shuts the door.*

☞ **Points to Note**

- The play is set in Hilljoy Square, Dublin - an ironic touch, considering the bleakness and poverty reflected by the set, which lacks any sign of joy.
- The bunch of flowers, symbolising Davoren's poetic ambitions, provides an ironic contrast to the grim disarray of the room. Also, the religious statues and the crucifix which belong to Shields contrast sharply with his true nature.
- The contrasts between Shields' pronouncements on the 'Irish People' and his behaviour provide us with the first example of comic, dramatic irony.
- Davoren compares himself to the poet Shelley and to Prometheus, a figure from Shelley's most famous work. Percy Bysshe Shelley (1792-1822) was born of an aristocratic background, against which he rebelled. *Prometheus Unbound* is a verse-drama which reflects his revolutionary ideals. The poem draws on Greek mythology. Prometheus stands for all that is finest in humanity and for the spirit of patient and heroic resistance to oppression. Jupiter, the god, stands for the oppressor and inflicts great pain and suffering on Prometheus. As the play unfolds you may judge if the comparison between Davoren and Prometheus is justified.
- O'Casey's views on religion are reflected in Davoren's words - "Bah. You know as little about truth . . . ."
- There is humorous and ironic contrast between Shields' words on the braces and their actual quality. Note also his comments on washing.
- Maguire is a man of few words.
- Shields declares "I don't want to boast about myself" and promptly begins to do just that. He comments on the fitness of the Irish People for self-government. Clearly Shields is unaware of his own failings, which he projects on to other people and criticises them.
- The landlord episode is very comical and again it ironically underscores Shields' true nature. It also serves to reveal for us the rumours about Davoren that have been circulating among the occupants of the house.

The Shadow of a Gunman

The Landlord (*outside*). Mind you, I'm in earnest; you'll not stop in this house a minute longer than the twenty-eighth.

Seumas (*with a roar*). Ah, go to hell!

Davoren (*pacing the room as far as the space will permit*). What in the name of God persuaded me to come to such a house as this?

Seumas It's nothing when you're used to it; you're too thin-skinned altogether. The oul' sod's got the wind up about you, that's all.

Davoren Got the wind up about me!

Seumas He thinks you're on the run. He's afraid of a raid, and that his lovely property'll be destroyed.

Davoren But why, in the name of all that's sensible, should he think that I'm on the run?

Seumas Sure they all think you're on the run. Mrs. Henderson thinks it, Tommy Owens thinks it, Mrs. an' Mr. Grigson thinks it, an' Minnie Powell thinks it too. (*Picking up his attaché case*) I'd better be off if I'm goin' to do anything today.

Davoren What are we going to do with these notices to quit?

Seumas Oh, shove them up on the mantelpiece behind one of the statues.

Davoren Oh, I mean what action shall we take?

Seumas I haven't time to stop now. We'll talk about them when I come back.... I'll get me own back on that oul' Mulligan yet. I wish to God they would come an' smash his rookery to pieces, for it's all he thinks of, and, mind you, oul' Mulligan would call himself a descendant of the true Gaels of Banba - (*as he goes out*):

Oh, proud were the chieftains of famed Inisfail.
Is truagh gan oidher 'na Vfarradh.
The stars of our sky an' the salt of our soil -

Oh, Kathleen ní Houlihan, your way's a thorny way! [*He goes out.*

Davoren (*returning to the table and sitting down at the typewriter*) Oh, Donal Og O'Davoren, your way's a thorny way. Your last state is worse than your first. Ah me, alas! Pain, pain ever, for ever. Like thee, Prometheus, no change, no pause, no hope. Ah, life, life, life! (*There is a gentle knock at the door.*) Another Fury come to plague me now!

[*Another knock, a little louder.*

Davoren You can knock till you're tired.

[*The door opens and Minnie Powell enters with an easy confidence one would not expect her to possess from her gentle way of knocking. She is a girl of twenty-three, but the fact of being forced to earn her living, and to take care of herself, on account of her parents' early death, has given her a force and an assurance beyond her years. She has lost the sense of fear (she does not know this), and, consequently, she is at ease in all places and before all persons, even those of a superior education, so long as she meets them in the atmosphere that surrounds the members of her own class. Her hair is brown, neither light nor dark, but partaking of both tints according to the light or shade she may happen to be in. Her well-shaped figure — a rare thing in a city girl — is charmingly dressed in a brown tailor-made costume, her stockings and shoes are a darker brown tint than the costume, and all are crowned by a silk tam-o' shanter of a rich blue tint.*

Minnie Are you in, Mr. Shields?

Davoren (*rapidly*). No, he's not, Minnie; he's just gone out - if you run out quickly

The Shadow of a Gunman

you're sure to catch him.

Minnie Oh, it's all right, Mr. Davoren, you'll do just as well; I just come in for a drop o' milk for a cup o' tea; I shouldn't be troublin' you this way, but I'm sure you don't mind.

Davoren *(dubiously).* No trouble in the world; delighted, I'm sure. *(Giving her the milk.)* There, will you have enough?

Minnie Plenty, lashins, thanks. Do you be all alone all the day, Mr. Davoren?

Davoren No, indeed; I wish to God I was.

Minnie It's not good for you then. I don't know how you like to be by yourself - I couldn't stick it long.

Davoren *(wearily).* No?

Minnie No, indeed; *(with rapture)* there's nothin' I'm more fond of than a Hooley. I was at one last Sunday - I danced rings round me! Tommy Owens was there - you know Tommy Owens, don't you?

Davoren I can't say I do.

Minnie D'ye not? The little fellow that lives with his mother in the two-pair back - *(ecstatically)* he's a gorgeous melodeon player!

Davoren A gifted son of Orpheus, eh?

Minnie *(who never heard of Orpheus).* You've said it, Mr. Davoren: the son of poor oul' Battie Owens, a weeshy, dawny, bit of a man that was never sober an' was always talkin' politics. Poor man, it killed him in the long run.

Davoren A man should always be drunk, Minnie, when he talks politics - it's the only way in which to make them important.

Minnie Tommy takes after the oul' fellow, too; he'd talk from morning till night when he has a few jars in him.

[*Suddenly; for like all of her class, Minnie is not able to converse very long on the one subject, and her thoughts spring from one thing to another.*

Poetry is a grand thing, Mr. Davoren, I'd love to be able to write a poem - a lovely poem on Ireland an' the men o' '98.

Davoren Oh, we've had enough of poems, Minnie, about '98, and of Ireland, too.

Minnie <u>Oh, there's a thing for a Republican to say! But I know what you mean : it's time to give up the writing an' take to the gun.</u> *(Her roving eye catches sight of the flowers in the vase.)* What's Mr. Shield's doin' with the oul' weeds?

Davoren Those aren't Shields', they're mine. Wild flowers is a kindlier name for them, Minnie, than weeds. These are wild violets, this is an *Arum maculatum*, or Wake Robin, and these are Celandines, a very beautiful flower related to the buttercups. *(He quotes):*

One day, when Morn's half-open'd eyes
Were bright with Spring sunshine -
My hand was clasp'd in yours, dear love,
And yours was clasp'd in mine -
We bow'd as worshippers before
The Golden Celandine.

The Shadow of a Gunman

Minnie Oh, aren't they lovely, an' isn't the poem lovely, too! I wonder, now, who she was.

Davoren (*puzzled*). She, who?

Minnie Why, the . . . . (*roguishly*) Oh, be the way you don't know.

Davoren Know? I'm sure I don't know.

Minnie It doesn't matter, anyhow - that's your own business; I suppose I don't know her.

Davoren Know her - know whom?

Minnie (*shyly*). Her whose hand was clasped in yours, an' yours was clasped in hers.

Davoren Oh, that - that was simply a poem I quoted about the Celandine, that might apply to any girl - to you, for instance.

Minnie (*greatly relieved, coming over and sitting beside* Davoren). But you have a sweetheart, all the same, Mr. Davoren, haven't you?

Davoren I? No, not one, Minnie.

Minnie Oh, now, you can tell that to some one else; aren't you a poet an' aren't all the girls fond o' poets?

Davoren That may be, but all the poets aren't fond of girls.

Minnie They are in the story-books, ay, and fond of more than one, too. (*With a questioning look*) Are you fond of them, Mr. Davoren?

Davoren Of course I like girls, Minnie, especially girls who can add to their charms by the way in which they dress, like you, for instance.

Minnie Oh, now, you're on for coddin' me, Mr. Davoren.

Davoren No, really, Minnie, I'm not; you are a very charming little girl indeed.

Minnie Then if I'm a charmin' little girl, you ought to be able to write a poem about me.

Davoren (*who has become susceptible to the attractiveness of Minnie, catching her hand*). And so I will, so I will, Minnie; I have written them about girls not half so pretty as yourself.

Minnie Ah, I knew you had one, I knew you had one now.

Davoren Nonsense. Every girl a poet writes about isn't his sweetheart; Annie Laurie wasn't the sweetheart of Bobbie Burns.

Minnie You needn't tell me she wasn't; "An' for bonnie Annie Laurie I'd lay me down an' die". No man ud lay down an' die for any but a sweetheart, not even for a wife.

Davoren No man, Minnie, willingly dies for anything.

Minnie Except for his country, like Robert Emmet.

Davoren Even he would have lived on if he could; he died not to deliver Ireland. The British Government killed him to save the British nation.

Minnie You're only jokin' now; you'd die for your country.

Davoren I don't know so much about that.

Minnie You would, you would, you would - I know what you are.

Davoren What am I?

Minnie (*in a whisper*). A gunman on the run!

Davoren (*too pleased to deny it*). Maybe I am, and maybe I'm not.

Minnie Oh, I know, I know, I know. Do you never be afraid?

Davoren Afraid! Afraid of what?

Minnie Why, the ambushes of course; *I'm all of a tremble when I hear a shot go off, an' what must it be in the middle of the firin'?*

Davoren (*delighted at* Minnie's *obvious admiration; leaning back in his chair, and lighting a cigarette with placid affectation*) I'll admit one does be a little nervous at first, but a fellow gets used to it after a bit, till, at last, a gunman throws

The Shadow of a Gunman

a bomb as carelessly as a schoolboy throws a snowball.

Minnie *(fervently).* I wish it was all over, all the same. *(Suddenly, with a tremor in her voice.)* You'll take care of yourself, won't you, Donal - I mean, Mr. Davoren?

Davoren *(earnestly).* Call me Donal, Minnie; we're friends, great friends now - *(putting his arm around her)* go on, Minnie, call me Donal, let me hear you say Donal.

Minnie The place badly needs a tidyin' up . . . . Donal - there now, are you satisfied? *(Rapidly, half afraid of Davoren's excited emotions).* But it really does, it's an awful state. Tomorrow's a half-day, an' I'll run in an' straighten it up a bit.

Davoren *(frightened at the suggestion).* No, no, Minnie, you're too pretty for that sort of work; besides, the people of the house would be sure to start talking about you.

Minnie An' do you think Minnie Powell cares whether they'll talk or no? She's had to push her way through life up to this without help from any one, an' she's not goin' to ask their leave, now, to do what she wants to do.

Davoren *(forgetting his timidity in the honest joy of appreciating the independent courage of Minnie).* My soul within art thou, Minnie! A pioneer in action as I am a pioneer in thought. The two powers that shall "grasp this sorry scheme of things entire, and mould life nearer to the heart's desire". Lovely little Minnie, and brave as well; brave little Minnie, and lovely as well.

[*His disengaged hand lifts up her bent head, and he looks earnestly at her; he is stooping to kiss her, when* Tommy Owens *appears at the door, which* Minnie *has left partially open.* Tommy *is about twenty-five years of age. He is small and thin; his words are uttered in a nasal drawl; his voice is husky, due to frequent drinks and perpetual cigarette-smoking. He tries to get rid of the huskiness by an occasional cough.* Tommy *is a hero-worshipper, and, like many others, he is anxious to be on familiar terms with those who he thinks are braver than he is himself, and whose approbation he tries to win by an assumption equal to their own. He talks in a staccato manner. He has a few drinks taken - it is too early to be drunk - that make him talkative. He is dressed in a suit of dungarees, and gives a gentle cough to draw attention to his presence.*

Tommy I seen nothin' - honest - thought you was learnin' to typewrite - Mr. Davoren teachin' you. I seen nothin' else - s'help me God!

Minnie We'd be hard put to it if we minded what you seen, Tommy Owens.

Tommy Right, Minnie, Tommy Owens has a heart - Evenin', Mr. Davoren - don't mind me comin' in - I'm Tommy Owens - live up in the two-pair back, workin' in Ross an' Walpole's - Mr. Shields knows me well; you needn't be afraid o' me, Mr. Davoren.

Davoren Why should I be afraid of you, Mr. Owens, or of anybody else?

Tommy Why should you, indeed? We're all friends here - Mr. Shields knows me well - all you've got to say is, "Do you know Tommy Owens?" an' he'll tell you the sort of a man Tommy Owens is. There's no flies on Tommy - got me?

Minnie For goodness' sake, Tommy, leave Mr. Davoren alone — he's got enough burgeons on him already.

Tommy Not a word, Minnie, not a word - Mr. Davoren understands me well, as man to man. It's "Up the Republic" all the time - eh, Mr. Davoren?

Davoren <u>I know nothing about the Republic; I have no connection with the politics of the day, and I don't want to have any connection.</u>

Tommy You needn't say no more - a nod's as good as a wink to a blind horse - you've no meddlin' or makin' with it, good, bad, or indifferent, pro nor con; I know it an' Minnie knows it - give me your hand. *(He catches* Davoren's *hand).* Two firm hands clasped together will all the power outbrave of the heartless English tyrant, the Saxon coward an' knave. That's Tommy Owens' hand, Mr. Davoren, the hand of a man, a man - Mr. Shields knows me well.

[*He breaks into song.*

High upon the gallows tree stood the noble-hearted three,
By the vengeful tyrant stricken in their bloom;
But they met him face to face with the spirit of their race,
And they went with souls undaunted to their doom!

Minnie *(in an effort to quell his fervour).* Tommy Owens, for goodness' sake . . . .

Tommy *(overwhelming her with a shout):*

God save Ireland ses the hayros, God save Ireland ses we all,
Whether on the scaffold high or the battle-field we die.
Oh, what matter when for Ayryinn dear we fall!

(Tearfully) Mr. Davoren, I'd die for Ireland!

Davoren I know you would, I know you would, Tommy.

Tommy I never got a chance - they never gave me a chance - but all the same I'd be there if I was called on - Mr. Shields knows that - ask Mr. Shields, Mr. Davoren.

Davoren There's no necessity, Tommy; I know you're the right stuff if you got the chance, but remember that "he also serves who only stands and waits".

Tommy *(fiercely).* <u>I'm bloody well tired o' waitin' — we're all tired o' waitin'. Why isn't every man in Ireland out with the I.R.A.?</u> Up with the barricades, up with the barricades; it's now or never, now an' for ever, as Sarsfield said at the battle o' Vinegar Hill. Up with the barricades - that's Tommy Owens - an' a penny buys a whistle. Let them as thinks different say different - what do you say, Mr. Davoren?

Davoren I say, Tommy, you ought to go up and get your dinner, for if you wait much longer it won't be worth eating.

Tommy Oh, damn the dinner; who'd think o' dinner an' Ireland fightin' to be free - not Tommy Owens, anyhow. It's only the Englishman who's always thinkin' of his belly.

Minnie Tommy Owens!

Tommy Excuse me, Miss Powell, in the ardure ov me anger I disremembered there was a lady present.

[*Voices are heard outside, and presently* Mrs. Henderson *comes into the room, followed by* Mr. Gallogher, *who, however, lingers at the door, too timid to come any further.* Mrs. Henderson *is a massive woman in every way; massive head, arms, and body; massive voice, and a massive amount of self-confidence. She is a mountain of good nature, and during the interview she behaves towards* Davoren *with deferential self-assurance. She dominates the room, and seems to occupy the whole of it. She is dressed poorly but tidily, wearing a white apron and a large shawl.* Mr. Gallogher, *on the other hand, is*

The Shadow of a Gunman

a spare little man with a spare little grey beard and a thin, nervous voice. He is dressed as well as a faded suit of blue will allow him to be. He is obviously ill at ease during his interview with Davoren. *He carries a hard hat, much the worse for wear, under his left arm, and a letter in his right hand.*

Mrs. Henderson *(entering the room)*. Come along in, Mr. Gallicker, Mr. Davoren won't mind; it's him as can put you in the way o' havin' your wrongs righted; come on in, man, an' don't be so shy - Mr. Davoren is wan ov ourselves that stands for government ov the people with the people by the people. You'll find you'll be as welcome as the flowers in May. Good evenin', Mr. Davoren, an' God an' His holy angels be between you an' all harm.

Tommy *(effusively)*. Come on, Mr. Gallicker, an' don't be a stranger - we're all friends here - anything special to be done or particular advice asked, here's your man here.

Davoren *(subconsciously pleased, but a little timid of the belief that he is connected with the gunmen)*. I'm very busy just now, Mrs. Henderson, and really . . . .

Mrs. Henderson *(mistaking the reason of his embarrassment)*. Don't be put out, Mr. Davoren, we won't keep you more nor a few minutes. It's not in me or in Mr. Gallicker to spoil sport. Him an' me was young once, an' knows what it is to be strolling at night in the pale moonlight, with arms round one another. An' I wouldn't take much an' say there's game in Mr. Gallicker still, for I seen, sometimes, a dangerous cock in his eye. But we won't keep you an' Minnie long asunder; he's the letter an' all written. You must know, Mr. Davoren - excuse me for not introducin' him sooner - this is Mr. Gallicker, that lives in the front drawin'-room ov number fifty-five, as decent an' honest an' quiet a man as you'd meet in a day's walk. An' so signs on it, it's them as 'ill be imposed upon - read the letter, Mr. Gallicker.

Tommy <u>Read away, Mr. Gallicker, it will be attended to, never fear; we know our own know, eh, Mr. Davoren?</u>

Minnie Hurry up, Mr. Gallicker, an' don't be keeping Mr. Davoren.

Mrs. Henderson Give him time, Minnie Powell. Give him time. You must know in all fairity, Mr. Davoren, that the family livin' in the next room to Mr. Gallicker - the back drawin'-room, or, to be more particular - am I right or am I wrong, Mr. Gallicker?

Mr. Gallogher You're right, Mrs. Henderson, perfectly right, indeed - that's the very identical room.

Mrs. Henderson Well, Mr. Davoren, the people in the back drawin'-room, or, to be more particular, the residents - that's the word that's writ in the letter - am I right or am I wrong, Mr. Gallicker?

Mr. Gallogher You're right, Mrs. Henderson, perfectly accurate - that's the very identical word.

Mrs. Henderson Well, Mr. Davoren, the residents in the back drawin'-room, as I aforesaid, is nothin' but a gang o' tramps that oughtn't to be allowed to associate with honest, decent, quiet, respectable people. Mr. Gallicker has tried to reason with them, and make them behave themselves - which in my opinion they never will - however, that's only an opinion, an' not legal — ever since they have made Mr. Gallicker's life a Hell! Mr. Gallicker, am I right or am I wrong?

Mr. Gallogher I'm sorry to say you're right, Mrs. Henderson, perfectly right - not a word of exaggeration.

Mrs. Henderson Well, now, Mr. Gallicker, seein' as I have given Mr. Davoren a fair account ov how you're situated an' ov these tramps' cleverality, I'll ask you to read the letter, which I'll say, not because you're there, or that you're a friend o' mine, is as good a letter as was decomposed by a scholar. Now, Mr. Gallicker, an' don't forget the top sayin'.

[*Mr. Gallogher prepares to read; Minnie leans forward to listen; Tommy takes out a well-worn note-book and a pencil stump, and assumes a very important attitude.*

Tommy One second, Mr. Gallicker, is this the twenty-first or twenty-second?
Mr. Gallogher The twenty-first, sir.
Tommy Thanks; proceed, Mr. Gallicker.
Mr. Gallogher (*with a few preliminary tremors, reads the letter. Reading*):

"To All to Whom These Presents Come,
   Greeting
   'Gentlemen of the Irish
   Republican Army . . .'

Mrs. Henderson There's a beginnin' for you, Mr. Davoren.
Minnie That's some swank.
Tommy There's a lot in that sayin', mind you; it's a hard wallop at the British Empire.
Mrs. Henderson (*proudly*). Go on, Mr. Gallicker.
Mr. Gallogher (*reading*):

"I wish to call your attention to the persecution me and my family has to put up with in respect of and appertaining to the residents of the back drawing-room of the house known as fifty-five, Saint Teresa Street, situate in the Parish of St. Thomas, in the Borough and City of Dublin. This persecution started eighteen months ago - or to be precise - on the tenth day of the sixth month, in the year nineteen hundred and twenty."

Mrs. Henderson That's the word I was trying to think ov - precise - it cuts the ground from under their feet - so to speak.
Mr. Gallogher (*reading*):

"We, the complainants, resident on the ground floor, deeming it disrespectable . . . ."

Mrs. Henderson (*with an emphatic nod*). Which it was.
Mr. Gallogher (*reading*):

"Deeming it disrespectable to have an open hall door, and to have the hall turned into a playground, made a solemn protest, and, in consequence, we the complainants aforesaid has had no peace ever since. Owing to the persecution, as aforesaid specified, we had to take out a summons again them some time ago as there was no Republican Courts then; but we did not proceed again them as me and my wife - to wit, James and Winifred Gallogher - has a strong objection to foreign Courts as such. We had peace for some time after that, but now things have gone from bad to worse. The name calling and the language is something abominable . . . ."

Mrs. Henderson (*holding out her hand as a constable would extend his to stop a car that another may pass*). Excuse me, Mr. Gallicker, but I think the word "shockin'" should be put in there after abominable; for the language used be these tramps has two ways o' bein'

The Shadow of a Gunman

looked at - for it's abominable to the childer an' shockin' to your wife - am I right or am I wrong, Mr. Davoren?

Tommy (*judicially*). Shockin' is a right good word, with a great deal o' meanin', an'....

Mrs. Henderson (*with a deprecating gesture that extinguishes* Tommy). Tommy, let Mr. Davoren speak; whatever Mr. Davoren ses, Julia Henderson'll abide be.

Davoren (*afraid to say anything else*). I think the word might certainly be introduced with advantage.

Mrs. Henderson Go over there, Mr. Gallicker, an' put in the word shockin', as aforesaid.

[Gallogher *goes over to the table, and with a great deal of difficulty enters the word.*

Tommy (*to Mr. Gallogher as he writes*). Ey, there's two k's in shockin'!

Mr. Gallogher (*reading*):

"The language is something abominable and shocking. My wife has often to lock the door of the room to keep them from assaulting her. If you would be so kind as to send some of your army or police down to see for themselves we would give them full particulars. I have to be always from home all day, as I work with Mr. Hennessy, the harness maker of the Coombe, who will furnish all particulars as to my unvarnished respectability, also my neighbours. <u>The name of the resident-tenant who is giving all this trouble and who, pursuant to the facts of the case aforesaid, mentioned, will be the defendant, is Dwyer.</u> The husband of the aforesaid Mrs. Dwyer, or the aforesaid defendant, as the case may be, is a seaman, who is coming home shortly, <u>and we beg The Irish</u>

Republican Army to note that the said Mrs. Dwyer says he will settle us when he comes home. While leaving it entirely in the hands of the gentlemen of The Republican Army, the defendant, that is to say, James Gallogher of fifty-five St. Teresa Street, ventures to say that he thinks he has made out a Primmy Fashy Case against Mrs. Dwyer and all her heirs, male and female as aforesaid mentioned in the above written schedule.

N.B. - If you send up any of your men, please tell them to bring their guns. I beg to remain the humble servant and devoted admirer of the Gentlemen of the Irish Republican Army.

Witness my hand this tenth day of the fifth month of the year nineteen hundred and twenty.

James Gallogher"

Mr. Gallogher *(with a modest cough).* Ahem.

Mrs. Henderson There's a letter for you, Mr. Davoren!

Tommy It's the most powerfullest letter I ever heard read.

Minnie It wasn't you, really, that writ it, Mr. Gallicker?

Mrs. Henderson Sinn Féin Amhain: him an' him only, Minnie. I seen him with me own two eyes when me an' Winnie - Mrs. Gallicker, Mr. Davoren, aforesaid as appears in the letter - was havin' a chat be the fire.

Minnie You'd never think it was in him to do it.

Mrs. Henderson An' to think that the likes ov such a man is to have the sowl-case worried out ov him by a gang o' tramps; but it's in good hands now, an' instead ov them settlin' yous, Mr. Gallicker, it's yous 'ill settle them. Give the letter to Mr. Davoren, an' we'll be goin'.

[*Gallogher gives the letter to* Davoren.

Mrs. Henderson *(moving towards the door).* I hope you an' Mr. Shields is gettin' on all right together, Mr. Davoren.

Davoren Fairly well, thanks, Mrs. Henderson. We don't see much of each other. He's out during the day, and I'm usually out during the evening.

Mrs. Henderson I'm afraid he'll never make a fortune out ov what he's sellin'. He'll talk above an hour over a pennorth o' pins. Every time he comes to our place I buy a package o' hairpins from him to give him a little encouragement. I 'clare to God I have as many pins now as ud make a wire mattress for a double bed. All the young divils about the place are beginnin' to make a jeer ov him, too; I gave one ov them a mallavogin' the other day for callin' him oul' hairpins!

Mr. Gallogher *(venturing an opinion).* Mr. Shields is a man of exceptional mental capacity, and is worthy of a more dignified position.

Mrs. Henderson Them words is true, Mr. Gallicker, and they aren't. For to be wise is to be a fool, an' to be a fool is to be wise.

Mr. Gallogher *(with a deprecating tolerance).* Oh, Mrs. Henderson, that's a parrotox.

Mrs. Henderson It may be what a parrot talks, or a blackbird, or, for the matter of that, a lark - but it's what Julia Henderson thinks, any . . . . whisht, is that a *Stop Press*?

[*Outside is heard the shriek of a newsboy calling "Stop Press".*

Mrs. Henderson Run out, Tommy, an' get it till we see what it is.

Tommy I haven't got a make.

Mrs. Henderson I never seen you any

The Shadow of a Gunman

other way, an' you'll be always the same if you keep follyin' your Spearmints, an' your Bumble Bees an' your Night Patrols. *(Shouting to someone outside)* Is that a *Stop Press*, Mrs. Grigson?

Voice outside Yis; an ambush out near Knocksedan.

Mrs. Henderson That's the stuff to give them. *(Loudly)* Was there anybody hurted?

Voice outside One poor man killed - some chap named Maguire, the paper says.

Davoren *(agitated)*. What name did she say?

Minnie Maguire; did you know him, Mr. Davoren?

Davoren <u>Yes — no, no; I didn't know him, no, I didn't know him, Minnie.</u>

Minnie I wonder is it the Maguire that does be with Mr. Shields?

Davoren Oh no, not at all, it couldn't be.

Mrs. Henderson Knocksedan? That's in the County Sligo, now, or I'm greatly mistaken - am I right, Mr. Gallicker, or am I wrong?

Mr. Gallogher *(who knows perfectly well that it is in the County Dublin, but dare not correct Mrs. Henderson)*. That's where it is - Knocksedan, that's the very identical county.

Mrs. Henderson Well, I think we better be makin' a move, Mr. Gallicker; we've kep' Mr. Davoren long enough, an' you'll find the letter'll be in good hans.

[Mr. Gallogher *and* Mrs. Henderson *move towards the door, which when he reaches it* Mr. Gallogher *grips, hesitates, buttons his coat, and turns to* Davoren.

Mr. Gallogher Mr. Davoren, sir, on behalf ov meself, James Gallicker, an' Winifred, Mrs. Gallicker, wife ov the said James, I beg to offer, extend an' furnish our humble an' hearty thanks for your benevolent goodness in interferin' in the matter specified, particularated an' expanded upon in the letter, mandamus or schedule, as the case may be. An' let me interpretate to you on behalf ov meself an' Winifred Gallicker, that whenever you visit us you will be supernally positive ov a hundred thousand welcomes - ahem.

Mrs. Henderson *(beaming with pride for the genius of her friend)*. There's a man for you, Mr. Davoren! You forgot to mention Biddy and Shaun, Mr. Gallicker - *(to* Davoren*)* his two children - it's himself has them trained well. It ud make your heart thrill like an alarm clock to hear them singin' "Faith ov Our Fathers" an' "Wrap the Green Flag Roun me".

Mr. Gallogher *(half apologetically and half proudly)*. Faith an' Fatherland, Mrs. Henderson, Faith and Fatherland.

Mrs. Henderson Well, good-day, Mr. Davoren, an' God keep you an' strengthen all the men that are fightin' for Ireland's freedom.

[*She and* Gallogher *go out.*

Tommy I must be off too; so-long, Mr. Davoren, an' remember that Tommy Owens only waits the call.

[*He goes out too.*

Davoren Well, Minnie, we're by ourselves once more.

Minnie Wouldn't that Tommy Owens give you the sick - only waitin' to hear the call! Ah, then it'll take all the brass bands in the country to blow the call before Tommy Owens ud hear it. *(She looks at her wristlet watch.)* Sacred Heart, I've only ten minutes to get back to work! I'll have to fly! Quick, Mr. Davoren, write me name in typewritin' before I go - just "Minnie".

[Davoren *types the name.*

The Shadow of a Gunman

Minnie *(shyly but determinedly).* Now yours underneath - just "Donal". *(Davoren does so.)* Minnie, Donal; Donal, Minnie; good-bye now.
Davoren Here, what about your milk?
Minnie I haven't time to take it now. *(Slyly)* I'll come for it this evening.
　　　　[*They both go towards the door.*

Davoren Minnie, the kiss I didn't get.
Minnie What kiss?
Davoren When we were interrupted; you know, you little rogue, come, just one.
Minnie Quick, then.

[*Davoren kisses her and she runs out. Davoren returns thoughtfully to the table.*

Davoren Minnie, Donal; Donal, Minnie. <u>Very pretty, but very ignorant. A gunman on the run! Be careful, be careful, Donal Davoren. But Minnie is attracted to the idea, and I am attracted to Minnie. And what danger can there be in being the shadow of a gunman?</u>

　　　Curtain

☞ **Points to Note**

- Minnie Powell gives the gloomy and depressing world of the tenement slums a ray of light and hope. Her charm, self-confidence and honesty are remarkable by the fact that she is surrounded by quarrelling, ignorance, hypocrisy and insincerity.
- She makes the approach to Davoren, believing him to be a rebel gunman on the run. The love scene is the result of her admiration for someone that she mistakenly regards as a heroic patriot. Davoren, delighted by her admiration, does not tell her the truth. There is dramatic irony both in her misjudgement of Davoren and his misleading of Minnie. Had she known the truth - that he was a harmless poet and not a gunman - she would not have approached him.
- Davoren's question to Tommy Owens - *"Why should I be afraid of you Mr. Owens, or anybody else?"* - is uttered to impress Minnie. Davoren is clever enough to know how Tommy Owens will respond to the question. The question is uttered by Davoren in order to give extra weight to the (false) rumour that he is a gunman on the run.

The Shadow of a Gunman

- A similar utterance is made by Davoren moments later when he declares - *"I know nothing . . . . any connection"*. There is irony here as Davoren states the truth but intends that the other characters believe the opposite.

RHETORIC
- Rhetoric is the art of speaking persuasively for or against an idea. The term **Rhetoric** also describes language which is enriched with colourful poetic devices. **Empty rhetoric** is a term used to describe language with words which sound very impressive and rich but contain little or no coherent message or intelligent thought. In this regard, note the conversation between Owens and Davoren.
- Tommy Owens' declaration that he would *'die for Ireland'* is not an attempt to deceive others but rather himself. He goes on to claim that *'they'* never gave him a chance, which is pathetic nonsense.
- When Mrs. Henderson arrives with Mr. Gallogher in tow, Owens assumes control of the situation. His manner is intended to suggest that he is an important and close friend of Davoren. Again the situation is rich in dramatic irony and humour, as we can see beyond the respective poses of both Owens and Davoren.

MALAPROPISMS
- A *malapropism* is the incorrect use of a word, with comic results. The term comes from Mrs. Malaprop, a character from a play by Sheridan. Malapropisms generally occur when characters are trying to give an impression of being intelligent and educated. However, their misuse of words or the use of incorrect forms of words reveals the characters' pretensions. Many of the characters in the play use malapropisms, giving the play an extra humorous dimension. We encounter the first of many in the opening lines when Shields declares *"I was fast in the arms of Morpheus"*.

- Mrs. Henderson's language is rich in; *idioms* - *"Mr. Davoren is wan of ourselves"*; *malapropisms* - "in all *fairity*" and repeated *cliches* - "am I right or am I wrong". The effect is comic.
- Tommy Owens' foolish comment on the opening words of the letter is *ironic*. The words, by any stretch of the imagination, could not be regarded as *"a hard wallop at the British Empire"*.
- Mr. Gallogher's letter is extremely *verbose* and laden with legal *jargon* to the point that it sounds utterly ridiculous. *Verbose* is an adjective and means the use of more words than are necessary to convey an idea. *Jargon* is the special language of a certain group or profession. It is frequently pretentious, obscure and unintelligible to ordinary people. In the letter Gallogher attempts to strike the tone of a formal legal document. However, its misuse of words, its incorrect grammar and syntax, its jargon and its idioms reveal a good deal about the character of its author. He is under the false illusion that he is intelligent and literate. Gallogher's illusions are further strengthened by the praise and admiration of Tommy Owens and Mrs. Henderson.

The Shadow of a Gunman

- While the letter episode is comic drama at its funniest, it also provides us with a bitter reminder that illiteracy and lack of educational opportunities are the by-products of poverty and deprivation.
- Mr. Gallogher's opinion on Shields is a gem in itself and provides an apt, ironic comment on both of them.

PARADOX

- A *paradox* is a statement which *appears* to *contradict* itself. It is used in order to focus the attention of the reader on the point being stated. A simple example of a paradox is the proverb - "One must be cruel to be kind". The description of Shields as a 'wise fool' arises from Mrs. Henderson's observation on Shields.

- The title of the play comes from Davoren's words in the final lines of Act I. A gunman on the run is an illusion which is not of Davoren's own making - yet he goes along with it, enjoying the respect and admiration that the illusion brings. The closing words also reveal Davoren as a character who realises that he may be treading a dangerous path.

? Questions and Assignments

1. Write briefly on each of the pieces of dialogue that are underlined. Your answers should include (a) a brief explanation (b) what the words reveal about their speaker and other characters (c) where dramatic irony occurs, you should identify and explain it.

2. Describe your impressions of each of the characters in Act I. Refer to the text to support your views.

3. What part of Act I did you consider most humorous? Explain your answer.

4. O'Casey is renowned for his ability to capture the 'flavour' of the speech of ordinary Dubliners. Is there evidence of this in Act I? Explain with reference to the text.

5. "At no point in Act I are we allowed to forget the poverty and misery of the scene." Do you agree with this view? Explain your answer.

ACT II

The same as in Act I. But it is now night. Seumas *is in the bed that runs along the wall at back.* Davoren *is seated near the fire, to which he has drawn the table. He has a fountain-pen in his hand, and is attracted in thought towards the moon, which is shining in through the windows. An open writing-pad is on the table at* Davoren's *elbow. The bag left by* Maguire *is still in the same place.*

Davoren
The cold chaste moon, the Queen of Heaven's bright isles,
Who makes all beautiful on which she smiles;
That wandering shrine of soft yet icy flame,
Which ever is transformed yet still the same.

Ah, Shelley, Shelley, you yourself were a lovely human orb shining through clouds of whirling human dust. "She makes all beautiful on which she smiles." Ah, Shelley, she couldn't make this thrice accursed room beautiful. Her beams of beauty only make its horrors more full of horrors still. There is an ugliness that can be made beautiful, and there is an ugliness that can only be destroyed, and this is part of that ugliness. Donal, Donal, I fear your last state is worse that your first.

[*He lilts a verse, which he writes on the pad before him.*

When night advances through the sky with slow
And solemn tread.
The queenly moon looks down on life below,
As if she read
Man's soul, and in her scornful silence said:
All beautiful and happiest things are dead.

Seumas (*sleepily*). Donal, Donal, are you awake? (*A pause*). Donal, Donal, are you asleep?

Davoren   I'm neither awake nor asleep: I'm thinking.

Seumas   I was just thinkin', too - I was just thinkin', too, that Maguire is sorry now that he didn't come with me instead of going to Knocksedan. He caught something besides butterflies - two of them he got, one through each lung.

Davoren   The Irish people are very fond of turning a serious thing into a joke; that was a serious affair - for poor Maguire.

Seumas (*defensively*) Why didn't he do what he arranged to do? Did he think of me when he was goin' to Knocksedan? How can he expect me to have any sympathy with him now?

Davoren   He can hardly expect that now that he's dead.

Seumas   The Republicans 'll do a lot for him, now. How am I goin' to get back the things he has belongin' to me, either? There's some of them in that bag over there, but that's not quarter of what he had; an' I don't know where he was stoppin', for he left his old digs a week or so ago - I suppose there's nothing to be said about my loss; I'm to sing dumb.

Davoren   I hope there's nothing else in the bag, besides thread and hairpins.

Seumas   What else ud be in it? . . . . I can't sleep properly ever since they put on this damned curfew. A minute ago I thought I heard some of the oul' ones standin' at the door; they won't be satisfied till they bring a raid on the house; an' they never begin to stand at the door till after curfew . . . . Are you gone to bed, Donal?

Davoren   No; I'm trying to finish this poem.

Seumas   (*sitting up in bed*). If I was you I'd give that game up; it doesn't pay a working-man to write poetry. <u>I don't profess to know much about poetry</u> - I don't profess to know much about poetry - about poetry - I don't know much about the pearly glint of the morning dew, or the damask sweetness of the rare wild rose, or the subtle greenness of the serpent's eye - but I think a poet's claim to greatness depends upon his power to put passion in the common people.

Davoren Ay, passion to howl for his destruction. The People! Damn the people! <u>They live in the abyss, the poet lives on the mountain-top</u>; to the people there is no mystery of colour : it is simply the scarlet coat of the soldier; the purple vestments of a priest; the green banner of a party; the brown or blue overalls of industry. To them the might of design is a three-roomed house or a capacious bed. To them beauty is for sale in a butcher's shop. To the people the end of life is the life created for them; to the poet the end of life is the life that he creates for himself; life has a stifling grip upon the people's throat - it is the poet's musician. The poet ever strives to save the people; the people ever strive to destroy the poet. The people view life through creeds, through customs, and through necessities; the poet views creeds, customs, and necessities through life. The people . . . .

Seumas *(suddenly, and with a note of anxiety in his voice)*. Whisht! What's that? Is that the tappin' again?

Davoren Tappin'. What tappin'?

Seumas *(in an awed whisper)*. This is the second night I heard that tappin'! I believe it bodes no good to me. There, do you hear it again - a quiet, steady, mysterious tappin' on the wall.

Davoren I hear no tappin'.

Seumas It ud be better for me if you did. It's a sure sign of death when nobody hears it but meself.

Davoren Death! What the devil are you talking about, man?

Seumas I don't like it at all; there's always something like that heard when one of our family dies.

Davoren I don't know about that; but I know there's a hell of a lot of things heard when one of your family lives.

Seumas God between us an' all harm! Thank God I'm where I ought to be - in bed . . . . It's always best to be in your proper place when such things happen - Sacred Heart! There it is again; do you not hear it now?

Davoren Ah, for God's sake go asleep.

Seumas Do you believe in nothing?

Davoren I don't believe in tappin'.

Seumas Whisht, it's stopped again; I'll try to go asleep for fear it ud begin again.

Davoren Ay, do; and if it starts again I'll be sure to waken you up.   [*A pause.*

Seumas It's very cold to-night. Do you feel cold?

Davoren I thought you were goin' asleep?

Seumas The bloody cold won't let me . . . You'd want a pair of pyjamas on you. *(A pause)*. Did you every wear pyjamas, Donal?

Davoren No, no, no.

Seumas What kind of stuff is in them?

Davoren *(angrily)*. Oh it depends on the climate; in India, silk; in Italy, satin; and the Eskimo wears them made from the skin of the Polar bear.

Seumas *(emphatically)*. If you take my advice you'll get into bed - that poem is beginnin' to get on your nerves.

Davoren *(extinguishing the candle with a vicious blow)*. Right; I'm going to bed now, so you can shut up.

[*Visibility is still maintained from the light of the moon.*

Seumas I was goin' to say something when you put out the light - what's this it was? - um, um, oh, ay : when I was comin' in this evenin' I saw Minnie Powell goin' out. If I was you I wouldn't have that one comin' in here.

Davoren She comes in; I don't bring her in, do I?

Seumas The oul' ones'll be talkin', an' once they start you don't know how it'll end. Surely a man that has read Shelley couldn't be interested in an ignorant little bitch that thinks of nothin' but jazz dances, fox-trots, picture theatres an' dress.

Davoren Right glad I am that she thinks of dress, for she thinks of it in the right way, and makes herself a pleasant picture to the eye. Education has been wasted on many persons, teaching them to talk only, but leaving them with all their primitive instincts. Had poor Minnie received an education she would have been an artist. She is certainly a pretty girl. I'm sure she is a good girl, and I believe she is a brave girl.

Seumas A Helen of Troy come to live in a tenement! You think a lot about her simply because she thinks a lot about you, an' she thinks a lot about you because she looks upon you as a hero - a kind o' Paris . . . . she'd give the world an' all to be gaddin' about with a gunman. An' what ecstasy it ud give her if after a bit you were shot or hanged; she'd be able to go about then - like a good many more - singin', "I do not mourn me darlin' lost, for he fell in his Jacket Green". An' then, for a year an' a day, all round her hat she'd wear the Tricoloured Ribbon O, till she'd pick up an' marry someone else - possibly a British Tommy with a Mons Star. An' as for bein' brave, it's easy to be that when you've no cause for cowardice; I wouldn't care to have me life dependin' on brave little Minnie Powell - she wouldn't sacrifice a jazz dance to save it.

Davoren (*sitting on the bed and taking off his coat and vest, preparatory to going to bed*). There; that's enough about Minnie Powell. I'm afraid I'll soon have to be on the run out of this house, too; it is becoming painfully obvious that there is no peace to be found here.

Seumas Oh, this house is all right; barrin' the children, it does be quiet enough. Wasn't there children in the last place you were in too?

Davoren Ay, ten; (*viciously*) and they were all over forty.

[*A pause as Davoren is removing his collar and tie.*

Seumas Everything is very quiet now; I wonder what time is it?

Davoren The village cock hath thrice done salutation to the morn.

Seumas Shakespeare, Richard the III, Act Five, Scene III. It was Ratcliff said that to Richard just before the battle of Bosworth . . . . How peaceful the heavens look now with the moon in the

The Shadow of a Gunman

middle; you'd never think there were men prowlin' about tryin' to shoot each other. I don't know how a man who has shot any one can sleep in peace at night.

Davoren   There's plenty of men can't sleep in peace at night now unless they know that they have shot somebody.

Seumas   I wish to God it was all over. The country is gone mad. Instead of counting their beads now they're countin' bullets; their Hail Marys and paternosters are burstin' bombs - burstin' bombs, an' the rattle of machine-guns; petrol is their holy water; their Mass is a burnin' buildin'; their De Profundis is "The Soldiers' Song", an' their creed is, I believe in the gun almighty, maker of heaven an' earth - an' it's all for "the glory o' God an' the honour o' Ireland".

Davoren   I remember the time when you yourself believed in nothing but the gun.

Seumas   <u>Ay, when there wasn't a gun in the country; I've a different opinion now when there's nothin' but guns in the country</u> . . . . An' you daren't open your mouth, for Kathleen ní Houlihan is very different now to the woman who used to play the harp an' sing "Weep on, weep on, your hour is past", for she's a ragin' divil now, an' if you only look crooked at her you're sure of a punch in th' eye. But this is the way I look at it - I look at it this way : You're not goin' - you're not goin' to beat the British Empire - the British Empire, by shootin' an occasional Tommy at the corner of an occasional street. Besides, when the Tommies have the wind up - when the Tommies have the wind up they let bang at everything they see - they don't give a God's curse who they plug.

Davoren   <u>Maybe they ought to get down off the lorry and run to the Records Office to find out a man's pedigree before they plug him.</u>

Seumas   It's the civilians that suffer; when there's an ambush they don't know where to run. Shot in the back to save the British Empire, an' shot in the breast to save the soul of Ireland. I'm a Nationalist meself, right enough - a Nationalist right enough, but all the same - I'm a Nationalist right enough; I believe in the freedom of Ireland, an' that England has no right to be here, but I draw the line when I hear the gunmen blowin' about dyin' for the people, when it's the people that are dyin' for the gunmen! With all due respect to the gunmen, I don't want them to die for me.

Davoren   Not likely; you object to any one of them deliberately dying for you for fear that one of these days you might accidently die for one of them.

Seumas   You're one of the brave fellows that doesn't fear death.

Davoren   Why should I be afraid of it? It's all the same to me how it comes, where it comes, or when it comes. I leave fear of death to the people that are always praying for eternal life; "Death is here and death is there, death is busy everywhere".

Seumas   Ay, in Ireland. Thanks be to God I'm a daily communicant. There's a great comfort in religion; it makes a man strong in time of trouble an' brave in time of danger. No man need be afraid with a crowd of angels round him; thanks to God for His Holy religion!

Davoren   You're welcome to your angels; philosophy is mine; philosophy that makes the coward brave; the sufferer defiant; the weak strong; the . . .

[*A volley of shots is heard in a lane that runs parallel with the wall of the back-yard. Religion and philosophy are forgotten in the violent fear of a nervous equality.*

Seumas Jesus, Mary, an' Joseph, what's that?

Davoren My God, that's very close.

Seumas Is there no Christianity at all left in the country?

Davoren Are we ever again going to know what peace and security are?

Seumas If this continues much longer I'll be nothing but a galvanic battery o' shocks.

Davoren It's dangerous to be in and it's equally dangerous to be out.

Seumas This is a dangerous spot to be in with them windows; you couldn't tell the minute a bullet ud come in through one of them - through one of them, an' hit the - hit the - an' hit the . . . .

Davoren (*irritably*). Hit the what, man?

Seumas The wall.

Davoren Couldn't you say that at first without making a song about it?

Seumas (*suddenly*). I don't believe there's horses in the stable at all.

Davoren Stable! What stable are you talking about?

Seumas There's a stable at the back of the house with an entrance from the yard; it's used as a carpenter's shop. Didn't you often hear the peculiar noises at night? They give out that it's the horses shakin' their chains.

Davoren And what is it?

Seumas Oh, there I'll leave you!

Davoren Surely you don't mean . . . .

Seumas But I do mean it.

Davoren You do mean what?

Seumas I wouldn't - I wouldn't be surprised - wouldn't be surprised - surprised . . . .

Davoren Yes, yes, surprised - go on.

Seumas I wouldn't be surprised if they were manufacturin' bombs there.

Davoren My God, that's a pleasant contemplation! The sooner I'm on the run out of this house the better. How is it you never said anything about this before?

Seumas Well - well, I didn't want - I didn't want to - to . . . .

Davoren You didn't want to what?

Seumas I didn't want to frighten you.

Davoren (*sarcastically*). You're bloody kind!

[*A knock at the door; the voice of* Mrs. Grigson *heard.*

Mrs. Grigson Are you asleep, Mr. Shields?

Seumas What the devil can she want at this hour of the night? (*To* Mrs. Grigson) No, Mrs. Grigson, what is it?

Mrs. Grigson (*opening the door and standing at the threshold. She is a woman about forty, but looks much older. She is one of the cave dwellers of Dublin, living as she does in a tenement kitchen, to which only an occasional sickly beam of sunlight filters through a grating in the yard; the consequent general dimness of her abode has given her a habit of peering through half-closed eyes. She is slovenly dressed in an old skirt and bodice; her face is grimy, not because her habits are dirty - for, although she is untidy, she is a clean woman - but because of the smoky atmosphere of her room. Her hair is constantly falling over her face, which she is as frequently removing by rapid movements of her right hand*). He hasn't turned up yet, an' I'm stiff with the cold waitin' for him.

Seumas Mr. Grigson, is it?

Mrs. Grigson Adolphus, Mr. Shields, after takin' his tea at six o'clock - no, I'm tellin' a lie - it was before six, for I remember the Angelus was ringin' out an' we sittin' at the table - after takin' his tea he went out for a breath o' fresh air, an' I haven't seen sign or light of him

The Shadow of a Gunman

since. 'Clare to God me heart is up in me mouth, thinkin' he might be shot be the Black an' Tans.

Seumas Aw, he'll be all right, Mrs. Grigson. You ought to go to bed an' rest yourself; it's always the worst that comes into a body's mind; go to bed, Mr. Grigson, or you'll catch your death of cold.

Mrs. Grigson I'm afraid to go to bed, Mr. Shields, for I'm always in dread that some night or another, when he has a sup taken, he'll fall down the kitchen stairs an' break his neck. Not that I'd be any the worse if anything did happen to him, for you know the sort he is, Mr. Shields; sure he has me heart broke.

Seumas Don't be downhearted, Mrs. Grigson; he may take a thought one of these days an' turn over a new leaf.

Mrs. Grigson Sorra leaf Adolphus 'll ever turn over, he's too far gone in the horns for that now. Sure no one ud mind him takin' a pint or two, if he'd stop at that, but he won't; nothin' could fill him with beer, an' no matter how much he may have taken, when he's taken more he'll always say, "Here's the first today".

Davoren (*to Seumas*). Christ! Is she going to stop talking there all the night?

Seumas 'Sh, she'll hear you; right enough, the man has the poor woman's heart broke.

Davoren And because he has her heart broken, she's to have the privilege of breaking everybody else's.

Mrs. Grigson Mr. Shields.

Seumas Yes?

Mrs. Grigson Do the insurance companies pay if a man is shot after curfew?

Seumas Well, now, that's a thing I couldn't say, Mrs. Grigson.

Mrs. Grigson (*plaintively*). Isn't he a terrible man to be takin' such risks, an' not knowin' what'll happen to him? <u>He knows them Societies only want an excuse to do people out of their money</u> - is it after one, now, Mr. Shields?

Seumas Aw, it must be after one, Mrs. Grigson.

Mrs. Grigson (*emphatically*). Ah, then, if I was a young girl again I'd think twice before gettin' married. Whisht! There's somebody now - it's him, I know be the way he's fumblin'.

[*She goes out a little way. Stumbling steps are heard in the hall.*

Mrs. Grigson (*outside*). Is that you, Dolphie, dear?

[*After a few moments* Adolphus, *with* Mrs. Grigson *holding his arm, stumbles into the room.*

Mrs. Grigson Dolphie, dear, mind yourself.

Adolphus (*he is a man of forty-five, but looks, relatively, much younger than* Mrs. Grigson. *His occupation is that of a solicitor's clerk. He has all the appearance of being well fed; and, in fact, he gets most of the nourishment,* Mrs. Grigson *getting just enough to give her strength to do the necessary work of the household. On account of living most of his life out of the kitchen, his complexion is fresh, and his movements, even when sober, are livelier than those of his wife. His is comfortably dressed; heavy top-coat, soft trilby hat, a fancy coloured scarf about his neck, and he carries an umbrella*). I'm all right; do you see anything wrong with me?

Mrs. Grigson Of course you're all right, dear; there's no one mindin' you.

Adolphus Grigson Mindin' me, is it, mindin' me? He'd want to be a good thing that ud mind me. There's a man here - a man, mind you, afraid av nothin'

The Shadow of a Gunman

- not in this bloody house anyway.

Mrs. Grigson *(imploringly)*. Come on downstairs, Dolphie, dear; sure there's not one in the house ud say a word to you.

Adolphus Grigson Say a word to me, is it? He'd want to be a good thing that ud say anything to Dolphus Grigson. *(Loudly)* Is there anyone wants to say anything to Dolphus Grigson? If there is, he's here - a man, too - there's no blottin' it out - a man.

Mrs. Grigson You'll wake everybody in the house; can't you speak quiet?

Adolphus Grigson *(more loudly still)*. What do I care for anybody in the house? Are they keepin' me : are they givin' me anything? When they're keepin' Grigson it'll be time enough for them to talk. *(With a shout)* I can tell them Adolphus Grigson wasn't born in a bottle!

Mrs. Grigson *(tearfully)*. Why do you talk like that, dear? We all know you weren't born in a bottle.

Adolphus Grigson There's some of them in this house think Grigson was born in a bottle.

Davoren *(to Seumas)*. A most appropriate place for him to be born in.

Mrs. Grigson Come on down to bed, now, an' you can talk about them in the mornin'.

Grigson I'll talk about them, now; do you think I'm afraid of them? Dolphus Grigson's afraid av nothin', creepin' or walkin', - if there's any one in the house thinks he's fit to take a fall out av Adolphus Grigson, he's here - a man; they'll find that Grigson's no soft thing.

Davoren Ah me, alas! Pain, pain ever, for ever.

Mrs. Grigson Dolphie, dear, poor Mr. Davoren wants to go to bed.

The Shadow of a Gunman

Davoren Oh, she's terribly anxious about poor Mr. Davoren, all of a sudden.

Grigson *(stumbling towards Davoren, and holding out his hand).* Davoren! He's a man. Leave it there, mate. You needn't be afraid av Dolphus Grigson; there never was a drop av informer's blood in the whole family av Grigson. I don't know what you are or what you think, but you're a man, an' not like some of the goughers in this house, that ud hang you. Not referrin' to you, Mr. Shields.

Seumas I know that, Mr. Grigson; go on down, now, with Mrs. Grigson, an' have a sleep.

Grigson I tie myself to no woman's apron-strings, Mr. Shields; I know how to keep Mrs. Grigson in her place; I have the authority of the Bible for that. I know the Bible from cover to cover, Mr. Davoren, an' that's more than some in this house could say. And what does the Holy Scripture say about woman? It says, "The woman shall be subject to her husband", an' I'll see that Mrs. Grigson keeps the teachin' av the Holy Book in the letter an' in the spirit. If you've ever in trouble, Mr. Davoren, an' Grigson can help - I'm your man - have you me?

Davoren I have you, Mr. Grigson, I have you.

Grigson Right; I'm an Orangeman, an' I'm not ashamed av it, an' I'm not afraid av it, but I can feel for a true man, all the same - have *you* got me, Mr. Shields?

Seumas Oh, we know you well, Mr. Grigson; many a true Irishman was a Protestant - Tone, Emmet an' Parnell.

Grigson Mind you, I'm not sayin' as I agree with them you've mentioned, Mr. Shields, for the Bible forbids it, an' Adolphus Grigson 'll always abide be the Bible. Fear God an' honour the King - that's written in Holy Scripture, an' there's no blottin' it out. *(Pulling a bottle out of his pocket.)* But here, Mr. Davoren, have a drink, just to show there's no coolness.

Davoren No, no, Mr. Grigson, it's late now to take anything. Go on down with Mrs. Grigson, and we can have a chat in the morning.

Grigson Sure you won't have a drink?

Davoren Quite sure - thanks all the same.

Grigson *(drinking).* Here's the first today! To all true men, even if they were born in a bottle. Here's to King William, to the battle av the Boyne; to the Hobah Black Chapter - that's my Lodge, Mr. Davoren; an' to the Orange Lily O.

[*Singing in a loud shout:*

An' dud ya go to see the show, each rose an' pinkadilly O,
To feast your eyes an' view the prize won be the Orange Lily O.
The Vic'roy there, so debonair, just like a daffadilly O,
With Lady Clarke, blithe as a lark, approached the Orange Lily O.
    Heigh Ho the Lily O,
      The Royal, Loyal Lily O,
Beneath the sky what flower can vie with Erin's Orange Lily O!

Davoren Holy God, isn't this terrible!

Grigson *(singing):*

The elated Muse, to hear the news, jumped like a Connaught filly O,
As gossip Fame did loud proclaim the triumph av the Lily O.
The Lowland field may roses yield, gay heaths the High-lands hilly O,
But high or low no flower can show like Erin's Orange Lily O.
    Heigh Ho the Lily O,
      The Royal, Loyal Lily O,
Beneath the sky what flower can vie with Erin's Or . . . .

The Shadow of a Gunman

While Grigson *has been singing, the sound of a rapidly moving motor is heard, faintly at first, but growing rapidly louder, till it apparently stops suddenly somewhere very near the house, bringing* Grigson's *song to an abrupt conclusion. They are all startled, and listen attentively to the throbbing of the engines, which can be plainly heard.* Grigson *is considerably sobered, and anxiously keeps his eyes on the door.* Seumas *sits up in bed and listens anxiously.* Davoren, *with a shaking hand, lights the candle, and begins to search hurriedly among the books and papers on the table.*

Grigson (*with a tremor in his voice*). There's no need to be afraid, they couldn't be comin' here.

Mrs. Grigson God forbid! It ud be terrible if they came at this hour ov the night.

Seumas You never know now, Mrs. Grigson; they'd rush in on you when you'd be least expectin' them. What, in the name o' God, is goin' to come out of it all? Nobody now cares a traneen about the orders of the Ten Commandments; the only order that anybody minds now is, "Put your hands up". Oh, it's a hopeless country.

Grigson Whisht; do you hear them talking outside at the door? You're sure of your life nowhere now; it's just as safe to go everywhere as it is to anywhere. An' they don't give a damn whether you're a loyal man or not. If you're a Republican they make you sing "God save the King", an' if you're loyal they'll make you sing the "Soldiers' Song". The singin' ud be all right if they didn't make you dance afterwards.

Mrs. Grigson They'd hardly come here unless they heard something about Mr. Davoren.

Davoren About me! What could they hear about me?

Grigson You'll never get some people to keep their mouths shut. I was in the Blue Lion this evening, an' who do you think was there, blowin' out av him, but that little blower, Tommy Owens; there he was tellin' everybody that *he* knew where there was bombs; that *he* had a friend that was a General in the I.R.A.; that *he* could tell them what the Staff was thinkin' av doin'; that *he* could lay his hand on tons av revolvers; that they wasn't a mile from where he was livin', but that *he* knew his own know, an' would keep it to himself.

Seumas Well, God blast the little blower, anyway; it's the like ov him that deserves to be plugged! (*To* Davoren) What are you lookin' for among the books, Donal?

Davoren A letter that I got today from Mr. Gallogher and Mrs. Henderson; I'm blessed if I know where I put it.

Seumas (*peevishly*). Can't you look for it in the mornin'?

Davoren It's addressed to the Irish Republican Army, and, considering the possibility of a raid, it would be safer to get rid of it.

[*Shots again heard out in the lane, followed by loud shouts of "Halt, halt, halt!"*

Grigson <u>I think we had better be gettin' to bed, Debby; it's not right to be keepin' Mr. Davoren an' Mr. Shields awake.</u>

Seumas An' what made them give you such a letter as that; don't they know the state the country is in? An' you were worse to take it. Have you got it?

Davoren I can't find it anywhere; isn't this terrible!

Grigson Good-night, Mr. Davoren; good-night, Mr. Shields.

Mrs. Grigson Good-night, Mr. Shields; good-night, Mr. Davoren.

The Shadow of a Gunman

[*They go out.* Seumas *and* Davoren *are too much concerned about the letter to respond to their good-nights.*

Seumas What were you thinkin' of when you took such a letter as that? Ye gods, has nobody any brains at all, at all? Oh, this is a hopeless country. Did you try in your pockets?

Davoren (*searching in his pockets*). Oh, thanks be to God, here it is.

Seumas Burn it now, an', for God's sake, don't take any letters like that again.... There's the motor goin' away; we can sleep in peace now for the rest of the night. Just to make sure of everything now, have a look in that bag o' Maguire's : not that there can be anything in it.

Davoren If there's nothing in it, what's the good of looking?

Seumas It won't kill you to look, will it?

[Davoren *goes over to the bag, puts it on the table, opens it, and jumps back, his face pale and limbs trembling.*

Davoren My God, it's full of bombs, Mills bombs!

Seumas Holy Mother of God, you're jokin'!

Davoren If the Tans come you'll find whether I'm jokin' or no.

Seumas Isn't this a nice pickle to be in? St. Anthony, look down on us!

Davoren There's no use of blaming St. Anthony; why did you let Maguire leave the bag here?

Seumas Why did I let him leave the bag here; why did I let him leave the bag here! How did I know what was in it? Didn't I think there was nothin' in it but spoons an' hairpins? What'll we do now; what'll we do now? Mother o' God, grant there'll be no raid to-night. I knew things ud go wrong when I missed Mass this mornin'.

Davoren Give over your praying and let us try to think of what is best to be done. There's one thing certain : as soon as morning comes I'm on the run out of this house.

Seumas Thinkin' of yourself, like the rest of them. Leavin' me to bear the brunt of it.

Davoren And why shouldn't you bear the brunt of it? Maguire was no friend of mine; besides, it's your fault; you knew the sort of a man he was, and you should have been on your guard.

Seumas Did I know he was a gunman; did I know he was a gunman, did I know he was a gunman? Did....

Davoren Do you mean to tell me that...

Seumas Just a moment....

Davoren You didn't know...

Seumas Just a moment....

Davoren That Maguire was connected with....

Seumas (*loudly*). Just a moment; can't...

Davoren The Republican Movement? What's the use of trying to tell damn lies?

[Minnie Powell *rushes into the room. She is only partly dressed, and has thrown a shawl over her shoulders. She is in a state of intense excitement.*

Minnie Mr. Davoren, Donal, they're all round the house; they must be goin' to raid the place; I was lookin' out of the window an' I seen them; I do be on the watch every night; have you anything? If you have....

[*There is heard at street door a violent and continuous knocking, followed by the crash of glass and the beating of the door with rifle-butts.*

Minnie There they are, there they are, there they are!

The Shadow of a Gunman

[Davoren *reclines almost fainting on the bed;* Seumas *sits up in an attitude of agonised prayerfulness;* Minnie *alone retains her presence of mind. When she sees their panic she becomes calm, though her words are rapidly spoken, and her actions are performed with decisive celerity.*

Minnie What is it; what have you got; where are they?

Davoren Bombs, bombs, bombs; my God! in the bag on the table there; we're done, we're done!

Seumas Hail, Mary, full of grace - pray for us miserable sinners - Holy St. Anthony, do you hear them batterin' at the door - now an' at the hour of our death - say an act of contrition, Donal - there's the glass gone!

Minnie I'll take them to my room; maybe they won't search it; if they do aself; they won't harm a girl. Goodbye . . . . Donal.

[*She glances lovingly at Donal - who is only semi-conscious - as she rushes out with the bag.*

Seumas <u>If we come through this I'll never miss a Mass again!</u> If it's the Tommies it won't be so bad, but if it's the Tans, we're goin' to have a terrible time.

[*The street door is broken open and heavy steps are heard in the hall, punctuated with shouts of "'Old the light 'ere", "Put 'em up", etc. An* Auxiliary *opens the door of the room and enters, revolver in one hand and electric torch in the other. His uniform is black, and he wears a black beret.*

The Auxiliary 'Oo's 'ere?
Seumas *(as if he didn't know).* Who - who's that?

The Shadow of a Gunman

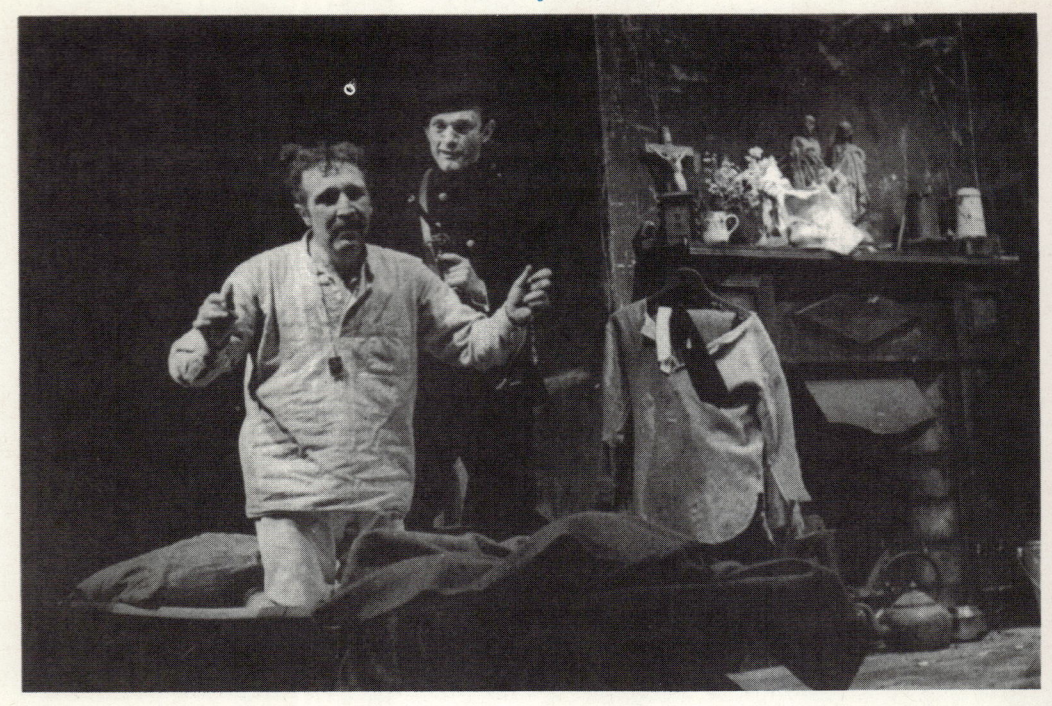

The Auxiliary (*peremptorily*). 'Oo's 'ere?

Seumas Only two men, mister; me an' me mate in t'other bed.

The Auxiliary Why didn't you open the door?

Seumas We didn't hear you knockin', sir.

The Auxiliary You must be a little awd of 'earing, ay?

Seumas I had rheumatic fever a few years ago, an' ever since I do be a - I do be a little deaf sometimes.

The Auxiliary (*to* Davoren) 'Ow is it you're not in bed?

Davoren I was in bed; when I heard the knockin' I got up to open the door.

The Auxiliary <u>You're a koind blowke, you are. Deloighted, like, to have a visit from us, ay? Ah?</u> (*Threatening to strike him*) Why down't you answer?

Davoren Yes, sir.

The Auxiliary What's your name?

Davoren Davoren. Dan Davoren, sir.

The Auxiliary You're not an Irishman, are you?

Davoren I-I-I was born in Ireland.

The Auxiliary Ow, you were, were you; Irish han' proud of it, ay? (*To Seamus*) What's your name?

Seumas Seuma . . . . Oh no; Jimmie Shields, sir.

The Auxiliary Ow, you're a selt (*he means a Celt*), one of the seltic race that speaks a lingo of its ahn, and that's going to overthrow the British Empire - I don't think! 'Ere, where's your gun?

Seumas I never had a gun in me hand in me life.

The Auxiliary Now; you wouldn't know what a gun is if you sawr one, I suppowse. (*Displaying his revolver in a careless way*) 'Ere, what's that?

Seumas Oh, be careful, please, be careful.

The Auxiliary Why, what 'ave I got to be careful abaht?

178

The Shadow of a Gunman

Seumas The gun; it-it-it might go off.

The Auxiliary An' what prawse if it did; it can easily be relowded. Any ammunition 'ere? What's in that press?

[*He searches and scatters the contents of press.*

Seumas Only a little bit o' grub; you'll get nothin' here, sir; no one in the house has any connection with politics.

The Auxiliary Now? I've never met a man yet that didn't say that, but we're a little bit too ikey now to be kidded with that sort of talk.

Seumas May I go an' get a drink o' water?

The Auxiliary You'll want a barrel of watah before you're done with us. (*The Auxiliary goes about the room exaimining places*) 'Ello, what's 'ere? A statue o' Christ! An' a Crucifix! You'd think you was in a bloomin' monastery.

[*Mrs. Grigson enters, dressed disorderly and her hair awry.*

Mrs. Grigson They're turning the place upside-down. Upstairs an' downstairs they're makin' a litter of everything! I declare to God, it's awful what law-abidin' people have to put up with. An' they found a pint bottle of whiskey under Dolphie's pillow, an' they're drinkin' every drop of it - an' Dolphie'll be like a devil in the mornin' when he finds he has no curer.

The Auxiliary (*all attention when he hears the word whiskey*). A bottle of whiskey, ay? 'Ere, where do you live - quick, where do you live?

Mrs. Grigson Down in the kitchen - an' when you go down will you ask them not to drink - oh, he's gone without listenin' to me.

[*While Mrs. Grigson is speaking the Auxiliary rushes out.*

Seumas (*anxiously to* Mrs. Grigson). Are they searchin' the whole house, Mrs. Grigson?

Mrs. Grigson They didn't leave a thing in the kitchen that they didn't flitter about the floor; the things in the cupboard, all the little odds an' ends I keep in the big box, an . . . .

Seumas Oh, they're a terrible gang of blaguards - did they go upstairs? - they'd hardly search Minnie Powell's room - do you think, would they, Mrs. Grigson?

Mrs. Grigson Just to show them the sort of a man he was, before they come in, Dolphie put the big Bible on the table, open at the First Gospel of St. Peter, second chapter, an' marked the thirteenth to the seventeenth verse in red ink - you know the passages, Mr. Shields - (*quoting*) :

"Submit yourselves to every ordinance of man for the Lord's sake : whether it be to the king, as supreme; or unto governors, as unto them that are sent by him for the punishment of evildoers, an' for the praise of them that do well.

. . . . Love the brotherhood. Fear God. Honour the King."

An' what do you think they did, Mr. Shields? They caught a hold of the Bible an' flung it on the floor - imagine that, Mr. Shields - flingin' the Bible on the floor! Then one of them says to another - "Jack," says he, "have you seen the light; is your soul saved?" An' then they grabbed hold of poor Dolphie, callin' him Mr. Moody an' Mr. Sankey, an' wanted him to offer up a prayer for the Irish Republic! An' when they were puttin' me out, there they had the poor man sittin' up in bed, his hands crossed on his breast, his eyes lookin' up at the ceilin', an' he singin' a hymn - "We shall meet in the Sweet Bye an' Bye" - an' all the time, Mr. Shields, there they were drinkin' his whiskey; there's torture for you, an' they all laughin' at poor Dolphie's terrible sufferin's.

Davoren In the name of all that's sensible, what did he want to bring whiskey home with him for? They're bad enough sober, what'll they be like when they're drunk?

Mrs. Grigson (*plaintively*). He always brings a drop home with him - he calls it his medicine.

Seumas (*still anxious*). They'll hardly search all the house; do you think they will, Mrs. Grigson?

Mrs. Grigson An' we have a picture over the mantelpiece of King William crossing the Boyne, an' do you know what they wanted to make out, Mr. Shields, that it was Robert Emmet, an' the picture of a secret society!

Seumas She's not listenin' to a word I'm sayin'! Oh, the country is hopeless an' the people is hopeless.

Davoren For God's sake tell her to go to hell out of this - she's worse than the Auxsie.

Seumas (*thoughtfully*). <u>Let her stay where she is; it's safer to have a woman in the room. If they come across the bombs I hope to God Minnie'll say nothin'.</u>

Davoren We're a pair of pitiable cowards to let poor Minnie suffer when we know that we and not she are to blame.

Seumas What else can we do, man? Do you want us to be done in? If you're anxious to be riddled, I'm not. Besides, they won't harm her, she's only a girl, an' so long as she keeps her mouth shut it'll be all right.

Davoren I wish I could be sure of that.

Seumas D'ye think are they goin', Mrs. Grigson? What are they doin' now?

Mrs. Grigson (*who is standing at the door, looking out into the hall*). There's not a bit of me that's not shakin' like a jelly!

Seumas Are they gone upstairs, Mrs. Grigson? Do you think, Mrs. Grigson, will they soon be goin'?

Mrs. Grigson When they were makin' poor Dolphie sit up in the bed, I 'clare to God I thought every minute I'd hear their guns goin' off, an' see poor Dolphie stretched out dead in the bed - whisht, God bless us, I think I hear him moanin'!

Seumas You might as well be talkin' to a stone! They're all hopeless, hopeless, hopeless! She thinks she hears him moanin'! It's bloody near time somebody made him moan!

Davoren (*with a sickly attempt at humour*). He's moaning for the loss of his whiskey.

[*During the foregoing dialogue the various sounds of a raid - orders, the tramping of heavy feet, the pulling about of furniture, etc. - are heard. Now a more definite and sustained commotion is apparent. Loud and angry, commands of "Go on", "Get out and get into the lorry", are heard, mingled with a girl's voice - it is Minnie's - shouting bravely, but a little hysterically, "Up the Republic".*

Mrs. Grigson (*from the door*). God save us, they're takin' Minnie, they're takin' Minnie Powell! (*Running out*) What in the name of God can have happened?

Seumas Holy Saint Anthony grant that she'll keep her mouth shut.

Davoren (*sitting down on the bed and covering his face with his hands*). We'll never again be able to lift up our heads if anything happens to Minnie.

Seumas For God's sake keep quiet or somebody'll hear you; nothin'll happen to her, nothin' at all - it'll be all right if she only keeps her mouth shut.

Mrs. Grigson *(running in)*. They're after gettin' a whole lot of stuff in Minnie's room! Enough to blow up the whole street, a Tan says! God tonight, who'd have ever thought that of Minnie Powell!

Seumas Did she say anything, is she sayin' anything, what's she sayin', Mrs. Grigson?

Mrs. Grigson She's shoutin' "Up the Republic" at the top of her voice. An' big Mrs. Henderson is fightin' with the soldiers - she's after nearly knockin' one of them down, an' they're puttin' her into the lorry too.

Seumas God blast her! Can she not mind her own business? What does she want here - didn't she know there was a raid on? Is the whole damn country goin' mad? They'll open fire in a minute an' innocent people'll be shot!

Davoren What way are they using Minnie, Mrs. Grigson; are they rough with her?

Mrs. Grigson They couldn't be half rough enough; the little hussy, to be so deceitful; she might as well have had the house blew up! God tonight, who'd think it was in Minnie Powell!

Seumas Oh, grant she won't say anything!

Mrs. Grigson There they're goin' away now; ah, then I hope they'll give that Minnie Powell a coolin'.

Seumas God grant she won't say anything! Are they gone, Mrs. Grigson?

Mrs. Grigson With her fancy stockin's, an' her pompoms, an' her crepe de chine blouses! I knew she'd come to no good!

Seumas God grant she'll keep her mouth shut! Are they gone, Mrs. Grigson?

Mrs. Grigson They're gone, Mr. Shields, an' here's poor Dolphie an' not a feather astray on him. Oh, Dolphie, dear, you're all right, thanks to God; I thought you'd never see the mornin'.

Grigson *(entering without coat or vest)*. Of course I'm all right; what ud put a bother on Dolphie Grigson? - not the Tans anyway!

Mrs. Grigson When I seen you stretched out on the bed, an' you . . . . singin' a hymn . . . .

Grigson *(fearful of possible humiliation)*. Who was singin' a hymn? D'ye hear me talkin' to you - where did you hear me singin' a hymn?

Mrs. Grigson I was only jokin', Dolphie, dear; I . . . .

Grigson Your place is below, an' not gosterin' here to men; down with you quick!

[*Mrs. Grigson hurriedly leaves the room.*

Grigson *(nonchalantly taking out his pipe, filling it, lighting it, and beginning to smoke)*. Excitin' few moments, Mr. Davoren; Mrs. G lost her head completely - panic-stricken. But that's only natural, all women is very nervous. The only thing to do is to show them that they can't put the wind up you; show the least sign of fright an' they'd walk on you, simply walk on you. Two of them come down - "Put them up", revolvers under your nose - you know, the usual way. "What's all the bother about?" says I, quite calm. "No bother at all," says one of them, "only this gun might go off an' hit somebody - have you me?" says he. "What if it does," says I; "a man can only die once, an' you'll find Grigson won't squeal". "God, you're a cool one," says the other, "there's no blottin' it out."

Seumas That's the best way to take them; it only makes things worse to show that you've got the wind up. "Any ammunition here?" says the fellow that come in here. "I don't think so," says I, "but you better have a look." "No back talk," says he, "or you might get plugged." "I don't know of any clause," says I, "in the British Constitution that makes it a crime for a man to speak in his own room," - with that, he just had a look round, an' off he went.

Grigson If a man keeps a stiff upper front - Merciful God, there's an ambush!

[*Explosions of two bursting bombs are heard on the street outside the house, followed by fierce and rapid revolver fire. People are heard rushing into the hall, and there is general clamour and confusion.* Seumas *and* Davoren *cower down in the room;* Grigson, *after a few moments' hesitation, frankly rushes out of the room to what he conceives to be the safer asylum of the kitchen. A lull follows, punctured by an odd rifle-shot; then comes a peculiar and ominous stillness, broken in a few moments by the sounds of voices and movement. Questions are heard being asked:* "Who was it was killed?", "Where was she shot?" *which are answered by:* "Minnie Powell"; "She went to jump off the lorry an' she was shot"; "She's not dead, is she?"; "They say she's dead - shot through the buzzom!"

Davoren (*in a tone of horror-stricken doubt*). D'ye hear what they're sayin', Shields d'ye hear what they're sayin' - Minnie Powell is shot.

Seumas For God's sake speak easy, an' don't bring them in here on top of us again.

Davoren Is that all you're thinking of? Do you realise that she has been shot to save us?

Seumas Is it my fault; am I to blame?

Davoren It is your fault and mine, both; oh, we're a pair of dastardly cowards to have to let her do what she did.

Seumas She did it off her own bat - we didn't ask her to do it.

[Mrs. Grigson *enters. She is excited and semi-hysterical, and sincerely affected by the tragic occurrence.*

Mrs. Grigson (*falling down in a sitting posture on one of the beds*). What's goin' to happen next! Oh, Mr. Davoren, isn't it terrible, isn't it terrible! Minnie Powell, poor little Minnie Powell's been shot dead! They were raidin' a house a few doors down, an' had just got up in their lorries to go away, when they was ambushed. You never heard such shootin'! An' in the thick of it, poor Minnie went to jump off the lorry she was on, an' she was shot through the buzzom. Oh, it was horrible to see the blood pourin' out, an' Minnie moanin'. They found some paper in her breast, with "Minnie" written on it, an' some other name they couldn't make out with the blood; the officer kep' it. The ambulance is bringin' her to the hospital, but what good's that when she's dead! Poor little Minnie, poor little Minnie Powell, to think of you full of a life a few minutes ago, an' now she's dead!

Davoren Ah me, alas! Pain, pain, pain ever, for ever! It's terrible to think that little Minnie is dead, but it's still more terrible to think that Davoren and Shields are alive! Oh, Donal Davoren, shame is your portion now till the silver cord is loosened and the golden bowl be broken. Oh, Davoren, Donal Davoren, poet and poltroon, poltroon and poet!

Seumas (*solemnly*). I knew something ud come of the tappin' on the wall!

CURTAIN

The Shadow of a Gunman

👉 Points to Note

- ACT II, like ACT I, begins with Davoren quoting poetry and Shields in bed. Now that it is night, the gloomy and melancholy mood of the scene is emphasised even more.
- There is much black humour in Shields' comments on Maguire's death. He adopts a self-righteous 'it serves him right' tone.
- Though Maguire only makes a brief appearance in the play he is still an important character. He serves as a ***contrast*** with most of the other figures in the play. We, the audience, can see that their 'big talk' does not match their actions. Maguire, on the other hand, presents himself as a harmless pedlar who takes a day off to go out hunting butterflies. Beneath this front was an underground fighter who was convinced of the necessity of his actions.

    Unlike the other characters, (with the exception of Minnie Powell) Maguire was prepared to suffer the consequences of his beliefs.

    This portrayal of Maguire should not be seen as support by O'Casey for Maguire's political beliefs. He is important not because he is fighting for Ireland's independence but rather because he dies for his beliefs.
- The exchanges between Shields and Davoren on poetry reveal an important side of Davoren's character. He regards himself as above the ordinary people because of his poetic gifts. He dislikes contact with other humans. He barely tolerates Shields, curses visitors and treats their requests with scorn. He accepts Gallogher's letter simply to give credence to the 'gunman on the run' rumour and impress Minnie Powell. Even Minnie's advances are initially rejected by Davoren.
- *"I wouldn't care to have my life depending on brave little Minnie Powell - she wouldn't sacrifice a jazz dance to save it"* declares Shields. There is **double irony** here. Shields accuses Minnie of cowardice - yet it is she who saves his life. Nevertheless, there is an unintentional truth in his words for Minnie would certainly not sacrifice her life for somebody like Shields.
- In the exchanges between Shields and Davoren there are some examples of clever verbal irony. Note Shields' observation - *"I don't know how a man who has shot any one can sleep in peace at night"* and Davoren's witty rejoinder. Note also Shields' comment on *"the gunmen blowin' about dyin' for the people, when it's the people that are dyin' for the gunmen!"* Both of these observations (equally relevant to the present time) reflect O'Casey's vision of war through the sufferings of the ordinary people and not through the haze of sentimental patriotism. However, these observations by Shields do not cast him in the role of the conscientious pacifist. They are merely justifications for his own cowardice.
- Responding to Shields' taunt, Davoren declares - *"Why should I be afraid of it? (death) It's all the same to me how it comes, where it comes or when it comes."* In the light of subsequent events there is tragic irony in his words, i.e. he believes them to be true but they prove not to be.
- There is comic irony in their fine words on the sources of their courage - religion in the case of Shields and philosophy in the case of Davoren - when we observe their fearful reaction to the shots outside.

The Shadow of a Gunman

- Mrs. Grigson's concern is not merely about her husband's safety. His arrival marks the beginning of another very amusing episode in the play. He speaks about himself - frequently in the third person - as he imagines (or wishes?) others to do so. The dramatic irony here is that Mr. Grigson too is unable to see himself as he really is.
- Grigson's comments on Tommy Owens reveal Owens as a foolish and untrustworthy braggart.
- During the raid Grigson is prepared to humiliate himself in order to humour the soldiers. After it is over he provides an utterly untruthful version of how he dealt with the soldiers, unaware of his wife's truthful report. Unknowingly, he reveals himself as a coward, a liar and a boaster.
- Shields matches Grigson's account of how he behaved towards the soldiers with an equally fictitious story.
- His repeated response to Minnie's action - *"... if only she keeps her mouth shut ..."* yet again reveals the low nature of Shields' character.
- During the raid Minnie Powell proves herself true to her convictions. Impulsively she takes on a task that she must know to be extremely risky. She rises even more in our estimation by the fact that others who are utterly worthless, speak disparagingly of her.
- While Minnie Powell's death is the most tragic event in the play, the tragedy is deepened by the fact that she died for an illusion. Her admiration for Davoren, whom she imagined to be somebody he was not, led her to sacrifice her life not only for her lover but for someone she thought was a self-sacrificing patriot.
- None of the play's characters who are caught in a web of their own illusions ever succeed in gaining any insight into the kind of people they really are. We, the audience, see them as they are and for us they become figures of fun - except for Minnie who arouses our compassion. This is the ***dramatic irony*** that is present throughout the play.
- In this respect, however, Davoren cannot be included. The central character in the play and always on stage, Davoren ultimately sees the meaning of his own behaviour and its tragic results - *"We're a pair of pitiable cowards to let poor Minnie suffer when we know that we and not she are to blame!"*

The play closes with Davoren declaring the shame he feels - *"O Donal Davoren, shame is your portion now till the silver cord is loosened . . . ."* One wonders though if he is sincere or just toying with an idea for a new poem.

? Questions and Assignments contd.

6. Write briefly on each of the pieces of dialogue that are underlined. Your answers should include (a) a brief explanation, (b) what the words reveal about their speaker and other characters and (c) where dramatic irony or figurative speech occurs, you should identify and explain them.
7. Write a full character sketch on each of the characters in the play.
8. Describe (a) the raid and (b) the circumstances of Minnie Powell's death.

The Shadow of a Gunman

9. Imagine that the soldiers discovered the bombs in Shields' room and write the dialogue for this episode.
10. Here are some common audience responses to plays - laughter; anger; inspiration; compassion; new understanding; satisfaction; unease and tension. Which of these responses did you feel when studying the play?
    Write at least 150 words explaining why you felt as you did.
11. Study each of the black and white photographs (on pages 149, 161, 164, 173, 177 and 178) and (i) write an accurate description of each photograph (ii) identify, as precisely as possible, the part of the play each photograph depicts. Give reasons for your answer.

✓ Q.1 — Sample Answer

"You're too thin-skinned altogether" - Shields to Davoren.

(i) Shields tells this to Davoren after the landlord's visit. Davoren is threatening to leave the house. Shields is probably worrying about no longer getting whatever rent Davoren pays him. Although there is no mention in the play of Davoren paying Shields' rent it is unlikely that Shields allows him to stay for nothing. Shields is not worried about the landlord's threats and means that Davoren shouldn't be either.

(ii) The words point to a difference between Shields and Davoren. Shields is certainly not a thin-skinned character - he cares nothing about anybody. He regards 'thin-skin' as a flaw in a personality.

(iii) 'Thin-skinned' is an idiom that means sensitive.

✓ Q.2 — Sample Answer

Tommy Owens is an utterly contemptible person. His first words are a lie. He tries to impress on Davoren that he is a trustworthy fellow. He tells Davoren to check him out with Mr. Shields. Mr. Shields is not the type of person from whom anyone with sense would seek a recommendation.

He speaks in nods and winks and relies on idioms - *"no flies on Tommy - got me?"* and *"a nod's as good as a wink"*.

He whinges on about never being given 'the chance' to die for Ireland. This is nonsense as all he had to do was join up - if they'd have him. When Mrs. Henderson and Mr. Gallogher arrive, Owens pretends to be a close friend of Davoren and tries to give the impression of being important.

We later learn that he was bragging in the pub about how close he was to the top Republicans. As well as being utter lies this shows how unreliable he would be as a member of that organisation.

Our last impression of him is when he declares that he hasn't the price of a paper - *"I haven't got a make"*. This was obviously a lie but it also shows him to be someone who wasn't ready to sacrifice a halfpenny *(make)* let alone his life.

✓ Q.6 — Sample Answer

(i) *"He knows them Societies only want an excuse to do people out of their money"* - Mrs. Grigson to Shields.

    Mrs. Grigson arrives in Shields' room around one in the morning. She claims that she is worried about her husband's safety as he still has not returned home. However, these words reveal the real cause of her worry - will the insurance company pay out if Mr. Grigson is shot after curfew? There is dramatic irony in her words as she reveals her true nature in them. There is also a touch of black humour in her words. She is almost saying *"Why hasn't my husband the sense to get killed in broad daylight?"* and *". . . to do people out of their money"* is a colloquialism meaning 'to defraud people'.

(ii) *"Your place is below and not gosterin' here to men; down with you quick"* - Grigson to his wife.

    Mr. Grigson is speaking to his wife. It is after the raid. She is in Shields' room and she has told Shields and Davoren, in great detail, how the Tans treated her husband. He now arrives just as she is referring to the hymn that he was forced to sing. He orders his wife back downstairs, afraid that she would humiliate him in front of Davoren and Shields. However, Grigson does not realise that they have already been told what happened.

    The words are those of a bully. Grigson has been shown up to be a coward but in order to show his 'toughness' he speaks to his wife like one would speak to a dog. Courage is not about pushing around those who are weaker than yourself. The words *"down below"* refers to Grigson's room but could also reflect Grigson's attitude towards his wife - her place was in a lower rank to the men. "Gosterin' " (Gostering) is obviously a piece of slang meaning chatting or gossiping. It is not used today, except by some older people.

ERNIE'S INCREDIBLE ILLUCINATIONS

—Alan Ayckbourn

> As well as being a play to read and enjoy, *Ernie's Incredible Illucinations* offers plenty of scope for a production by a class. Its large cast gives everybody in the class an opportunity to get involved in acting. The play also provides scope for an imaginative approach to set construction, costume design and sound effects.
>
> A small number of slight changes in the script are all that is needed to give the play an Irish setting. For all budding playwrights, the loose plot of the play allows for the adaptation of existing scenes or the addition of new ones (see **Questions and Assignments**). This edition of the play has been divided into five scenes for classroom/study purposes. It is suggested that the play be read in full before any of the Questions and Assignments are attempted.

Characters

Ernie	Man
Mum	Woman
Dad	Kid Saracen
Receptionist	Second Man
Doctor	Lady
Officer	Library Attendant
Auntie May	Girl Librarian
First Barker	Lady Librarian
Second Barker	A Tramp
Third Barker	Patients
Fourth Barker	Soldiers
Referee	Crowds
Timekeeper	Boxers

The action takes place in a doctor's waiting-room and surgery - and elsewhere.

Time - the present

I

At one side of the stage is a doctor's waiting-room. It is filled with an assortment of miserable-looking patients, coughing, wheezing, sneezing and moaning. Amongst them sit Mr. and Mrs. Fraser and their son, Ernie.

Ernie *(to the Audience, after a second)* If you ever want to feel ill - just go and spend a happy half-hour in a doctor's waiting-room. If you're not ill when you get there, you will be when you leave.

A man enters, having seen the doctor. He is moaning. He crosses the waiting-room and goes out. The other patients look at him and sorrowfully shake their heads. The Receptionist enters.

Receptionist   Mr. and Mrs. Fraser.

Mum and Dad rise

Doctor will see you now.
Mum Thank you. Come on, Ernie.

Mum and Dad and Ernie follow the Receptionist across the stage to the Doctor who sits behind a table.

'Morning Doctor.

The Receptionist leaves

Ernie's Incredible Illucinations

> **? Questions and Assignments**
>
> 1. Write a set of more detailed stage directions for the 'miserable-looking patients'. You should specify how many of them were in the waiting-room as well as details of the costume and behaviour of each. You should also include details of 'props'. Such a scene could provide two or three minutes of comic theatre without any dialogue whatsoever.
> 2. Give a set of clear directions on how this opening scene could be staged. You will have to consider what happens to the people in the waiting-room. Do they leave the stage? Where will the doctor be positioned? You may illustrate your answer with a sketch or diagram.

II

Doctor Ah. Ah. Mr. and Mrs. Fraser. Is that it?
Mum That's right. I'm Mrs. Fraser - and this is my husband, Mr. Fraser - and this is our son - Ernie.
Doctor Ah yes. Ernie. I've been hearing all sorts of things about you, young Ernie. Now, what have you been up to, eh?
Dad Illucinations.
Doctor I beg your pardon?
Dad Illucinations.
Doctor Oh, yes, illuci - quite, yes.
Mum What my husband means, Doctor, is that Ernie has been creating these illusions.
Doctor Ah.
Mum Well, they're more than illusions, really.
Dad I'll say.
Doctor Beg Pardon?
Dad I'll say.
Mum He's been causing that much trouble. At school, at home, everywhere he goes. I mean we can't go on like this. His dad's not as strong as he was, are you, Albert?
Dad No.
Doctor What?
Dad No.
Doctor Perhaps it would be better if you told me a little more about it. When did you first notice this . . . .?
Mum Ah well . . . .
Dad Ah.
Mum Now then . . . .
Dad Now . . . .
Mum He'd have been . . . . well, it'd have been about . . . . near enough . . . er . . .
Doctor Go on.

Ernie steps forward. During his speech Mum and Dad remain seated. The Doctor moves to the side of the stage, produces a notebook and makes notes on what follows

Ernie It started with daydreams. You know, the sort everybody gets. Where you suddenly score a hat trick in the last five minutes of the Cup Final, or you bowl out the West Indies for ten runs — or saving your granny from a blazing helicopter, all that sort of rubbish. It was one wet Saturday afternoon and me and my mum and my dad were all sitting about in the happy home having one of those exciting afternoon rave-ups we usually have in our house.

Ernie sits at the table in the Doctor's chair and starts to read a book. Mum has started

Ernie's Incredible Illucinations

knitting and Dad just sits, gazing ahead of him. There is a long silence.

Ernie It was all go in our house.

Pause

Mum I thought you'd be at the match today, Albert.

Dad Not today.

Mum Not often you miss a game.

Dad They're playing away.

Mum Oh.

Dad In Birmingham. I'm damned if I'm going to Birmingham. Even for United.

Ernie Meanwhile - while this exciting discussion was in progress, I was reading this book about the French wartime resistance workers and of the dangers they faced - often arrested in their homes. I started wondering what would happen if a squad of soldiers turned up at our front door, having been tipped off about the secret radio transmitter hidden in our cistern - when suddenly . . . .

? Questions and Assignments

1. In the last piece of dialogue in this section Ernie refers to *'this exciting discussion'*. To what discussion was he referring? Why did he describe it as 'exciting'?
2. Write an alternative 'discussion' to that referred to by Ernie, but make it equally 'exciting'. You may make it longer than the original piece.

III

The tramp of feet, and a squad of soldiers comes marching on and up to their front door.

Officer Halte! *(He bangs on the door)*

Pause

Dad That the door?
Mum What?
Dad The door.
Mum Was it?
Officer Open zis door. Open the door! *(He knocks again)*
Mum Oh, that'll be the milkman wanting his money. He always comes round about now. Albert, have you got ten bob?
Dad *(fumbling in his pockets)* Ah . . . .
Officer *(shouting)* Open zis door immediately. Or I shall order my men to break it down! *(He bangs on the door again)*

Ernie's Incredible Illucinations

Mum Just a minute. Coming.
Dad Should have one somewhere . . . .
Officer We know you're in there, English spy! Come out with your hands up . . . .!
Mum What's he shouting about? Oh, I'd better ask him for three pints next week, if Auntie May's coming . . . .
Officer Zis is your last chance . . . . *(He knocks again)*
Mum Oh shut up . . . .

The Officer signals his men. Two of them step back, brace their shoulders and prepare to charge the door

I'm coming - I'm coming.

Ernie I shouldn't go out there, Mum . . . .
Mum What?
Ernie I said don't go out there.
Mum What . . . .?
Ernie It's not the milkman. It's a squad of enemy soldiers.
Mum Who?
Ernie They've come for me . . . .
Mum Who has?
Ernie The soldiers. They've found out about the radio transmitter.
Mum What radio?
Dad Hey, here, that's a point. Have you paid our telly licence yet, Ethel? It might be the detector van.
Mum Oh, sit down, Albert. Stop worrying. It's just Ernie. Shut up, Ernie.
Ernie But Mum . . . .
Dad I think I'll take the telly upstairs. Just in case . . . .

The Soldiers charge at the door. A loud crash.

Ernie Don't go out, Mum.
Mum Shut up!
Dad *(picking up the television, struggling with it)* Just take it upstairs.

Ernie *(to Mum)* Don't go!
Mum I can't leave him out there. The way he's going he'll have the door off its hinges in a minute . . . . *(She moves to the door)*
Dad Mind your backs. Out of my way . . .
Ernie Mum . . . .

Mum opens the door just as the two Soldiers are charging for the second time. They shoot past her, straight into the hall, collide with Dad and land in a heap with him. Dad manages to hold the television above his head and save it from breaking.

Mum Hey . . . .
Dad Oy!

The Officer and the other Soldiers enter. Ernie crouches behind the table.

Officer Ah-ha! The house is surrounded.
Mum Who are you?
Officer Put up your hands. My men will search the house.
Dad *(feebly)* Hey . . . .
Officer *(shouting up the stairs)* We know you're hiding in here, you can't get away...
Dad Hey - *hey* - HEY!
Officer Ah-ha. What have we here?
Dad Oh. It's the telly. The neighbour's telly. Not mine.
Officer Ah-ha.
Dad Just fixing it for him, you see . . . .
Officer Outside.
Dad Eh?
Officer You will come with me.
Dad What, in this? I'm not going out in this rain.
Officer Outside or I shoot.
Dad Here . . . .
Mum Albert . . . .
Ernie Hold it! Drop those guns!
Officer Ah, so . . . . *(He raises his gun)*

Ernie's Incredible Illucinations

> **? Questions and Assignments**
>
> 1. This scene is the result of Ernie reading a book about French wartime resistance workers. Imagine, instead, that he had been watching a horror film or a cowboy film and rewrite this scene.

Ernie Da-da-da-da-da-da-da-da-da-da-da.

The Soldiers collapse and are strewn all over the hall. Mum screams. Then there is a silence

Mum Oh, Ernie. What have you done?
Ernie Sorry, Mum.
Dad Oh, lad . . . .
Mum Are they - dead?
Dad Yes.

Mum screams again

    Steady, steady. This needs thinking about.

Mum What about the neighbours?
Dad Could create a bit of gossip, this could.
Mum What about the carpet? Look at it.
Dad Hasn't done that much good.
Mum What'll we do with them?
Dad Needs a bit of thinking about.

Ernie steps forward. As he speaks and during the next section, Dad and Mum carry off the bodies

Ernie Well, Mum and Dad decided that the best thing to do was to pretend it hadn't happened. That was usually the way they coped with all emergencies . . . .

The Doctor steps forward

Mum *(struggling with a body)* We waited till it got dark, you see . . . .

Doctor Yes? And then . . . .?
Dad We dumped 'em.
Doctor I beg your pardon?
Dad We dumped 'em. Took 'em out and dumped 'em.
Doctor Dumped them? Where, for heaven's sake?
Dad Oh - bus shelters - park benches . . . .
Mum Corporation car-park.
Dad Left one in the all-night cafeteria.
Mum And one in the Garden of Rest.
Dad Caused a bit of a rumpus.
Doctor I'm not surprised.
Mum We had the police round our way for days - trying to sort it out . . . .
Dad They never did get to the bottom of it, though.
Doctor Extraordinary. And then?
Ernie *(stepping forward)* And then - Auntie May arrived to stay. I liked my Auntie May.

IV

Auntie May enters

The Doctor steps back again

Auntie 'Ullo, Ernie lad. Have a sweetie.
Ernie Ta, Auntie. And Auntie May took me to the fair.

The stage is filled with jostling people, barkers and fairground music. The Barkers speak simultaneously

Ernie's Incredible Illucinations

First Barker Yes, indeed, the world's tallest man! He's so tall, madam, his breakfast is still sliding down him at tea time. Come along now, sir. Come inside now . . . .

Second Barker Ladies and gentlemen. I am prepared to guarantee that you will never again, during your lifetimes, see anything as unbelievably amazing as the Incredible Porcupine Woman. See her quills and get your thrills. Direct from the unexplored South African Jungle . . .

Third Barker Try your luck - come along, madam - leave your husband there, dear, he'll still be there when you come back - tell you what - if he isn't I can sell you a replacement - five shots for sixpence - knock 'em all down and pick up what you like . . . .

Ernie Can I have a go on that, Auntie?

Auntie Not now, Ernie.

Ernie Oh go on, Auntie May.

Auntie I want a cup of tea.

Ernie Have an ice-cream.

Auntie I've had three. I can't have any more. It'll bring on my condition . . . .

Ernie What condition, Auntie?

Auntie Never you mind what. But I should never have had that candy floss as well. I'll suffer for it.

Fourth Barker Just about to start, ladies and gentlemen. A heavyweight boxing bout, featuring the one and only unofficial challenger for the heavyweight championship of the world - Kid Saracen. The Kid will be fighting this afternoon, for the very first time, a demonstration contest against the new sensation from Tyneside, Eddie "Grinder" Edwards. In addition, ladies and gentlemen, the Kid is offering fifty pounds - yes, fifty pounds - to any challenger who manages to last three three-minute rounds . . . .

Ernie Oh, come on, Auntie. Let's go in and watch.

Auntie What is it?

Ernie Boxing.

Auntie Boxing? I'm not watching any boxing. I don't mind wrestling but I'm not watching boxing. It's bloodthirsty.

Ernie Auntie . . . .

Auntie Nasty stuff, boxing . . . .

Fourth Barker Come along, lady. Bring in the young gentleman. Let him see the action . . . .

Auntie Oh no . . . .

Fourth Barker Come along. Two is it?

Ernie Yes please. Two.

Fourth Barker Thank you, son.

Auntie Eh?

Ernie This way, Auntie.

Before Auntie May can protest, she and Ernie are inside the boxing-booth. The Crowd have formed a square around the ring in which stand Kid Saracen, Eddie Edwards and the Referee

Referee Ladies and gentlemen, introducing on my right, the ex-unofficial challenger for the World Heavyweight Championship - KID SARACEN . . . .

Boos from the Crowd

And on my left, the challenger from Newcastle upon Tyne - EDDIE EDWARDS . . . .

The Crowd cheers

(To the boxers) Right, I want a good, clean fight, lads. No low blows and when I say "break" - stop boxing right away. Good luck.

Timekeeper Seconds out.

The bell rings. The Crowd cheers as the boxers size each other up. They mostly

Ernie's Incredible Illucinations

cheer on Edwards - "Come on, Eddie", "Murder him, Eddie", etc. The boxers swap a few punches.

Auntie Oooh! I can't look.

The man next to her starts cheering

Man Flatten him, Eddie!
Auntie peers out from behind her hands in time to see the Kid clout Eddie fairly hard

Auntie Hey, you stop that!
Man Get at him, Eddie . . . .!
Auntie Yes, that's right, get at him!
Man Hit him!
Auntie Knock him down!
Man Smash him!
Auntie Batter him! *(She starts to wave her arms about in support of Eddie, throwing punches at the air)*
Man That's it, missis. You show 'em.
Auntie I would, I would.
Man Give 'em a run for their money, would you?
Auntie I'm not that old . . . .
Man Eddie!
Auntie Come on, Eddie!
Ernie Eddie!

In the ring the Kid throws a terrific blow which brings Eddie to his knees

Referee One - two - three -
Man Get up, Eddie . . . .
Auntie Get up . . . . get up . . . .
Referee - four . . . .

Eddie rises and blunders round the ring. The Kid knocks him clean out. The Referee counts him out. The Crowd boos wildly. The Kid walks smugly round the ring, his hands raised above his head in triumph.

Auntie You brute.

Man Boo. Dirty fight . . . .
Auntie Bully . . . .
Referee *(quietening the Crowd)* And now, ladies and gentlemen, the Kid wishes to issue a challenge to any person here who would like to try his skill at lasting three rounds - any person here. Come along now - anybody care to try . . . .

Muttering from the Crowd

Auntie *(to the Man)* Go on then.
Man Who, me?
Auntie What are you frightened of, then?
Man I'm frightened of him . . . .
Referee Come along now. We're not asking you to do it for nothing. We're offering fifty pounds - fifty pounds, gentlemen . . .
Auntie Go on. Fifty quid.
Man I'd need that to pay the hospital bill...
Auntie Go on . . . .
Man It's all right for you, lady - just standing there telling other people to go and get their noses broken.
Auntie All right, then. I'll go in myself. Excuse me . . . . *(She starts to push through the Crowd towards the ring)*
Man Hey . . . .

193

Ernie's Incredible Illucinations

Ernie Auntie, where are you going?
Auntie Out of my way . . . .
Man Hey, stop her - she's off her nut . . .
Ernie Auntie!
Auntie (*hailing the Referee*) Hey, you . . .
Referee Hallo, lady, what can we do for you? Come to challenge him, have you?

Laughter from the Crowd

Auntie That's right. Help me in.
Referee Just a minute, lady, you've come the wrong way for the jumble sale, this is a boxing-ring . . . .
Auntie I know what it is. Wipe that silly smile off your face. Come on then, rings out of your seconds . . . .

The Crowd cheers

Referee Just a minute. Just a minute. What do you think you're playing at . . . .?
Auntie You said anyone could have a go, didn't you?
Woman That's right. Give her a go, then.
Referee (*getting worried*) Now. listen . . . .
Kid Saracen Go home. There's a nice old lady . . . .

The Crowd boos

Auntie You cheeky ha'porth.
Second Man Hit him, grandma.

The Crowd shouts agreement

Referee Tell you what, folks. Let's give the old lady fifty pence for being a good sport . . . .
Auntie I don't want your fifty pence . . . . Come on.
Woman Get the gloves on, granny.
Auntie I don't need gloves. My hands have seen hard work. I was scrubbing floors before he was thought of . . . .
Woman That's right, love.

Ernie (*stepping forward*) And then suddenly I got this idea. Maybe Auntie May could be the new heavyweight champion of the world . . . .

The bell rings. Auntie May comes bouncing out of her corner flinging punches at the Kid, who looks startled. The Crowd cheers

Auntie Let's have you.
Kid Saracen Hey, come off it!

The Referee tries vainly to pull Auntie May back but she dances out of reach

Kid Saracen Somebody chuck her out.

The Kid turns to appeal to the Crowd. Auntie May punches him in the back

Auntie Gotcher!
Kid Saracen Ow!

Auntie May bombards the Kid with punches

Ernie (*commentator style*) And Auntie May moves in again and catches the Kid with a left and a right to the body and there's a right-cross to the head - and that really hurt him - and it looks from here as if the champ is in real trouble . . . as this amazing sixty-eight-year-old challenger follows up with a series of sharp left-jabs - one, two, three, four jabs. . .

The Kid is reeling back

And then, bang, a right-hook and he's down . . . . !

The Kid goes down on his knees. The Crowd cheers

Auntie (*to the Referee*) Go on. Start counting.

Ernie's Incredible Illucinations

Crowd One - two - three - four - five - six

The Kid gets up again

Ernie And the Kid's on his feet but he's no idea where he is - and there's that tremendous right uppercut - and he's down again . . . . !

The Crowd counts him out. Auntie May dances round the ring with glee. The Crowd bursts into the ring and Auntie May is lifted on to their shoulders
The Crowd go out with Auntie May, singing "For She's a Jolly Good Fellow"

The Referee and the Kid are left

Referee Come on. Get up - Champ.
Kid Saracen Ooooh. *(He staggers to his feet)*

The Kid goes out, supported by the Referee

? Questions and Assignments

1. Write a piece of speech for a *fifth 'barker'* who is inviting the people to challenge the 'T.V. Quiz Champion of the World'.

2. Now rewite the above scene, outlining what happens when Ernie and his Auntie May take up the challenge of the *fifth barker.*

V

Ernie, Dad, Mum and the Doctor are left

Doctor *(still writing, excitedly)* Absolutely incredible!
Mum Terrible it was. It took it out of her, you know. She was laid up all Sunday.
Dad And we had all those fellows round from the Amateur Boxing Association trying to sign her up to fight for the Combined Services.
Mum So I told his dad on the Monday, seeing as it was half-term, "Take him somewhere where he won't get into trouble," I said. "Take him somewhere quiet".

Dad So I took him down to the library.

The Doctor retires to the side of the stage again

Dad, Mum and Ernie exit

The scene becomes the Public Library. It is very quiet. Various people tip-toe about. At one end sits an intellectual-looking Lady with glasses, reading; at the other, an old Tramp eating his sandwiches from a piece of newspaper. One or two others. A uniformed Attendant walks up and down importantly. The Lady with glasses looks up at the lights. She frowns

? Questions and Assignments

1. Extend the stage directions here to include another two people in the Public Library.

Ernie's Incredible Illucinations

Lady Excuse me . . . .
Attendant Sssshhh!
Lady Sorry. *(Mouthing silently)* The light's gone.
Attendant *(mouthing)* What?
Lady *(whispering)* I said the light's gone over here.
Attendant *(whispering)* What?
Lady New bulb.

The Attendant shakes his head, still not understanding.

(Loudly) UP THERE! YOU NEED A NEW BULB - IT'S GONE. I CAN'T SEE!

People   Sssshhhh!
Attendant *(whispering)* Right.
Lady *(whispering)* Thank you.

The Attendant tip-toes out as Dad and Ernie tip-toe in
Dad *(to Ernie)* Sssshhhh!

Ernie nods. They tip-toe and sit

Ernie *(to the Audience)* I didn't really think much of this idea of my mum's . . . .
People Ssssshhhh!
Ernie *(whispering)* I didn't really think much of this idea of my mum's. It was a bit like sitting in a graveyard only not as exciting. The trouble is, in library reading-rooms some bloke's pinched all the best magazines already and you're left with dynamic things like *The Pig Breeder's Monthly Gazette* and suchlike. I'd got stuck with *The Bell Ringer's Quarterly.* Which wasn't one of my hobbies. Nobody else seemed to be enjoying themselves either. Except the bloke eating his sandwiches in the corner. I reckoned he wasn't a tramp at all, but a secret agent heavily disguised, waiting to pass on some secret documents to his contact who he was to meet in the library and who was at this very moment lying dead in the Reference Section, a knife in his ribs. Realising this, the tramp decides to pick on the most trustworthy-looking party in the room — my dad!

The Tramp gets up stealthily and moves over to Dad. As he passes him he knocks his magazine out of his hand

Dad Hey!
Tramp Beg pardon, mister. *(He bends to pick up the magazine and hands it back to Dad. As he does so he thrusts his newspaper parcel into Dad's hands)* Sssshhhh. Take this. Quickly! They're watching me. Guard it with your life.
Dad Eh?

The Tramp hurries away. A sinister man in a mackintosh gets up and follows him out.

Who the heck was that?
Ernie Dunno, Dad.
Dad *(examining the parcel)* What's all this, then?
Ernie Dunno.
Dad I don't want his sandwiches. Spoil my dinner. *(As he unwraps the parcel)* Hey!
Ernie What is it?
Dad Looks like a lot of old blue-prints and things. Funny. This anything to do with you?
Ernie *(innocently)* No, Dad.

The Attendant enters with a step-ladder. He places it under the light. A Girl Librarian who has entered with him steadies the step-ladder. The Attendant produces a bulb from his pocket and starts to climb the step-ladder.

Ernie's Incredible Illucinations

(*Watching the Attendant*) And now, as Captain Williams nears the summit of this, the third highest mountain in the world, never before climbed by man . . . .

Wind noises start

He pauses for a moment through sheer exhaustion . . . .

The Attendant, feeling the effects of the wind, clings to the step-ladder for dear life. It sways slightly.

Attendant (*shouting down to the Librarian*) More slack. I need more slack on the rope . . . . !
Librarian (*shouting up to him*) More slack. Are you all right?
Attendant I - think - I can - make it.
Librarian Be careful. The rock looks treacherous just above you.
Attendant It's all right. It's - quite safe - if I - just aaaaaaahhh!
(*He slips and holds on with one hand*)

Lady Captain! What's happened!
Attendant Damn it. I think I've broken my leg . . . .
Lady Oh, no.
Librarian How are we going to get him down?

Dad rises

Ernie And here comes Major Fraser, ace daredevil mountaineer, to the rescue.
Dad Give me a number three clambering-iron and a hydraulic drill-lever, will you? I'm going up.
Librarian Oh no, Major.
Dad It's the only way.
Lady Don't be a fool, Major.
Dad Someone's got to go. Give me plenty of line . . . . (*He starts to climb*)

Librarian Good luck.
Lady Good luck.

A sequence in which Dad clambers up the ladder, buffeted by the wind

Dad Can you hold on?
Attendant Not - much - longer.
Dad Try, man, try. Not much longer . . . .
Lady Keep going, man.

Dad reaches the Attendant. People cheer. The two men slowly descend the ladder

Ernie And here comes the gallant Major Fraser, bringing the injured Captain Williams to safety . . . .

Dad and the Attendant reach the floor. More cheers and applause from the onlookers. The Attendant is still supported by Dad with one arm round his neck. There is a general shaking of hands. The wind noise stops

197

Ernie's Incredible Illucinations

Attendant *(coming back to reality, suddenly)* Hey, hey! What's going on here? *(To Dad)* What do you think you're doing?
Dad Oh.
Attendant Let go of me.
Dad Sorry, I . . . .
Attendant Never known anything like it. This is a public building, you know . . . .
Dad Ernie . . . .
Ernie Yes, Dad?
Dad Did you start this?
Ernie *(innocently)* Me, Dad?
Dad Now listen, lad . . . .

A Second Librarian enters, screaming

Second Librarian Oh, Mr. Oats, Mr. Oats. . . .
Attendant What's the matter girl? What's the matter?
Second Librarian There's a man in the Reference Section.
Attendant Well?
Second Librarian He's dead.
Lady Dead?
Second Librarian Yes. I think he's been killed. There's a knife sticking in his ribs. . . .

The First Librarian screams

The Attendant hurries out, followed by the others

Ernie and Dad are left

Dad Ernie!
Ernie Sorry, Dad.

The Doctor moves in. Mum joins them

Doctor Incredible.
Dad Embarrassing.
Doctor Yes, yes.

> **? Questions and Assignments**
>
> 1. Describe Ernie's illucination in the library and tell what sparked it off.

VI

The scene is now back to where it was at the beginning, with the four in the Doctor's room on one side and the waiting-room full of patients on the other

Mum Can you do anything, Doctor?
Doctor Mmmm. Not much, I'm afraid.
Mum No?
Doctor You see, it's not really up to me at all. It's up to you. An interesting case. Very. In my twenty years as a general practitioner I've never heard anything quite like it. You see, this is a classic example of group hallucinations . . . .
Dad Illucinations, yes.
Doctor Starting with your son and finishing with you all being affected . . .
Mum All?
Doctor All of you. You must understand that all this has happened only in your minds.
Dad Just a minute. Are you suggesting we're all off our onions?
Doctor Off your . . . .?
Dad You know. Round the thing. Up the whatsit.
Doctor No . . . .
Dad My missis as well?
Doctor No. No.
Dad Then watch it.
Doctor I was just explaining . . . .
Dad You don't need. It's Ernie here, that's all. He imagines things and they happen.
Doctor Oh, come now. I can't really accept that.

Ernie's Incredible Illucinations

Dad Why not?
Doctor It's - impossible. He may *imagine* things....
Dad He does.
Doctor But they don't *really* happen. They *appear* to, that's all.
Dad Is that so?
Doctor Of course.

A slight pause

Dad Ernie.
Ernie Yes, Dad.
Dad Imagine something. We'll see who's nutty.
Ernie What Dad?
Dad Anything, son, anything. Just to show the doctor.
Mum Nothing nasty, Ernie. Something peaceful....
Dad How about a brass band? I like brass bands.
Mum Oh dear. Couldn't it be something quieter? Like - a mountain stream or something....
Dad Don't be daft, Ethel. The doctor doesn't want a waterfall pouring through his surgery. Go on, lad. A brass band.
Ernie Right, Dad. *(He concentrates)*

A pause

Doctor Well?
Dad Give him a chance.

A pause

Mum Come on Ernie. *(Pause)* He's usually very good at it, Doctor.
Dad Come on, lad.
Ernie It's difficult, Dad, I can't picture them.
Doctor Yes, well I'm afraid I can't afford any more time just now, Mr. and Mrs. Fraser. I do have a surgery full of people waiting to see me - *(he calls)* - Miss Bates! - so you will understand I really must get on.

The Receptionist enters

Receptionist Yes, Doctor?
Doctor The next patient, please, Miss Bates.
Receptionist *(going)* Yes, Doctor.

The Receptionist exits

Doctor *(getting up and pacing up and down as he speaks)* What I suggest we do is, I'll arrange an appointment with a specialist and - he'll be able to give you a better diagnosis - *(his steps become more and more march like)* — than I will. I'm quite sure - that - a - few - sessions - with a trained - psychiatrist - will - be - quite - sufficient - to - put - everything - right - right - left - right - left - left - left - right - left....

The Doctor marches to the door of his room, does a smart about-turn and marches round his desk

The Patients from the waiting-room enter and follow him, some limping, some marching and all playing, or as if playing, brass instruments

L-e-e-e-f-t.... Wheel....

After a triumphal circuit of the room everyone marches out following the Doctor, who has assumed the rôle of drum major

Ernie *(just before he leaves)* It looks as though the Doctor suffers from illucinations as well. I hope you don't get 'em. Ta-ta.
Ernie marches out jauntily, following the band, as -
the CURTAIN *falls*

Ernie's Incredible Illucinations

❓ Questions and Assignments

1. 'You must understand that all this has happened in your own minds' the doctor tells Ernie and his parents. Is the doctor proved wrong? Explain.

2. Imagine that you have been to a performance of the play. Write a 250 word review for a local newspaper. Your review should include aspects of the play that impressed you or disappointed you. A newspaper review of a play aims to help the public to decide whether the play is worth going to see or not. Therefore, your review should not divulge too much of the plot (see **Reviews - Mass Media** section).

3. Identify the parts of the script which would need to be re-written to give the play an Irish setting and re-write these.

4. Using your imagination, write two extra scenes which could be added to the play. Here are a few suggestions - Ernie in school; Ernie in the Principal's office; Ernie on the Late Late Show; Ernie visits the Dáil.

A Villa on Venus

— *Kenneth Lillington*

Introduction

While *A Villa on Venus* is primarily a humorous play, it explores some issues that are of great concern to modern man.

The play offers scope for some imaginative props, costumes and sets - although it can also be staged with the minimum of these. With some minor adjustments to the script, the play can also be performed by an all-girl cast or a mixed cast.

Drama Scripts - Layout

Plays written for stage, radio or television are set out differently from short stories and novels. Because most of the words in plays are dialogue, lots of inverted commas would be needed. This would cause much confusion for the actors.

Instead (i) the characters' names are clearly marked at the side or in the margin to help the actors to see clearly when to speak (ii) no quotation marks (" ") are used but all other punctuation rules are observed (iii) stage directions, which indicate how lines are to be spoken and what actions are to be performed, are printed in italics and/or brackets. When writing drama script assignments you should bear these points in mind.

Cast

Sham ⎫
Gimble ⎭ Citizens of the Planet Venus

Frank Fearless ⎫
Bill Bold ⎬ Visitors from the Planet Earth
Dick Dreadnought ⎭

Spiv ..... A salesman from the Planet Mercury

First B.E.M. ⎫
Second B.E.M. ⎪
Third B.E.M. ⎬ Bug-Eyed Monsters
Fourth B.E.M. ⎪
Fifth B.E.M. ⎪
Sixth B.E.M. ⎭

SCENE

The curtain rises on a landscape in northern Venus which, though distinctly unworldly, is not unfamiliar to us, for we have seen similar scenes often enough on the covers of science-fiction magazines. The background is a conglomeration of futuristic machinery and exotic vegetation. Down left is an equally futuristic seat, and up right, a Reflector, which resembles a large shaving-mirror mounted on a revolving stand. Into this **Sham** *is gazing intently.*

Sham Gimble!
Gimble *(off-stage, left)* Yes, boss?
Sham Come here a minute, will you?
Gimble *(off-stage)* All right, All right!
   (Enter **Gimble**. *He and* **Sham**, *whose flesh is a bright golden colour, are both dressed in simple Grecian tunics.* **Sham**, *much the older of the two, is a genial little creature, cultured in voice, kindly and worldly-wise in manner.* **Gimble** *is young, brisk efficient; and he speaks, curiously enough, in a strong Dublin accent.)*
Gimble What is it? Someone landing?
Sham Yes, and I don't like the look of it.

A Villa on Venus

Take a look in the reflector, Gimble, will you? Your eyes are better than mine.
(He crosses to the seat, left.)
Gimble *(manipulating the reflector)* Can't see a thing... Ah, wait a bit, though. Yes, I can.
Sham Where are they from, that's the point?
Gimble Hard to say. Not Jupiter.
Sham No.
Gimble Not Mars, either.
Sham No.
Gimble Well, really, I've never seen a crate like this before. Looks as if it's come out of the Ark. In fact, I'm not sure it *isn't* the Ark... Do you know, it may sound crazy, but -
Sham Well?
Gimble I think they're from the Earth!
Sham *(grimly)* Exactly! The Red Planet.
Gimble Oh, but they couldn't be. They're living in the Dark Ages down there!
Sham That's no argument. It'd be just like them to invent some fantastic craft centuries after all the other planets have done it, and then think themselves lords of the Universe. What do you bet me they start offering us coloured beads when they get here?
Gimble They might not get here! You should see this thing rocking about!
Sham Well, I wish them no harm, but I don't like this. I've watched the Earth through the instrument for years, and I wouldn't exactly call the natives friendly.
Gimble Act rather strange, don't they?
Sham They're raving mad, my son. They keep blowing one another to bits.
Gimble Oh, well, that's all right, then. They'll blow one another to bits, and we'll go on living our dignified lives.
Sham No, you don't quite understand. What I mean is -
Gimble *(with a shout)* They're through! They going to land!... Easy, now,

A Villa on Venus

Earthmen. Gently does it... Nose her down... Steady, steady... They're going to crash!

*(He dives off, left, in alarm, with **Sham** after him. From off-stage right there is an ear-splitting crash, several rolling echoes, and a series of flashes. The faces of **Sham** and **Gimble** appear cautiously from the wings.)*

Gimble What a rotten landing!
Sham Sh! Here they come.

*(They withdraw their heads. Enter **Frank Fearless**, **Dick Dreadnought**, and **Bill Bold**, tugging off their space-helmets. Their dress is as familiar as the scenery: for they are wearing the space-suits we have seen so often in magazines and on the screen. They place their helmets on the ground, well to the rear, stretch, and inhale deeply.)*

Frank Thank goodness to get that thing off! Some fool cleaned the inside with paraffin!
Dick Awfully hot, isn't it?
Bill *(waving an arm at the scenery)* We're in the South, I imagine.
Sham *(off-stage)* Lucky for you you're not!
Frank Strange! I thought I heard a voice!
Dick So did I.
Bill An echo, no doubt.
Dick Now that's just silly. You said, 'We're in the South, I imagine.' How could that echo back as 'Lucky for you you're not'?
Gimble *(off-stage)* Shows he's thinking, anyway.
Frank *(casting an eye over the immensely complicated machinery in the background)* It's possible, I suppose, that there may be *life* here, in a primitive form.
Sham *(off-stage)* Thank you, sir.
Dick There it is again - that sound!
Bill *(resolutely)* I'm going to investigate this!
Sham *(emerging, followed by **Gimble**)* Don't bother. Good evening, gentlemen.
Frank Good Lord! Things from Another World!
Gimble *(irritated)* Cheek! Who got here first?
Dick It speaks English!
Bill *(roaring with laughter)* Ha, ha, ha! Look at its face!
Frank Steady, fellows. I shall try to speak to it. Er - greetings, creatures.
Sham Greetings to you. Have a toffee.
Dick Steady, Frank. May be poisoned.
Frank No, no. We must humour them. Er - how does one eat this sort of thing?
Gimble Well, one puts it in one's mouth, one moves one's jaws about, and finally one swallows.
Frank *(with dignity)* I see. And now - how it is that you are speaking English?
Sham *(to **Gimble**, with a gesture of resignation)* Oh, it's like talking to a savage! *(to **Frank**)* Well, you see, the air here is charged with rays which turn our thoughts into a common language. To you, I may seem to be speaking English - to me, you seem to be speaking *my* language.
Frank Ah, I see. We have something of the sort on the Earth.
Dick It's called United Nations.
Sham If it isn't a personal question, why

A Villa on Venus

have you come to Venus?

Dick We are here in the name of Progress.

Sham Oh. We're here in the name of *(introducing* **Gimble**) Gimble, and *(bowing)* Sham. *(He points to the ray-guns which the* **Earthmen** *are holding.)* And what are those?

Bill *(flourishing gun)* These are ray-guns. They can blow an elephant to bits at a distance of two miles.

Gimble And you've got those in the name of Progress, too, I suppose?

Frank Yes, of course. The natives must be shown who is their master. But don't worry - you seem friendly little beings. We shan't shoot you.

Gimble That's very kind of you.

Frank We are driven by an insatiable craving for Progress. All our race have this urge. We are the first Men on Venus, but soon, others will come, spurred by our example -

Sham How delightful!

Frank They will overrun the Solar System. They will embrace the great nebulae. They will take the sun.

Gimble Well, be careful where you take it, pal. It's useful.

Dick *(eagerly)* Frank's right. Before long, every housewife on the Earth will own a villa on Venus.

Gimble And what about us?

Bill Ah, to you will fall the honour of being Man's first interplanetary assistants.

Sham Well, well, well… Anyway, it's a good job you didn't land in the South.

Dick So you said before. Why?

Sham The B.E.Ms live in the South.

Frank B.E.Ms?

Gimble The B.E.Ms - the Bug-Eyed Monsters.

Frank Come off it! Bug-Eyed Monsters exist only in the cheapest fiction.

Sham I'm afraid life's rather like the cheapest fiction, pal.

Bill But what are they like - the B.E.Ms?

Gimble Er… like nothing on Earth.

Sham But don't worry. They never come here.

Dick Now that's a pity. These creatures must be most interesting phenomena. We might have got some pictures of them.

Gimble *(furiously)* Look, pal, the B.E.Ms are not going to pose for you while you tell 'em to watch the birdy! They're really nasty, those things are, and we don't want 'em here, right?

Frank Well, they don't come here anyway, according to you.

Gimble You never know. *They* might want to take pictures of *you*.

Sham Come, this is getting us nowhere. I think that before you gentlemen make any more - er - progress, you'd better have some supper.

Gimble It won't be poison. We don't eat poison.

Sham Come, Gimble. Sit down, gentlemen. We'll call you when supper's ready.

(Exit **Sham** *and* **Gimble***. The* **Earthmen** *sit on the seat, left.)*

Frank Quaint little creatures, aren't they? Almost human.

Dick Very simple-minded though.

Bill You can say that again. All that nonsense about Bug-Eyed Monsters.

(Enter, left, a **Bug-Eyed Monster***. It wears a long green cloak, black tights, and a green hood, from which stares a green and demoniac face. Grinning wickedly, it lurks behind the* **Earthmen***, listening as they chat.)*

Dick Pure children's-comic stuff!

Frank Oh, I entirely agree. I for one don't believe in the B.E.Ms for a moment.

(The **B.E.M.** *moves silently to centre, and beckons. Enter five more* **B.E.Ms***, exactly*

A Villa on Venus

*like the first, from right. They form a line, centre to right. The **First B.E.M.** stands downstage, a little apart from the others.)*

Dick I intend to write an article about the childish beliefs of the beings on Venus.

Bill I wonder if this supper's ready? I expect - *(in consternation)* Hey! Look, lads - look!

*(The **Earthmen** spring to their feet, see the **B.E.Ms** and back away apprehensively.)*

First B.E.M. Greetings, Earthmen!

Frank *(gulping)* Er-yes, of course. Greetings.

First B.E.M. We observed your arrival, and hurried here to greet you.

Dick V-very good of you.

First B.E.M. Good? Please don't use that unpleasant language here. We despise goodness.

Bill But what do you want to do?

B.E.Ms *(exultantly)* WE WORK FOR THE DESTRUCTION OF MANKIND.

Second B.E.M. *(stepping forward)* Yes. For many years we have had visitors to Venus from other planets - Mercury, Mars, Jupiter, Saturn. But they have all been creatures of peace, and have used their science to keep us away. Always have we turned our longing eyes on your planet, for you and we - ah! we can work together so beautifully for the death of man!

B.E.Ms *(joyfully)* DEATH! THE DEATH OF MAN!

Third B.E.M. *(stepping forward)* For your planet, the red planet, Earth, is the planet of Murder and Death.

B.E.Ms MURDER AND DEATH!

Fourth B.E.M. *(stepping forward)* Join us, Earthmen, in our great plan to destroy Mankind!

Fifth B.E.M. *(stepping forward)* Help us to launch the avalanche of our rage!

Sixth B.E.M. *(stepping forward)* Haste with us to the Day of Doom!

B.E.Ms DOOM!

*(But the **Earthmen** are extremely indignant.)*

Frank Now look here, you nasty little … nasties… you've got us all wrong!

Bill We wouldn't dream of joining your disgusting plot.

Dick You can just put your hands up, and don't try any tricks, because these guns can blow an elephant to bits at two miles.

First B.E.M. Ha ha! *(To the others.)* Hypnotise these men!

*(The **B.E.Ms** swing their arms rhythmically, crooning as they do so - Whoo… Whoo… Bonk! - and at the 'bonk' the **Earthmen** are struck rigid.)*

First B.E.M. Excellent! Now, in their trance, they will tell us all the secrets of their life on Earth! Right, men - On to Doom.

B.E.Ms ON TO DOOM!

*(They file out, leaving the **Earthmen** still transfixed. The last **B.E.M.** puts his head round the curtain.)*

B.E.M. Er- follow us, please.

*(Arms outstretched like sleepwalkers, the **Earthmen** follow. Re-enter **Sham** and **Gimble**, who carries a tray with three covered dishes on it.)*

Sham Well, here you are, gents… Well! Where have they gone to?

Gimble Gone exploring, maybe. *(He sets down the tray.)*

Sham After all our trouble, too. What bad manners.

Gimble *(sniffing the air)* Just a minute. Can you smell something?

Sham *(sniffing)* Yes, now that you mention it.

Gimble A bit like sulphur, isn't it?

Sham Yes, it is rather -

(They stare at each other, suddenly.)

Sham and **Gimble** *(together)* Sulphur!

Sham *(greatly alarmed)* The B.E.Ms have got them!

Gimble Talk about birds of a feather!

205

A Villa on Venus

Sham *(sitting down)* I suppose we ought to rescue them.

Gimble *(joining him on the seat)* Yes... We'll start tomorrow, shall we?

Sham Hello! *(pointing into wings, right)* There's someone coming.

Gimble Why, it's that salesman fellow from Mercury. It's old Spiv. Hi-ya, Spiv!

*(Enter **Spiv**. He is dressed like **Sham** and **Gimble**, and resembles them, but that he looks old and very weary. He lugs an enormous suitcase.)*

Sham *(going forward to shake his hand)* Hello, Spiv! I haven't seen you for ages!

Gimble *(with sympathy)* You look a bit tired. Come and sit down and rest your feet.

*(**Spiv** sinks down, planting the suitcase at his feet.)*

Spiv That's the way I feel. *(without hope)* You don't want to buy a death-ray, do you?

Sham No, thank you.

Spiv It'll wipe out a whole city.

Sham Well, when I want to wipe out a whole city, I'll remember you.

Spiv *(dejectedly)* They all talk like that nowadays.

Gimble Business is bad, is it pal?

Spiv Terrible. I go up and down the Solar System, calling on all the planets until I'm worn out, but no one wants to buy weapons any more. Peace and concord - nothing but peace and concord wherever I go. It's awful.

Gimble Not very nice, though, is it, selling things that kill people?

Spiv What can I do? It's my bread and butter. I suppose I could get another job, but that's not easy at my time of life.

Sham You might sell to the B.E.Ms.

Spiv *(shocked)* Oh, no, no. I've got some conscience left.

Sham Well - why don't you try the Earth?

Spiv *(considering)* The planet Earth?... No, not worth bothering about. They're too backward. *(He rises wearily.)* The fact is, I'm finished. *(He picks up his case and walks to centre.)* They just don't want machines of death any more. Books of poetry now - they sell like hot cakes.

Sham I do wish I could help you, Spiv.

Spiv I know you would if you could.

Gimble Perhaps a lovely war will break out somewhere. Keep your chin up.

Spiv No such luck. But thanks for listening. So long, fellows.

Sham and **Gimble** *(together)* So long, Spiv.

*(Exit **Spiv**.)*

Gimble Poor old Spiv, selling weapons in a peaceful Universe!

Sham *(gazing after him)* Yes, it's a shame... What! some more visitors? *(suddenly)* Gimble! Watch out! It's the B.E.Ms!

*(**Sham** and **Gimble** take up a defensive position behind the seat as the **B.E.Ms** troop in.)*

Gimble Now look here - if you want trouble you'll get it. We don't want the likes of you round here!

Sham Go on! Off with ye!

First B.E.M. *(anxiously)* No, listen, Sham -

Sham Sham? Who do you think you're talking to? Get out!

First B.E.M. No, please listen.

Sham Oh, all right. What is it?

First B.E.M. Please help us to get rid of these *ghastly* Earthmen!

Sham Why, what's wrong with them?

First B.E.M. *Wrong* with them? They're *unspeakable*.

Gimble Then why did you kidnap them?

First B.E.M. Oh, we were in the wrong, we admit it. but we didn't realise that anything could be so vile.

Sham I thought that you objects worked for 'the destruction of mankind', or something?

First B.E.M. Yes, yes, but there's a

A Villa on Venus

difference between healthy destruction and the horrors we've been told.

**Second B.E.M.   We put them in a trance, and they described their life on the Earth.

Third B.E.M.   Their squalid days!

Fourth B.E.M.   Their piggish nights!

Fifth B.E.M.   Their beastly world of business, and their poisonous ways of pleasure!

Sixth B.E.M.   Their repulsive insurance companies, banks and offices!

Second B.E.M.   Their ratlike houses, hotels and clubs!

Third B.E.M.   Their trains and tubes and buses and bicycles!

Fourth B.E.M.   Their prisons and palaces and aerodromes and asylums!

Fifth B.E.M.   Their luxury liners!

Sixth B.E.M.   Their cafes and cinemas!

Second B.E.M.   Their picnics on the beach!

Third B.E.M.   Their dances on the lawn!

Fourth B.E.M.   Their food, beds, funerals, baths!

Fifth B.E.M.   Their men!

Sixth B.E.M.   Their women!

B.E.Ms *(together)*   THEIR BEASTLY LIVES!

First B.E.M.   And after all that, what do you think one of them said? I'll tell you. He said, 'In time, every housewife on the Earth will own a villa on Venus!'

Sham   *(calmly)* Well, you've really let yourselves in for it this time, haven't you? **

First B.E.M.   It'll be just as bad for you.

Sham   Oh no, it won't. They all want to live in the South, you'll see. *(B.E.Ms groan.)*

First B.E.M.   *(deeply dejected)* Ah, well, we deserve it, I suppose. All right, men - on to Doom!

B.E.Ms   *(croaking dismally)* On to Doom. *(They begin to shamble away.)*

Sham   Wait! I've changed my mind!

B.E.Ms   *(returning jubilantly)* Hooray!

Sham   Quiet! Gimble, go after Spiv and bring him back, will you?

Gimble   Right, boss. *(Exit Gimble)*

First B.E.M.   You're really going to help us?

Sham   Yes. I never thought I'd have any fellow-feeling for a Bug-Eyed Monster, but circumstances alter cases. I'm going to sent the Earthmen right back to the Earth.

First B.E.M.   *(advancing with hand outstretched)* This is wonderful! How can I ever thank -

Sham   *(hastily)* Er - keep your distance, please. I don't want to stink of sulphur for the next week.

First B.E.M. *(retreating)* Oh. Sorry, I'm sure. No offence.

Sham   How soon can you send the Earthmen back to me?

First B.E.M.   At twice the speed of light.

Sham   That'll do. And now go away.

First B.E.M. With pleasure. What ho, lads, let's sing as we march, shall we? *(Exit B.E.Ms, gaily singing a marching song.)*

A Villa on Venus

Sham *(advancing to the footlights, to the audience)* I only hope I'm doing the right thing.
*(Re-enter **Gimble** with **Spiv**.)*
Gimble Here he is boss.
Sham Ah, Spiv! I think I might have some business for you after all.
Spiv That's really handsome of you, Sham.
Sham Not at all. Got your samples ready?
Spiv You bet!
Sham I think you're just about to make your fortune. Ah, here they come. Stand by.
*(Enter the three **Earthmen**.)*
Frank Hello, you funny little things! *(seeing **Spiv**)* Good Lord, there's another one of them!
Sham Good evening. Had a good time?
Dick We've met your Bug-Eyed Monsters.
Bill And taught them how civilised beings behave.
Sham Really? And what did they say?
Frank Oh, they were tremendously impressed. They're much more intelligent than you are, of course.
Sham Are they, indeed? How nice.
Dick When we explained what life was like on Earth, they were so ashamed that they crept away.
Bill We're going to educate them. We're going to open schools all over Venus.
Sham What a good idea! But allow me to introduce a friend of mine. Earthmen, Spiv; Spiv, Earthmen.
Frank And who is this odd little fellow?
**Sham Spiv's a scientist. He comes from Mercury.
Bill A scientist. How amusing!
Sham Show them your wares, Spiv.
*(**Spiv** brings forward his suitcase and opens it, while the **Earthmen** regard him with amusement, as visitors to the Zoo might watch the antics of a monkey.)*
Spiv *(fishing out a piece of apparatus)* Well, gents, this is a death-ray. It'll wipe out a whole city.
*(The attitude of the **Earthmen** undergoes a perceptible change.)*
Frank *(taking the death-ray in his hands and examining it closely)* I say... this really is brilliant.
Dick *(taking death-ray in his turn)* Civilisation of the highest order!
*(The **Earthmen** exchange an awkward glance.)*
Bill Er - please excuse us, sir, for being rude just now. We realise that you come from a very advanced planet.
Spiv Well, now, this *(producing another piece of apparatus)* is a disintegrator. It turns people's bodies to heaps of dust.
Frank Magnificent!
Dick How humble it makes me feel, to meet a really first-class brain!
Bill Don't interrupt. *(to **Spiv**)* Pray go on, sir.
Spiv And this *(he produces a helmet-shaped object)* is an annihilation-cap. You just put it on, think, and the whole area falls to bits.
Frank *(breathlessly)* Wonderful. Absolutely wonderful.
Bill Vastly superior to anything we've got on Earth.
Sham *(casually)* Spiv was thinking of visiting the Earth, as it happens.
Spiv Oh, no I -
Sham Sh-h!
Frank Really? What an honour for us!
Dick All the universities will give him a degree.
Bill He'll get the Nobel Prize!
Spiv The Nobel Prize? What's that for?
Sham Peace.
Spiv *(rather bewildered)* Well, it's very kind of you gents to offer me all these honours, but the point is, will I get any

A Villa on Venus

money, because you see -

Frank Money? My dear sir, on my planet we honour genius. You'll make an enormous fortune.

Spiv Oh, well, in that case -

Dick You'll come with us to the Earth?

Spiv Why, yes, I'd be glad to.

Frank Splendid! What a great day for the World!

Dick Look fellows, let's forget about the B.E.Ms. This is so much more important. **

Bill But when can we start? Our spaceship's wrecked.

Spiv You can come in mine, if you like. It's quite comfortable.

Frank May we? It's so very good of you.

Dick When can we start?

Spiv Well, now, if you like.

Earthmen *(together)* Yes, let's not waste a single minute!

Gimble Aren't you going to eat your supper?

Frank Supper? We've no time for supper while genius waits. Come on, fellows, let's off to show the Earth these brilliant machines of death!

(They pick up their space-helmets)

Bill *(bowing to **Spiv**)* You first, sir.

Spiv No, no after you. *(He waves **Bill** forward, and turns to **Sham** as the **Earthmen** exeunt.)* Sham, old friend - I don't know how to thank you!

Sham Oh, don't mention it. It's a pleasure. *(exit **Spiv**.)*

Sham Well, for once, everybody's happy. But for how long, I wonder?

Gimble And they didn't even eat their supper!

Sham Well, you know what to do about that. Come on, I'm hungry.

(They pick up the tray of food and go out as the CURTAIN falls.)

? Questions and Assignments

1. Retell the story of this play in approximately 300 words.

2. (i) What evidence is there in the play to suggest that Gimble and Sham are more intelligent than the Earthmen?
(ii) Do you think these characters add a comic touch to a performance of the play? Explain your answer.

3. (i) What event in the play shows the Earthmen to be suspicious types?
(ii) Do the Earthmen strike you as admirable people? Explain your answer.

4. Explain why the B.E.Ms do not want the Earthmen to remain on their planet.

5. (i) What are the "qualities of genius" according to the Earthmen?
(ii) **Bill** *He'll get the Nobel Prize!* Explain the irony in this statement.

6. Comment on the character of Spiv.

7. Is this play humorous or serious? Explain your answer.

8. Using your imagination, rewrite the dialogue in the sections of the play marked ** (beginning) to ** (end). While you may change the dialogue completely, you should in general, adhere to the original plot.

On page 110 is an idea for one approach to **Assignment 8**. It is not complete and you may wish to continue it or else work on your own idea. However, you should note carefully how handwriting is laid out in dramatic dialogue.

A Villa on Venus

<u>First B.E.M.</u>   We put them in a trance and they described their life on Earth.

<u>Third B.E.M.</u>   Their boring days!

<u>Fourth B.E.M.</u>   Their glitzy shopping centres.

<u>Fifth B.E.M.</u>   The tedious television quiz shows that they watch for hours on end.

<u>Sixth B.E.M.</u>   The fluff-brained celebrities that they pay homage to as if ....

III - POETRY

The Night Mail

This is the night mail crossing the border,
Bringing the cheque and the postal order,
Letters for the rich, letters for the poor,
The shop at the corner and the girl next door,
Pulling up Beattock, a steady climb -
The gradient's against her but she's on time.

Past cotton grass and moorland boulder,
Shovelling white steam over her shoulder,
Snorting noisily as she passes
Silent miles of wind-bent grasses;
Birds turn their heads as she approaches,
Stare from the bushes at her blank-faced coaches;
Sheepdogs cannot turn her course,
They slumber on with paws across;
In the farm she passes no one wakes
But a jug in a bedroom gently shakes.

Dawn freshens, the climb is done.
Down towards Glasgow she descends
Towards the steam tugs, yelping down the glade of cranes
Towards the fields of apparatus, the furnaces
Set on the dark plain like gigantic chessmen.
All Scotland waits for her;
In the dark glens, beside the pale-green sea lochs,
Men long for news.

The Night Mail

Letters of thanks, letters from banks,
Letters of joy from the girl and boy,
Receipted bills and invitations
To inspect new stock or visit relations,
And applications for situations,
And timid lovers' declarations,
And gossip, gossip from all the nations,
News circumstantial, news financial,
Letters with holiday snaps to enlarge in,
Letters with faces scrawled on the margin.
Letters from uncles, cousins and aunts,
Letters to Scotland from the South of France,
Letters of condolence to Highlands and Lowlands,
Notes from overseas to the Hebrides;
Written on paper of every hue,
The pink, the violet, the white and the blue,
The chatty, the catty, the boring, adoring,
The cold and official and the heart's outpouring,
Clever, stupid, short and long,
The typed and the printed and the spelt all wrong.

Thousands are still asleep
Dreaming of terrifying monsters
Or a friendly tea beside the band at Cranston's or Crawford's;
Asleep in working Glasgow, asleep in well-set Edinburgh,
Asleep in granite Aberdeen.
They continue their dreams
But shall wake soon and long for letters.
And none will hear the postman's knock
Without a quickening of the heart,
For who can bear to feel himself forgotten?

— *W. H. Auden*

Questions and Assignments

1. How does the poet depict the border countryside?
2. What impression do you get of the city of Glasgow? Base your answer on the details in the poem.
3. (i) List in your own words, the different kinds of letters that the train is carrying.
   (ii) Compose two different types of letter from the list.
4. The poet sometimes gives human attributes to the train. Quote some examples of this and say what effect each one has.

The Night Mail

5. The poet builds up a great deal of anticipation and excitement in the poem. How does he do this?
6. Comment on the use of the words "glade" in line 19, "fields" in line 20 and "plain" in line 21.
7. What idea do you think the poet wants to convey in each of these lines: -
   (i) "Stare from the bushes at her blank-faced coaches".
   (ii) "Sheepdogs cannot turn her course"?
8. Select two images from the poem that impress you and explain why.
9. Give some directions on how each of the sections should be read.

> ### ☞ Points to Note

RHYTHM

Rhythm is the regular beat that runs through a song, a dance or any piece of music. The drum, in all its forms, is probably the most used musical instrument. Rhythm is beaten out on a drum, so, to understand rhythm in poetry, you could imagine the kind of drumbeat that might accompany a reading of the poem.

Many everyday sounds have rhythm - such as footsteps, horses' hooves and various machines. You have only to read a line or two of this poem to hear how the rhythm carries it along. The rhythm of the opening lines echoes that of the train as it speeds towards Glasgow as dawn is breaking. The opening lines give the impression of speed and make the readers feel that they are aboard. This section will obviously be read at a rapid pace. As well as carrying a poem along with a beat, rhythm also allows the poet to emphasise key words.

This poem was spoken on the soundtrack of a film about the nightly journey of the London-Glasgow mail train.

✓ Q. 8 — Sample Answer

One image that impressed me was "the furnaces set on the dark plain like gigantic chessmen". From this comparison one can visualise the tall slender furnaces towering at regular intervals over the dark industrial landscape. They appear like "gigantic chessmen" because we are looking at them from above i.e. the top of the "climb".

Line 9 contains the word "snorting" — an excellent sound word to describe the noise made by the train as it attempts the climb. As well as effectively describing the noise of the train, the word "snorting" makes the train sound like an angry or a hard-working person. This is an example of the poet's use of personification.

Greer County

How happy am I when I crawl into bed -
A rattlesnake hisses a tune at my head,
A gay little centipede, all without fear,
Crawls over my pillow and into my ear.

My clothes is all ragged as my language is rough,
My bread is corn-dodgers, both solid and tough;
But yet I am happy, and live at my ease
On sorghum molasses, bacon, and cheese.

Good-bye to Greer County where blizzards arise,
Where the sun never sinks and a flea never dies,
And the wind never ceases but always remains
Till it starves us to death on our government claims.

Farewell to Greer County, farewell to the West,
I'll travel back East to the girl I love best,
I'll travel back to Texas and marry me a wife,
And quit cornbread for the rest of my life.

- Traditional American

Questions and Assignments

1. What is the mood of the cowboy in the first two stanzas? Base your answer on the details given in the poem.
2. Describe the life-story of the cowboy in Greer County.
3. Why does the cowboy leave Greer County?
4. What in the poem suggests that the ballad came down through the oral tradition.

Points to Note

- **BALLAD**

Today's pop singers are the modern counterparts of a tradition that goes back many, many centuries. The term "ballad" has its origin in the Middle Ages, where it meant dance-song. The old ballads told simple stories of love and adventure as well as local and national history.

We have no idea who wrote most of the old ballads. In many cases, in fact, they were not written at all. They were composed by a travelling singer or troubadour and then changed gradually as they passed on from generation to generation by word of mouth, until finally someone wrote them down. Those that survived did so because they told stories that had plenty of vivid details and exciting dramatic touches. They also have regular rhythm patterns which is not surprising when we remember their musical origins. Another reason why these

Greer County

ballads were remembered and passed on was their simple yet effective rhyming schemes. Most ballads consist of four line verses (stanzas) with an *abab* or *abcb* rhyming scheme. In this regard the rhyming scheme of *Greer County* is a little different - *aabb*.

- **ONOMATOPOEIA**

Consider the second line: "A rattlesnake hisses a tune at my head". As one reads the word "hisses" one can hear the actual sound made by the snake. Not only does the word "hiss" describe the noise made by the snake but it also sounds like that noise when spoken. There are very many words like that in English. Here are some examples - *buzz; mutter; rumble; moan*. Note that they all describe sounds. The term onomatopoeia (onomatopoeiac - adjective) is used to describe these kind of words. Can you think of any more?

The Discovery

There was an Indian, who had known no change,
    Who strayed content along a sunlit beach
Gathering shells. He heard a sudden strange
    Commingled noise; looked up; and gasped for speech.
For in the bay, where nothing was before,
    Moved on the sea, by magic, huge canoes,
With bellying cloths on poles, and not one oar,
    And fluttering coloured signs and clambering crews.

And he, in fear, this naked man alone,
    His fallen hands forgetting all their shells,
His lips gone pale, knelt low behind a stone,
    And stared, and saw, and did not understand,
Columbus's doom-burdened caravels
    Slant to the shore, and all their seamen land.

- J. C. Squire

The Discovery

❓ Questions and Assignments

1. Tell the story of this poem in your own words.
2. Comment on the phrase "who had known no change".
3. What features of the ships particularly astonished the Indian?
4. What type of person was the Indian? Support your answer by reference to the poem.
5. Are we made to sympathise with the Indian? Give reasons for your answer.
6. Why does the poet refer to Columbus' ships as "doom-burdened caravels"?
7. (a) How did the Indian first react to the sight of the ships?
   (b) How did he feel immediately afterwards?
8. What does the poet wish to convey by the use of the following adjectives: commingled, bellying, clambering, fallen.
9. Identify the alliteration in line 3. What letter-sound does it emphasise? Is this letter-sound noticeable in the next line? Where?
10. Write about this scene as Columbus might describe it.

☞ Points to Note

POINT OF VIEW

This poem gives an imaginary account of the arrival of Christopher Columbus to the New World, as seen through the puzzled and frightened eyes of a native.

We also see the event from the point of view of the poet. Unlike the Indian, the poet knew that the event would ultimately result in destruction and bloodshed for the natives of the New World.

SYMBOLS

Many of the images in the poem can be regarded as symbols. The "sunlit beach" could stand for an environment that is pleasant and free from evil. The shells could stand for the wealth of the Indians - wealth that nature provided freely as opposed to wealth acquired by greed and exploitation.

SONNET

This has been a very popular form of poem with its origins in 13th century European literature. A *sonnet* is a poem of fourteen lines and will have one of a restricted number of rhyming schemes. The two main types of sonnet are the *Petrarchan* called after the Italian poet Petrarch, and the *Shakespearean*. The Petrarchan form divides into an eight line stanza (octet or octave) and a six line stanza (sestet). The rhyming schemes vary a little, particularly in the sestet, though the following ones occur frequently (sometimes with slight variations) - *abbaabba cdcdcd* and *abbacddc cdecde*.

The Shakespearean form consists of three quatrains (four line sections) and a rhyming couplet *abab cdcd efef gg*.

The composition of a sonnet, unlike more modern modes, requires a great deal of writing skill and discipline. Here are two more sonnets for you to read and enjoy.

The Discovery

From you have I been absent in the spring,
When proud-pied April, dress'd in all his trim,
Hath put a spirit of youth in everything.
That heavy Saturn laugh'd and leap'd with him.
Yet nor the lays of birds, nor the sweet smell
Of different flowers in odour and in hue,
Could make me any summer's story tell,
Or from their proud lap pluck them where they grew;
Nor did I wonder at the Lily's white,
Nor praise the deep vermilion in the Rose;
They were but sweet, but figures of delight,
Drawn after you, you pattern of all those.
    Yet seem'd it Winter still, and, you away,
    As with your shadow I with these did play.

-W. Shakespeare

Nuns fret not at their convent's narrow room,
    And hermits are contented with their cells,
    And students with their pensive citadels;
Maids at the wheel, the weaver at his loom,
Sit blithe and happy; bees that soar for bloom,
    High as the highest peak of Furness fells,
    Will murmur by the hour in foxglove bells:
In truth the prison unto which we doom
Ourselves no prison is: and hence for me,
    In sundry moods, 'twas pastime to be bound
    Within the Sonnet's scanty plot of ground;
Pleased if some souls (for such there needs must be)
Who have felt the weight of too much liberty,
    Should find brief solace there, as I have found.

-William Wordsworth

The Tigress

They trapped her in the Indian hills
And put her in a box; and though so young
The dockers quailed to hear her voice
As she made war on every bolt and thong.

Now she paces, sleeps on her ledge,
Glares, growls, excretes, gnaws lumps of meat,
Sun and shadow in iron bars
Dropping about her and a listless mate.

- Clifford Dyment

Questions and Assignments

1. Explain the events on which this poem is based.
2. What kind of feelings are created in the first stanza? Which words capture these feelings best?
3. The second stanza creates a different feeling. Which words capture this feeling best? Describe the feeling and comment on the words you have chosen and the impact they have.
4. The sound of words in poetry is very important. Pick out parts of this poem where the sound of the words is very powerful. Explain your choice.
5. Why did the poet use the word "dropping" in the final line? Note the title.
6. Why do you think there is such a sudden stop after the word "box"? Why is there no other punctuation in that stanza?
7. Suggest an alternative title for the poem.

Points to Note

WORD POWER IN POETRY

When you look at how poets use words it is important to remember that there are three aspects to consider: (i) the literal meaning (ii) the sound of the word and what it might suggest (iii) any associated ideas. These are the ideas that come into your head when your hear a particular word: they may not have strong links with the literal meaning of the word.

In the final line of the first stanza of "The Tigress" the poet says that the tigress made "war" on every bolt and thong. At a literal level we understand that making war means attacking, resisting or fighting back. The sounds suggested by the word "war" are vicious roars and piercing cries. Ideas associated with the word "war" might include the showing of spirit, courage, anger and resentment at the loss of freedom.

The use of the verb "quailed" in line 3 creates a very vivid image of the reaction to the young tigress. Even dockers whom we would normally expect to be tough, hardened men, flinched when they heard her roar.

Anthem for Doomed Youth

What passing-bells for these who die as cattle?
    Only the monstrous anger of the guns.
    Only the stuttering rifles' rapid rattle
Can patter out their hasty orisons.
No mockeries for them from prayers or bells,
    Nor any voice of mourning save the choirs,
The shrill, demented choirs of wailing shells;
    And bugles calling for them from sad shires.

What candles may be held to speed them all?
    Not in the hands of boys, but in their eyes
Shall shine the holy glimmers of good-byes.
    The pallor of girls' brows shall be their pall;
Their flowers the tenderness of silent minds,
And each slow dusk the drawing-down of blinds.

-Wilfred Owen

Anthem for Doomed Youth

? Questions and Assignments

1. Examine each of the following words as they are used in the poem. In the case of each word say what idea the poet wishes to get across by choosing that particular word.

   - stuttering
   - sad
   - shrill
   - pallor

2. Comment briefly on the first line of the poem.
3. What message does the poet wish to convey in this poem?
4. The sound of words in poetry is very important. Identify parts of this poem where the sounds of words have a powerful impact.
5. Comment on the use of the following adjectives in the poem: monstrous, rapid, hasty, demented, wailing.
6. Discuss the aptness of the title. Suggest an alternative title for the poem.
7. Explain what the last line of the poem means. Does it have more than one meaning?
8. Describe the mood of the poem and say how the mood is achieved.

☞ Points to Note

RHETORICAL QUESTION

A *rhetorical* question does not seek information. It is used in writing and in speech to make a statement. A rhetorical question always implies an obvious response. The first lines of both the octet and the sestet are rhetorical questions.

When the poet asks "what candles may be held to speed them all?", we know the answer is "none!" The line implies that there are no religious rites - "candles" - to mark their deaths.

FORM

This poem is written in *sonnet form*. It is divided into an octet with a rhyming scheme of *ababcdcd* and a sestet with a rhyming scheme of *effegg*.

There is a change in tone between the octet and the sestet. In the octet the poet concentrates on the harsh sounds and savagery of the battlefield — the stuttering rifles' rapid rattle and the shrill, demented choirs of wailing shells — that disrespectfully mark the young boys' deaths. In the sestet he dwells on the softer, gentler things — the pallor of girls' brows and the tenderness of silent minds — that mark their passing with deep love and respect.

✓ Q. 2 — Sample Answer

A powerful simile is used in line 1 "What passing-bells for these who die as cattle?" The poet uses this image to show what little value is placed on the lives of young boys who are sent out to fight for their country. When an animal drops dead in a field it is considered no longer useful and is either removed without ceremony or just left to rot. When young soldiers die in action, they are, according to the poet, treated in a similar way. This is a very powerful comparison which is designed to evoke anger in the reader.

The Road Not Taken

Two roads diverged in a yellow wood,
And sorry I could not travel both
And be one traveller, long I stood
And looked down one as far as I could
To where it bent in the undergrowth;

Then took the other, as just as fair,
And having perhaps the better claim,
Because it was grassy and wanted wear;
Though as for that the passing there
Had worn them really about the same,

And both that morning equally lay
In leaves no step had trodden black.
Oh, I kept the first for another day!
Yet knowing how way leads on to way,
I doubted if I should ever come back.

I shall be telling this with a sigh
Somewhere ages and ages hence:
Two roads diverged in a wood, and I -
I took the one less travelled by,
And that has made all the difference.

- Robert Frost

? Questions and Assignments

1. What choice faces the poet in the first stanza?
2. Did the poet have any regrets? Explain.
3. Describe the two roads that face the poet.
4. Which road does the poet choose and why does he choose it?
5. Do you think the poet really means that he will return to the other road another day.
6. What do you think the roads represent?
7. Explain what the poet means by "Yet knowing how way leads on to way".
8. What is the mood of the poem? Explain how the particular mood is achieved.

The Road Not Taken

▶ **Points to Note**

ALLEGORY

An *allegory* is a story that operates on two levels. On the deeper level symbols are used to put across a complex idea or a message that would be difficult to express in concrete terms. *The Road Not Taken* could be regarded as an allegory. At first glance the poet seems to be describing a simple event - walking in the woods and choosing a road at a junction. At a deeper level the poem explores the problem faced by the poet in making an important choice about his life. The poem is rich in symbols - the two roads could represent two different lifestyles from which the poet had to choose. Can you find any more symbols in the poem?

The Man He Killed

> **THOMAS HARDY 1840 - 1928**
>
> Hardy is famous not only as a poet but also as a novelist. He was born in Dorset in England, the son of a builder. His rural English roots are reflected in much of his poetry, which is traditional in its tuneful rhyming lyrics. Many of his poems focus on some incident which is then portrayed in a vivid and dramatic way.

'Had he and I but met
    By some old ancient inn,
We should have sat us down to wet
    Right many a nipperkin!

'But ranged as infantry,
    And staring face to face,
I shot at him as he at me,
    And killed him in his place.

'I shot him dead because -
    Because he was my foe,
Just so: my foe of course he was;
    That's clear enough; although

'He thought he'd 'list, perhaps,
    Off-hand like - just as I -
Was out of work - had sold his traps -
    No other reason why.

'Yes; quaint and curious war is!
    You shoot a fellow down
You'd treat if met where any bar is,
    Or help to half-a-crown.'

- Thomas Hardy.

? Questions and Assignments

1. What point is being made in the first stanza? Where else in the poem is this point mentioned again?
2. In what circumstances has the speaker in the poem killed the man?
3. Why do you think the word 'because' is repeated in the third stanza?

The Man He Killed

4. What reasons had the "foe" for enlisting in the army? What do the reasons imply?
5. Would you agree with the speaker's opinion that war is "quaint and curious"? Explain your answer.
6. What is Hardy's message in this poem?
7. Write in dialogue form, the conversation that might have taken place in the inn had the two men (one a ghost, perhaps) an opportunity to meet.

Points to Note

DRAMATIC MONOLOGUE

A dramatic monologue is a poem written as though it is being spoken by one person, usually to another who does not speak. The speaker, while talking about other things, reveals a great deal about his or her own character. "The Man He Killed" is written in this form.

RHYME

Rhyme is the repetition of similar sounding words. If a stress is placed on the rhyming elements of words, those words are then doubly emphasised. Rhyme helps you to remember poems. It also holds the lines together and gives a poem a musical touch.

The Man He Killed

RHYME-SCHEME OR RHYMING SCHEME

The pattern of rhyme at the end of lines is called the *rhyme-scheme* or the *rhyming scheme*. To note this pattern we use the letters of the alphabet. The letter *a* is used for the first rhymed sounds, *b* for the second and so on.

The rhyme-scheme of the poem "The Man he Killed" is *abab* in each of the five verses

'Had he and I but met   *a*
By some old ancient inn,   *b*
We should have sat us down to wet   *a*
Right many a nipperkin!   *b*

Not all poetry rhymes. Poetry which does not rhyme is called *blank verse*.

ASSONANCE

Assonance occurs when two or more words share the same vowel sounds, though not the same consonants. In poetry, assonance is one of the most common methods of achieving a musical effect. Assonance in which the broad vowel sounds (a, o, u) e.g. "stared", "foe", "shoot" - are used, can sometimes give the poem a solemn or sad mood because they slow down the pace at which the words can be read. On the other hand, assonance in which the slender vowel sounds (e, i) are used can sometimes have the opposite effect on the mood because they can be read at a faster pace e.g. "And killed him in his place".

In "The Man He Killed" there are some examples of assonance - "And staring face to face". The repetition of the 'a' sound gives the line a musical effect and adds to the solemnity of the tone or mood. Another example occurs in line 4: "And killed him in his place". Here the repetition of the "i" sound both contributes to the musical quality of the line and quickens the pace at which the line is read.

To express the thoughts of a war veteran, the poet uses simple direct language which is conversational in tone. Words like "nipperkin" and "half-crown" would indicate that the poem was written in the past. The message, however, is as relevant today as it was when the poem was written, over fifty years ago.

Snow in the Suburbs

Every branch big with it,
Bent every twig with it;
Every fork like a white web-foot;
Every street and pavement mute:
Some flakes have lost their way, and grope back upward, when
Meeting those meandering down they turn and descend again.
The palings are glued together like a wall,
And there is no waft of wind with the fleecy fall.

A sparrow enters the tree,
Whereupon immediately
A snow-lump thrice his own slight size
Descends on him and showers his head and eyes,
And overturns him
And near inurns him,
And lights on a nether twig, when its brush
Starts off a volley of other lodging lumps with a rush.

The steps are a blanched slope,
Up which, with feeble hope,
A black cat comes, wide-eyed and thin;
And we take him in.

- *Thomas Hardy*

Snow in the Suburbs

? Questions and Assignments

1. What effect does the snow have on (a) the trees (b) the street (c) the palings (d) the steps outside the house?
2. Pick out two details from the first stanza that show it is very calm.
3. In the second stanza we are told the effect the snow has on a sparrow. Describe in detail what happens to the sparrow when he lands on the branch of a tree.
4. (a) Why does the poet introduce a black cat into the scene?
   (b) What details suggest that the black cat is a stray?
5. Explain exactly what the poet is trying to suggest in the use of the following words: web-foot, fleecy, grope, meandering, inurns, volley.

☞ Points to Note

SIMILE
A *simile* is a direct comparison made partly to clarify what is being said but also to give the statement more vigour and colour. A simile is easily recognised as it always employs one of the following words: *like, as, than*.

In this poem we find two examples of simile. Firstly in line 3: "Every fork like a white web-foot" and secondly in line 7: "The palings are glued together like a wall". Both of these similes give a picture of the snow occupying every available space.

METAPHOR
A *metaphor* is another form of comparison but not as obvious as a simile. Metaphors are very common in everyday speech - "a song *rockets* up the charts; prices *soar*; somebody leads a *dog's life*".

Metaphors are compressed similes. Instead of saying "a song went up the charts as rapidly as a rocket goes into space" we shorten it to the phrase above. Metaphors give writing and speech much of its colour and vigour.

In *"Snow in the Suburbs"* the poet uses two metaphors to create pictures of the snow. In line 8 the snow that has built up on the palings is referred to as a "fleecy wall". In line 17 the steps are said to be "a blanched slope".

ALLITERATION
Alliteration is the arranging of words in such a way that a repeated initial sound enhances the overall effect of the words. Alliteration is often used in advertisements for much the same purpose as it is used in poetry, that is, to catch the reader's attention.

Examples of alliteration used in *"Snow in the Suburbs"* occur in line 8: "And there is no waft of wind with the fleecy fall" and also in line 16: "Starts off a volley of other lodging lumps with a rush".

The language used in this poem is tight and concise. In each of the first four lines the verb is omitted but understood. Each word is carefully chosen to describe the effect of the snow, no word is superfluous.

At the Railway Station, Upway.

'There is not much that I can do,
    For I've no money that's quite my own!'
    Spoke up the pitying child -
A little boy with a violin
At the station before the train came in, -
'But I can play my fiddle to you,
And a nice one 'tis, and good in tone!'

    The man in the handcuffs smiled;
The constable looked, and he smiled, too,
    As the fiddle began to twang;
And the man in the handcuffs suddenly sang
        With grimful glee:
        'This life so free
        Is the thing for me!'
And the constable smiled, and said no word,
As if unconscious of what he heard;
And so they went on till the train came in -
The convict, and boy with the violin.

- Thomas Hardy

At the Railway Station, Upway

? Questions and Assignments

1. In your own words, describe the event outlined in the poem.
2. What was the little boy's attitude to the convict?
3. How did the convict react to the little boy's gesture?
4. The constable smiled on two occasions. Why do you think he smiled?
5. What is ironic about the choice of tune?
6. (a) How would you describe the mood of the poem?
   (b) How does the poet establish this mood?
7. Comment on the phrase "grimful glee".
8. The theme of a poem is the message the poet intends for the reader. What do you consider to be the theme of this poem?

☞ **Points to Note**

Through the episode at the station platform in *At the Railway Station, Upway* Hardy shows how music can often affect people in a way that words rarely can.

CONTRAST

Instead of using a comparison the poet sometimes creates an image or emphasises an idea by using words or ideas that are very different; this is called *contrast*. In comparing, we show likenesses; in contrasting, we show differences. Can you find examples of contrast in this poem?

✓ **Q. 7 — Sample Answer**

The phrase is used to describe the way the prisoner sang. At first the two words seem to contradict each other. *Glee* and *grimful* describe opposite moods. Perhaps the prisoner wanted to sing his way out of the unhappy mood he was in. On the other hand, the prisoner might have had a sense of humour and "put on" a gleeful act which he did not feel. He may have wanted to embarrass the policeman, singing about being free while handcuffed to him.

Heredity

I am the family face;
Flesh perishes, I live on,
Projecting trait and trace
Through time to times anon,
And leaping from place to place
Over oblivion.

The years-heired feature that can
In curve and voice and eye
Despise the human span
Of durance - that is I;
The eternal thing in man,
That heeds no call to die.

— *Thomas Hardy*

? Questions and Assignments

1. What does the poet wish to tell us in his poem "Heredity"?
2. Is the message of the poem hopeful? Explain your answer.
3. Explain what you think the poet means by
   (i) "And leaping from place to place over oblivion".
   (ii) "The years-heired feature".
   (iii) "The eternal thing in man,
        That heeds no call to die".

☞ Points to Note

The poem makes the point that, while individual family members die, certain physical features and personality traits continue to occur in all families from generation to generation. Heredity - the family face - speaks to us as if it were a person.

Thomas MacDonagh

He shall not hear the bittern cry
   In the wild sky, where he is lain,
Nor voices of the sweeter birds
   Above the wailing of the rain.

Nor shall he know when loud March blows
   Thro' slanting snows her fanfare shrill,
Blowing to flame the golden cup
   Of many an upset daffodil.

But when the Dark Cow leaves the moor
   And pastures poor with greedy weeds,
Perhaps he'll hear her low at morn
   Lifting her horn in pleasant meads*.

- Francis Ledwidge

* *meadows*

Thomas MacDonagh

? Questions and Assignments

1. What words in the first stanza tell us that Thomas MacDonagh is dead?
2. (a) According to the poet what things shall Thomas MacDonagh never experience again? (b) Say why you think the poet chose these particular things.
3. Explain the second stanza.
4. Select lines from the poem which appeal to you and say why you chose them.
5. Find examples of alliteration and assonance in the poem. Explain the effect each one has.
6. Describe the mood of this poem and how it is established.
7. Identify two contrasting images in the poem and comment briefly on the contrasts.

☞ Points to Note

MOOD AND TONE IN POETRY

Our moods are constantly changing. The different events, thoughts and experiences which we encounter in life affect our moods. At different times in our lives we experience fear, anger, joy, nostalgia, sorrow, hope etc... Often you will encounter references to the *mood* or *tone* of a poem. Identifying this is quite easy. To begin, it is important to remember that all poems are inspired by some feelings or emotions. A poet may be angered, saddened, amused or awed by some event or experience and may then respond by writing a poem on it. The poem is likely to reflect the mood of the poet at the time of the experience. Therefore, if you can sense the poet's attitude to the subject matter, you will be well on the way towards identifying the mood of the poem. All poets aim to have the reader not only share the underlying ideas of a poem but also its mood. Tone and Mood are terms that are broadly interchangeable. For example, a poem with a sad mood should be spoken in a tone of voice that reflects this sadness.

How Mood is established

(i) *Subject Matter* - the poet's attitude towards the subject of the poem will be reflected in the mood of the poem. The execution of Thomas MacDonagh, a friend of the poet, gives this poem a mood of sorrow.

(ii) *Images* - these also help to set the tone of a poem. Pay particular attention to similes, metaphors and adjectives and the feelings they evoke. "The bittern cry", "the wild sky", "the wailing of the rain" are all images that suggest bleakness and loneliness.

(ii) *Sound Effects* - the actual sounds of words also establish the mood of a poem. Pay particular attention to assonance, alliteration and rhyme. In *Thomas MacDonagh,* the repetition of the long vowel sounds in the first stanza - wild sky; lain, wailing, rain; - help to establish a mournful mood.

(iv) *Rhythm* - a quick lively rhythm in a poem generally establishes a light-hearted mood, while a slow rhythm establishes a more serious mood.

CHANGING MOODS

It is important to remember that the mood may change over the course of a poem. In the final stanza of *Thomas MacDonagh* there is a mood of optimism as Ledwidge suggests that Ireland will achieve freedom from oppression and the spirit of MacDonagh will rejoice in this.

LAMENT

A *lament* is a poem that mourns a death. This lament shares many characteristics of Gaelic verse including some internal rhymes. Note how the final word in the first line rhymes with the word "sky" in line two. Can you trace any similar patterns throughout the poem?

To Simon

You'll never see your thirteenth birthday now
Nor trouble this demanding world again
With unexpected bursts of rage
And, yet, you talked to grown ups
With all the grave precociousness of youth
And though you fought with peers,
You were observed with younger boys,
Blowing bubbles on the sunlit green
The day before you hurried off.

Why shouldn't you have raged
Being made to fit a world
Where businessmen cut down the woods
And neighbours throw old fridges in the streams?
And if you too had lived
We would have taught you fiercer loves
Than loosing bubbles on the air
Like new created, futile globes.

- Patrick Devaney

1. Outline briefly your response to this poem.

Basking Shark : Achill Island

Where bogland hillocks hid a lake
we placed a tom-cat on a raft; our guns
clawed pellets in his flesh until, his back
arching to an ancient jungle fear, he drowned.
We fished for gulls with hooks we'd hide
in bread and when they swallowed whole we'd pull;
screaming they sheared like kites above a wild
sea; twine broke and we forgot; until
that day we swam where a great shark
glided past, dark and silent power
half-hidden through swollen water; stunned
we didn't shy one stone. Where seas lie calm
dive deep below the surface; silence there
pounds like panic and moist fingers touch.

- John F. Deane

Basking Shark : Achill Island

? Questions and Assignments

1. What two cruel deeds does the poet recall having done in the past?
2. How do we know from the poem that the youngsters did not think much about their cruel deeds?
3. What impression do you get of the shark? How does the poet convey this impression?
4. The poet uses three unusual verbs, "clawed", "sheared" and "shy". Comment on their use in the poem.
5. Is there a message in the poem? Explain.

☞ Points to Note

IMAGES

An *image* in poetry is a word or phrase that paints a vivid picture in our imagination or helps us to imagine a sound, or some other sensation. Images are frequently based on metaphors or similes.

The images in the poem *Basking Shark : Achill Island* are very vivid and powerful. "Our guns clawed pellets in his flesh" makes the reader imagine the pellets tearing like claws at the flesh of the cat. "His back arching to an ancient jungle fear, he drowned" powerfully conveys the pain experienced by the cat before he drowned, as well as the savage nature of his death.

The poet uses a simile to describe the way the gulls darted in pain, about the sky, after they swallowed the hooks: "screaming they sheared like kites above a wild sea".

In the final line the fear experienced by the youngsters is made real by the image or picture of the boys' hands perspiring beneath the water: "moist fingers touch".

✓ Q. 3 — Sample Answer

The impression I get of the shark is that he is a huge, powerful and terrifying creature.

The poet uses the word "great" which suggests the size and strength of the shark. The word "glide" expresses the ease of movement of this powerful creature. "Dark" could refer to more than the shark's colour. It could suggest a sinister nature. "Silent" suggests the silence and stealth of the shark stalking its prey - it had no need to use sound to instil fear. The fact that it was just "half-hidden through swollen water" also indicates its size. Its terrifying nature is conveyed by the reaction of the boys. They were totally panic-stricken.

The Early Purges

I was six when I first saw kittens drown.
Dan Taggart pitched them, 'the scraggy wee shits',
Into a bucket: a frail metal sound.

Soft paws scraping like mad. But their tiny din
Was soon soused. They were slung on the snout
Of the pump and the water pumped in.

'Sure isn't it better for them now?' Dan said.
Like wet gloves they bobbed and shone till he sluiced
Them out on the dunghill, glossy and dead.

Suddenly frightened, for days I sadly hung
Round the yard, watching the three sogged remains
Turn mealy and crisp as old summer dung

Until I forgot them. But the fear came back
When Dan trapped big rats, snared rabbits, shot crows
Or, with a sickening tug, pulled old hens' necks.

Still, living displaces false sentiments
And now, when shrill pups are prodded to drown
I just shrug. 'Bloody pups'. It makes sense:

'Prevention of cruelty' talk cuts ice in town
Where they consider death unnatural.
But on well-run farms pests have to be kept down.

— *Seamus Heaney*

The Early Purges

? Questions and Assignments

1. List the words in the first two stanzas that suggest the weak and defenceless nature of the kittens.
2. (a) What effect had the drowning of the kittens on the six-year old boy?
   (b) How does his reaction to the killing of animals change as he matures?
3. What was Dan Taggart's attitude to animals?
4. (a) Why do you think the poet mentions
       (i) "false sentiments"
       (ii) "where they consider death unnatural"?
   (b) In what way are these two expressions connected?
5. The poet quotes Dan Taggart twice and himself, as an adult, once. What effect does this have on the poem?
6. Discuss the impact of each of the following verbs in the poem:
   pitched, soused, slung, bobbed, sluiced, prodded.
7. Comment on the effectiveness of the following adjectives in the poem: glossy, mealy, crisp, sickening.

☞ Points to Note

Tales of cruelty, whether it is intentional or not, always awaken the attentions and feelings of readers. How did you respond to this poem?

RUN-ON LINES

Run-on lines of verse occur where the structure and meaning carry the reader's eye and ear directly over to the next line without a break. They are frequently found in modern poetry. Their use takes away the sing-song effect of rhymes and prevents words at the end of a line being over-emphasised.

Several run-on lines can be found in "The Early Purges" e.g.
"Soft paws scraping like mad. But their tiny din
Was soon soused. They were slung on the snout
Of the pump and the water pumped in."

CONSONANCE

Consonance occurs when words in close proximity have the same consonant sound.
An example of consonance occurs in line 2 of *"The Early Purges"*.
"Dan Taggart pitched them, 'the scraggy wee shits'," the repeated "gg" and "r" sound is harsh and unmusical. This conveys the harsh, insensitive nature of Dan Taggart and the deed he carried out.

Another example occurs in line 5 where the repeated 's' sound helps us to hear, in our minds, the rush of the water from the pump.

The Early Purges

✓ Q. 6 — Sample Answer

The verb "pitched" conveys not just the idea of the kittens having been placed in the bucket but also Dan Taggart's attitude towards them. We gather from the choice of verb that he had no regard for the kittens - he flung them from him as one would fling vermin.

The verb "soused" gets across the idea of the drowning-out of the feeble sounds of the kittens by the force of the water coming from the pump. We can almost hear the sound of the water overpowering the weak sounds made by the kittens as the bucket filled. The "s" sound in the word "soused" also helps to convey a sense of something being quietened.

Like the verb "pitched" the use of the verb "slung" highlights Dan Taggart's off-hand approach to the job of getting rid of the kittens. He is casual both in his actions and his attitude.

The use of the verb "bobbed" makes one feel sorry for the kittens. One pictures their helpless little bodies rising and falling in the cold water before they die.

We normally associate the word "sluiced" with waste and dirt. The choice of this verb again tells as much about Dan Taggart's attitude as it does about his action. He flushed them out because he regarded them as pests.

The use of the verb "prodded" suggests that the person disposing of the pups would not touch them with his hand. He would use a stick or possibly a pitch-fork so that he would remain at a distance from the wretched things.

Interruption to a Journey

The hare we had run over
Bounced about the road
On the springing curve
Of its spine.

Cornfields breathed in the darkness.
We were going through the darkness and
The breathing cornfields from one
Important place to another.

We broke the hare's neck
And made that place, for a moment,
The most important place there was,
Where a bowstring was cut
And a bow broken for ever
That had shot itself through so many
Darknesses and cornfields.

It was left in that landscape.
It left us in another.

- Norman MacCaig

Interruption to a Journey

? Questions and Assignments

1. Examine each of the following words as they are used in the poem. In the case of each word say what idea the poet wishes to get across by choosing that particular word.

   - bounced
   - springing
   - breathing
   - shot

2. Why do you think the poet chose the title "Interruption to a Journey"? What other title might you give the poem?
3. Explain the comparison in the last four lines of the third stanza. Is it a metaphor or a simile? What is the purpose of the comparison? Is it effective?
4. Describe in a short paragraph, the event that inspired this poem.
5. What do you think the poet means when he says that the cornfields *"breathed in the darkness"*?
6. Why do you think the place where the hare dies is "the most important place there was"?
7. What do you think the poet means by the last two lines?

☞ Points to Note

The mood of this poem could be described as sombre because in it the poet reflects on the accidental killing of a hare.

The image he creates of the hare after it was hit is very powerful. It shows that the poet was deeply disturbed by what had happened. In the third stanza he openly expresses his regret about having put an end to the hare's life "And a bow broken for ever /That had shot itself through so many /Darknesses and cornfields."

The final line of the poem leaves the reader in no doubt as to the extent to which the poet was affected by the incident.

The poem is typical of the modern mode of poetry writing in that it has no end rhyme, its form is irregular and its lines vary in length.

Boy at the Window

Seeing the snowman standing all alone
In dusk and cold is more than he can bear.
The small boy weeps to hear the wind prepare
A night of gnashings and enormous moan.
His tearful sight can hardly reach to where
The pale-faced figure with bitumen eyes
Returns him such a god-forsaken stare
As outcast Adam gave to Paradise.

The man of snow is, nonetheless, content
Having no wish to go inside and die.
Still, he is moved to see the youngster cry.
Though frozen water is his element,
He melts enough to drop from one soft eye
A trickle of the purest rain, a tear
For the child at the bright pane surrounded by
Such warmth, such light, such love, and so much fear.

- Richard Wilbur

Boy at the Window

? Questions and Assignments

1. Having read the poem can you suggest why the poet chose the word "weeps" rather than "cries", in line 3?

2. Why does the small boy pity the snowman?

3. Explain why the poet compares the snowman to Adam.

4. (a) Why does the snowman pity the boy?
   (b) How does he show his feelings?

5. Say what you think the poet means by the following expressions: -
   (i) "Bitumen eyes".
   (ii) "Though frozen water is his element".

6. Comment on the final line of the poem.

☞ Points to Note

The subject of the boy's pity is rather unusual. In line 4 the poet uses two interesting sound words: "A night of gnashings and enormous moan". The words "gnashings" and "moan" echo the sounds they describe and so can be taken as onomatopoeiac words.

Although this poem has a rhyming scheme which gives it a lyrical tone, it also has run-on lines which makes a reading of it sound like a continuous story.

✓ Q. 1 — Sample Answer

He chose "weeps" as the word shows the extent of the sadness felt by the boy. "Weeps" also forms an alliteration with "wind", giving the line a better sound. "Cries" would sound too harsh and it would convey the idea of noise and pain which goes against the mood of the poem.

Harvest Hymn

We spray the fields and scatter
    The poison on the ground
So that no wicked wild flowers
    Upon our farm be found.
We like whatever helps us
    To line our purse with pence;
The twenty-four-hour broiler-house
    And neat electric fence.

All concrete sheds around us
    And Jaguars in the yard,
The telly lounge and deep-freeze
    Are ours from working hard.

We fire the fields for harvest,
    The hedges swell the flame,
The oak trees and the cottages
    From which our fathers came.
We give no compensation,
    The earth is ours today,
And if we lose on arable,
    Then bungalows will pay.

All concrete sheds around us
    And Jaguars in the yard,
The telly lounge and deep-freeze
Are ours from working hard.

- John Betjeman

Harvest Hymn

? Questions and Assignments

1. What idea does the poet wish to convey in *Harvest Hymn*?
2. This poem is a parody of a famous hymn *We plough the fields and scatter the good seed on the land.* Is there anything in the poem that suggests this?
3. What is the tone of the poem? Sincere? Mocking? Happy? How does the poet achieve this tone?
4. Comment on the use of the following words in the poem: poison, pence, compensation, bungalows, Jaguars.
5. What do the following phrases mean to you - "wicked wild flowers"; "to line our purse"; "the hedges swell the flame"?
6. Write a parody on a well-known poem or song.

☞ Points to Note

PARODY

A *parody* is a piece of writing which achieves a humorous effect by imitating the characteristics of a writer's style or of a written form.

The poem, *Harvest Hymn*, written by the former Poet Laureate of England, attacks the selfish and destructive methods of modern farming by mocking them. In this hymn-parody the modern farmers sing their own praises of their methods and their new-found wealth.

MUSIC

The poem has a number of examples of alliteration which help to retain the musical quality of the original hymn and also help to emphasise certain words: -

"wicked wild flowers"; "Upon our **f**arm be **f**ound"; "To line our **p**urse with **p**ence"; "We **f**ire the **f**ields for harvest";

- the use of assonance also contributes to the musical quality of the poem: -

"And Jaguars in the yard"; "The telly lounge and deep-freeze".

246

The Windmill

Behold! a giant am I!
Aloft here in my tower
With my great jaws I devour
The maize, and the wheat, and the rye,
And grind them into flour.

I look down over the farms;
In the fields of grain I see
The harvest that is to be,
And I fling to the air my arms,
For I know it is all for me.

I hear the sound of flails
Far off, from the threshing-floors
In barns, with their open doors
And the wind the wind in my sails,
Louder and louder roars.

I stand here in my place,
With my foot on the rock below,
And which ever way it may blow
I meet it face to face,
As a brave man meets his foe.

And while we wrestle and strive,
My master, the miller, stands
And feeds me with his hands;
For he knows who makes him thrive,
Who makes him lord of lands.

On Sundays I take my rest;
Church-going bells begin
Their low, melodious din;
I cross my arms on my breast
And all is peace within.

- H. W. Longfellow

The Windmill

❓ Questions and Assignments

1. Examine each of the following words as they are used in the poem. In the case of each word say what idea the poet wishes to get across by choosing that particular word.

• place	• giant	• hands	• roars
• fling	• arms	• devour	

2. Identify two examples of musical language in this poem.
3. What human characteristics has the poet given the windmill in the first stanza?
4. In the second stanza what human things does the windmill do?
5. What human faculty has 'The Windmill' acquired in the third stanza?
6. (a) What word suggests that the wind is also human?
   (b) Describe the relationship the windmill has with the wind.
7. What is the windmill's relationship with the miller?
8. What actions of the windmill in the final stanza suggest that it is human?
9. Which line suggests that the windmill is in harmony with its surroundings?

👉 Points to Note

PERSONIFICATION

Personification is a particular kind of metaphor in which an object, an animal or an emotion is described or addressed as if it were a person.

In this poem the poet describes the windmill as if it were a person - a person of great size and strength - a giant. He actually has the windmill speak directly to us. In every stanza except the fifth, the windmill uses the word "I" at least once. This serves as a constant reminder that the windmill is a person telling us about himself. In the fifth stanza the windmill speaks of the wind as if it too were a person. The word "we" is used when he talks about them both.

RHYMES

The poem consists of six five-line stanzas. The rhyming scheme is regular in each stanza - *abbab*. These rhymes help to emphasise words that are important in the poem. They also make the poem sound musical when it is read aloud.

The Unknown Citizen

(To JS/07/M/378
This Marble Monument
Is Erected by the State)

He was found by the Bureau of Statistics to be
One against whom there was no official complaint,
And all the reports on his conduct agree
That, in the modern sense of an old-fashioned word, he was a saint,
For in everything he did he served the Greater Community.

Except for the War till the day he retired
He worked in a factory and never got fired,
But satisfied his employers, Fudge Motors Inc.
Yet he wasn't a scab or odd in his views,
For his Union reports that he paid his dues,
(Our report on his Union shows it was sound)
And our Social Psychology workers found
That he was popular with his mates and liked a drink.
The Press are convinced that he bought a paper every day
And that his reactions to advertisements were normal in every way.
Policies taken out in his name prove that he was fully insured,
And his Health-card shows he was once in hospital but left it cured.
Both Producers Research and High-Grade Living declare
He was fully sensible to the advantages of the Instalment Plan
And had everything necessary to the Modern Man,
A phonograph, a radio, a car and a frigidaire.
Our researchers into Public Opinion are content
That he held the proper opinions for the time of year;
When there was peace, he was for peace; when there was war, he went.
He was married and added five children to the population,
Which our Eugenist says was the right number for a parent of his generation,
And our teachers report that he never interfered with their education.
Was he free? Was he happy? The question is absurd:
Had anything been wrong, we should certainly have heard.

- W. H. Auden

The Unknown Citizen

❓ Questions and Assignments

1. Why, in your opinion, had the unknown citizen a number rather than a name inscribed on his tombstone?
2. Why do you think the state erected a monument to the unknown citizen?
3. What does the line "he worked in a factory and never got fired" suggest about the unknown citizen?
4. What features of modern life are being satirised in this poem?
5. Would you consider that the unknown citizen was happy and free? Explain your answer.
6. What is the poet's message to the reader in *The Unknown Citizen*?
7. Suggest another title for the poem and explain your choice.
8. How would you describe the language used by the poet?
9. Describe the rhythm and rhyming scheme of the poem.

👉 Points to Note

SATIRE

Satire is a form of humorous writing which holds up to ridicule the vices and follies of mankind. The satirist sometimes tries to influence the reader in order to bring about change. Such a writer might criticise our attitudes, our values or our behaviour. *The Unknown Citizen* is a satirical poem. In this poem is W. H. Auden satirising the way of life of an ordinary man or is he satirising those who gather the statistics?

IRONY

Irony is the use of language in which apparent or literal meaning and the true meaning are different and sometimes opposite. Irony, however, is not meant to deceive. The writer using irony intends that the clever and sensitive reader will easily discover the real meaning. Sarcasm is a form of irony.

The final two lines of the poem, *The Unknown Citizen* contain a measure of irony: -

"Was he free? Was he happy? The question is absurd:
Had anything been wrong, we should certainly have heard."

Do you think they would?

A Christmas Childhood

> **PATRICK KAVANAGH 1905 - 1967**
>
> Patrick Kavanagh was a native of Co. Monaghan. His formal education ended at fourteen when he started work on the small family farm under the stern but encouraging supervision of his mother. Largely as a result of the guile and determination of his mother, they acquired extra land. It was poetry however and not farming that interested Kavanagh and in 1939 he left for Dublin to try his hand as a full-time poet and writer. There he earned a meagre living as a contributor to magazines and newspapers. In 1952 he founded a weekly magazine, entitled *Kavanagh's Weekly*, in which he offered opinions on an extremely varied range of topics. Sadly, *Kavanagh's Weekly* was not a commercial success.
>
> His life in Monaghan provided the inspiration for much of his poetry. You can read more about Kavanagh in his autobiography *The Green Fool* and in the autobiographical novel *Tarry Flynn*.

I

One side of the potato-pits was white with frost -
How wonderful that was, how wonderful !
And when we put our ears to the paling-post
The music that came out was magical.

The light between the ricks of hay and straw
Was a hole in Heaven's gable. An apple tree
With its December-glinting fruit we saw -
O you, Eve, were the world that tempted me

To eat the knowledge that grew in clay
And death the germ within it ! Now and then
I can remember something of the gay
Garden that was childhood's. Again

The tracks of cattle to a drinking-place,
A green stone lying sideways in a ditch
Or any common sight the transfigured face
Of a beauty that the world did not touch.

II

My father played the melodeon
Outside at our gate ;
There were stars in the morning east
And they danced to his music.

A Christmas Childhood

Across the wild bogs his melodeon called
To Lennons and Callans.
As I pulled on my trousers in a hurry
I knew some strange thing had happened.

Outside the cow-house my mother
Made the music of milking ;
The light of her stable-lamp was a star
And the frost of Bethlehem made it twinkle.

A water-hen screeched in the bog,
Mass-going feet
Crunched the wafer-ice on the pot-holes,
Somebody wistfully twisted the bellows wheel.

My child poet picked out the letters
On the grey stone,
In silver the wonder of a Christmas townland,
The winking glitter of a frosty dawn.

Cassiopeia was over
Cassidy's hanging hill,
I looked and three whin bushes rode across
The horizon - the Three Wise Kings.

A Christmas Childhood

And old man passing said :
"Can't he make it talk " -
The melodeon. I hid in the doorway
And tightened the belt of my box-pleated coat.

I nicked six nicks on the door-post
With my penknife's big blade -
There was a little one for cutting tobacco.
And I was six Christmases of age.

My father played the melodeon,
My mother milked the cows,
And I had a prayer like a white rose pinned.
On the Virgin Mary's blouse.

- Patrick Kavanagh

Questions and Assignments

1. This poem is a child's view of Christmas. What details and images in the poem show this?
2. What effect has the repetition of the word "wonderful" in the second line?
3. As a young child the poet is very aware of the presence of God around him. Where in the poem do you see this?
4. Select three images from the poem that you like and say why they appeal to you.
5. The language in the poem is a mixture of childish language and adult language. Find examples of both and say what effect this mixture of language has on the poem.
6. On the evidence in the poem describe the type of life the poet experienced as a child.

Points to Note

THEMES

This poem touches on a number of themes which recur often in Kavanagh's poetry. The first is the regret he frequently felt, as an adult, for the loss of the innocence of childhood. This idea is explored a little in the first part of the poem, which you may find a little obscure. He is comparing his situation with that faced by Adam. Adam was tempted and ate the fruit of the forbidden tree. He was then banished from Paradise and lost his state of innocence. Instead he gained "knowledge" of a world where hardship and death were a reality - both unknown in the innocent world of Paradise. Therefore, what was gained was ultimately valueless.

This brings us to the other theme that also recurs in much of Kavanagh's poetry - the beauty, magic and mystery of the ordinary things about us; "any common sight". For Kavanagh, childhood was a "gay garden" in comparison to the stale world of adulthood. The child sees wonder in such things as the frosted potato-pits, the tracks of cattle or "a green stone lying sideways in a ditch" - sights that hold no interest for the adult.

In Memory of My Mother

I do not think of you lying in the wet clay
Of a Monaghan graveyard; I see
You walking down a lane among the poplars
On your way to the station, or happily

Going to second Mass on a summer Sunday -
You meet me and you say:
"Don't forget to see about the cattle -"
Among your earthiest words the angels stray.

And I think of you walking along a headland
Of green oats in June,
So full of repose, so rich with life -
And I see us meeting at the end of a town

On a fair day by accident, after
The bargains are all made and we can walk
Together through the shops and stalls and markets
Free in the oriental streets of thought.

O you are not lying in the wet clay,
For it is a harvest evening now and we
Are piling up the ricks against the moonlight
and you smile up at us - eternally.

- Patrick Kavanagh

In Memory of My Mother

❓ Questions and Assignments

1. What sort of woman was the poet's mother on the evidence of the poem?
2. Describe the relationship the poet had with his mother.
3. The poet states twice in the poem that he does not think of his mother "lying in the wet clay". Why do you think he does this?
4. The poet associates ordinary things with exotic and romantic things. Find two examples of this and comment on their purpose and effect.
5. Describe the quality and effect of the language in the following lines: -
    (i) "Among your earthiest words the angels stray."
    (ii) "So full of repose, so rich with life -"
    (iii) "Free in the oriental streets of thought."
6. Describe the mood of the poem and say how this mood is achieved.

☞ Points to Note

In this poem the poet addresses his dead mother to tell her how he remembers her. Speaking directly to her, in colloquial language has the effect of making his mother seem present to receive his tribute.

As in many of Patrick Kavanagh's poems, ordinary and commonplace things are spoken of as if they were wonderful and exotic. The headland in the field of oats and the streets of the town on a fair day are ascribed beauty and wonder above the ordinary.

The poem is made up of five four-line stanzas. It contains a number of run-on lines and it lacks a regular metre and rhyme pattern. The structure of the lines and the absence of a rhyme pattern help to give the poem a colloquial tone of everyday speech.

✓ Q. 1 — Sample Answer

The poet's mother seems to be a very active type of person. All the references to her in the poem show her to be doing something or going somewhere. She is pictured on her way to the station, going to Mass, walking the streets on a fair day and helping with the harvest. These details give a picture of a woman who is not bound to the house but takes an active part in running the farm. The picture of her at the headland is one of a serene and contented woman. Perhaps she is happy with the progress of the crop of oats. Her reminder to Patrick to "see about the cattle" might reveal a bossy or a fussy side to her. The image of her smiling up at him - he is on a rick of straw and she is on the ground - gives us the impression of the warm and loving side of the woman.

Q. 5 (I)

The word "angels" could stand for (symbolise) goodness and care, while the phrase "earthiest words" may mean "bad" language. In this line Kavanagh may be trying to get across the idea that, even if his mother used sharp or vulgar language, there was no malice or evil behind it.

Epic

I have lived in important places, times
When great events were decided: who owned
That half a rood of rock, a no-man's land
Surrounded by our pitchfork-armed claims.
I heard the Duffys shouting "Damn your soul"
And old McCabe stripped to the waist, seen
Step the plot defying blue cast-steel -
"Here is the march* along these iron stones."
That was the year of the Munich bother. Which
Was most important? I inclined
To lose my faith in Ballyrush and Gortin
Till Homer's ghost came whispering to my mind.
He said: I made the Iliad from such
A local row. Gods make their own importance.

boundary ditch

- Patrick Kavanagh

Epic

? Questions and Assignments

1. To what "great events" is the poet referring in the opening lines? Do you think that the adjective "great" is a suitable one? Explain.
2. Comment on the behaviour of McCabe and the Duffys.
3. What do you understand by the term "no-man's land"? Is there any other reference in the poem that links with the phrase "no-man's land"? Explain.
4. Comment on the phrase "the Munich bother".
5. Comment on the use of Irish place names in the poem.
6. Kavanagh poses a question in the poem. Outline, in your words, the question and his response. Do you agree with him? Explain why.

☞ Points to Note

The subject matter of this short poem echoes an episode from *Tarry Flynn* which describes neighbours in bitter dispute over land. It seems to be based on an incident where Tarry Flynn faced the anger of the Duffys and their ally, McCabe.

The poem is written in sonnet form though the rhyme is "loose" in places. In the octet Kavanagh recalls a squabble over land. In the sestet he looks back at the event, recalling that it took place in "the year of the Munich bother" - 1938. In that year Hitler, Mussolini, Chamberlain and Daladier signed an agreement which made significant changes to national boundaries in Europe. In this regard the events were similar.

The poet is "inclined" to see local feuds over land as unworthy of poetry until he considers that Homer himself composed the *Iliad* from a local "row" in Troy. In the end he concludes that small events can provide material for great poems.

On Raglan Road

(*Air:* The Dawning of the Day)

On Raglan Road on an autumn day I met her first and knew
That her dark hair would weave a snare that I might one day rue;
I saw the danger, yet I walked along the enchanted way,
And I said, let grief be a fallen leaf at the dawning of the day.

On Grafton Street in November we tripped lightly along the ledge
Of the deep ravine where can be seen the worth of passion's pledge,
The Queen of Hearts still making tarts and I not making hay -
O I loved too much and by such, by such is happiness thrown away.

I gave her gifts of the mind, I gave her the secret sign that's known
To the artists who have known the true gods of sound and stone
And word and tint. I did not stint for I gave her poems to say
With her own name there and her own dark hair like clouds over fields of May.

On a quiet street where old ghosts meet I see her walking now
Away from me so hurriedly my reason must allow
That I had wooed not as I should a creature made of clay -
When the angel woos the clay he'll lose his wings at the dawn of day.

— *Patrick Kavanagh*

? Questions and Assignments

1. Explain what you think is meant by "weave a snare that I might one day rue".
2. What is the danger the poet saw?
3. What, according to the poet, is the result of loving too much?
4. What gifts did the poet give to the girl?
5. (i) Was the poet successful in his quest for the girl's love?
   (ii) Can you explain what he tells us in the last verse?

"Morning Song"

Love set you going like a fat gold watch.
The midwife slapped your footsoles, and your bald cry
Took its place among the elements.

Our voices echo, magnifying your arrival. New statue.
In a drafty museum, your nakedness
Shadows our safety. We stand round blankly as walls.

I'm no more your mother
Than the cloud that distils a mirror to reflect its own slow
Effacement at the wind's hand.

All night your moth-breath
Flickers among the flat pink roses. I wake to listen:
A far sea moves in my ear.

One cry, and I stumble from bed, cow-heavy and floral
In my Victorian nightgown.
Your mouth opens clean as a cat's. The window square

Whitens and swallows its dull stars. And now you try
Your handful of notes;
The clear vowels rise like balloons.

- *Sylvia Plath*

"Morning Song"

❓ Questions and Assignments

1. What ideas do the first three lines suggest to you?
2. The poet is obviously delighted with her baby. This delight is mixed with wonder. Show how she communicates this delight and wonder by close reference to the poem.
3. Some people might say, "This is not a proper poem: it doesn't rhyme." Answer this criticism by explaining how "Morning Song" succeeds as a poem.
4. Comment on the following words as they are used in the poem: bald, shadows, flickers, swallows.
5. Comment on the title of the poem.
6. *Morning Song* and *Born Yesterday* have a newborn baby as the subject matter. In what ways are these poems similar and in what ways are they different?
7. The poet uses a number of comparisons. Identify four of these and comment briefly on each of them.

👉 Points to Note

The poem "Morning Song" is written in the form of a dramatic monologue. In it the poet speaks to her newborn baby. As she reveals her delight and wonder, she gives the reader an insight into the great love she feels towards the child.

The poem consists of six three-line stanzas which have no regular metre or rhyme pattern.

✓ Q. 7 — Sample Answer

(i) In Line 1: "Love set you going like a fat gold watch." The poet uses this comparison to create a picture in our minds of an outside force - love - setting the baby's life in motion. The beating of the heart is likened to the ticking of the watch. The word "fat" suggests the plumpness of the baby and the word "gold" conveys the idea of the preciousness of life.

(ii) In line 6 "We stand round blankly as walls". This simile conveys the sense of wonder of those present with the newborn child. They are overcome with awe.

(iii) In line 15: "Your mouth opens clean as a cat's". This comparison suggests the size, colour and shape of the open mouth of the baby as she awaits her food.

(iv) In line 18: "The clear vowels rise like balloons". The baby's cries are compared to balloons. This simile suggests the lightness and fragile nature of the child's cries. It may also suggest that, to the poet (the mother) the cries of the baby bring joy rather than annoyance.

All the comparisons listed above are similes.

Born Yesterday

for Sally Amis

Tightly-folded bud,
I have wished you something
None of the others would:
Not the usual stuff
About being beautiful,
Or running off a spring
Of innocence and love -
They will all wish you that,
And should it prove possible,
Well, you're a lucky girl.

But if it shouldn't, then
May you be ordinary;
Have, like other women,
An average of talents:
Not ugly, not good-looking,
Nothing uncustomary
To pull you off your balance,
That, unworkable itself,
Stops all the rest from working.
In fact, may you be dull -
If that is what a skilled,
Vigilant, flexible,
Unemphasised, enthralled
Catching of happiness is called.

— Philip Larkin

? Questions and Assignments

1. What, by the end of the poem, do you understand to be the poet's main wishes for the girl as she grows up?
2. What do you find unusual about what the poet wants for the baby?
3. The poet realises that what he is wishing for the baby is rather unusual. What do you think were the reasons for the poet's wishes?
4. The phrase "Tightly-folded bud", in the first line, is a good phrase to use about a baby. What does it suggest to you?
5. The writer uses some expressions which are typical of conversational English. Quote two of these and explain why you think the poet uses this conversational style.
6. If you were the mother or father of this baby girl, would you be pleased by what the poet is wishing for your baby daughter? Base your answer mainly on the poem.

Born Yesterday

✓ **Q. 3 — Sample Answer**

In "Born Yesterday" the poet not only reveals what he wishes for his godchild but also reveals something of himself. Obviously this poet is not a "dull" person, in the sense of an unimaginative, or stupid, or uninteresting type of person. Therefore, it is a little ironic that he wishes her to have "an average of talents" and to be "dull". Philip Larkin is a famous and talented poet, yet he seems to be suggesting that his gift and his lack of "dullness" brought him no happiness or joy. He seems to believe that any talent or other gift that puts people above the ordinary may bring more trouble than rewards.

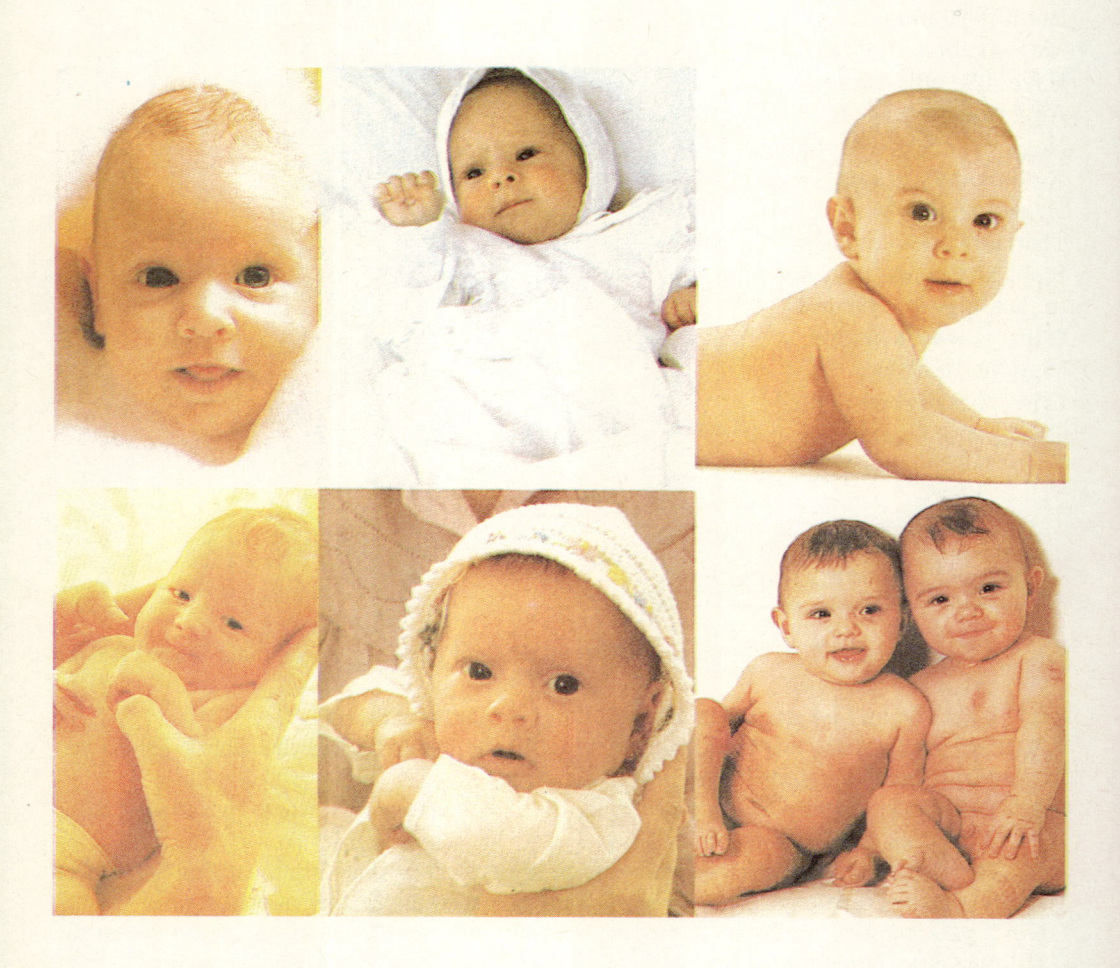

My Grandmother

She kept an antique shop - or it kept her.
Among apostle spoons and Bristol glass,
The faded silks, the heavy furniture,
She watched her own reflection in the brass
Salvers and silver bowls, as if to prove
Polish was all, there was no need of love.

And I remember how I once refused
To go out with her, since I was afraid.
It was perhaps a wish not to be used
Like antique objects. Though she never said
That she was hurt, I still could feel the guilt
Of that refusal, guessing how she felt.

Later, too frail to keep a shop, she put
All her best things in one long, narrow room.
The place smelt old, of things too long kept shut,
The smell of absences where shadows come
That can't be polished. There was nothing then
To give her own reflection back.

And when she died I felt no grief at all,
Only the guilt of what I once refused.
I walked into her room among the tall
Sideboards and cupboards - things she never used
But needed: and no finger-marks were there,
Only the new dust falling through the air.

- Elizabeth Jennings

My Grandmother

? Questions and Assignments

1. Examine each of the following words as they are used in the poem. In the case of each word say what idea the poet wishes to get across by choosing that particular word.

• frail	• faded	• brass
• felt	• hurt	• used

2. What are the 'shadows' referred to in the third stanza?
3. What facts about the grandmother's life are to be found in the poem?
4. What type of relationship had the poet with her grandmother?
5. Explain the two references to "reflection" that are found in the poem.
6. Describe the mood of the poem and say how it is achieved.

☞ Points to Note

The poem, which explores the bond between an old woman and her possessions, consists of four six-line stanzas, each of which has a regular rhyming scheme of *ababcc*.

It is written in the form of a dramatic monologue. In it, the speaker, (the grand-daughter) speaks about her grandmother and the relationship she had with her. While speaking about her grandmother she reveals a great deal about her own character.

✓ Q. 4 — Sample Answer

The poet allows us to see the grandmother only through the eyes of her grand-daughter. The girl saw her grandmother as someone who was very removed from people, someone who had little need of love. The grandmother surrounded herself with the antiques she kept in her shop. The girl felt that the antiques meant everything to her grandmother.

The girl recalls an occasion when she refused to go out with her grandmother because she did not want to be used like the antiques. Afterwards she always felt guilty because she knew she had misunderstood and hurt her grandmother. She realised what she had done as she saw her grandmother grow old and surround herself with keepsakes - things that reminded her of friends in the past - "things she never used/But needed".

Silver

Slowly, silently, now the moon
Walks the night in her silver shoon;
This way, and that, she peers, and sees
Silver fruit upon silver trees;
One by one the casements catch
Her beams beneath the silvery thatch;
Couched in his kennel, like a log,
With paws of silver sleeps the dog;
From their shadowy cote the white breasts peep
Of doves in a silver-feathered sleep;
A harvest mouse goes scampering by,
With silver claws, and silver eye;
And moveless fish in the water gleam,
By silver reeds in a silver stream.

- Walter de la Mare

Silver

? Questions and Assignments

1. One word from each of the pairs below is used in the poem. In each case say why you think the poet did not choose the alternative word given.

   - cote/shed
   - still/moveless
   - quietly/silently
   - scampering/running
   - trees/bushes
   - house/kennel
   - slumber/sleep
   - rays/beams
   - peers/stares

2. List all the things "seen" by the moon in this poem.
3. What effect has the frequent repetition of the word "silver" in the poem?
4. Find an example of simile in the poem and say what effect it has.
5. Select the image from the poem that most appeals to you and explain your choice.
6. Write a poem similar in theme and structure but with a modern urban setting.

☞ Points to Note

The moon here could be regarded as a sculptress surveying her work.

SOUND EFFECTS

This poem is rich in sound effects. It contains many examples of assonance, consonance and alliteration. Many of these are created by the repetition of "s" and "l" sounds. These sounds help to emphasise the stillness of the moonlit scene.

Snow

No breath of wind,
No gleam of sun -
Still the white snow
Whirls softly down -
Twig and bough
And blade and thorn
All in an icy
Quiet, forlorn,
Whispering, rustling,
Through the air,
On sill and stone,
Roof - everywhere,
It heaps its powdery
Crystal flakes
Of every tree
A mountain makes;
Till pale and faint
At shut of day,
Stoops from the West
One wintry ray,
And, feathered in fire,
Where ghosts the moon,
A robin shrills
His lonely tune.

- *Walter De La Mare*

Snow

? Questions and Assignments

1. What does the poet tell us in the first four lines?
2. Why do you think the poet uses the word "forlorn" to describe the effect of the snow on twig, bough, blade and thorn?
3. The words "whispering" and "rustling" are used to describe the sounds of the falling snowflakes. Do you consider these words appropriate? Explain your answer.
4. Select the image you like best in the poem and explain your choice.
5. Comment on the use of the verb "whirls" in line 4 and the verb "shrills" in line 23.
6. Explain what you think the poet wishes to convey in the lines: -
   (i) "Of every tree
       A mountain makes"
   (ii) "And, feathered in fire
        Where ghosts the moon."
7. (a) Compare this poem with Emily Dickinson's poem "The Snow".
   (b) State which of the two poems you prefer and give reasons for your choice.

☞ Points to Note

The poet uses hyperbole in lines 15 and 16: *"Of every tree / A mountain makes."*

Here the poet exaggerates for the sake of effect. He does this in order to emphasise the enlarged appearance of the trees after a fall of snow.

Examples of alliteration occur in : - *"On sill and stone"* ; *"A mountain makes"*; *"And feathered in fire"*. These help to draw attention to certain words and to enrich the sound patterns of the poem.

✓ Q. 3 — Sample Answer

Yes, in this case these words are appropriate as the poet emphasises the utter silence of the scene - "no breath of wind"; "whirls softly down"; "all in an icy quiet" - and therefore the very gentle sounds of the falling snowflakes could be heard as they alight on trees, roofs, window sill etc. Both words are onomatopoeiac and describe gentle sounds. The echo of the "r" and "s" sounds in them adds further to their gentle cadence.

The Snow

It sifts from leaden sieves,
It powders all the wood,
It fills with alabaster wool
The wrinkles of the road.

It makes an even face
Of mountain and of plain, -
Unbroken forehead from the east
Unto the east again.

It reaches to the fence,
It wraps it, rail by rail,
Till it is lost in fleeces;
It flings a crystal veil

On stump and stack and stem, -
The summer's empty room,
Acres of seams where harvests were,
Recordless, but for them.

It ruffles wrists of posts,
As ankles of a queen, -
Then stills its artisans like ghosts,
Denying they have been.

- Emily Dickinson

The Snow

? Questions and Assignments

1. What are the 'leaden sieves' to which the poet refers?
2. What effect has the snow on the fence and on the field?
3. Human characteristics are given to a number of objects in the poem. List the objects and the human characteristic given to each of them.
4. Identify the verbs in the poem which you feel are well chosen. In the case of each, explain why you regard it as an apt choice.
5. Select the three images from the poem that you consider most striking and explain your choice.
6. What do you think the poet means by each of the following phrases: "The summer's empty room", "It ruffles wrists of posts"?
7. Compare and contrast this poem with Thomas Hardy's poem "Snow in the Suburbs".

☞ Points to Note

In this poem metaphorical language is used to describe the snow. In the first stanza the poet calls the snow "alabaster wool". This term compares the snow to a soft powdery white material which fills up all the depressions and cracks in the road. In line 11 the poet refers to the snow as "fleeces". She makes this comparison because we normally associate softness and bulkiness with a fleece of wool. In line 12 she speaks of the snow as a lady with a "crystal veil". This comparison focuses our attention on the cover the snow gives and also on the texture and sheen of the surface layer of snow.

An example of alliteration appears in line 13: "On stump and stack and stem". The use of the "s" sound at the beginning of the three words in the line draws attention to the items covered by the snow, adds to the musical quality of the line and emphasises the silence of the scene.

The Fog

I saw the fog grow thick,
    Which soon made blind my ken;
It made tall men of boys,
    And giants of tall men.

It clutched my throat, I coughed;
    Nothing was in my head
Except two heavy eyes
    Like balls of burning lead.

And when it grew so black
    That I could know no place,
I lost all judgement then,
    Of distance and of space.

The street lamps, and the lights
    Upon the halted cars,
Could either be on earth
    Or be the heavenly stars.

A man passed by me close,
    I asked my way, he said,
'Come, follow me, my friend' -
    I followed where he led.

He rapped the stones in front,
    'Trust me,' he said, 'and come';
I followed like a child -
    A blind man led me home.

        - W. H. Davies

The Fog

? Questions and Assignments

1. One word from each of the pairs below is used in the poem. In each case say why you think the poet did not choose the alternative word given.

   - lead/metal
   - people/men
   - halted/parked
   - held/clutched
   - rapped/struck
   - heavenly/shining
   - balls/lumps
   - went/followed
   - landmark/place
   - get/grow
   - led/went

2. Write a short story based on the events in the poem.

☞ Points to Note

HYPERBOLE
- *Hyperbole* is an obvious exaggeration or overstatement used, not to deceive the reader, but to emphasise a point.
  In this poem the poet uses this figure of speech in the first and fourth stanzas. In the first stanza he says that the fog

  > 'made tall men of boys
  > And giants of tall men'.

  In the fourth stanza, in order to give an idea of how disorientated he was by the fog, the poet again exaggerates about the street lights and the lights on the halted cars.

  > 'The street lamps and the lights
  > Upon the halted cars,
  > Could either be on earth
  > Or be the heavenly stars'.

- The **repetition** of the word "tall" in line 2 emphasises the point that the poet is making about the effect of the fog.

- There are two examples of *simile* in the poem. In the second stanza the poet makes a comparison between his eyes and balls of burning lead in order to show that his eyes were stinging from strain.
  > 'Except two heavy eyes
  > Like balls of burning lead'.

- In the final stanza he speaks of following the blind man "like a child" to show that he was as willing as a lost child to be led home.

- The sound of the word "rapped" in the first line of the final stanza is similar to the sound made by the stick of the blind man as it struck the stones. "Rapped" could be termed an *onomatopoeiac* word.

From Trabzon to Gumushane

I travelled like a Sultan
in a caravan on wheels
from Trabzon to Gumushane.

The weather sweated and cooled
the brow
at stops along the Lordly peaks
of Zigana pass and Dag.

At Caliphs halts and camels stops
the children say hello and
smile from dirty mouths
and ragged clothes at
hairy whited tourists legs
in search of names and rest.

Our caravan passed like Xeniphon
in conquest trails
and where his men embraced in joy
we drank a cola from a tin
and watched the glare of ragged kids
at tourist flash
and poses of the trendy new.

Tourist Sir what is your search?
with pills and tan and billy can
answer that and travel home
and know yourself for real.

      - *Bernard Kennedy*

From Trabzon to Gumushane

❓ Questions and Assignments

1. What type of weather did the traveller experience on his journey? Give a reason for your answer.
2. Why do you think the poet describes the peaks as "Lordly"?
3. (a) Describe the children the traveller saw en route.
   (b) What were their reactions to the tourists?
4. What message do you think the poet wishes to convey?
5. Use an encyclopaedia to write a brief note on Xeniphon.

☞ Points to Note

SETTING

The *Setting* is a term used to describe when and where the action of a poem takes place. The setting may be (a) geographical — where the poem is set (b) the time of day, of year or even the year itself in which the poem is set (c) the social environment from which the poem's speaker or characters come or (d) any combination of these three.

The poem *From Trabzon to Gumushane* has a definite geographical setting. In it the poet describes a journey made into the less trodden parts of inland Turkey. Allthough this journey took place in recent times, the poet links it with journeys made by Sultans and by Xeniphon in the past.

The poem is an example of *free verse* form, because like much modern poetry it has no regular metre or rhyme pattern.

The Tom-cat

At midnight in the alley
    A Tom-cat comes to wail,
And he chants the hate of a million years
    As he swings his snaky tail.

Malevolent, bony, brindled,
    Tiger and devil and bard,
His eyes are coals from the middle of Hell
    And his heart is black and hard.

He twists and crouches and capers
    And bares his curved sharp claws,
And he sings to the stars of the jungle nights,
    Ere cities were, or laws.

Beast from a world primeval,
    He and his leaping clan,
When the blotched red moon leers over the roofs
    Give voice to their scorn of man.

He will lie on a rug to-morrow
    And lick his silky fur,
And veil the brute in his yellow eyes
    And play he's tame and purr.

But at midnight in the alley
    He will crouch again and wail,
And beat the time for his demon's song
    With the swing of his demon's tail.

- Don Marquis

The Tom-cat

❓ Questions and Assignments

1. Examine each of the following words as they are used in the poem. In the case of each word say what idea the poet wishes to get across by choosing that particular word.

• bony	• veil	• clan	• chants	• wail
• hard	• snaky	• scorn	• silky	• claws

2. Find evidence in the poem to show that the Tom-cat is seen as a demonic-like figure.
3. Discuss the points of contrast between the daytime cat and the midnight cat.
4. What is the cat's attitude to humans?
5. Say why you think the poet used the following phrases:-
   (i) "sings to the stars".
   (ii) "red moon leers".
   (iii) "His eyes are coals from the middle of Hell".
6. What do you consider is the purpose of the final stanza?
7. Select three images from the poem that appeal to you and say why you like them.
8. Comment on (a) the following adjectives: malevolent, brindled, black, hard, primeval, blotched. (b) The following verbs: - twists, crouches, capers - as they are used in the poem.

☞ Points to Note

This poem has the pace and rhythm of a chant. Line 3 of each verse has extra syllables and more varied musicality. In each stanza the end word of the second line rhymes with the end word of the fourth line. This rhyme helps to bring ideas or images in the poem together and to draw more attention to the words themselves. For example, in stanza 5 the two words that rhyme are *"fur"* and *"purr"*. These two words portray the cat as a soft, gentle and lovable animal.

✓ Q. 4 — Sample Answer

The poet presents the night-time cat as a devilish creature with a snaky tail. He has the cat emerge from the darkness wailing and chanting hate. The night-time cat's appearance is bony and his eyes are like coals from the middle of Hell. The overall picture is that of a primitive, threatening, aggressive creature.

By contrast, the daytime cat shows a tame domestic presence. Instead of wailing he purrs; instead of twisting and crouching he licks and lies. The daytime cat shows off his silky fur. He uses it to camouflage the bony form and sharp claws of the night.

Q.6 (iii)

(iii) In the third line of the second stanza the poet uses a metaphor: *"His eyes are coals from the middle of Hell"*. In comparing the cat's eyes with coals from the middle of Hell the poet presents us with a picture of the cat as a devil-like creature whose eyes emit evil into the night.

Travelling Through the Dark

Travelling through the dark I found a deer
dead on the edge of the Wilson River road.
It is usually best to roll them into the canyon:
that road is narrow; to swerve might make more dead.

By glow of the tail-light I stumbled to the back of the car
and stood by the heap, a doe, a recent killing;
she had stiffened already, almost cold.
I dragged her off; she was large in the belly.

My fingers touching her side brought me the reason -
her side was warm; her fawn lay there waiting,
alive, still, never to be born.
Beside that mountain road I hesitated.

The car aimed ahead its lowered parking lights;
under the hood purred the steady engine.
I stood in the glare of the warm exhaust turning red;
around our group I could hear the wilderness listen.

I thought hard for us all - my only swerving -
then pushed her over the edge into the river.

- William Stafford

Travelling Through the Dark

? Questions and Assignments

1. Describe the event on which this poem is based.

2. "I thought hard for us all". What thoughts would you imagine went through the poet's mind at that moment?

3. Explain what you think the poet means by

    (i) "Around our group I could hear the wilderness listen".

    (ii) "My only swerving".

4. (a) Describe the mood of the poem.

    (b) How is the mood established?

Hide and Seek

Call out. Call loud: 'I'm ready! Come and find me!'
The sacks in the toolshed smell like the seaside.
They'll never find you in this salty dark,
But be careful that your feet aren't sticking out.
Wiser not to risk another shout.
The floor is cold. They'll probably be searching
The bushes near the swing. Whatever happens
You mustn't sneeze when they come prowling in.
And here they are, whispering at the door;
You've never heard them sound so hushed before.
Don't breathe. Don't move. Stay dumb. Hide in your blindness.
They're moving closer, someone stumbles, mutters:
Their words and laughter scuffle, and they're gone.
But don't come out just yet; they'll try the lane
And then the greenhouse and back here again.
They must be thinking that you're very clever,
Getting more puzzled as they search all over.
It seems a long time since they went away.
Your legs are stiff, the cold bites through your coat;
The dark damp smell of sand moves in your throat.
Push off the sacks. Uncurl and stretch. That's better!
Out of the shed and call to them: 'I've won!'
The darkening garden watches. Nothing stirs.
The bushes hold their breath; the sun is gone.
Yes, here you are. But where are they who sought you?

- Vernon Scannell

Hide and Seek

> **? Questions and Assignments**

1. Where was the child hiding?
2. Why do you think the searchers "scuffled"?
3. Why did the searchers laugh?
4. How did the game end?
5. Why wasn't the hiding child found?
6. Describe what you imagine were the feelings of the boy after he decided to leave his hiding place.
7. Choose three images from the poem which you find particularly vivid. Give reasons for your choice.

> **☞ Points to Note**

A famous writer once said that it is better to be deceived by one's friends rather than deceive them. In relation to this point of view has this poem something to say?

A *simile* is used in line 2:

"The sacks in the toolshed smell like the seaside".

This simile gets across the idea that the sacks contain something - most likely sand - that was taken from the seaside. This image appeals strongly to our sense of smell and conveys the damp atmosphere of the shed where the child is hiding.

A type of *paradox* occurs in line 10:

"You've never heard them sound so hushed before".

"Sound" means that a noise is produced while "hushed" suggests silence. Although the phrase "sound so hushed" appears to contradict itself, the line more than succeeds in describing the control exercised by the boys as they enter the shed.

Personification is used in line 24:

"The bushes hold their breath"

This expression is used to show that there was absolute stillness. It also gives the idea that the bushes, like the child, await something to happen.

> **✓ Q. 3 — Sample Answer**
>
> The poem does not explain this and it is up to the reader to guess why the seekers laughed. I think that they laughed because they spotted the one who was hiding but they pretended not to have done so. He, meanwhile, thinks that he has outsmarted them. He imagines that they are continuing to search for him. It is in the last few lines that both he and the readers begin to realise that the seekers have abandoned their search. The seekers probably laughed because they outsmarted the child in hiding.

Sea

I am patient, repetitive, multi-voiced,
Yet few hear me
And fewer still trouble to understand

Why, for example, I caress
And hammer the land.
I do not brag of my depths

Or my currents, I do not
Boast of my moods or my colours
Or my breath in your thought.

In time I surrender my drowned,
My appetite speaks for itself,
I could swallow all you have found

And open for more,
My green tongues licking the shores
Of the world

Like starved beasts reaching for men
Who will not understand
When I rage and roar

When I bellow and threaten
I am obeying a law
Observing a discipline.

This is the rhythm
I live.
This is the reason I move

In hunger and skill
To give you the pick of my creatures.
This is why I am willing to kill,

Chill every created nerve.
You have made me a savage master
Because I know how to serve.

    - *Brendan Kennelly*

Sea

> **? Questions and Assignments**

1. In this poem the sea has a human voice. How does the poet make us continually aware of this?
2. List the qualities of the sea that are mentioned in the poem.
3. What human qualities does the poet give the sea?
4. (a) To whom is the sea addressing itself?
   (b) What tone does it adopt?
5. Explain what you think the poet means by
   (i) "I caress and hammer the land".
   (ii) "I surrender my drowned"
   (iii) "You have made me a savage master
         Because I know how to serve".
6. Select lines from the poem that appeal to you and say why you like them.
7. What action of the sea might the irregular length of the lines suggest?

> **☞ Points to Note**

CONTRAST

The poet uses *contrast* in lines 4 and 5: -
"Why, for example, I caress
And hammer the land."

This use of contrast suggests the sea's most extreme moods. When the sea is calm and gentle it caresses the land. When it is rough and angry it hammers the land.

In line 14 the poet uses a *metaphor*: "My green tongues licking the shores".

This comparison of the waves with green tongues creates a vivid image that suggests the colour, shape and movements of a wave. The word *"licking"* extends the metaphor - the erosive action of a wave is compared to the licking of a tongue. Can you suggest another aspect of this comparison?

The Coming of the Cold

The ribs of leaves lie in the dust,
The beak of frost has picked the bough,
The briar bears its thorn, and drought
Has left its ravage on the field.
The season's wreckage lies about,
Late autumn fruit is rotted now.
All shade is lean, the antic branch
Jerks skyward at the touch of wind,
Dense trees no longer hold the light,
The hedge and orchard grove are thinned.
The dank bark dries beneath the sun,
The last of harvesting is done.
All things are brought to barn and fold.
The oak leaves strain to be unbound,
The sky turns dark, the year grows old,
The buds draw in before the cold.

- Theodore Roethke

The Coming of the Cold

? Questions and Assignments

1. One word from each of the pairs below is used in the poem. In each case say why you think the poet did not choose the alternative word given.

   - barn/shed
   - jerks/moves
   - moist/dank
   - lean/thin
   - decayed/rotted
   - marked/picked
   - damage/ravage
   - dark/grey
   - ribs/skeletons
   - beneath/under
   - thick/dense

2. Write a paragraph entitled "The Coming of Winter" using the poem for inspiration.
3. What idea do you think the poet wants to convey in the phrase "season's wreckage"?
4. This poem consists of a series of images that signal the approach of winter. Pick out the two images that you find most effective and explain your choice.
5. Pick out an example of the use of contrast in the poem and say what effect this has.
6. Describe the setting of the poem in a sentence or two.
7. Write a poem, similar in form and structure to *The Coming of the Cold* on one of the following titles: The Coming of Spring; The Coming of Christmas; The Coming of Autumn; The Coming of Night.

☞ Points to Note

IMAGES

In this poem, the poet, through a series of well-drawn images, reminds us that winter is upon us. The poet's unusual but very apt choice of words merits close study. When he speaks of the *"beak of frost"* having *"picked"* the bough he makes the frost seem bird-like. The use of the words *"ravage"*, *"wreckage"* and *"rotted"* conveys a picture of everything having been destroyed. The reference to the trees further emphasises the change that has taken place.

An example of consonance occurs in line 11: "dank bark". The repetition of the 'k' sound enriches the sound pattern of the line and also helps to draw more attention to the words themselves and consequently to the image they create.

Uncle Jack and the Other Man

I know a man who works on the land
Has a barrel for a chest and a huge flat hand
Can hurl a wheat-bag over a fence.

I like to watch him working in the sun
And see the little drops of perspiration run
Like bright flies slowly down his arms.

There was a story once that he took
A tight grip of the London phone book
And pulled it in half - but I don't believe it

Because he *never* boasts - it was Bongo Grass
Who invented that story, he's the worst in class
For pranks and fibs and exaggerations.

But he's certainly strong, and a little strange too:
When you pass him by he hardly speaks to you,
But pats his dogs or makes a cigarette.

He takes no interest in a conversation.
Not like my Uncle Jack. He works at the station
And is always talking when he finds a chance.

If you pay him a visit in his room at night
He'll build up the fire and in the leaping light
He'll tell you stories of ghosts and devils.

Sometimes I stay for hours.
      Uncle Jack
Has skinny white legs and a painful back:
He can't lift a bag or tear the phone book

And yet, he's always interesting. I suppose
I'd like to be like Uncle Jack because he knows
So much ... but I'd also like to grow - so I can
Hurl things about like that other man.

      - Keith Harrison

Uncle Jack and the Other Man

? Questions and Assignments

1. One word from each of the pairs below is used in the poem. In each case say why you think the poet did not choose the alternative word given.

• jumping/leaping	• grow/develop	• fascinating/interesting
• throw/hurl	• sweat/perspiration	• beads/drops
• skinny/thin	• half/two	• brags/boasts
• composed/invented	• strong/robust	• conversation/talk
• also/too		

2. Write about the poem under the following headings :-
   (i) The contrast between Uncle Jack and the Other Man.
   (ii) The structure and rhyming scheme of the poem.

☞ **Points to Note**

- A *metaphor* is used in the first stanza to describe the chest of the Other Man :
    he 'has a barrel for a chest'.
  The poet uses this metaphor to emphasise the strength and bulk of the Other Man.

- A *simile* is used in the second stanza to describe the drops of perspiration running down the Other Man's arms :
    'And see the little drops of perspiration run
    Like bright flies slowly down his arms'.
  This comparison also emphasises the strength and power of the Other Man. The drops of sweat look as small as flies on his arms. The movements of the drops resemble the spurts of movements that flies make on skin.

Hard Cheese

The grown ups are all safe,
Tucked up inside,
Where they belong.

They doze into the telly,
Bustle through the washing-up,
Snore into the fire,
Rustle through the paper.

They're all there,
Out of harm's way.

Now it's *our* street:
All the back yards,
All the gardens,
All the shadows,
All the dark corners,
All the privet hedges,
All the lamp-posts,
All the doorways.

Here is an important announcement:
The army of occupation
Is confined to barracks.
Hooray.

We're the natives.
We creep out at night,
Play everywhere,
Swing on *all* the lamp-posts,
Slit your gizzard?

Then, about nine o'clock,
They send out search parties.

We can hear them coming.
And we crouch
In the garden-sheds,
Behind the dustbins,
Up the alleyways,
Inside the dustbins,
Or stand stock-still,
And pull ourselves in,
As thin as a pin,
Behind the lamp-posts.

Hard Cheese

And they stand still,
And peer into the dark.
They take a deep breath -
You can hear it for miles -
And then, they bawl,
They shout, they caterwaul:
'J-i-i-i-i-mmeeee!'
'Timeforbed. D'youhearme?'
'M-a-a-a-a-a-reeee!'
'J-o-o-o-o-o-hnneeee!'
'S-a-a-a-a-mmeeee!'
'Mary!' 'Jimmy!'
'Johnny!' 'Sammy!'
Like cats. With very large mouths.

Then we give ourselves up,
Prisoners - of - war.
Till tomorrow night.

But just you wait.
One of these nights
We'll hold out,
We'll lie doggo,
And wait, and wait,
Till they just give up
And mumble
And go to bed.
You just wait.
They'll see!

- Justin St. John

? Questions and Assignments

1. What is the speaker's attitude to grown-ups? Refer to lines in the poem to support your answer.
2. Comment on the choice of verbs in the second stanza.
3. What features of the street attract the poet?
4. Comment on the phrase "as thin as a pin".
5. What do you think the poet wishes to convey by the phrases:-
   - "The army of occupation "
   - "Where they belong"
   - "They'll see!"
   - "Is confined to barracks."
   - "We're the natives".
   - "Out of harm's way. "
   - "Prisoners-of-war".
6. Select three words from the poem which convey both sound and sense and, in the case of each, comment on its effectiveness.

Hard Cheese

7. Say whether you like or dislike this poem. Give reasons for your answer.

> 👉 **Points to Note**

Few playgrounds can offer the same scope for fun and adventure as the streets of your neighbourhood at dark. Parents are portrayed here, in a lighthearted way, as tyrants, intent on spoiling the fun - but have they a choice?

EXTENDED METAPHOR

There are a number of metaphors in this poem. The poet describes the grown-ups as the "army of occupation". The metaphors that are used to describe the later events and situations of the poem are all linked to or extend from the comparison between the grown-ups and "an army of occupation". The grown-ups are indoors - i.e. "confined to barracks"; the children are "the natives". What other linking metaphors can you find? What situations or events are they describing?

> ✓ **Q. 4 — Sample Answer**
>
> This is a phrase to describe how thin the children seem to become as they try to hide behind lamp-posts. It is a simile that is a little exaggerated, like many similes. However, it is original. Most people say "thin as a rake" but the "thinness" of a pin is more obvious than that of a rake. Also "thin as a pin" has a nice rhyme.

Haiku

A crimson berry
Splattering softly down on
The frost white garden.

- Masoaka Shiki

👉 Points to Note

Haiku is a form of tightly structured Japanese poetry which properly has seventeen syllables arranged in three lines of five, seven and five syllables. This rule is often broken in translations of haiku into English, where stress rather than syllable counting is more important.

A haiku usually consists of two simple images or ideas which our imagination brings together. Note the contrast between the bright red berry and the white frost. The splattered berry may symbolise blood spilled, which would suggest death and the onset of winter. Here are some more examples.

Flashing neon light
Blurred through a steaming window:
A concert of colours!

- J. W. Hackett

Alone I cling to
The freezing mountain and see
White cloud - below me

- Ian Serraillier

Robin

As heavy snow falls
He's a red-vested Batman
On a garden fence.

❓ Questions and Assignments

1. Write an appreciation of each of them.
2. Try writing your own haiku on a subject of your choice.

Praise of a Collie

She was a small dog, neat and fluid -
Even her conversation was tiny:
She greeted you with *bow*, never *bow-wow*.

Her sons stood monumentally over her
But did what she told them. Each grew grizzled.
Till it seemed he was his own mother's grandfather.

Once, gathering sheep on a showery day,
I remarked how dry she was. Pollóchan said, 'Ah,
It would take a very accurate drop to hit Lassie.'

And her tact - and tactics! When the sheep bolted
In an unforeseen direction, over the skyline
Came - who but Lassie, and not even panting.

She sailed in the dinghy like a proper sea-dog.
Where's a burn*? - she's first on the other side.
She flowed through fences like a piece of black wind.

But suddenly she was old and sick and crippled …
I grieved for Pollóchan when he took her a stroll
And put his gun to the back of her head.

- Norman MacCaig

* *stream*

Praise of a Collie

? Questions and Assignments

1. Examine each of the following words as they are used in the poem. In the case of each word say what idea the poet wishes to get across by choosing that particular word.

   - grizzled
   - monumentally
   - flowed
   - skyline
   - fluid
   - conversation
   - bolted
   - unforeseen

2. Read the poem carefully and write as much as you can about (i) the dog and (ii) the poet. Choose your examples from the poem carefully, to support what you say. You will find it helpful to consider the poet's choice of words and the way the ideas in the poem are organised.

3. (a) Compare the two similes used in the poem - "like a proper sea-dog" and "like a piece of black wind".
   (b) Why does the poet include them?

4. What feelings does the last stanza arouse in you?

☞ Points to Note

An example of the use of *hyperbole* occurs in lines 5 and 6: "Each grew grizzled / Till it seemed he was his own mother's grandfather".

Here the poet exaggerates how old the collie's offspring looked, in order to emphasise how young she looked, even when she was very old.

Since prehistoric times, dogs have been the most loyal and affectionate of all domestic animals - and the collie is one of the most popular breeds. Collies are renowned for their friendly and warm natures and are also dependable working dogs. This poem is a warm tribute to a loved collie.

✓ Q. 4 — Sample Answer

The poet uses the adjective "fluid" to describe Lassie's litheness. From the use of the word "fluid" we get the impression that her movement was as smooth as the movement of a liquid. In the fifth stanza the poet extends this image by stating that the collie "flowed" through fences.

Vegetarians

Vegetarians are cruel unthinking people.
Everybody knows that a carrot screams when grated
That a peach bleeds when torn apart.
Do you believe an orange insensitive
to thumbs gouging out its flesh?
That tomatoes spill their brains
painlessly? Potatoes, skinned alive
and boiled, the soil's little lobsters.
Don't tell me it doesn't hurt
when peas are ripped from their overcoats,
the hide flayed off sprouts,
cabbage shredded, onions beheaded.

Throw in the trowel and lay down the hoe.
Mow no more. Let my people go!

- *Roger McGough*

? Questions and Assignments

1. What is the theme of this poem?
2. How does the poet support the claim he makes in the first line?
3. In the case of some of the fruit and some of the vegetables, the poet speaks of them as if they had feelings. Quote from the poem to show where this happens and say how it influences the message the poet wishes to convey.
4. Select lines from the poem that appeal to you and say why you like them.
5. Identify and explain the pun in the second last line.

☞ Points to Note

This poem gives a lighthearted twist to the preachings of some vegetarians and animal-rights campaigners.

In the first line he categorises vegetarians as unthinking people and then proceeds to give characteristics to fruit and vegetables. In the final line he asks the vegetarians to "let my people go."

The poet use a *metaphor* in lines 7 and 8, when he calls potatoes "the soil's little lobsters". He makes this comparison to point out that it is just as cruel to boil potatoes as it is to place live lobsters in boiling water.

Child on Top of a Greenhouse

The wind billowing out the seat of my britches,
My feet crackling splinters of glass and dried putty,
The half-grown chrysanthemums staring up like accusers,
Up through the streaked glass, flashing with sunlight,
A few white clouds all rushing eastward,
A line of elms plunging and tossing like horses,
And everyone, everyone pointing up and shouting!

- *Theodore Roethke*

? Questions and Assignments

1. Who is the speaker in this poem?
2. Describe the mood of the speaker.
   Support your answer by reference to the poem.
3. What does the speaker hear and see from his vantage point?
4. What effect does the repetition of the word "everyone" in the last line, have?
5. The poet creates an impression of movement in the poem. How does he achieve this?
6. How important is the title of this poem?

☞ Points to Note

The word "billowing" in line 1 and the word "crackling" in line 2 are examples of *onomatopoeiac* words. The sound of the word "billowing" echoes the sound made by the wind as it blows out the seat of the child's britches. The word "crackling" conveys an idea of the sound made by the child's feet on the broken glass.

Two *similes* are used in the poem. (i) In line 3:
"The half-grown chrysanthemums staring up like accusers."
The child mentions that the flowers look like "accusers" because he can see their faces looking up at him like the faces of all the shouting people on the ground.
(ii) In line 6:
"A line of elms plunging and tossing like horses."
To the child the movement of the elm trees in the wind seems like the wild movement of horses, as he is eye-level with the tops of the trees.

Both of these similes remind us that the child has a very unusual perspective on things - as he looks down from his vantage point above.

The Bat

By day the bat is cousin to the mouse.
He likes the attic of an ageing house.

His fingers make a hat about his head.
His pulse beat is so slow we think him dead.

He loops in crazy figures half the night
Among the trees that face the corner light.

But when he brushes up against a screen,
We are afraid of what our eyes have seen:

For something is amiss or out of place
When mice with wings can wear a human face.

 - Theodore Roethke

? Questions and Assignments

1. What impression do you get of the bat (a) by day and (b) by night?
2. Comment briefly on the third line.
3. What figure of speech does the poet use when he refers to bats as "mice with wings". Explain why you think he uses this particular figure of speech.
4. Write out the rhyme-scheme of the poem and say what effect it has on the poem.
5. Explain the use of the word "cousin" in line 1 and "screen" in line 7.
6. In the last four lines the poet introduces a strange idea. Can you explain what he is referring to when he mentions "afraid" and a "human face"?

☞ Points to Note

COUPLET

A *couplet* is a pair of lines, usually of the same metre, which have a common rhyme as in this poem.

✓ **Q. 2 — Sample Answer**

Having never seen a sleeping bat, I have to take the poet's word that *"His fingers make a hat about his head"*. The poet uses this metaphor in order to create a picture in our minds of the appearance of the bat as he sleeps. While the bat's fingers wrapped about his head do not make a hat, the effect looks like a hat. The line would suggest that the poet is an attentive observer of nature.

He Wishes for the Cloths of Heaven

WILLIAM BUTLER YEATS (1865 - 1939)

W. B. Yeats is Ireland's most famous poet. He was born in Dublin but spent much of his childhood in London. His holidays were often spent in Sligo with his mother's people. He became interested in both poetry and things Irish - culture and politics - during his teens. He fell in love with Maud Gonne when he was in his early twenties and this love affair provided him with inspiration for many of his poems. However, Maud Gonne did not return Yeats' love and she eventually married John McBride, a rebel leader.

Yeats founded the Abbey Theatre in 1904 and wrote a number of verse-plays which were produced. He is remembered chiefly for his poetry. It was Ireland, its legends, its heroes, its landscape, its politicians and its people which provided him with inspiration for most of his poetry. Some of the poetry of his later years is a little difficult and obscure. He is regarded as the greatest English speaking poet of the twentieth-century and was awarded the Nobel Prize for literature in 1923. He died in France in 1939 but his body was returned to Ireland and buried in Drumcliff in Sligo in 1948.

Had I the heaven's embroidered cloths,
Enwrought with golden and silver light,
The blue and the dim and the dark cloths
Of night and light and the half-light,
I would spread the cloths under your feet:
But I, being poor, have only my dreams;
I have spread my dreams under your feet;
Tread softly because you tread on my dreams.

                 - W. B. Yeats

? Questions and Assignments

1. What are the "embroidered cloths" to which the poet refers?
2. "Embroidered cloths" is a metaphor. Trace the development of this metaphor down through the poem.
3. Describe the structure of the poem.
4. What is the tone of the poem? What phrases create the tone?
5. What does the last line suggest about the type of relationship the poet had with his beloved?
6. There is a series of repetitions in this poem. What effect do these repetitions have?

He Wishes for the Cloths of Heaven

☞ Points to Note

This is a love poem addressed to Maud Gonne. W. B. Yeats was deeply in love with this beautiful woman who had committed herself to the Irish revolutionary movement of her time. For years, Yeats sought her love and her hand in marriage but his efforts were in vain. The disappointed Yeats found solace in his poetry.

The language of the poem is tight and concise - there is not an unnecessary word used.

Though the poet uses words economically and keeps the length of the poem to eight lines, he still succeeds in making a very strong statement about the depth of his feeling for his beloved.

In line 4 the poet uses internal rhyme: *"Of night and light and the half-light"*. This creates a very pleasing sound pattern as does the use of assonance in line 7: *"I have spread my dreams under your feet;"*

The Wild Swans at Coole

The trees are in their autumn beauty,
The woodland paths are dry,
Under the October twilight the water
Mirrors a still sky;
Upon the brimming water among the stones
Are nine-and-fifty swans.

The nineteenth autumn has come upon me
Since I first made my count;
I saw, before I had well finished,
All suddenly mount
And scatter wheeling in great broken rings
Upon their clamorous wings.

I have looked upon those brilliant creatures,
And now my heart is sore.
All's changed since I, hearing at twilight,
The first time on this shore.
The bell-beat of their wings above my head,
Trod with a lighter tread.

Unwearied still, lover by lover,
They paddle in the cold
Companionable streams or climb the air;
Their hearts have not grown old;
Passion or conquest, wander where they will,
Attend upon them still.

But now they drift on the still water,
Mysterious, beautiful;
Among what rushes will they build,
By what lake's edge or pool
Delight men's eyes when I awake some day
To find they have flown away?

- William Butler Yeats

The Wild Swans ot Coole

? Questions and Assignments

1. Why does the poet feel sad when he looks at the swans again, after nineteen years?
2. What lines in the poem tell us that
   (i) the poet was much younger when he first saw the swans
   (ii) the swans remain ageless and untiring
   (iii) the swans are constant in their love
   (iv) the swans retain their passion and spirit?
3. Find, in the poem, lines that suggest fast movement and lines that suggest stillness.
4. Taking the swans as symbols, say what you think they represent.
5. What is the mood of the poem? What images, details and sounds build up this mood?
6. Comment on the effectiveness of the following phrases as they are used in the poem: "autumn beauty . . . mirrors a still sky"; "brimming water"; "clamorous wings"; "bell-beat"; "companionable streams".
7. What comment is the poet making on human love in this poem?

☞ Points to Note

It was on a lake in the grounds of Coole Park, Gort, Go. Galway that W. B. Yeats saw the swans that inspired him to write this poem. Coole Park was the home of Lady Augusta Gregory who was a great friend and patron of the poet. In 1897 Yeats first saw the swans and counted fifty nine. Nineteen years later he counted them again to find the same number. To him it appeared that the swans had not changed. This led him to reflect on how much his life had changed in that nineteen-year period.

The poem is made up of five six-line stanzas. The rhyming scheme for each stanza is the same. The second line rhymes with the fourth and there is a strong concluding rhyme in the fifth and sixth lines.

The rhythm is slow, giving the poem a sad and melancholy tone. The long vowel sounds - autumn, water, stones, nine - also help to emphasise the poem's mournful tone and the repeated "l" sounds - "woodland, twilight, still (stanza 1), brilliant, all's, bell-beat, lighter (stanza 3) - add to the impression of the still evening.

IV - MASS MEDIA

Newspapers

I — Making The Headlines Hit!

👉 Points to Note

THE FRONT PAGE

The aim of banner headlines (i.e. the main front page headlines) is to persuade people to buy the newspaper. An effective headline captures the attention of the intended readers and arouses their curiosity.

❓ Questions and Assignments

Below are a selection of banner headlines. In the case of each headline :-

(i) Outline briefly the kind of report or story that you would expect to follow the headline.
(ii) List at least three questions which you would expect to be answered in that report.
(iii) Say whether you think it came from a serious newspaper or a newspaper that deals with more sensational stories. Give a brief reason for your answer in each case.

1. **Home Loan Costs Set to Rise**
2. **New Bid to save Erin Foods Jobs**
3. **Exam Chaos Looms**
4. **Corrib Pollution Threat**
5. **Farmers In Brussels Protest**
6. **Smith faces no confidence Motion**
7. **Minister Optimistic on Job Trends**
8. **Mandy's Mum in NiteClub Brawl**
9. **Waitress Tracy is left a cool Million!**
10. **Phew! Jason lets off steam!**

Read All About It!

👉 Points to Note

All headlines in a newspaper must indicate the subject matter of the reports and stories that follow. They are always written with the *interests* and *attitudes* of the paper's readership in mind.

The sub-editors who compose the headlines make frequent use of certain words because these words are (i) **short** and save page space (ii) are particularly **dramatic, vivid** and **descriptive.**

A selection of these words is listed in the box below.

NOUNS AND VERBS

Some of these words can only be used as nouns while others can only be used as verbs. However, many of the words can be used as both verbs and nouns. For example, the word 'link', meaning 'connection' or 'connect', can be used

— as a noun — JEWEL THEFT : TERRORIST LINK SUSPECTED

— as a verb — NEW TOLL ROAD TO LINK TOWNS

❓ Questions and Assignments

1. In the case of each word in the list, explain its meaning and say whether it can be used as (i) a verb only (ii) a noun only (iii) both as a noun and as a verb.
2. Taking the words that can be used as nouns and verbs, write headlines to show them in both forms (see example above).

• Deal	• Held	• Smash	• Fear	• Chief
• Bug	• Quiz	• Curb	• Probe	• Slam
• Rap	• Drama	• Snubbed	• Chaos	• Win
• Haul	• Axes	• Hits	• Net	• Spark
• Quit	• Looms	• Ordeal	• Threat	• Seeks
• Crook	• Clash	• Soar	• Toll	• Ban
• Shock	• Blast	• Rise	• Aid	• Boss
• Flee	• Boost	• Riddle	• Press	• No
• Plea	• Kid	• Link	• Weds	• Bid
• Boom	• Horror	• Plunge	• Storm	• Tragedy
• Killing	• Pledge	• Drive	• Urge	• Cuts
• Scare	• Mob	• Row	• Call	• Backs
• Alert	• Find			

Newspapers

? Questions and Assignments

A word has been omitted from each of the following headlines. Study the brief descriptions of the stories which the headlines introduce and then select suitable words from the list on page 302 to complete the headlines.

Headline	Topic of Report
1 Pay _____ Off	an agreement on wages abandoned.
2 Flu _____ Warning	a 'flu' virus that is likely to spread.
3 Three die in _____	an explosion in which three people were killed.
4 Politicians _____ on Budget	two politicians in disagreement on details of the budget.
5 Diplomat _____	a foreign diplomat who is treated in a cold and distant manner.
6 Safety _____ to continue	a campaign for road safety that is to be continued beyond its original timescale.
7 Woman dies in River _____	a woman who is drowned when the car in which she was travelling is driven off a quayside.
8 Interest Rates to _____	bank interest rates to increase significantly.
9 Limerick _____	an incident of manslaughter or murder in the Limerick area.
10 Port Strike _____ Exports	a strike by dockers which results in goods for export not being shipped.
11. Wife's _____ to Kidnappers	the wife of a kidnap victim strongly requesting the safe release of her husband.
12 Gardaí _____ escapees	gardaí capturing two men who escaped from custody.
13 Schoolboy in Zoo _____	a schoolboy who climbs into lions' cage.
14 Rail Strike _____	the likely possibility of a strike by railworkers taking place shortly.
15 Pop-star _____ in Paris	a pop-star who got married in Paris.
16 _____ in foreign _____ condemned	a bishop who condemns reductions in the government's programme for assisting poorer nations.
17 Libyan _____ in arms _____	a large consignment of illegal guns found by gardaí and the possibility that the guns were imported from Libya.

Making the Headlines Hit

> **? Questions and Assignments — Headlines**

(i) Use the words in the box on page 302 to complete the headlines for each of the following stories. In some cases you may have to change the form of the word given in the box.

(ii) **Correcting Proofs:** In each report there are a number of errors in punctuation, use of capital letters and spelling. Identify these and correct them.

Councillors ____ Corporation

City Councillors last night critised Dublin Corporation for the disgracefull state it has left a disused city church where children are said to be playing with skulls and bones in its vaults.

St. lukes church in the Liberties is said to be in an extremely vandalised state and local resident's are calling on . . . .

Baby, Father in ____

A twenty-nine year old Dublin man and his eighteen-month old daughter were killed in a traffic acident last night.

The man was standing at the gateway of his home with the child in his arms when they were struck by an articulated truck.

Holidaymakers ____ Resorts

Holidaymakers on campsites in a number of resorts in the South of France were forced to leave the sites as forest fires threatened to engulf the entire area.

Chairman ____ in Port ____

Mr. Peter Smith. chairman of the ardlea port authority resigned last night following a disagreement between him and other Members of the authority over plans for a new pier.

Water Shortages ____

The country is on course fo the dryest spring on record and all ready potatos are sufering from lack of rain. Farmers are expecting a dismal second cut of silage and a number of county councils are planing to introduce water rationing.

Minister ____ to Delay Road Plan

A member of the Castlederry Urban Council had appealed to the minister for the environment to reconsider plans for reconsider plans for a new by-pass for the town. Work on the by-pass is due to commence shortly and . . .

Report ____ Hospital Consultants

A report published in todays edition of the british Medical Journal has strongly condemned some over they're failure to come to hospital wards when called

---

Reforms ____ Food Panic in Russia

People mobbed food stores in cities throughout the Soviet Union yesterday as panic buying followed the announcment of a goverment plan to increase prices.

Athens ____

Greeks were advised to stay off the streets of Athens yesterday after air pollution sent hundreds of people to hospital. high temperatures and lack of wind have contributed to nitrogen dioxide levels of close to 500 milligrams per cubic metre of air, the point at which government emergency measures must be introduced

---

T.D. ____ Support

Mr. Michael McNisp T.D. for Tipperary West has promised to support demands from residents in the Athmore area for mining activity to cease. Peter O'Dell, Chariman of the athmore community council had earlier this week called on Mr. McNisp for his suport.

Newspapers

Verbs in Headlines

☞ **Points to Note**

Bus Fares ___

A spokesman for Bus Eireann today confirmed that bus fares are to be increased by around 5%.

The verb is missing from the headline of this story. The main point of the story is that bus fares are to be increased. Look at the list of verbs in the box below. The verb which has a similar meaning to 'increase' is 'rise'.

The fares have not yet been increased - but they will be in the future. Therefore, the verb which appears in the headline is **'to rise'** - the infinitive form of the verb 'rise'.

T.V. Host ___

Dave Smyle, the popular host of the HTV quiz show WHAT DAY IS TODAY has died in a Cardiff hospital after a short illness.

The verb is missing from this headline. The report is about somebody who died very recently, probably the day before the report. In headlines that deal with events that have just happened, sub-editors use the present tense. Therefore, the verb appears in the headline above as **'dies'**. This form of the verb gives the headline a more dramatic and up-to-date look - almost as if the event was happening while the report was being written.

Garda ___ by raider Court told

During the second day of the trial of Gordon McLout the court was told that Detective Garda Seán O'Brien was shot in the ankle during a raid on the Bank of Leinster at . . .

The verb is missing from this headline. The shooting of the garda took place some months before but the details are only now being revealed. In this type of report the past tense is used. Therefore, the verb appears in the headline above as **'shot'**.

❓ Questions and Assignments

1. Read the articles on page 306 and choose appropriate verbs from the list below to complete the headlines. You may have to change the forms or tenses of some of the verbs.
2. **Proof Corrections:** In each report there are a number of errors in punctuation, use of capital letters and spelling. Identify these and correct them.

• Went	• Quit	• Travel	• Sell	• Starve	• Shoot
• Tour	• Fail	• Find	• Arrest	• Seek	• Marry
• Leave	• Loose	• Plead	• Win	• Jail	• End
• Come	• Fine	• Rise	• Die	• Shoot	• Soar

Making the Headlines Hit

Tivoli Owner ____ Licence

A former Liberties boy. who never forgot his boyhood assosiation with the tivoli cinema on francis Street, Dublin later poured £400,000 of his money into refurbishing it as a uniqeu theater, a court was told yesterday, as he sought a drinks license for the facility.

Cubans ____

Four cubans who entered the Italian ambassador's residanse in Havana on 17 july have left. after Italy obtained garantees for their safety, the foreign ministry said yesterday.

Opponents ____

An opponent to Iraqi President saddam hussein was quoted as saying Yesterday that the Iraqi leader was using the us-imposed trade embargo to starve people in areas of the country hostile to his regime.

"Once the embargo was announced, Saddam issued his dicision to starve the areas where the popalation opposses him," Mohammed Haidari, member of the Consultive Council of the Islamic Revolution in Iraq told newsmen.

Students ____ Border

A group of students from trinity college have announsed plans for a bus tour along the border.

Jane Fonda ____

Jane Fonda is to marry a us media billionair, Mr Ted Turner "in the new year". The actress's publicist said. Ted picked out an opal-and-daimond ring and-daimond ring at Tiffany's and will present it to the actress at her birthday on December 21st.

Plotters ____

Nigeria yesterday execoted 42 convicted coup plotters by Firing Squad.

Warren ____ to Show Up

Boxing prommoter Frank Warren missed an appearance on the Jonathan Ross chat show on Channel 4 last night because he was stuck in a Traffic Jam.

It was the first time that Mr. Warren was scheduled to speak in public since former boxing champian Terry Marsh was cleared at the Old Bailey of attempting to murder him.

Belfast man ____ for Five Years

A Belfast man who formully served with both the irish and British Armies was jailed for five years yesterday at belfast crown court after ammitting allowing the IRA to use his home to make bombs.

Teenager ____ Guilty

A british teenager, Ms Karen Smith, pleaded guilty to charges of posseccing 5.9lb of heroin. Ms Smith (19) was arrested on July 18th with her componian, Ms Patricia Cahill (17) from Birmingham at banqok's international airport.

police found over 70lb of pure heroin in the luggage of the two young women. and charged them with trying to smuggle it on a flight to gambia.

River Polluters ____

Magistrates at Newton Abbot ordered award-winning Finlake Leisure to pay a £500 fine with £300 costs after Raw Sewage from its campsite near Chudleigh poluted the river teign. The firm said its new £50,000 tretment system had been jammed by a cola can.

Driver ____ Sack of Cash

A British motorist who found £80,000 in a sack lying in the road has recieved a £1,000 reward after handing it to the Police.

Mr. Ian Flindall was amased when he opened the sack of used notes. which fell from a securicor van between Stanton-by-Bridge and Melbourne, Derbyshire. He went striaght to police with the money.

Word Play in Headlines

> **Points to Note**

Headline writers often 'play' with words when they want to indicate that a story is in some way amusing or light-hearted. The techniques they use to do this fall broadly into four categories.

(i) Puns
- They use a word — such as *night* — which has the same pronunciation as another word — such as *knight* e.g. GOOD KNIGHT. However, both words must be in some way relevant to the story.
- A variation on this is to use a word which sounds fairly similar to another when both have obvious links to the story. An example of this was a report on a young mother who mislaid her handbag while shopping. She later found it under a pile of nappies in her local supermarket. The story was headed 'NAPPY ENDING'. An equally appropriate title for the story of course would have been 'HAPPY ENDING'.
- It is often said that sarcasm is the lowest form of wit. Puns would also rank fairly low, it would appear, to judge from the groans with which they are frequently received.

(ii) Rhyme
- Rhyming words are also used. For example, 'CELL BELL' was the headline of a story about a remand prisoner who sought bail on the grounds that the bells of a nearby church kept him awake while he was being remanded in custody.

(iii) Alliteration
- Alliteration is another device which you will frequently come across in headlines. 'CHOP CHAMP CHIPS IN' headlined a story about a karate champion making a donation to charity.

(iv) Variations on Cliches and Everyday Phrases
- IT'S SNOW JOKE, TANK YOU MAM, NOT THE FULL DOLLAR, T.D. RAISES ROOF DURING HOUSING DEBATE are just a few examples of headlines in this category. Their links with everyday phrases and cliches will be obvious.

Each of these four types of headlines appear frequently in the 'popular' tabloid newspapers, However, sub-editors on the 'quality' papers also use these devices to signal that a story has a touch of humour to it. While these types of headline may not always be funny, it is worth noting that a fair degree of imagination and ingenuity is needed by sub-editors to make them up.

Making the Headlines Hit

? Questions and Assignments

1. (i) Compose a headline which contains some word play for each of the stories below.
   (ii) When you are finished, you can compare your efforts to the originals by correctly linking each of the words or phrases in Box A on page 310 with the appropriate one in Box B on page 310.
2. Comment on the word play used in each of the original headlines.
3. What words or phrases are used in each of the stories which indicate that the stories are written in a conversational style rather than a formal style?
4. Make up a short news story inspired by each of the following headlines :-

   Bear Cheek   *Rob-a-Job*   *Steve Soaks Sean*   *Weigh for it*
   Cold as Rice   *Copper Hopper*   *A Pocketful of Pie*   *Won for the Road.*

??

Crooks stole two new £35,000 Mercedes saloons from Ballylee, Co. Mayo - by driving straight through a showroom's plate glass window.

??

Mary Robinson has posed an extremely difficult dilemma for one of Ireland's last great male bastions.

The President of Ireland has in the past automatically become a member of the ritzy Portmarnock Golf Club, which does NOT allow women to become full members.

??

Poet Tony Reid, of Kilkenny, was lost for words yesterday after a thief broke into his car and stole 100 poems he had scribbled on old envelopes.

??

Wrinkly robber Alfred Glessinger was so past it he could only hobble away from raids because of an old rupture.

Glessinger (63) of Glenmore, Co. Cork, was jailed for six years at Cork Court yesterday for hold-ups at three building societies.

??

Wacky British wine lovers are to make the Beaujolais Nouveau run in reverse — taking empty bottles back to France.

Each November teams race to bring the new vintage to England.

But club owner John Pfeffer of Colchester, Essex, said : "We wanted to do something different".

??

Little Anthony Sutton got a rocket yesterday after he built a bonfire — at the top of the stairs.

Anthony (7) set fire to rubbish at his home in Rossmore, badly burning the carpet.

Dad, Patrick, who called the fire brigade, said : "It could have been much worse".

??

Waterford Crystal workers are going to lose a "bonanza" deal that in the past earned them an extra £1,450 a year on average.

But now the Labour Court has ruled that the practice should be discontinued.

??

Singer Janet Jackson, sister of Michael, has splashed out £2 million in cash to buy herself a second home.

She has snapped up a six-bedroom, six-bathroom Los Angeles mansion.

Newspapers

??

Novice angler Dave Murphy amazed chums by hooking three sharks on his first fishing trip.

Dave (42) had never held a fishing rod before the jaunt off the Sligo coast.

But while his pals netted tiddlers, he landed a 85lb blue shark, followed by two more weighing 65 and 45lbs.

*

??

Officials in a Dallas aquarium are worried about the health of Denis, a killer shark, who is on loan to the centre from the San Francisco Aquatic Centre. The trouble with Denis is that he appears to be a little off colour.

"He just mooches around in his tank looking glum" remarked aquarium boss, Chuck Bean, "his killer instinct seems to be gone." In San Francisco, he was used to the company of other sharks in his tank. Here he is in a tank of his own. He probably misses the company.

??

Sky satellite channels are more popular than BBC1 and BBC2, according to audience research on homes with both types of telly.

??

Romantic Tim Bent hired a cinema's illuminated display board yesterday to ask his girlfriend : "Will you marry me?"

Jeanne Blaszcak saw the proposal light up in Taunton, Somerset, near her home, and phoned Tim (30) at work in Stirling, Scotland, to accept!

??

People who tell lies on the telephone are sure to be found out, according to research published yesterday.

The sound of your own voice will give you away, say psychologists Guy Fielding and David Lewis.

Mr. Fielding says : "When you lie your voice automatically rises and this is very obvious to the person listening at the other end of the telephone".

??

The lovely Lisa Aziz really is a perfect stand-in for Anne Dimwit on TV-am reports.

She is cool, pleasant and clever. In fact would anyone care if precious Ms Diamond never came back?

??

Forest owners are spraying trees with essence of skunk to stop thieves nicking them for Christmas.

American inventor John Boddicker said : "It's a smell no one would have in their house and hangs about for weeks".

??

A cut-price war has erupted between two of the country's biggest supermarket chains.

But only shoppers in the Tallaght Town Centre will avail of the bargains.

Dunnes Stores and Crazy Prices have slashed the prices on some of their products in their stores in the new multi-million pound centre.

??

Kylie Minogue popped into a posh shop to buy a dress - and was mistaken for a tourist. She was only recognised when she pulled out her credit card.

Virginia Bates, owner of the shop in Kensington, West London, said : "This tiny little girl came in and I just assumed she was an Australian tourist.

"She bought a lace Victorian dress. It really suited her".

Making the Headlines Hit

??

Hawaii 5-0 star Jack Lord, is saying Aloha to a fortune. For since putting down his gun, he's picked up a paint brush to become one of the world's top artists.

His water colour and oil paintings sell for a minimum £10,000.

And his works hang in 40 museums around the world.

Jack (60) quit showbiz after Hawaii 5-0 was axed ten years ago and is now earning bigger money in his new profession.

??

Residents of a tiny village awoke yesterday to find thousands of fish lying all over the plaice.

The invasion of the small fry occured in the village of Grange in Co. Sligo. Locals thought somebody was codding when they discovered their main street was covered in fish.

But is turned out that there was nothing fishy about it.

A truck carrying thousands of baby fish had crashed into a pole in the village during the night, spilling its contents all over the street.

The fingerlings had been on the way to a fish farm when the accident happened.

A

- Dave so quick _____
- Golf Rules go _____
- Number up for _____
- Xmas tree pong _____
- Janet's splash _____
- **Fishy Plaice** _____
- Cash _____
- Store _____
- Ode _____
- **Tim gets his dame** _____
- **Drawing** _____
- It's Kylie _____
- Sail _____
- The strain _____
- **Bonfire** _____
- Liza's _____
- Sky give _____
- Blow _____
- **Loan** _____

B

- _____ to glass staff
- _____ and return
- _____ wars
- _____ phone fibbers
- _____ dear
- _____ robber
- _____ boring Beeb a bashing
- _____ Shark
- _____ ka-putt
- _____ on the jaws
- _____ of cash
- _____ a shiner
- _____ 'n grab
- _____ needles thieves
- _____ no codding
- _____ a fortune
- _____ in lights
- _____ surprising
- _____ fright boy

310

Newspapers

✓ **Sample Answer** (Report * page 309)

1. (i) No Tank Mate *or* Shark Blues.
   (ii) Loan Shark.
2. "Loan Shark" is a common phrase which describes people who lend money illegally and usually at very high rates. In the story the shark was on *loan* to the Dallas aquarium so the word *loan* is used in the headline. The word *loan* is also a pun on the word *lone*. He was the only shark in the tank — a *lone* shark.
3. The phrase "a little off colour" is a chatty way of saying "slightly ill" or "slightly unwell". Also the word "boss" is a conversational word meaning "manager". These expressions give the story a conversational style rather than a formal one.

Newspapers

II - Writing News Reports

Sentences - The Long and the Short

👉 Points to Note

SENTENCES - CLAUSES - PHRASES

It is important to note the difference between a *Sentence*, a *Clause* and a *Phrase*. A **Sentence** is a group of words with at least one subject and one predicate. A **sentence** may or may not have an object.

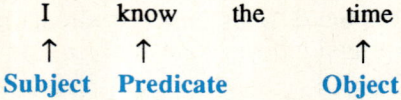

$$\begin{array}{ccc} \text{I} & \text{know} & \text{the time} \\ \uparrow & \uparrow & \uparrow \\ \textbf{Subject} & \textbf{Predicate} & \textbf{Object} \end{array}$$

In the case of each of the following sentences, identify (i) the subject, (ii) the predicate and (iii) the object (if one is included).

- He trained every morning.
- The President left for Paris.
- Gardaí arrested a number of men.
- The boy told the story to the class.
- A number of men were arrested by Gardaí.
- The teacher announced the news of a half day.
- After the match, the crowd left the grounds quietly.
- The thief sold most of the paintings on the continent.
- Two people were killed in a collision between a truck and a car.
- The Minister praised young people in Dublin for their efforts to restore an old church.

A **clause** is like a sentence within a larger sentence. It makes a statement, though not a complete one. Each clause has its own subject and predicate e.g. — The girl *who won the race* was presented with a trophy.

The clause in this sentence is printed in italics. Its subject is 'who' and its predicate is 'won'.
A **phrase** is a group of words which occur together but do not make a complete statement e.g. — a sharp left turn; ripe old age; golden curls; the much admired politician.

Types of Sentences

SIMPLE SENTENCES
- *Maria and Jill went on holidays.*
- *The jet crashed.*
- *The teacher and the pupils returned to the school.*

All the examples above are *simple* sentences as they each have only one *predicate*. Two of them, however, have two subjects each.

312

Writing News Reports

DOUBLE OR MULTIPLE SENTENCES

A double or multiple sentence is made up of *co-ordinate clauses*. A clause is said to be co-ordinate when it can be separated from another so that each makes an independent sentence and gives independent sense,

    e.g. —   *(i) Sinéad McGee went to Florida and Clare Glynn went to Cork.*
             (ii) Tom came first, Peter came second but Noel only came third.

COMPLEX SENTENCE

A **complex sentence** consists of a *main (or principal)* clause and one or more *subordinate* clauses.

A *subordinate clause* is one which depends on the main clause for its meaning,

        e.g — The farmer *who had some cattle to sell* brought them to the mart.

The words in italics form a sub-ordinate clause.

Types of Subordinate Clauses

NOUN CLAUSES

- A **noun clause** takes the place of a noun and is usually either the subject or object of the principal clause of the sentence. In the examples below, the noun clauses are printed in italics.

In each of the following sentences, the **subject** is a noun clause.
(i) *What she saw* frightened her.
(ii) *Everything that Tom suggested* was opposed by Nuala.
(iii) *Why the accident occurred* is still not clear.

In each of the following sentences, the **object** is a noun clause.
(i) The boy imagined *that he was a space-man.*
(ii) He cannot remember *what I told him.*
(iii) The Taoiseach was asked *when the government would meet again.*

ADJECTIVE CLAUSES

- An **adjective clause** tells us more about a noun or a pronoun belonging to some other clause and is generally used where a suitable adjective cannot be found,

    e.g. — (i) The detectives *who had arrived on the scene* arrested two men for questioning.
           (ii) The house *where the money was found* was later searched by armed gardaí.
           (iii) That drink is made from fruit *that is grown in Ireland.*

ADVERB CLAUSES

- An **adverb clause** does the work of an adverb. It tells us more about a verb, an adjective or an adverb.

    e.g. — (i) The minister left for Brussels *when the meeting ended.*
           (ii) He ran for election *because he was encouraged by a number of TDs.*
           (iii) *Because it is very valuable,* the painting is kept in a special display case.

Newspapers

Sentence Structure in News Reports

The opening sentence of a news report is the most important sentence in it. The opening sentence must grab the attention of the reader and make him/her want to read on. To do this the opening sentence must be packed with information. It will usually contain the key elements of the story - the *who?, what?, when?, where?, why?* and *how?* or as much of these as is possible. The remainder of the story will elaborate more on each of these. **Therefore, the opening sentences of news reports are nearly always complex sentences.** At later stages in the report the journalist may use some simple sentences.

? Questions and Assignments

1. Read each of the following opening sentences of news reports and list as much of the following as possible — *who?; what?; when? where?; why?* and *how?*
2. In the case of each sentence pick out the main clause and each of the subordinate clauses. Say what type of subordinate clause each one is.
3. Rewrite each of the sentences in alternative form but without omitting any information that was contained in the original.
4. Using your imagination, add two further sentences to each of the original ones. In each case maintain the same style as the original. These sentences should (a) elaborate in some way on the information in the opening sentence or (b) give the reaction of a person who is in some way involved.
5. Compose two or three word headlines for each story.
6. Each story has one spelling or punctuation error. Identify and correct each one.

1. NEARLY 600 dolphins were butchered for meat on a Japanese island after fishermen had forsed them onto a beach on Saturday.

2. Floods in the midwestern US forced more than 1,000 people from there homes and closed several stretches of highway.

3. SCHOOL ended early yesterday for thousands of Junior Certificate students who were given a half-day of to celebrate this year's exam results.

4. AN INTERNATIONAL relief effort continued to bring suplies to areas of Namibia that are in the grip of a severe drought.

5. THE CRISIS which has hit Dublin's water supply since mid-summer is far from over, dublin Corporation has again warned.

6. A 27-year-old dublin man, who left the country after he was the victim of a stabbing incident failed to turn up for the trial yesterday.

Writing News Reports

7 The Progressive Democrats have described the latest unemployment figures, which show a rise for the third month in a row, as "very disapointing".

8 THIEVES who carry out "snatch and run" handbag robberies on women motorists will in future go to jial, the new President of the District Court warned yesterday.

9 TWO Dublin women vowed to picket what they termed a Man Only bar after their legel challenge against it failed in Dublin District Court yesterday.

10 METEOROLOGICAL experts in India say this season's southwest monsoon has been "good", having brought ample rainfall to agricultural areas that depend on its four months of normaly drenching rains.

11 TWO MEN and a 10-year-old boy were detained in hospital last night after a three-car collision on the Stillorgan dual carraigeway.

12 LETTERS writen by the notorious murderer Dr. Crippen went for three times their estimated value when they were sold for £7,500 in London yesterday.

👉 Points to Note

ADJECTIVE AND ADVERB PHRASES

Instead of using adjective and adverb clauses, journalists frequently use *adjective phrases* and *adverb phrases* so that more information can be contained in a smaller space. This style of writing is described as *economical*. For example the sentence — Peter McNeill, **who was born in Sligo** emigrated in 1979 to Canada **where he now heads a computer company** / **which specialises in radar equipment** — contains three adjective clauses (highlighted in bold lettering). By substituting adjective phrases for the clauses the sentence can be shortened from 24 words to 19 words — e.g. *Sligo-born Peter McNeill emigrated in 1979 to Canada where he now heads a computer company specialising in radar equipment.*

WORK on the new National Sports Centre at the Custom House Docks, costing up to £60m, will begin next year, the Minister for Sport indicated yesterday.

STAFF at Dublin's Dogs and Cats Home are to return to normal working on Monday next following a two month protest in which they occupied the Grand Canal Quay premises.

TALENTED Derry City striker Liam Coyle has signed for Irish League club Coleraine on a one-month contract and makes his debut this afternoon against Cliftonville at the Showgrounds.

EUGENE McGee, manager of the Irish football team to tour Australia, said yesterday that he was perturbed by reports that Michael Mooney, Donegal's sole representative in the squad, had been sent to the line during a club match on Sunday.

The Belfast-based band have recorded a new album due for release next month.

The stone-throwing crowd surrounded the building where the meeting was taking place.

Newspapers

> **? Questions and Assignments**

1. Identify an adjective phrase or an adverb phrase in each of the 6 extracts on the bottom of page 315 and rewrite the report using an equivalent clause.
2. Examine each of the news items numbered 1 to 12 on pages 314 and 315 and rewrite any four in a more economical style, using adjective and/or adverb phrases instead of clauses. Take care not to omit any item of information when you rewrite each of the items.

> ✓ **Q. 2 — Sample Answer (Report No. 5)**
>
> The water crisis affecting Dublin since midsummer is far from over, Dublin Corporation has again warned.

News Reports - Different Styles

> ☞ **Points to Note**

- In general, the 'quality' newspapers adhere to a *formal* style in their news reports, while reporters in the 'popular' newspapers tend to go for a more *descriptive* and *colourful* style of reporting.
- The 'quality' newspapers also aim for a neutral approach to news. They set out to give the facts without comment or prejudice, letting the readers form their own opinions.

> Detectives are still seeking two youths who assaulted a uniformed garda......

- The 'popular' papers use very descriptive language in many of their news reports. Frequently, these descriptive words and phrases can also be highly emotive.

> Detectives are still seeking two louts who savagely attacked a young garda......

- When this happens the reporter is conveying her/his attitudes towards the people and events in the news report. The language used is also likely to shape and influence the feelings of the reader. Sometimes this style of writing can result in a reporter transmitting her/his own prejudices and lack of understanding of an event on to the readers.
- Most Irish papers, in general, tend to avoid this style of reporting. However, many British newspapers go in for reports that make use of highly emotive language and these newspapers — mainly 'popular' tabloids — have quite high readership in Ireland.

Writing News Reports

Nevertheless, it would be unfair to regard all news reports in tabloid papers as biased and hysterical. Much of their coverage of events is honest and balanced and presented in a snappy, colourful and chatty style that is easier, for many people, to digest.

The following reports show how different papers deal with the same story.

French driver badly beaten

A French lorry driver was attacked and had his skull fractured in Britain yesterday in what looks like a reprisal for French raids on British meat trucks, police said.

Eric Gunther (28), was transporting a load of chemical products along a motorway in Kent, southern England, when three men in a car stopped him and beat him with a baseball bat.

He was left by the roadside with a fractured skull and other injuries and is now recovering in hospital.

The attack comes a day after French farmers campaigning against foreign imports seized nearly 400 British sheep and burned them in front of a French government building.

French farmers have hijacked at least 19 lorries carrying foreign livestock and meat since June, including a dozen with British cargo.

In Paris, British ambassador Ewan Ferguson lodged a formal protest with the government over lorry attacks by French farmers.

— *The Irish Press*

Ban Frog Nosh and Save Dosh!

Make the frogs hopping mad by leaving their goods off your shopping list — and you'll save money into the bargain.

Here are some you can boycott, plus a list of their British alternatives....

— *The Sun*

? Questions and Assignments

1. Compare and contrast both stories under the following headings :-
   (i) Facts reported   (ii) Reaction reported (iii) Style of language
   (iv) Comments made by reporters.

French trucker KOd by lamb war "avengers"

Three thugs hijacked a French lorry on the M2 yesterday and beat up the driver — sparking fears that the lamb war has spilled onto Britain's roads.

The ambush came just hours after French farmers burned 400 British lambs in protest at cheap meat imports.

Police think the French lorry may have been attacked in revenge.

They said last night: "Many people have been sickened by the French farmers' outrages against British lorry drivers."

Trucker Eric Gunther, 28, was driving along the London-bound carriageway from France to Manchester when a blue Fiesta swerved in front, forcing him to stop.

The yobs leaped out and smashed his windscreen with lumps of woods. He was flung onto the ground and the inside of his cab wrecked.

The three then sped off — without stealing any of his load of medicine.

Eric, from Montigny in France, was in Medway hospital, Kent, last night with a fractured skull. He is recovering.

Stefan Giraud, the boss of Eric's freight company, said: "It was a cowardly attack."

"The French farmers are even more angry. I hate to think what might happen next."

One British trucker stormed: "It's disgusting we've sunk to the same brutality as the French."

You can get your own back on French farmers who have carried out 12 attacks on British loads of meat and livestock.

Simply boycott French goods and buy British.

One supermarket owner in Welshpool, Roger Hughes, has banned French goods from his Spar shelves.

He wants other stores to do the same.

— *The Sun*

Newspapers

Town's water fear after big fish kill

Serious polution of the River Dee in Co. Louth may have also contanimated the water supply for Ardee which is drawn from the river, it was feared last night.

Over one thousand fish, mainly trout. Were killed when a four-mile stretch was polluted yesterday.

fishery officers, who examined the river last night, said they thought the source of pollution could be chemical. "The water was decidedly toxic," said Dee and Glyde Fishing Association chairman, Padge Reilly.

"This is a time of year for spraying to kill weeds in potatoes. Every single year since 1973 we have been hammered with pollution on the Dee."

Town Commissioner Val kerr (FF) described the Dee as "a total write-off" and said he feared the town's water supply had been effected by pollution.

"It appears the source of pollution may be in an area which could be very serious for our supply of drinking water," he said.

Council area engineer paul gallagher was last night inspecting the local pumping station to see if the supply had being effected.

In this report the facts are presented in an economical, clear and neutral manner. The report also contains some comments from people involved in, or affected by, the situation. The reporter does not offer any comment on the events.

? Questions and Assignments

1. **Proof Corrections**: Part of a sub-editor's duties in a newspaper is to make sure that stories are printed without any misspellings or other errors such as punctuation errors. In reprinting this story, we have inserted some errors. Identify and correct each one.

2. What do you regard as the most important point in this report?

3. "*. . . . it was feared last night . . .* " What is the significance of this clause at the end of the first sentence?

4. Were there fish other than trout killed? Refer to the report to support your answer.

5. (a) Why is the phrase *a total write-off* in quotation marks?

   (b) What is meant by the phrase?

6. Rewrite this report as it might be written for an angling magazine.

318

Writing News Reports

Here we examine how reporters and newspapers vary the language and focus of their stories to appeal to the particular interests and attitudes of their readers.

A

??

LONDON - Vincent Van Gogh's 1889 painting "View of the Asylum and the Chapel of saint-remy", belonging to the actress Elizabeth Taylor, will be sold at auction on december 3rd by Christies' auction house, it was announced yesterday.

The painting, to be displayed today in Paris before beginning a world tour, is valued at £8-£10 million. Her father bought the painting for her in 1963 for £92,000.

B

??

A Van Gogh belonging to actress Elizabeth Taylor is expected to fetch up to £10m when it goes under the hammer at a London auction later this year.

Acording to Christies. who will be selling the work, the star paid £92,000 for it in 1963 after saying she wanted it "no matter what".

A Christies' representative in New York said the sale was for "entirely personal reasons". miss Taylor is not expected to attend the December 3 sale.

The work, The Asylum and the Chapel at St. Remy, was painted in 1889 after the artist had committed himself to the asylum.

C

??

SUPERSTAR Liz Taylor is set to pocket £10 million - by selling a painting she bought for just £92,000.

Liz (58) snapped up the Van Gogh masterpiece in 1963 when she was maried to Richard Burton.

Christies' in London said she was selling for "purely personal reasons". But pals insist she does NOT need the money.

The painting - The Asylum and the Chapel at St. Remy - was completed in 1889 after Van Gogh had comitted himself to a mental home. Art fan Liz decided she had to one it, "no matter what".

She is not expected to attend the auction next month.

In May, Van Gogh's Portrait of Dr. Gachet sold for a world record £49.1 million.

- Liz to sell Van Gogh.
- Taylor to sell Van Gogh.
- Van Gosh! Liz to make £10m on a Van Gogh.

P.S. The picture was actually withdrawn from auction. The highest bid was under £6m.

? Questions and Assignments

1. **Proof Reading:** Each story contains three errors. Identify each of these and correct them.
2. Match each of the headlines to one of the reports.
3. (a) Which of the headlines is the most formal in style? Explain why.
   (b) Comment on one feature of the style of each of the other two headlines.
4. Do all three reports focus on the same aspect of the news item? Explain.
5. Are all the reports consistent in the facts they present? Explain.
6. (a) Which of the stories is written in a very 'chatty' and informal style?
   (b) What techniques does the reporter use to achieve this style?
7. The sentence "Liz has millions stashed away from a Hollywood career spanning almost 50 years." was omitted from one of the reports. Which report do you think it was omitted from? Explain your answer.
8. Are reports A and C aimed at 2 different types of reader? Give reasons for your answer.

Newspapers

Paragaphs

Written material is alway divided into paragraphs. These help the reader by allowing him or her to digest the material in small sections. Paragraphs also make a piece of written material more attractive. Paragraphs are not created at random. In a piece of writing, a new paragraph comes when, for example, a scene changes or a new topic is introduced. Paragraphs usually start with a sentence that gives an indication of what the remainder of the paragraph is about. This is called the **topic** sentence. Occasionally the topic sentence comes at the end of a paragraph, summing up what has gone before. In newspapers, paragraphs tend to be short — to enable material to be taken in by readers in a hurry. However, in a book, a string of short paragraphs gives a sense of breathlessness.

Health warning as heat continues

As temperatures continue to (1) _____ , the public has been (2) _____ by health authorities to take extra (3) _____ when handling food in the aftermath of rising incidents of salmonella poisoning, and to be vigilant with the care of animals. According to the Department of Health, and the Environmental Health Officers Association, the (4) _____ spell of hot weather is creating ideal growth conditions for harmful bacteria. There has been an unusually high concentration of salmonella poisoning in the Cork area and an increase in reported cases in the south-eastern and mid-western regions of the country. Consumers have been (5) _____ to check refrigerator temperatures, to cook eggs and poultry (6) _____ , and to wash hands and utensils after touching meat. Meanwhile, the Dogs and Cats Home in Dublin has reported they are receiving daily calls complaining of dogs being locked in cars in stifling heat. Ms. Thérèse Cunningham, executive officer at the home, told *The Irish Times* the latest case to come to their (7) _____ happened yesterday at Findlater Place, near Cathal Brugha Street, when tourists left two dogs in a vehicle in a car park. The attendant rang the Dogs and Cats Home whose staff arrived to find one dog dead and the other badly dehydrated. Mr. John Costello, a vet with the home, said that dogs locked in cars without enough (8) _____ quickly used up all available oxygen and could die in a very distressed condition. The (9) _____ service has predicted a continuation of the hot weather. Yesterday's highest temperature was recorded at Casement Aerodrome, at 25.2 degrees Celsius. Temperatures throughout the country yesterday were lower than that at Casement Aerodrome, with winds keeping conditions cooler along the west and south coasts in particular. It was 19.1 degrees Celsius at Roches Point in Cork; 20 degrees at Belmullet, Co. Mayo and 21 degrees at Cahirciveen, Co. Kerry. Temperatures rose somewhat as one moved eastwards or into sheltered areas. The Mullingar weather station reported temperatures of 24.6 degrees while Kilkenny basked in 23.2 degrees. Dublin Airport enjoyed blissful weather, also, at 24.2 degrees. The good news is that these temperatures are likely to continue their upwards climb. A (10) _____ for the Met Office said that while it was too early to (11) _____ predict conditions over the Bank Holiday weekend, they were hoping for a sizzler.

Writing News Reports

? Questions and Assignments

1. Select suitable words from the box below to fill each of the spaces in the report above.

• asked	• thoroughly	• warned	• neatly
• precisely	• weather	• care	• soar
• decrease	• spokesman	• urged	• attention
• unusual	• ordered	• precautions	• meteorological
• air	• current	• ventilation	

2. The news report, in its original form, was divided into eight separate paragraphs. Indicate where you think each paragraph should begin and end. In each case, explain your choice by outlining, in a few words, the topic of each of the paragraphs.
3. (a) Where in the story does the reporter give a personal comment on the subject of the report?
   (b) The style of reporting here is mainly formal. Where in the story is there an exception to this?
4. Rewrite the story in a style suitable for a popular tabloid newspaper.

Union chief calls for aid for ex-Arigna miners

Two of the three collieries in Arigna, Co Roscommon, shut down for good this week. A total of 208 unemployed miners will now be (1) _____ with emigration, unless an Enterprise Fund is set up by the government to help (2) _____ alternative employment, says Charlie Hopkins, chairman of the local section of SIPTU. The smaller Wynne's Colliery in nearby Aughnacashel, which (3) _____ 28 miners, closed last Friday and another 40 from the Flynn & Leheny Colliery will be let go on the first of August. The early (4) _____ this week of the Arigna Collieries, the largest of the three mining companies operating in the area with 140 workers on its pay roll, "was inevitable" and left workers "dismayed", said Mr. Hopkins. There was (5) _____ sinister about the early closure of the Arigna mine, however, according to Brendan Leyden of Arigna Collieries. All the underground work has stopped, he said. It was a matter of logic as the last of the stockpile had to be cleared out. The miners, the majority of whom have large mortgage repayments to meet each month, now face the dole or (6) _____ . The local Fine Gael TD, John Ellis, along with several other Opposition deputies, urged the Government this week to retain the Arigna collieries. "I do not think any of the people concerned wish to receive social welfare payments, rather they wish to see employment maintained and that they be given the opportunity to continue to (7) _____ in the area," he said. The mines which were set up in 1958 to (8) _____ an ESB power station at Lough Allen are no longer feasible, says the ESB, which claims to be losing close to £3,000,000 annually by purchasing Arigna coal and operating a (9) _____ station with an efficiency rate at least 15% below that of modern stations.

— *The Sunday Tribune*

Newspapers

? Questions and Assignments

1. Select suitable words from the box below to fill each of the spaces in the report above.

• emigration	• closure	• employs	• leave	• something
• nothing	• work	• create	• power	• employed
• faced	• supply	• maintain	• run	• railway

2. Answer each of these questions with one complete sentence :-
   (a) What shut down for good?
   (b) What does Charlie Hopkins want the government to do?
   (c) What will happen on the first day of August?
   (d) What left the workers 'dismayed'?
   (e) What do the miners of Arigna now face?
   (f) What are the views of John Ellis, TD, on the situation?
3. Explain why the Arigna mines were forced to close.
4. Write a letter to the editor of the newspaper, outlining your response to this report.

☞ Points to Note

IDIOMS

If we say somebody is *all ears* we mean that the person is paying close attention to what is being said. If we ask a person to *put her shoulder to the wheel* what we are asking is that she make a greater effort.

Many expressions such as these are used in our everyday conversation. They are called *idioms*.

Here is a random selection of *idioms* :-

- bury the hatchet
- throw in the towel
- in hot water
- draw the line
- turn the tables
- the cold shoulder
- don't bug me
- smell a rat

The meaning of each one will be obvious to you.

Yet, for those learning English as a foreign language, the everyday idioms that we use are puzzling and confusing. Can you suggest why?

An *idiom* can be defined as a common phrase or expression whose meaning is not always clear even if the individual words are understood. The origins of many idioms are very old — e.g. *we are keeping our powder dry* means that *we are prepared*. Can you suggest the origin of this idiom?

SLANG AND COLLOQUIALISMS

These are similar in many ways to idioms. Slang words and phrases give colour and vigour to our conversation but are out of place in formal writing. Slang words and phrases tend to go out of date and may be understood in one area only or by one group of people only. In Dublin, you *mitch* or *go on the hop;* in Cork you *go on the lang.*

Writing News Reports

A *colloquialism* is a piece of slang that has survived for a generation or so. Essentially it is a less extreme form of slang. *They're bunched*, meaning they are tired or defeated, is an example of a colloquialism. Journalists use idioms, colloquialisms and slang to give their reports an informal and conversational tone. News reporters in the 'quality' papers make very little use of idioms, colloquialisms and slang. However, the 'popular' tabloid papers rely heavily on these devices.

MICHAEL Heseltine declared last night that he would not stand against Margaret Thatcher for the Conservative leadership this month as the Tory high command moved to crush any potential challenge.

The former defence secretary's leadership ambitions appeared to be severely blunted after his constituency party implicitly rebuked him for his attack on Mrs. Thatcher and publicly avowed its support for her.

Mrs. Thatcher brought forward the date of any leadership contest to November 20, giving potential rivals only until next Thursday to declare themselves. The timing is a clear indication of Mrs. Thatcher's desire to end speculation about her future as soon as possible. The decision was made in consultations with Cranley Onslow, chairman of the backbench 1922 Committee, after the prime minister returned from the world climate conference in Geneva. Mr. Onslow, who is in charge of the arrangements, said it was "very undesirable" that there should be a contest.

TORY rebel Michael Heseltine threw in the towel last night as Premier Margaret Thatcher called his bluff.

She flushed "Tarzan" out by demanding a short sharp leadership contest with just ONE WEEK for challengers to face up to her.

And the former Defence supremo was forced to announce he would NOT be in the fight.

He said from Tel Aviv : "I have said I am not going to take part in that process. I have said it so often that I am embarrassed to repeat it."

But for the first time, Westminster cynics believe he means it.

Mr. Heseltine's dream of seizing the Tory throne turned sour as his own supporters publicly denounced him.

? Questions and Assignments

1. Compare and contrast these reports under the following headings :-
   (a) content and (b) style.   (see **Points to Note** - *Idioms*)

Newspapers
III - Commenting on the News

Editorials

In all democracies, newspapers play an important role in informing and shaping public opinion. They do this not only by reporting the news but also by analysing and commenting on the events that make the news. One means of doing this is through the 'editorial' (sometimes called the leading article or the 'leader') which reflects the views of the paper's editor on issues facing the nation and the world.

Editorials usually contain elements of criticism or praise as well as advice. Senior editorial staff of a newspaper meet to decide the topic and direction of its editorials.

Tragedies

It is a sad fact of Irish life that public holidays and an increase in the number of road deaths go hand in hand. This weekend has been no different as our reports show. It would be tasteless, to say the least, to try to establish the reasons for these recent deaths - inquiries, inquests and court cases will eventually provide us with all that information.

What baffles everyone concerned with safety on the roads is the inability to produce an approach which will reduce the number of tragedies. Governments have warned, the Gardaí have patrolled and advice has been handed out. But to no avail. The tragedies continue - and the reported ones do not even refer to those accidents in which no one was killed but which have inflicted injuries which will stay with many people for the rest of their lives.

— *Irish Independent Editorial on June Bank Holiday Road Tragedies.*

? Questions and Assignments

1. Outline, in your own words, the main points of this editorial.
2. Consider the point made in the last sentence and write a news feature illustrating the effects of a non-fatal traffic accident on a (fictitious) family.

The most alarming aspect of the Dublin-Dundalk mail train robbery was the ease with which it was carried out. Given the current troubles on that particular line - the Dáil had been debating the IRA bomb threats just hours before the raiders struck - it is hard to credit that not even the most elementary precautions had been taken to protect a train carrying so much registered mail.

The Minister for Justice says it has not been the practice to provide Garda protection for such trains, an omission that helped provide some easy pickings for the gang involved. It is possible to argue that given the current strain on Garda resources, there is neither the money nor manpower to provide regular shotgun patrols. But to accept that is akin to extending an open invitation to armed gangs to strike when and as they please.

Contd...

Commenting on the News

> Security in such cases should be mandatory with the bills being picked up by An Post, which has overall responsibility for the mail. Similarly, the provision of Garda security for banks and other commercial concerns should be paid for by those involved, which woulease the pressure on tight Garda budgets. The critics of the obvious lack of security following this raid, inevitably have the benefit of hindsight.
>
> But the reality is that unless lessons are learned - and acted upon - from what happened, mail trains will come to be regarded as soft targets by all criminal gangs, both paramilitary and otherwise.
>
> — *The Irish Press*

? Questions and Assignments

1. Outline the (i) criticisms and (ii) the suggestions made in this editorial.

Death Watch

> The deaths of four Fishery Board Officers following the sinking of their small and totally unsuitable fibreglass boat will now be investigated by the Government. A lot of questions have to be asked and answered.
>
> First the public will want to know why it took so long to find the men. It seems impossible that they did not have a regular system of communicating with their base.
>
> Secondly it has come to light that two boats, any one of which could safely have been used by the men, had been sabotaged by poachers. Hence the use of the fibreglass boat. This brings to the public's attention the activities of poachers whose viciousness knows no bounds. Poaching is big business for them, and their methods of fighting the law are ruthless. The Gardaí must divert more men to (a) finding these poachers and getting them into court and (b) finding the people who are buying poached fish - and getting them into court as well.
>
> Thirdly it has become evident that the fishery protection service is not as well equipped or manned as it should be. Half measures are worse than no measures in this area because poachers operating against people with insufficient resources are bound to have successes and are therefore certain to try again.
>
> — *Irish Independent*

? Questions and Assignments

1. Outline the main points of this editorial.

2. Write a letter to the editor responding to the editorial.

Newspapers - Editorials

> Newspapers rarely choose rival competitors as subjects for editorial comment. However, in July 1990, when the Irish Press group of newspapers seemed certain to close, other papers responded editorially. The dispute which threatened closure was settled at a very late stage.

Editorial - (1)

It is always sad, it is always tragic when the newspaper community loses even one of its established titles. This morning, it is confirmed that not one but three such titles are to disappear with the closure of the Irish Press, the Evening Press and the Sunday Press.

It is sad and tragic whatever the reasons may have been for such a sad tragedy. Hundreds of employees - journalists, printers, administrative and commercial staff now face redundancy. To them we express our heartfelt sympathy.

As well, the Irish newspaper-reading public have lost a trio of publications that have served as one of the great pillars of choice that has stood for at least two generations in the services of Irish democracy. That is a serious loss.

And while we, as one of the other great pillars of choice, regret the passing of one of our vigorous rivals, the question will inevitably be asked: why was this loss allowed to happen; could it have been avoided?

The Irish Press group was born in 1931, the brainchild of Eamon de Valera for the stated express purpose of affording the Irish public a republican media organ. The daily paper was unequivocally republican in its viewpoints and perspectives and just as unequivocally and almost confessional supporter of Mr. de Valera's Fianna Fáil party.

For decades, the Irish Press prospered within these editorial parameters, while at the same time projecting a level of professional expertise that quickly thrust the paper into the front rank of journalism.

Eighteen years later saw the launch of the soon-to-be market leader Sunday Press, and in 1954 the Evening Press was added to the group. Just as the daily paper had achieved earlier, these too were to experience a high level of commercial success.

But since the decades between the early 1930s and the early 1960s, Irish society changed utterly. From a largely agrarian, conservative-minded community, the metamorphosis has been towards a more open, cosmopolitan ethos.

The emergence of television, the availability of higher standards of education to greater numbers and the affordability of travel abroad to more than just the privileged few all contributed to that metamorphosis.

Yet, surprisingly, the Press newspapers seemed to be oblivious to these developments and their sea-change effects on the media industry for a long time. The papers - particularly the daily paper - continued to operate as if Irish society had not changed at all, that the simplicities of political faith and the drabness of social patterns and attitudes were still with us.

Clearly, it is to that seminal stage in the life of the Irish Press newspapers that the decline and ultimate fall can be traced, though it was scarcely recognised at the time in Burgh Quay.

For it was not until the late 1960s and early 1970s that the penalties began to be paid in terms of falling circulation and advertising revenue. Company executives, still certain in

Contd...

their clearly outdated convictions, failed to even attempt to identify those sectors of the modern Irish market at which their newspapers should be targetted.

The newspapers themselves, though retaining their high standard of news reportage, continued to retain a political profile that appealed to fewer and fewer. Their designs continued to be dull and unimaginative and the range of news and features services offered to their customers were not expanded to meet the competition.

It was only in the late 1970s that this state of affairs became apparent to the decision-makers and by then, of course the decline was describing a steeper course.

Difficulties and disagreements over what was to be done erupted within the management structure, frequent disputes arose with the trade unions (on one occasion leading to a damaging lock-out), introduction of modern print technology was delayed. In 1986, the daily paper went tabloid - a predictably unsuccessful hybrid broadsheet superimposed upon a tabloid format.

From then onwards, the die was irrecovably cast. Enormous trading losses forced the de Valera-led management to call in aid - the American Ingersols for a fresh injection of capital in return for a 50 pc equity stake in a new publishing subsidiary.

Then came the crunch. Just under two years ago, the unions were presented with a survival package they regarded as far too draconian to stomach. Whether the employees should have accepted those proposals to save their papers and save their jobs is an issue that will be debated for years to come.

Whether in the future any or all of these titles can be resuscitated by the parent company or by alternative investors and if so when, are all matters for another day.

But this morning we are sure that everyone connected with the media industry, together with the general public, will join us in mourning the passing of the Press.

— *Irish Independent*

Editorial - (2)

The demise of The Irish Press is a cause of sadness to very many people: obviously the workers and shareholders, a large section of the public and a great deal of people in the newspaper business, many of whom have worked with The Irish Press at some stage in their careers.

There are clearly opportunities for rival publishing houses arising from the closure of these titles but these opportunities seem insignificant in the context of the loss that is being sustained.

Management, both commercial and editorial, in The Irish Press group have made many mistakes over the last 20 years and have contributed significantly to the commerical failure of the organisation.

Management has also contributed to an industrial relations climate within The Irish Press which has led to the obduracy of the workers over the last week.

But this is not the whole story. If The Irish Press group of newspapers was a magnificent editorial and commercial success, the workers and, most particularly, the journalists, would be claiming a great deal of credit for such success.

Indeed it would be ungenerous, in such circumstances, not to acknowledge the contribution of the workers, including the journalists, to such a success, no matter how skilled managers and editors were.

Contd...

By the very same token, the failure of the organisation cannot be attributed solely to management. The failure is also that of the workers themselves, including the journalists.

The Irish Press newspaper itself has not been in editorial decline for 20 years just because of bad management and weak editors. The journalists have also contributed to this decline and they should accept responsibility for this.

The state of morale within the company is not entirely conditioned by management, it is also a function of the competence, dedication and professionalism of the workers, including the journalists. Thus the poor morale that presently exists is partly the fault of the journalists working there.

— *Sunday Tribune*

? Questions and Assignments

1. Having read the editorials above, write briefly on each of the following topics :-
   - The history of the Irish Press group of newspapers.
   - The difficulties faced by the group and the cause of these difficulties.
   - The attitudes of both the Irish Independent and the Sunday Tribune to the prospect of the closure of the Irish Press group.

> In this editorial, The Irish News, published in Belfast, turns its attention to another "newspaper" - The Sun.

About Time To Act Your Age

On Saturday the British tabloid The Sun will be celebrating its 21st birthday.

Yesterday, Roy Greenslade, a former Sun journalist who now edits the Daily Mirror leapt smartly to the defence of the paper: "The Sun is a public two fingers to every institution - be it government, civil service, trade unions or aristocracy," he writes "And you can win money by playing its game! What more would you ask?"

He is, however, prepared to concede that the paper has one weakness: "There is the danger . . . when the reader in the pub sees that last week's alcohol-induced brain wave from the punter on the corner bar stool turn into yesterday's Sun leader and wakes up to find it's today's government policy."

It is time Mr. Greenslade and his tabloid chums caught themselves on. The Sun is not a "public two fingers to every institution." Quite the reverse. It has proved itself to be one of the present government's staunchest supporters.

Mrs. Thatcher has shown her gratitude. The man who created the "soaraway Sun" Larry Lamb, now has a knighthood for his pains.

And Mrs. Thatcher was one of the first to congratulate the present editor Kelvin MacKenzie on the 21st birthday: "The Sun has become a great British institution. If it can come up fresh and bubbling and vital every day for 21 years then so can I. And I shall do so."

Contd. . .

Commenting on the News

Kenneth Baker, chairman of the Conservative Party was even more gushing. He actually penned a poem to mark the occasion: "There was a Sun reader called Ken / Who worked somewhere close to Big Ben / When he wanted the news / And some up to date views / He gave The Sun ten out of ten."

You do not have to be a genius to see why the government is so delighted with The Sun. It has consistently supported Mrs. Thatcher and has proved her staunchest ally in a period when she is under intense pressure.

The Sun wields enormous political influence not least because its readers are by and large those least interested in politics.

They are therefore far more susceptible to having their opinions influenced by the press than those who are politically alert.

In the British general election the largest swing to the Conservatives was amongst Sun readers, Mrs. Thatcher and Mr. Baker have good reasons to be so grateful to the Sun.

Even now in Thatcher's darkest hour the Sun is in there fighting. When Sir Geoffrey Howe resigned from the Cabinet because he could no longer stomach her opposition to European unity the Sun launched its "Up Yours Delors" campaign designed to incite hostility towards the French.

But it is the hostility displayed towards Irish people that should concern everyone on this island. Through its ill-will and its prejudice The Sun has helped keep British people in ignorance of events in Ireland. It has stirred up ancient hatreds, gloated over the fate of innocents held in prison, gloried in death and slaughter. It has perpetuated the stereotype of the Irishman as a malevolent ignoramus with a pint of Guinness in one hand and an armalite in the other. It has done nothing to promote the cause of peace.

Instead the Sun's impressionable readers have been bombarded with gung-ho editorials calling on the British government to allow the SAS to "take the gloves off" and cross the border to kill all those it believes are members of the IRA.

When Paul Hill, who was wrongly convicted of having taken part in the Guildford bombings, got married the Sun carried a banner headline: "IRA Pig to Wed". It has consistently scoffed at the Birmingham Six's claims to innocence and suggested that anyone critical of the British legal system is somehow a traitor and a supporter of the IRA.

We do not therefore join Mrs. Thatcher and Mr. Baker in wishing The Sun a happy birthday. It is not a harmless comic, it is a dangerous, deceitful rag that has plumbed new depths for British journalism.

? Questions and Assignments

1. Explain clearly "the danger" that is referred to in the third paragraph.
2. (i) Why is The Sun important to the Conservative Party in Britain?
   (ii) How is this importance acknowledged?
3. ". . . The Sun has helped keep British people in ignorance of events in Ireland . . . stirred up ancient hatreds . . ." Show how the writer supports this argument.
4. From your reading of this editorial, outline your impressions of a typical Sun reader.
5. Write a letter to the editor of The Irish News responding to this editorial.

Newspapers - Editorials

> In the "quality" papers leader writers generally make their cases by presenting both sides of the argument and then defending, in a calm and reasoned way, the side with which they agree. They back up their points with evidence and link their ideas in a logical way. They appeal to the readers' intelligence rather than emotions.
>
> However, in some of the sensational tabloids, leader writers tend to make their case by stating only one side of the argument in a forcible and assertive way.
>
> The points are often made in one sentence paragraphs and are frequently emphasised by techniques such as the use of heavy typeface or underlining. Slang and idioms are also frequently used. This type of comment appeals to the readers' emotions rather than to their intelligence and reason. Often the effect is of a loud-mouthed bore loudly venting his gut feelings.
>
> Such writing exploits ignorance and feeds off a section of people who, by and large, are educationally and intellectually deprived.

Poll Facts
THE Sun makes two fearless forecasts.

ONE: There will be no referendum on Europe.

It is not necessary. Margaret Thatcher is carrying out the policies on which she was elected.

TWO: Michael Heseltine will not fight her for the leadership.

He knows that if he did, he would get such a derisory vote that people would stop talking about him.

Remember — you read it here first.

Try, try again
THE Falklands War ended 1-0 to Britain.

Now in the happier days, the Argentines come to Twickenham to play rugby. They go down 51-0.

They still aren't ready for us!

Fruitcakes
DID you know that carrots are a fruit?

The EC have ruled that jam can be made only from fruit.

As the Portuguese make jam from carrots this means that the carrot is now classified as a fruit.

How would we describe the Euro-bureaucrats?

Easy. Fruit and nut cases, all of them!

Hands Off
HERE is the first task for the new Irish President.

Arrange a referendum to change the constitution so that Ireland no longer claims Ulster as an integral part of the country.

At a stroke, this would disown the IRA after half a century.

It is the decent, civilised thing to do.

? Questions and Assignments

1. In the light of the comments in the Irish News editorial, "About time to act your age", comment briefly on each of the Sun "editorials."

Letters to the Editor

The letters to the Editor page of a newspaper gives readers the opportunity to comment on the variety of issues which affect their lives and the opportunity to comment on the actions of all those who exercise power in our society.

Sir — I am concerned about the loss of the Amazon rainforests.

We can't live without the trees because they produce a massive amount of oxygen and without oxygen we can't exist.

The oxygen prevents a build-up of carbon dioxide that the factories, cars, etc. exhale.

Many people live in the forests, and they cannot survive outside them.

Since the loggers started to cut down the rainforests many Indian tribes have disappeared. I think that's the same as murder!

The Amazonian forest gives us 50 per cent of the world's annual production of oxygen, so if they cut down the forests we are going to die as well.

— Yours etc.

Sir — It is stultifying to find that on return to my native land I am confronted with a mindless bureaucracy. A simple matter of an application for a driving licence is magnified to monstrous proportions. I produced a valid South Australian Licence to the Waterford Borough Council and applied for an Irish Licence. I was informed that it was not acceptable, nor was a Hong Kong nor a Malaysian nor an out of date U.K. licence. Only a valid EC Licence is acceptable.

I therefore applied to the U.K. for a licence and found that my South Australian Licence is acceptable.

The mind boggles!

Perhaps, the Minister for the Environment might like to comment on such bureaucratic lunacy?

— Yours etc.

Sir — I understood that it has been accepted now for several centuries that our planetary system is heliocentric. However, according to RTE's six o'clock news (August 17th), it now appears to be Dublinocentric. We were told that the recent eclipse of the moon all "began high over Dublin's Three Rocks Mountain".

Funny, I actually saw it over Waterford's Comeragh Mountains from a base in the South Riding of Tipperary. I even heard that somebody saw it in Cork City. Is this a record?

— Yours etc.

Sir — Public awareness of environmental problems is increasing, but so is public confusion, as illustrated by some entries in your Weekly Verse Competition on the topic of the greenhouse effect (June 4th).

The enhanced greenhouse effect causes the heating up of the world and rapid climate changes. A separate problem is the hole in the ozone layer which causes skin cancer and reduces crop yields. Both are caused by gases we let into the atmosphere, and confusion arises because some of these gases - CFCs - contribute to both effects.

We must keep clear about the problems so that we can be clear about the solutions.

— Yours etc.

Letters to the Editor

Sir — AS DUBLIN is the European Capital City of Culture next year, and as it's the 75th anniversary of the 1916 Rising, as a fitting tribute to such an occasion, may I suggest the idea of a monument and sculpture in memory of Padraig Pearse and those who died in the rebellion.

I thought that such a monument could be placed where once stood Nelson's Column, as it is a very appropriate and suitable site, adjacent to the GPO where the rebellion began. This new monument would be a great landmark and attraction for the city.

Such a monument would be of the same height, dimensions and classical style as Nelson's Column, which would be in keeping with the surrounding buildings and scale of the city. In Dublin of the auld times, Nelson's Column served as a focal point for O'Connell Street and indeed the whole city, and since it was destroyed the city has lacked that very visual object which marked the very heart and centre of Dublin.

I thought that the new pillar could be similar to the old, but with various modifications, i.e. steps leading up to a cube base but on which would have inscribed the Proclamation of the Republic both in Irish and English, decoratively both in Irish and English, decoratively embellished with Celtic designs. From this could rise the column, again which could have Celtic carvings, on which would stand at the very top a bronze statue figure of Pearse reading the Proclamation aloud as he did that Easter Sunday 1916, outside the GPO.

Such a monument would be very appropriate as the bloody rebellion is seen as the last great struggle against imperialism, from which arose the birth of the new Ireland, the modern, free and democratic republic we have today, despite the horrible murder and brutality in the North.

This new monument could be adopted by our government to hold a commemorative service each year as the rebellion is unashamedly an important part of the heritage not only of Dublin city but of Ireland.

Looking at other major European cities, they are laden with such monuments to the "glorious dead," and I feel that such a major national monument is greatly needed here in Dublin to the men and women who fought and died for what we have today.

— Yours etc.

Sir — I assume from the reader's letter (August 17th), that he has never allowed a friend to smoke in his house, always uses lead free petrol in his car and avoids other extreme pollutants such as buses and aeroplanes. I am sick of anti-smokers who while, expressing their disgust of cigarette smoking, eagerly endorse other forms of pollution.

— Yours etc.

Letters to the Editor

Sir — Comparing our government's response to two separate problems involving accommodation was most interesting.

Firstly, Peter Byrne reported (May 10th) that the Irish soccer squad's hotel problems were solved by a Government Minister who travelled to Rome and Sardinia at the behest of the Taoiseach, Charles Haughey. Apparently this action was taken because Mr. Haughey was so moved by the Irish squad's plight.

Secondly, the Rev. Peter McVerry (letter, May 10th) provides us with a graphic account of the plight of a 13-year-old homeless boy who is sleeping on the floor of a voluntary organisation's hostel because our government chooses to ignore his situation. Priorities! — Yours etc.

Sir — The Rev. Peter McVerry, SJ, asks the question does anyone in government care about homelessness? The answer is yes. This Government is extremely committed to resolving homelessness in all its forms. Why just last Wednesday it was announced that the Minister of State for Sport, Mr. Frank Fahy, had travelled to Rome at the behest of the Taoiseach to resolve the potential homelessness of the Irish team (income of a mere £400,000+ per home game) during the opening weeks of the World Cup.

Now, if Peter McVerry could get his squad of 14 teenagers (currently training together in his three bedroomed flat) to qualify for the 1994 World Cup, then perhaps Mr. Haughey might discover the problem, which would then become in the immortal words of another politician, "no problem" at all.

Short of that, it looks like the Rev. McVerry will have to wait until Frank Fahy becomes Taoiseach before anyone in government will care about the issue.

— Yours etc.

Sir — I am totally in agreement with letters (dated July 20th) regarding smoking in cinemas.

I was fortunate enough to work in New York for four years and a visit to the cinema was always a pleasure. Invariably, smoking was totally prohibited or at least severely restricted. This ensured a high degree of comfort for patrons.

In a country where one in three adults are said to smoke, the majority, in general, have to put up with the smoking habits of the minority. Does this make sense? Two hours in a packed, smoke-filled cinema is more than I care to endure. It's no wonder that the video rental industry is so successful.

I still find it difficult to understand why people smoke in defiance of all the negative medical implications for smokers. More importantly, from my perspective, the problem of passive smoking has also been highlighted and I certainly don't want to have my health affected by the habits of others.

Full marks to CIE/Dublin Bus for its efforts to make the travels of non-smokers more pleasant. — Yours etc.

? Questions and Assignments

1. In the case of each of these letters outline
   - (a) the topic of the letter
   - (b) the letter-writer's attitude towards the topic
   - (c) the argument put forward to support the view expressed.

2. In the case of each of the letters, write a response supporting **or** opposing the views expressed.

Features

The term "feature" describes an article that falls outside the category of hard news. In the features pages can be found bright and chuckly pieces, odds and ends of scholarship, memoirs, short bursts of preaching or moaning, amusing anecdotes as well as regular features on subjects such as gardening, motoring and fashion. In general, the features pages of Irish newspapers are wide-ranging, well-written, informative and entertaining and offer a treasure trove of inspiration for all essay writing.

Also included in features are pieces by regular columnists, published usually on a weekly basis. Usually entertaining and thought-provoking (although sometimes irritating) these columnists help to establish a paper's identity and to attract a regular readership.

Taking Children For Long Walks Is An Uphill Battle

Foreigners are not like us. And there is nothing like foreign travel to confirm one's preconceived notions about them.

For years, I suspected that, unlike us, the French are essentially a law-abiding people. Then, on holiday in France I found myself following a coastal track around magnificent headlands where gorse and heather bloomed.

Its resemblance to a similar track around the promontaries of Co. Kerry was startling. Except for one vital detail. In Kerry the track is known locally as the Smugglers' Walk whereas, in Northern France, the track, originally used for the same nefarious purposes, is called The Walk Of The Customs And Excise Officers.

At last I have got to a stage in life when walking has become a pleasure again. After years of grappling with the dubious delights of the family walk in the country I look back and wonder what drives us parents to exercise our children in this way - whatever about exercising our patience.

Is it simply because when we were young, our parents took us up the mountains? The traditional habits of the Dublin middle classes are so ingrained that we automatically inflict the same on our children - no matter what - until they get old enough to rebel.

And even as they rebel, you have this certainty that by the time they get to be adults they will be dragging their unwilling children up the same mountains and having the same Pinteresque conversations as they go.

"I'm tirrrred...."
"Not much further to go."
"I'm hunnggry...."
"Nearly there now."
"I'm borrrrred...."
"Look, here we are, at the top of the mountain!"
"Does that mean we can go home now?"

Contd...

Features

Small children never walk in a straight line anyway. Instead they scuttle around like crabs, sideways and backways. Only on the rarest occasion do they move forward.

Mostly they wait until you're within spitting distance of the summit of the mountain and then they sit down and demand to be carried the five miles back to the car. Tell them that walking is good for them and they will react like you've just pulled their eyelids inside out.

Adolescence brings an end to the whole sorry business. They go their way, into the bowels of HMV and the Virgin Megastore and leave the mountains for you to enjoy. Who knows what and how much exercise adolescents take - football, discos, jumping up and down at pop concerts? Most of the time you'd be afraid to ask.

Recently a team of British researchers decided to find out the answer to that question. They studied how much exercise children aged from 11 to 16 take.

If their findings are correct it is the adolescents whom we should be forcing out for long walks and not the little ones after all. The first scientific study ever in Britain into whether adolescents take enough exercise has just been completed and the results confirm what most parents have suspected for years. Adolescents do not take enough exercise and that is official.

The children were found to have low levels of physical activity and many of them seldom undertook the volume of activity necessary to benefit their hearts and lungs.

Adolescent girls were found to take even less exercise than boys although overweight children were found to be no less active than the rest.

The assessment is based on hundreds of measurements of heart rates taken over an extended period. Understanding the complexities of adolescence the researchers make allowances for the fact that heart rate is not just affected by exercise. It is also altered by the child's metabolic rate, climactic condition and what they call transient emotional state.

Transient emotional state! — what a pretty portmanteau phrase to encapsulate all the ups and downs of the age; the tantrums, the rages, the broken hearts, the crying spells, the head-to-head confrontations about money, money, money, money . . . .

Precisely the same mental gymnastics, come to think of it, that exercise parents to distraction.

— *Liz McManus (The Sunday Tribune)*

? Questions and Assignments

1. What confirmed the writer's notion that the French were a law-abiding race?

2. What were the "dubious delights" of the family walk in the country-side?

3. Outline the writer's response to the findings of the study made by British researchers.

4. Write a letter to the editor responding to this article.

Features

In this extract from an article by David Hanly, he writes about the advantages of living in a city. David Hanly writes a weekly column for The Sunday Tribune.

One Man in Search of the Good Life

I lived for five years in a country village trying to make a living as a creative writer. I failed. Since my return to Dublin almost 10 years ago I've been asked many times whether I would like to return to what most people seem to think was a "rustic idyll".

The short answer is that I would not. In giving reasons for my answer, I'm inclined to advance my need for what I call a "critical climate". I need challenge and disagreement. I need arrogant economists to stop me in my tracks and tell me I'm talking horse manure: I'm not short of them. I need historians to "revise" my view of our own and others' history. I need new information the way a junkie needs dope. I'm scared of complacency, of a kind of atrophying of the self-critical faculty which can all too often creep up on one in the absence of constant challenge.

Of course, in an era of instant communication, all of these things are available, but in a blunted, third-party way: for all the information that was on tap during the world-changing events of the past year - and the less profound but equally invigorating happenings here in the past month - I would hate to have been without the nightly buzz of reaction about my ears.

For all that I claim self-sufficiency, I need people and I need difference. Above all, difference, and that difference is available in quantity, in my experience, only in the city.

On the other hand, maybe I just like cities. One way or the other, I was moved to think again upon these matters by a booklet which I received from Jim Connolly in Kilbaha in Clare. Although I never knew him, I remember him well as the leader of the Monarchs Showband in Limerick (yeah, that far back). The title of the booklet is *Moving to the West,* which sounds autobiographical but ain't: it is in fact a modest proposal arising out of Jim's own experience as one who gave up the music business and moved to West Clare to make his living as a self-employed craftsman.

— *David Hanly (The Sunday Tribune)*

Questions and Assignments

1. Outline, in your own words, the advantages David Hanly sees in city life.

2. Do you agree with his views? Give reasons for your answer.

Features

> In this extract from an article by Nuala O'Faoláin, she offers some thought-provoking observations on the cliche that "the true spirit of Christmas has been replaced by materialism. Nuala O'Faoláin is a columnist with The Irish Times.

Mundane and the Magical

It doesn't make sense that only a handful of all the people on earth can really matter to you. You should care as much that your neighbours are all right, or the tramp who drinks down at the taxi-rank, or the people of Sudan. But Christmas shows up the limitations of our hearts. Tomorrow I'll be imagining just my own brothers and sisters and a few friends. Counting the blessings they have, and trying to forget the bad bits.

Those blessings will largely be material. I keep hearing people giving out about all the materialism at Christmas, but believe me I'd rather that the people I care about had loads of money and things at Christmas than that they hadn't. You don't begin the accounting with that. Obviously, the first thing is to be alive and healthy, and you can't buy that. To have some love in your life, and you can't buy that either.

But after that, I wish them all to be warm and to have wine in the fridge and to have the price of a taxi and presents to give their friends. For everything any of them have in that line, I'm grateful. Not being grateful wouldn't redistribute their good fortune.

Anyway, it is not as if one can choose between a "materialist" or a "spiritual" Christmas. One or the other is the more authentic for you. Most people will go to Mass and touch through it the ancient and the profound. And think that that's the spiritual bit done with.

They probably won't realise that family Christmases are full of ordinary spirituality. I see a family making the effort to express love and loyalty to each other. No such words are ever said, of course, or anything embarrassing like that. But what else is all the trouble they go to for each other?

You see the old people bombarded by information about Santa when the children come tumbling in. The children learning how their family does things at Christmas. The rituals, the fixed points, the songs that are always sung, the neighbours who always leave in a present. The generations intertwine, and find their own meaning in each other.

If you don't have parents or childen then you're at one remove. At the feast, but not of it. You're an aunt or a friend or some kind of spare part, which is perfectly all right, but not all that exciting, given what Christmas once was. It is all very well setting up a nice holiday for yourself, using all the shrewdness and resourcefulness you've acquired, but once, Christmas really was magical. The child inside still cries out for more than dry and reasonable pleasures.

Still. We have to grow up. Tomorrow could be haunted by what once was, or what might have been. But better to be grateful for what is. If you look around you tomorrow, you'll see the magic consists in having arrived at whatever you are. Did you ever think, when you were five years old, that tomorrow you'd be sitting down with those people in that place? Isn't everything pretty mysterious anyway, Santa or no Santa? Dull enough, tomorrow may be. Bit of a strain, even. But ordinary? No, it's never ordinary.

? Questions and Assignments

1. How according to the writer does Christmas "show up the limitations of our hearts"?
2. How does she support the point that "family Christmases are full of ordinary spirituality"?
3. Do you agree with the writer's views? Explain your answer.

Features

In this extract from a feature on one aspect of life in Britain, Maeve Binchy adopts the style and technique of the novel or short story. Maeve Binchy's column, *Maeve's Times*, is published on Saturdays in The Irish Times.

Four Faces of Tourism

The small mutinous girl was on half term and she was meeting her father's new friend. She didn't like the prospect. The school minibus dropped her outside Selfridges and her father identified himself. Her name was ticked off a list.

"Have a super time, Venetia" called the teacher.

"Ugh," said Venetia.

"Haven't you got tall," her father said.

"I suppose so. It happens. There are very few cases of people shrinking," she said.

"This is Emma" he said, his arm loosely around the neck of a girl ten years older than his daughter.

"Lovely to meet you," said Emma, "I've heard lots about you."

"I've heard nothing about you yet," Venetia said. "Are you the one after Susanna?"

Emma's eyes narrowed.

"I don't really know. I'd say there may have been one or two in between."

The lines were drawn. The man sighed.

"We were wondering about the London Dungeon," he ventured.

"You're not ancient enough, you've got to be very old before they put you in that place," Venetia said.

"Macdonalds?" he asked.

"I'm a vegetarian."

"Sorry." "No I'm sorry for *you* actually with all this fuss and everything."

"Do they let you read all about that at school?" Emma asked in what might have been her last attempt to establish a rapport with this child.

"No they wall us up and beat us with ropes if we read the papers," Venetia said.

"I meant sorry for not remembering you were a vegetarian," said her father.

"No reason why you should, I wasn't one the last time, at Easter."

"No," he said.

"With Susanna," she added helpfully.

"What *would* you like to do?"

"What we always do; the pictures, please." "It's a pity not to talk," he said.

"No it isn't. Could we go to the Krays?"

They bought an early *Evening Standard* to look up where the film was being shown.

? Questions and Assignments

1. Outline the circumstances of the scene.
2. Describe briefly each of the characters and their relationship to each other.
3. Using this extract as a model, write a similar piece on some aspect of Irish life.

Writer's Workshop

Essay Writing

The basic purpose of all forms of writing is to communicate a message from the writer to the reader. You may want to advise, tell a story, amuse, instruct, warn, recollect, persuade, describe . . . but you must have an interesting and worthwhile message to pass on to the reader. The message can be regarded as your raw material. It should consist of a good collection of interesting pieces of information and well-developed ideas.

GETTING IDEAS
While your own ideas are important, new ideas and facts can develop and sharpen your own views. Keep an open mind by :-
  (i)   *Listening to* news bulletins, discussions, documentaries, interviews, talks, reviews, drama and stories on radio and television.
  (ii) *Conversing with* friends, family, classmates, neighbours, teachers, etc. Learn to be a good listener. Practically everyone has something of interest to say and details of the experiences of others will often throw new light on your own experiences.
  (iii) *Watching* the world around you. Take notice of your environment and how it is changing, the people who inhabit it and the things they do. Question yourself about the things you see. The good writer is not content to merely observe - he or she asks *why?, how?, who?, what?, when?* The answers will provide ample material for writing.
  (iv) *Reading* books, magazines and newspapers is probably the most important source of ideas for your own writing. Most published material contains well-expressed responses to a variety of aspects of life from people with whom you are not personally acquainted. In their pages you will find many interesting and up-to-date facts, striking phrases, persuasive arguments and concise sentences.

THE PLAN
Planning your writing saves time. It should eliminate your stopping at the end of every sentence wondering what to write next.

A piece of writing that succeeds in grabbing and holding the attention of the reader can often appear to have flowed smoothly, effortlessly and spontaneously from the mind of the writer onto the page. Don't be deceived. Material that is interesting and easily read is generally the end product of careful planning, editing and redrafting by the writer.

Planning a piece of writing requires no more than a few sheets of roughwork paper. It involves deciding the topic of each paragraph or section, the points you will include in each and their order. Your plan should include references to any facts, figures, anecdotes or descriptions, that you intend to use.

STARTING OFF
The opening lines of your piece of writing must grab the interest of the reader. Make a collection of opening sentences of newspaper and magazine features, short stories and novels that you found particularly interesting. In each case, study the techniques used and adapt them to suit your own writing.

Writer's Workshop

To capture a reader's attention, writers often use the following techniques when composing introductions :-

- (i) a short anecdote. This may be clearly related to the topic or may, initially, have no apparent connection. However, its link with the topic will be established at an early stage.
- (ii) an interesting or unusual statement of fact,
- (iii) a relevant or apt quotation,
- (iv) a surprising statistic or comparison,
- (v) an opinion that initially appears extremely outrageous,
- (vi) a direct introduction to the action without any preamble,
- (vii) a question or rhetorical question.

Try to avoid introductions that :-
- (i) state obvious facts,
- (ii) define things which are generally understood,
- (iii) relate an incident or a series of events that have no real relevance to the action or piece of writing.

PARAGRAPHS

Write in paragraphs, beginning every paragraph on a new line and a little way in from the margin. Each paragraph should deal with one topic only.

THE RIGHT WORDS

Take care to choose the words and phrases that will convey your ideas in the clearest and most accurate way. Try to avoid using phrases and expressions that have become dull through over-use. A writer needs to have a good stock of words and phrases at her or his command. Reading helps to increase your vocabulary. When you read, note how various writers take different topics; the figures of speech they use, the verbs, adjectives and adverbs they select. Make notes of any words, phrases or sentences that strike you as being particularly effective. You will be able to adapt many of these to your own writing. Keep a note, also, of any original striking phrases coined by yourself.

FINISHING OFF

The closing paragraph should be short. Link it with the title by repeating a word or a phrase from the title. Alternatively you may be able to give the title a clever twist in the closing stages.

This is only one of many approaches and a study of a selection of newspaper features should provide you with plenty of ideas on how to give an essay a good finishing touch.

MAKING YOUR CASE

This type of writing involves expressing a judgement, making recommendations or outlining your vision on some controversial issue or problem. In your approach, you may find the following points worth considering :-

Writer's Workshop

- **Know your subject.** You will not be able to make a convincing case on a subject of which you have only a little vague knowledge.
- Be **clear and specific** when defining the problem and your views on it. Avoid phrases such as "The government must do more . . .", "Schools don't do enough to . . .", "A lot of . . .". By outlining your position in clear terms, you can test it in a realistic and reasoned manner.
- Imagine **somebody arguing against** your point of view. What kind of arguments would they offer? What evidence would they use to support their case?
- **Know your opponents' case** and state it honestly. If your position is sound you will be able to show how the opposite position is flawed - regardless of how persuasive their case is. Avoid making any insulting statements, inferences about the opposition - they only amount to an admission of weakness on your part.
- There are many **literary devices** - 'tricks of the trade' of writing, so to speak - that can be used in order to make your message more persuasive and acceptable. These include rhetorical questions, anecdotes, humour, graphic descriptions, comparisons and striking statistics. Use each of these sparingly.
- In a logical argument each step must be **linked to the previous one.** Here is a list of the more commonly use "link" words and phrases. They are generally used at the beginning of a sentence :-
  - (a) For example; For instance; In other words; As an illustration; Thus; (introducing examples/evidence after general statements).
  - (b) First; Second; Next; Then; Meanwhile; Finally; At last; Today; Tomorrow; (narrating/presenting a series of events).
  - (c) In addition; Also; Furthermore; Moreover; As a result; Therefore; Accordingly; Consequently; However; But; Nevertheless; On the other hand; On the contrary (debating/argumentative and analytical writing).

KEEPING A DIARY

Keep your own personal diary or journal and try to make at least one entry each week. Your journal or diary should be used to record details of, and responses to, a wide variety of situations and people. Don't try to describe everything that happens. Select those of most significance to you. As your journal or diary is a personal document, you should not be afraid to experiment with a variety of forms of expressions, such as poetry, dialogue, song lyrics and so on. You may also wish to use a section of it to record any phrases you encountered, either in reading or conversation, that struck you for their vividness, sharpness, aptness etc. Alternatively, you may wish to consider keeping a scrapbook of cuttings of interesting items from magazines or newspapers (Don't take cuttings from books!).

PRACTICE MAKES PERFECT

Writing is a craft. Like other crafts, the skills of writing cannot be mastered overnight. It requires constant practice on your own as well as a study of the work of established writers in order to learn how the masters of the craft approach the task. Like some craftsmen, writers, on occasions, produce works of art.

Writer's Workshop

A Last Word (from the Department of Education)

Students should be encouraged to engage in these procedures continually so they come to experience that the writing process is a thinking process :-

- give information in short cogent notes.
- compose captions, headlines and titles.
- fill in a variety of application forms.
- news reports.
- describe in a variety of forms, places, events and people.
- write personal letter; writer letter requesting/giving information.
- keep journal/diary on a range of experiences.
- write coherent narrative about self; compose fictional narrative.
- write simple dialogue or play-script.
- write in simple verse forms.
- comment/review literature read privately or read in class.
- comment/review films, television material and videos.
- write commentary and give response.
- engage in word-play to increase familiarity with the linguistic conventions of spellings, punctuation, grammar and syntax.

(Introduction to Junior Certificate English Dept. of Ed./N.C.C.A.)

Reviews

Almost all newspapers carry a wide selection of reviews. Books, films, concerts, records, radio and television programmes are reviewed each week. Your own reviewing techniques will be improved and developed by regular readings of the review sections of newspapers and magazines.

Television and Radio

Most newspapers have weekly television and radio columns where a regular columnist looks back on the high points — and the low points — of the week's radio and television programmes. These columnists frequently produce very witty writing and are recommended reading for those wishing to broaden their understanding of the techniques of television and radio.

Reviews

THE HORSE SHOW deprived us of this week's *Mission : Impossible*, so fans of hokum had to make do with an old *Mannix* (Network 2, Wednesday). A guy was found with a smoking gun in his hand, standing over a warm corpse. Open and shut.

But the guy's sister said the guy didn't do it; she knew because she did it. But the cops wouldn't believe her. Would Mannix please prove her brother innocent and herself guilty of murder.

A routine problem for Mike. There was the standard scene where he broke into someone's office and stole a confidential report from a filing cabinet. (He had no problem finding it; it had "Confidential Report" printed in huge letters on the cover.) And there was the standard scene where the gruff police lieutenant gave Mike 24 hours to come up with the solution to the case. There was the standard scene where the Real Nasties had Mike at gunpoint and he went *Swok! Smack!* and *Biff!* and stretched them both out just in time for the cops to arrive and arrest them.

Mike, of course, not only proved the guy was innocent. He also proved that the Real Nasties had poisoned the victim before the guy's sister came along and shot him. So, it turned out she shot a corpse and so she too was innocent.

And people say there's nothing on TV in the summer.

— *Gene Kerrigan (The Sunday Tribune)*

EVERYTIME I hear John McKenna on the wireless, my respect for the man shoots up like the hair on the base of my neck. Recently he stood in at an autopsy and gave a running commentary as a pathologist cut through the rib cage - went in up to his elbows in lungs, livers, intestines, he did. No, not McKenna, the pathologist.

That said, though, this week's edition of the series - the work of a psychic investigator - was the most ambitious flop since the setting up of the Youth Employment Agency.

Surely, I hear you say, that the 'manifestation' of a spectre on radio would have been another first for RTE Radio. One to go with Ronan Collins' Tap Dancing Competition for Radio, or the Famous Firework Extravaganza. I forget who was responsible for that one - Oh 'listen' to the Roman Candle! Did you 'hear' the great Catherine Wheel? But, yes, I hear you say, a ghost on radio. Just the thing to stir you out of that Monday torpor.

The show opened with the sound of an eerie organist playing in the shrubbery of a County Wicklow garden. In a ghost story there is always a chilling organ in the woodwork - no self-respecting ghost story would ever be without one. To the background of the chilly organ, the psychic investigator Tony Owens emptied the contents of his bag : A Bible, a crucifix, holy water "just in case" and, I didn't know psychics used them, a camera.

Yes, a camera. Once, while he was in Huntingdon Castle in Co. Wexford, Tony caught a cowled figure on camera. He showed the photograph to his friends. "Have a look at that," he said. What is it, his friends wanted to know? "Is it a monk?", "Is it a nun?", "Is it a ghost?" No, it's Wonderwo . . . .

But to get back to the haunted garden. A large black dog appeared, but he was dismissed as an innocent by-stander. Then it began to rain, so if and when the ghost put in an appearance, it was going to be a sorry sodden spectre.

"We're going to settle down and wait," said John with stoic dignity. Two hours later and the ghost still hadn't appeared. "We spent a long time under those trees," said John, as the show tortoised to a close.

Now I don't know how best to break this to you, but the sodden spectre - like Godot - never turned up. And it's no use blaming John or Tony. I mean to say how were they to know that the spectre was on a work-to-rule? Still, not to worry, John. Always look for the silver lining when never a shroud appears out of the blue.

— *Tom Widger (The Sunday Tribune)*

? Questions and Assignments

1. In the case of the television and radio reviews above (i) name the programme being reviewed, (ii) give some details about the content of the programme and (iii) say whether the reviewer was or was not impressed by the programme. Give reasons for your answer. You should pay particular attention to the tone of each of the reviews.

Mass Media
Book Reviews

> **? Questions and Assignments**

The following pages contain a selection of book reviews. In the case of each review: -
(i) Name the book being reviewed and the topic of that book.
(ii) Say whether the reviewer was *or* was not impressed by the book.
(iii) Write out any phrases used by the reviewer which praised *or* criticised the book being reviewed.

Rosemary Sutcliff has never tried to ingratiate herself with young readers by making her prose bland and easily digestible. The complexities of her style are not gratuitous, but reflect the depth and complexity of her subject-matter. Those without an innate historical sense or taste need to be encouraged to read her, because they discover that she not only makes bare facts "come alive" but attempts to make sense of them, and to illuminate legend, in human terms. She is also an extraordinarily rich, exciting and poetic writer. To those of my generation who thrilled to *The Eagle of the Ninth*, it is a pleasure to read her latest book, **The Shining Company** (Bodley Head £7.99), and find her still at the height of her powers.

The inspiration for it comes from the earliest northern British epic poem - such sources are often the triggers for her fiction - about 300 young, keen warriors belonging to the tribe of King Mynyddog in 600 AD who were brought together and trained for a year, as a fighting brotherhood, before being sent out against the invading Saxons. The hero is Prosper, son of Gerontius, a shieldbearer to one of them, and the story concerns him, his close friends and confederates, and his bond-slave. It is a remote time, and values and customs are completely alien to those of our own, particularly the concept of fealty and loyalty to a king, an individual lord, a blood brother. Rosemary Sutcliff gets under the skin of adventurous young men in trying to reveal what made them follow a leader and give their lives gladly in his service. It is as inspiring, and tragic, as any similar war story involving a "shining company" of golden boys, and this intricate, compellingly imagined and beautifully told story makes period and people sympathetic and comprehensible in our own time.

Double Vision by *Diana Hendry* (Julia MacRae Books £9.95) succeeds totally where very few books do, as a novel which bestrides the two worlds of adult and children's fiction with total success in both - though the areas of human understanding it explores would not be understood by readers much younger than 13 or so. Set in the 1950s, in a northern seaside resort - period and place marvellously pervade the whole - it is a story of two sisters growing up in very different ways, longing for adulthood, dreaming of real men and encountering callow youths, frustrated by stuffy, narrow horizons, astonished by the eccentricities of adult neighbours - all familiar ingredients of many novels. But it is the writing that is fully mature, subtle and assured, and unflashy - the stuff of which the very best fiction is wrought.

Book Reviews

School story series have certain unchanging ingredients and an equally long tradition, and *Jean Ure's* first book in a projected series about Peter High School, **Jo in the Middle** (Hutchinson £7.99), is a day-school successor to the old Malory Towers, Trebizon and Chalet School books. Friendships are made and loyalties strained, gangs form and break up, the games captain picks the house netball team and makes some controversial choices. Classroom characters are satisfyingly familiar - the good sport, the comic, the blue-stocking, the rebel, the single-minded, would-be ballerina. Not a pony or a mademoiselle in sight yet, but one lives in hope. Meanwhile, the central story about junior school friends Jo and Matty, growing up and changing as they make fresh encounters, is convincing and sensitive - the series will have many readers eager to empathise.

South of the Border by *Barbara Machin*

When books are written out of television series, characterisation often occurs. Regular viewers will have their own images of the two principal characters, Finn and Pearl, in this saga of intrigue and detection. The rest of us have to guess what makes them so likeable. The plotting is good though. Fundamentally, a union which wants to call a strike finds disturbing irregularities in its financial affairs. It has been using an advisor to help deal in works of art to try to get a higher rate of return than less speculative investments. Furthermore, a key union member has a villa in Spain, which he could not afford on his salary. Suspicions increase, but the union cannot afford to let the scandal leak. Finn and Pearl discreetly investigate, take a few knocks, and sort it all out (The Women's Press £4.95).

Squandering Eden by *Mort Rosenblum and Doug Williamson*

The combining gross domestic product of the whole continent of Africa is less than that of Italy. Natural resources are wasted or destroyed. Most of black Africa is desperately short of food. Often, foreign aid only makes the situation worse. Partly, this is because of corruption, and partly because it encourages a passive attitude amongst the Africans themselves. Mostly it is because the aid is given and administered by people who do not pause to consider the nature of the problems. Thus, grants allow farmers to produce mammoth crops of grain. Then, because there is no transport, they collapse under the costs of storage. This book looks in detail at the difficulties facing different countries. It does not suggest that money should be thrown at the problems out of post-colonial guilt, but that more sensitive help should be given to help Africans change their own values (Paladin £5.95).

I have read very little fiction this year, but was greatly taken with Penelope Fitzgerald's *The Gate of Angels* (Collins). I also much enjoyed *Son of Adam* (Deutsch), Denis Forman's nostalgic evocation of his boyhood in Dumfriesshire - especially Marnie the house-keeper, whose wig smelt of dead mouse and nutmeg.

- Ian MacIntyre

Book Reviews

The Village of Longing and Dancehall Days by *George O'Brien*

A vivid slice of Irish life, honest and unromanticised, these two volumes of autobiography were originally published separately, **The Village of Longing** winning the 1988 Irish Book Awards Silver Medal for Literature. O'Brien's reminiscences of his 1950s childhood in Lismore, County Waterford, in a matriarchal society reigned over by his grandmother, are evocative and thoughtful and run seamlessly into the second volume, about his teenage years in Dublin. There, avid for new experiences, he soon swaps J. Arthur Rank and banana fritters at the city's gleaming picture palaces for O'Casey at the Abbey Theatre; and at the Saturday night dancehalls discovers girls and soon finds that he "knew a fair few of the facts. It was life that was still a little obscure". Taking its young protagonist up to his arrival as an excited immigrant at Euston station, this is a delightful memoir which won the John Ederyn Hughes prize at the Sunday Times/Hay on Wye literary festival (Penguin £5.99).

The following are brief reviews of the general works of authors rather than of a particular book.

The Blyton books have been particularly criticised for sexism, racism and stereotyping. Mr Goon, the village policeman in "Mystery of the Burnt Cottage" ("Clear orf, you , Clear orf") would never pass editorial scrutiny today. Nor would Ann of the Famous Five, who chirps, "Fried things are so nice . . I love having two houses . . to look after," and who blushes with pride when Julian tells her "You're a very good little house-keeper." No Irish school resembled St. Clare's, Malory Towers, even less the Chalet School where gels wore smashing gentian tunics and had midnight feasts under their duvets. Irish playgrounds did not ring with cries of "Steady on, old girl" or "I say, you are a brick." Blyton and Brent Dyer's role models were unlikely ones for Irish children. Nevertheless, they introduced many to a lasting habit of reading and the notion of a good story.

By the early Seventies Roald Dahl regarded himself principally as a writer of children's stories, although he published an adult comic novel, *My Uncle Oswald*, in 1979. Dahl's vulgarity and childlike delight in excess made adults sceptical of his outstanding qualities as a storyteller and master of invention. Adults, when judging children's books, tend to be especially sensitive and protective about what children should and should not read. That he was controversial there can be no doubt. He could be cruel, savage even, when attacking things he did not like. His loathing of blood sports is given full rein in both *The Magic Finger* (1966) and *Danny, the Champion of the World* (1975). His intellectual snobbishness shows through time and time again, most notably in one of his last titles, *Matilda* (1988). He was accused of being anti-women for his book *The Witches* (1983), a charge he most strenuously denied. *Charlie and the Chocolate Factory* had distinctly racist over-tones in its first editions, an attitude that was corrected in later editions.

But Dahl had other sides, too, which can be found throughout his stories and give the lie to some of the charges laid against him. In *The Witches*, the most interesting and respected character is the grandmother, a woman of immense understanding and sympathy. No one who

Contd...

Book Reviews

despised women could invent a character like her. (She is also an illuminating antidote to the vile grandmother in *George's Marvellous Medicine*, 1981). The tenderness of the relationship between Danny and his father in *Danny, the Champion of the World* verges on the sentimental, making it one of Dahl's easiest books for adults as well as children to enjoy whole-heartedly. Similarly, in *The BFG* (1982) Dahl created a character, a tender-hearted giant with a penchant for an off-beam, invented vocabulary all of his own, who can only be loved by all. *Esio Trot* (1990), his last published title (there is one more *The Min Pins* awaiting publication as well as his manuscript of *The Vicar of Nibbleswicke* recently auctioned to raise money for the Dyslexia Society), is a wholly likeable and dotty story about a favourite tortoise.

All these books show that Dahl held many different views of the world. In his writing his aim was to delight children. To him, the importance of his success was that he helped the cause of children's reading. No one could dispute the huge role he played in getting children hooked into reading by offering them the kind of stories they really wanted to read. Stylistically, too, he helped new readers by using language simply and accurately. The quality of his writing is easily discernible by the fluency with which it can be read aloud.

Outside his own writing, his commitment to furthering the cause of children's reading was fulfilled in his role as honorary patron of Readathon, a nationwide sponsored reading event which not only raises money for the Malcolm Sargent Cancer Fund for Children but also encourages children throughout the country to read - and enjoy it. Dahl was gifted at talking to children at signing sessions where he was tireless in his commitment to making children feel genuine contact with him.

For many children Roald Dahl is synonymous with reading. He is the one author whose books are currency among children, being passed eagerly from hand to hand as soon as they appear. The absence of new Dahl titles will be a loss for many young readers.

Writers' Workshop

Writing your own Reviews

The purpose of a review is to present an assessment of a work (e.g. novel, film, record) or an event (e.g. play, concert, radio or television programme) so that the reader of the review can decide if she or he wishes to view or read the work being reviewed. Assume that your reader does not know as much as you do about the subject being reviewed.

Your review should deal with each of the following points: -

(i) The reader needs to have a reasonably good awareness of the subject before she or he will appreciate your assessment. Therefore you need to describe the subject clearly and accurately, including background details and explanations, where necessary.

(ii) Clarify for your reader, the purpose of the artist in creating the work under review. You should also, briefly clarify your own tastes and preferences in relation to the type of work being reviewed. This will allow the reader to put your review into perspective.

(iii) Try to be fair. Practically every work has some good points. Refer to these. A review which suggests that some work is utterly worthless will be suspect. Savaging a play, record, novel or film with your pen can be fun - but it is unlikely that this will give a balanced judgement. This is not to say that you should not mention the weak aspects of a work under review - just don't let them blind you to its good points. Aim to be honest, balanced and positive.

Crosswords

Crossword No. 1

Across
1. A young ___ ___ ___ lady set to go far (2 + 3 + 6).
7. A tree prone to disease.
9. Let's go - let's ___ ___ ___ (4 + 1 + 4).
10. Something of value on the marketplace.
11. One side; one aspect; one ___ .
14. Certainly not wild.
15. Accompanies bangers.
16. One being trained.
17. First aircraft.
19. Complain perhaps.
20. Some men think they are tough and ___ .
23. A shady leafy shelter in a wood.
26. Many musicians.
27. To make a mistake.
28. A master of ceremonies, a speechmaker.

Down
1. Can't be mistaken.
2. Requests.
3. Acted out on stage.
4. The Earth's protective layer.
5. He had an ___ for a great book.
6. Japanese club hostess.
8. Two things that go together (8 + 4).
11. Festival.
12. Hangs from a bracelet.
13. Picks you up when taken.
15. A brief memorandum.
18. To prevent, to impede.
21. A famous English racecourse.
22. Famous laugher.
24. A duty list.
25. Let it stand - like step - except for the end.

Crosswords

Crossword No. 2

Across

7. Mêlée.
8. A prickly plant.
9. To have something in view (2 + 5).
10. A type of male singer.
12. Whetting the appetite.
15. You'll be this - some day.
16. The speed at which . . . .
18. Holds up a blackboard.
19. Fashion, style.
21. See ahead.
22. Correct.

Down

1. To wipe out.
2. A brief stop.
3. Gives the spark.
4. In parts of Ireland one has moved, they claim.
5. Part of a town.
6. A cooking tool.
11. Consistency.
13. Having no pity whatsoever.
14. A quick glance.
16. Sorrow.
17. Hard and unyielding.
20. In a mess.

Crosswords

Crossword No. 3

Across

7. A violent strike (1 + 4).
8. Hanging ice.
9. Ties up.
10. The sum of.
12. Makes sure the figures add up.
15. Stretch factor.
18. Usually a Scottish musician.
19. Sleeping chamber.
21. A drama with music.
22. Direct a vehicle.

Down

1. Deeply dozing (4 + 6).
2. Test the flavour.
3. Lost because of a nail.
4. Total failure; breakdown.
5. Clearly different.
6. Flat top of mountain.
11. They're not early.
13. Waterfall.
14. A musical string puller.
16. To mend a shoe.
17. Clothes for a ceremonial occasion.
20. Rush.

Crossword No. 4

Across

9. Gave consent.
10. Great admiration by fan.
12. A safety pin has many ____ .
13. He ____ time.
14. Fail - abstract noun form.
15. Left over.
17. To remember.
18. No harmony; disagreement.
19. ____ day is a taxing one.
20. To insult by ignoring.
23. Without courage; missing bone.
25. Cranky (ness).
26. Hypocrisy.
27. Not quite a fracture.
29. Old ways of doing things.
32. Silent.
34. A wide and impressive view.
35. Tries to make bargain.
36. Tended.
37. Surprise; knock out briefly.
38. Famous for bad deeds.
39. Express disapproval of.

Down

1. Took place.
2. Break; interval.
3. Left high and dry.
4. Top person in newspaper.
5. Walked aimlessly.
6. Enough.
7. Ice cream flavour.
8. Can't be beaten.
11. To become used to hardship.
16. Removed creases from clothes.
19. If you're late you could miss it!
21. Not taking sides (3 + 9).
22. Nearer.
23. Fastest watch hand.
24. Phrase.
25. Play on a word.
28. Starts fires.
29. No respect.
30. Proposed by: ____ by.
31. He put out some ____ .
33. A bar of gold.
34. The soldiers often go on it.

Crosswords

Crossword No. 5

Across
9. Moving up (2 + 3 + 4).
10. A couple's afternoon order in a café (3 + 3 + 3).
12. Oval objects.
13. To remember.
14. After dinner course.
15. Rucksack.
17. It was ____ ____ and too late.
18. Not a small boy (4 + 3).
19. From Troy.
20. If you don't know then ____ .
23. Lights the back (4 + 5).
25. Forever.
26. Accomplished.
27. A little devil plus ALA.
29. Pines once again.
32. No egg, ____ ____ (2 + 7).
34. The ham that Peter owns.
35. Nationals of a large country.
36. Noticed and remembered (4 + 2).
37. Mire (anagram) or an Arab chief.
38. Spent more than he should have.
39. Something very surprising (3 + 6).

Down
1. Some what? This is easy.
2. Not really a villain - only an actor (5 + 7).
3. Grapes grow on it plus GARY.
4. Comment.
5. A slender heel.
6. A moody person is ___ ___ ___ (4 + 2 + 4).
7. A Ford model of the Sixties.
8. Without boots in the adjective form.
11. A pleasant surprise for a child.
16. Irreverent or indecent.
19. A tiny ____ .
21. Imagined : (3 + 2 + 3 + 4).
22. A hidden gunman.
23. Makes a horse move faster (6 + 4).
24. Minds the pheasants.
25. A period of history.
28. Make a note.
29. Fee paid to retain professional advice.
30. A wide-brimmed type of hat.
31. Illness.
33. Scold.
34. The evidence ____ him guilty.

IV - Advertising

In the past, if you wanted to tell people about goods you had for sale you walked through the streets shouting about it or else hired somebody to do the shouting for you. Here are examples of old street cries that were heard in cities and towns four or five hundred years ago.

"Fresh Dublin-Bay herrings,
Fine mackerel,
Sprats a penny a plate"

and

"Who wants some pudding nice and hot!
'Tis now the time to try it;
Just taken from the steaming pot
Free taste before you buy it"

This was the only means available of letting people know about goods and services that were for sale.

Nowadays it is almost impossible to escape from advertisements. They reach out to us from newspapers, magazines, radio, television, shop-windows, street hoardings, buses . . . . . all demanding our attention. Advertising is a big industry, with large sums of money being spent, telling the public about all the goods and services available and persuading them to buy or use the goods and services.

The typical modern advertisement differs greatly from the old street cries. The small ads in newspapers or on shop notice boards are the closest modern equivalent of the street cries, in that they describe the important features of the product in plain language. We use these small ads for many purposes e.g. to dispose of things such as a bicycle that we have outgrown or seek a kind person to take unwanted puppies or kittens. In these ways advertising can be very useful.

However, much of today's advertisements set out to persuade people to choose a certain brand of product or service from a range of almost identical products or services. What makes a certain brand of bread or soap or bank better than its competitors? Are there any significant differences between rival brands of say, porridge, chocolate, soft drinks? If so, do the advertisements identify these differences? Do they argue, in a plain logical way, why one brand is different from another?

The answer, in most cases, is "no". There are two reasons.
(i) The differences between rival brands are so slight as to be insignificant.
(ii) An advertisement, making a plain logical argument in favour of a certain product would probably make very dull reading.

These are the reasons why most advertisements offer little in the line of plain and solid arguments.

Instead they play on our emotions - those basic hopes, fears and needs that almost all humans have in common. We all like to look good, have friends, feel healthy, have a good time and have a share of the many goods and luxuries that modern life can offer.

Advertising

Very often advertisements link a product with friendship, success or popularity. A brand of lager is shown against the cosy comfort of a warm social occasion in a pub; a small car is driven by a smart, beautiful, well-dressed, confident person; a brand of chocolate is chosen by a pleasant caring mother for her neat and smiling children. For obvious reasons we are never shown the lager being consumed by a group of football hooligans, the car being driven by a hesitant, awkward type of person or a lazy, sloppy-looking mother feeding chocolate to some ill-tempered crying children.

In this section we are concerned with the way words and pictures are used in advertisements. The pictures are sometimes referred to as "illustrations". The words divide into two categories - the **"headline"** and the **"copy"**. Copy-writers are people who write the words for advertisements. They take great care in composing the headline and copy.

The purpose of the headline in an advertisement is the same as one in a news report - to get the attention of readers who are potential customers for the product or service being advertised. The headlines in advertisements have much in common with newspaper headlines. They may contain a straightforward piece of information; they may make use of alliteration, puns, rhymes, or other forms of word-play. They may be humorous, dramatic or sensational. Also, just like news headlines, advertisement headlines make frequent use of certain words and phrases.

FREE	NEW	SPECIAL	MOTHERS	INTRODUCING
LOOK YOUNGER		TOP PEOPLE	RELAX	MIRACLE
	SPECIAL OFFER		BARGAIN	

- This is just a random selection of these words and phrases.

In the main copy, certain words also keep cropping up. These would include: -

FRESH	BEST	NATURAL	NOURISHING	
	CARE	COUNTRY	CHOICE	CRISPY
GOODNESS	FUTURE	DISCOVER	YOU	TODAY	MODERN

? Questions and Assignments

1. Make a list of some other words which occur frequently in advertisements.

2. Compose an advertisement for each of the following products or services (a) a holiday in your district (b) tinned soup (c) a mountain bike (d) a soft-drink (e) jeans (f) a bank (g) an airline.

   Your answer should include (i) a headline (ii) approximately 100-200 words of body copy (iii) a detailed instruction to an artist or photographer on the illustrations required. Use fictional brand names in each case.

Advertisements

Who else would you trust to care for him the way you do?

Who else, but VHI. Because we've been taking care of people all over Ireland for over 30 years.

Once you become a member, you'll realise that the biggest benefit of all is a feeling of quiet confidence about the future.

Confidence that comes from knowing we guarantee comprehensive cover for hospital charges. And that you've got a thoroughly professional and experienced company looking after you.

Whenever you need it, you'll find our service friendly, expert and quick – about everything from answering small queries to settling large claims.

And we are constantly working at ways to make it even better. Like our recently introduced Direct Payment Service, which means we pay hospitals directly leaving you free from unnecessary paperwork.

And our innovative arrangement with An Post means there are now special VHI days each month in selected post offices so you can call in and see our staff closer to home.

Find out more about how VHI can work for you by completing the coupon below.

```
To: VHI, Freepost, VHI House,
Lower Abbey Street, Dublin 1.        FREEPOST
                                     No Stamp Required
Please send me more information
about Voluntary Health Insurance.
Name_____
Address_____
Telephone_____
```

VHI
Voluntary Health Insurance Board
AN BORD ÁRACHAIS SLÁINTE SHAORÁLAIGH

VHI - Working for you.

DUBLIN: VHI HOUSE, LOWER ABBEY STREET., DUBLIN 1. TEL: (01) 724599. CORK: VHI HOUSE, 70 SOUTH MALL, TEL: (021) 277188.
DUN LAOGHAIRE: 35/36 LOWER GEORGE'S ST., TEL: (01) 800306. GALWAY: ROSS HOUSE, VICTORIA PLACE, TEL: (091) 63715. LIMERICK: 62 O'CONNELL ST., TEL: (061) 316122.

Advertisements

V.H.I. Advertisement (See previous page)

? Questions and Assignments

1. Looking at the illustration and the headline, describe the type of person this advertisement is aimed at?
2. Comment on the opening sentence of the copy.
3. (i) What service is being advertised here?
   (ii) What features of the service are emphasised in the advertisement?

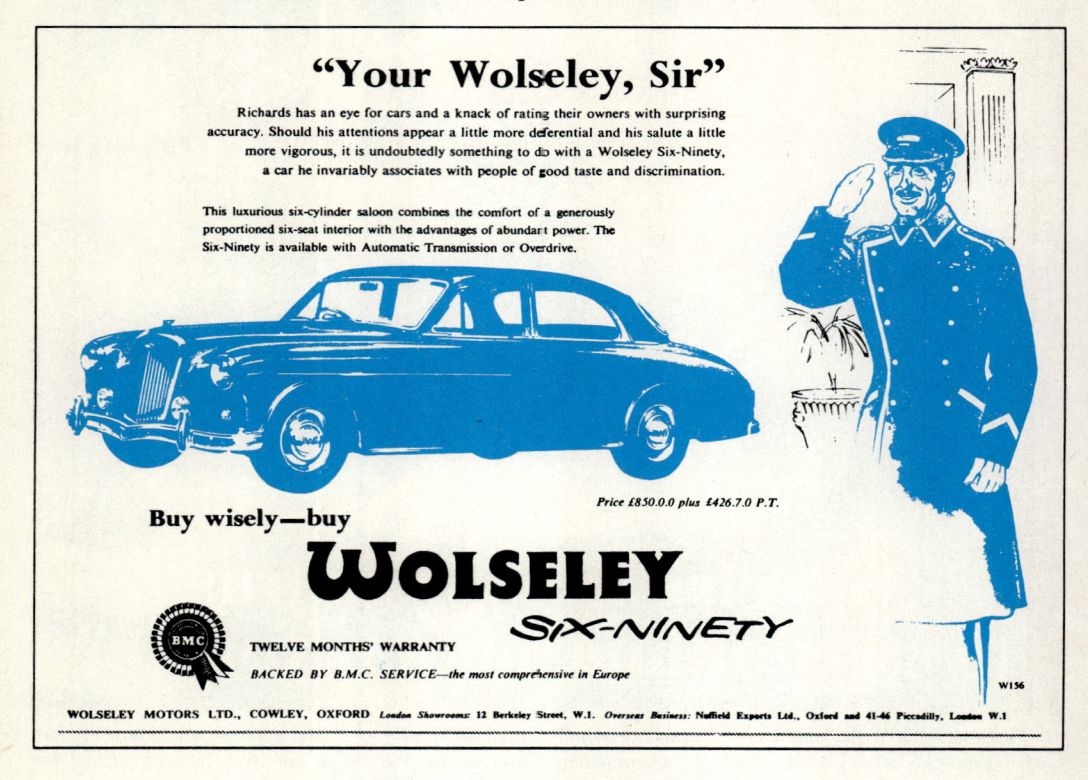

"Your Wolseley, Sir"

Richards has an eye for cars and a knack of rating their owners with surprising accuracy. Should his attentions appear a little more deferential and his salute a little more vigorous, it is undoubtedly something to do with a Wolseley Six-Ninety, a car he invariably associates with people of good taste and discrimination.

This luxurious six-cylinder saloon combines the comfort of a generously proportioned six-seat interior with the advantages of abundant power. The Six-Ninety is available with Automatic Transmission or Overdrive.

Price £850.0.0 plus £426.7.0 P.T.

Buy wisely—buy **WOLSELEY SIX-NINETY**

BMC — TWELVE MONTHS' WARRANTY
BACKED BY B.M.C. SERVICE—the most comprehensive in Europe

WOLSELEY MOTORS LTD., COWLEY, OXFORD   *London Showrooms:* 12 Berkeley Street, W.1.   *Overseas Business:* Nuffield Exports Ltd., Oxford and 41-46 Piccadilly, London W.1.

W156

Wolseley Advertisement

? Questions and Assignments

1. Comment on the headline "Your Wolseley, Sir" and explain its link with the person in the illustration.
2. What does this advertisement suggest about type of people who drive the Wolseley Six-Ninety motor car?
3. What is your impression of Richards? What features of the advertisement helped you to form this impression?
4. What facts about the car are contained in the advertisement?
5. Comment on the slogan "Buy wisely - buy Wolseley".

Advertisements
Simoniz Advertisement (see next page)

? Questions and Assignments

1. How is the link between car polish and tennis established in the headline? Is this link logical? Explain.
2. Do you think this advertisement appeals to people's vanity? Explain.
3. The word 'relax' is given a paragraph of its own. Can you suggest why.
4. What facts about the product are included in the advertisement?
5. Explain the illustration and its link with the product.

Super Valu Advertisement (see page 359)

? Questions and Assignments

1. Outline clearly what product or service is being advertised here.
2. What case does the advertisement make for the product being advertised?
3. What is unusual about the illustration?
4. The headline here is a little obscure. Briefly suggest its link with (a) the main copy and (b) the illustration.

Face Facts (Advertisement - see page 360)

? Questions and Assignments

1. Outline clearly the people at whom this advertisement is aimed.
2. Comment on the headline and its link with the copy.
3. What are the purposes of the three questions in the opening paragraph of the copy?
4. Is the illustration suitable for this advertisement? Explain.

Gordon's Advertisement (see page 361)

? Questions and Assignments

1. (a) What type of person is the Commander as portrayed in this advertisement?
   (b) What words and phrases help to establish his personality?
   (c) He appears in two separate illustrations. Can you suggest why.
   (d) Describe the photograph accurately, paying particular attention to the expression on the face of each of the characters.
2. Explain clearly what kind of need is exploited in this advertisement?
3. What facts are included about Gordon's which identify how it differs from other gins? (This advertisement was published in 1959.)

Advertisements

THE NEW SIMONIZ VALETING RANGE
FOR PEOPLE WHO WANT TO SHINE ON THE COURT AS WELL AS THE CAR

You know how good it feels to drive a perfectly polished car. But you know the effort that's needed, too.

Relax.

The new, easy to use SIMONIZ Valeting Range means that inside and out you can bring back that showroom shine and give long lasting protection to your car with the minimum of effort and hardly any fuss.

Wheels, windows, upholstery, tyres and trim—SIMONIZ will work wonders on your car. And it could do a lot for your backhand, too.

Game, set and match to SIMONIZ.

Simoniz aerosol products contain no CFCs

IT'S SIMPLE. IT'S SIMONIZ

PROTECTS • REFLECTS

358

Advertisements

REFRESHES THE PARTS OTHER SUPERMARKETS DON'T REACH

All round Ireland, in towns large and small, people who shop at Super Valu supermarkets are helping us pour more back into the local economy.

Because we not only buy quality Irish brands, but the very best Irish made products for our own Super Valu range. And the finest of fresh local produce, of course.

Every Super Valu supermarket is owned, managed and staffed by local people who are part of and essential to the community. Often their success brings new life and more employment all round. As well as the economies of Ireland's largest independently owned supermarket group.

So when you enjoy a glass of Super Valu mineral water you're doing yourself and everybody else a power of good.

Super Valu SUPERMARKETS

Advertisements

FACE FACTS!

Let's face it ... you want to reach a wide national audience of highly 'mobile' consumers with your advertising, right?
And you want to achieve that at a reasonable cost okay?
So you'll choose one of Commuter Advertising Networks Media Opportunities on your next Media Plan? Yes!
We deliver the audience with a high degree of impact, flexibility and choice ... whether it's using Dartcards, our Outdoor Poster Sites, Bus Advertising, Bridge Signs or any of our other options. Here's some facts –
100 Kerbsides achieved a 46% recall after only 2 weeks! 97% of 15 – 34 year olds are conscious of Bus Advertising, and 96% ABC1's are also conscious of Bus Advertising.*

So you see, if you face the facts, you'll choose Commuter Advertising Network everytime!
If you'd like to see our Video Presentation or discuss our opportunities in detail, telephone Stephen Murray, Sales Manager on 300712.
Delivering your audience – a fact worth taking on board!

*Behaviour & Attitudes Ltd.

can
Commuter Advertising Network
Delivering Your Audience!
35 Lower Abbey Street, Dublin 1. Telephone 300712
Fax 747324

Advertisements

A man who gives orders

At sea and ashore, the Commander is a man who knows how to give orders. He is a man with the power of command.

"We'll do that again...two Gordon's with orange, and two with tonic, please."

ON DUTY and off, the Commander gives clear orders swiftly. He commands instant attention even in the most crowded bar because he knows how to order.

You'll always hear men like the Commander naming the gin they want. The clean, fresh taste of Gordon's is unmistakable to them. And one of the great things about Gordon's is that you can be sure of getting it, wherever you go, so long as you ask for it by name.

Gordon's
the party spirit

Sciurus vulgaris

The Red Squirrel

Sciurus vulgaris

red squirrel   iora rua

Smaller and prettier than his more numerous Grey cousin, the Red Squirrel is, sadly, in decline in this country. A combination of a more specialised habitat (*Sciurus vulgaris* prefers conifers) and environmental changes has at once cut back on Red Squirrel numbers and allowed the larger Grey to colonise territory that was once the Irish Red Squirrel's domain and his alone.

While we might feel some empathy with a small native population overshadowed by a larger coloniser, feelings are not enough. The decline of *Sciurus vulgaris* is real, and it illustrates vividly the impact uncontrolled environmental change can have on a species - an impact which could scarcely have been foreseen by those who introduced the Grey Squirrel in the mid 19th century from its home in the hardwood forests of America.

Lack of foresight is no excuse today. Every one of us, in the way we live and work, has a potential impact on the environment of this island. With all the present day knowledge and research available to us, it is our duty to foresee the possible environmental effects our actions and operations may have upon the future.

That has been the ESB's policy since its inception. That is its policy today, actively carried out in day to day monitoring, research and long term planning.

ESB
ELECTRICITY SUPPLY BOARD
BORD SOLÁTHAIR AN LEICTREACHAIS

Advertisements

E.S.B. Advertisement (see pages 362 and 363)

? Questions and Assignments

1. Is this advertisement selling a product or service or has it another purpose? Explain.
2. What do we learn about squirrels from this advertisement?
3. What link is established between the squirrel and the E.S.B?
4. Do you think this type of advertisement is unnecessary? Give reasons.

Linguaphone Advertisement (see page 365)

? Questions and Assignments

1. What is being advertised here?
2. Who is this advertisement aimed at?
3. Explain the headline. Do you think it is a good one? Give reasons.
   (i) Do you think the aim of the opening paragraph of the copy is to worry readers? Explain your answer.
   (ii) "A vital weapon in your armoury". Explain this phrase.
4. What is the main point of the second paragraph?
5. What reassurance is offered in the third paragraph?
6. Can you identify "errors" in punctuation in the third and fourth paragraphs? Do you think the error is deliberate? Explain.
7. What is the principal message in the final paragraph?
   (See also **Accelerated Learning** Advertisement on page 368).
8. (i) Compare the **Linguaphone** and **Accelerated Learning** Advertisements under the following headings: (a) facts about the product. (b) the promises made.
   (ii) Which advertisement impressed you most? Explain.

Swimming in History Advertisement (see page 366)

? Questions and Assignments

1. Describe accurately, the illustration in this advertisement and explain its link with the headline.
2. What product is being advertised?
3. What facts about the product are included in the advertisement?

Canon Advertisement (See page 367)

? Questions and Assignments

1. Explain the headline in this advertisement. To whom does the word "we" refer?
2. Canon manufacture cameras. Does this advertisement promote the sale of Canon cameras? Explain your answer.
3. Comment on the link between the illustration and the copy.

Advertisements

CAN YOU SPEAK EUROPEAN?

With 1992 looming the pressure is on. Already competition is international. A threat or an opportunity? Depends on your attitude, your abilities. And, in future, a vital weapon in your armoury will be the way you communicate. With your clients, customers and competitors.

If you can't do it in their language, you're at a distinct disadvantage. Language literacy is even more important to you than computer literacy, because it's something you can't delegate. You have got to have 'Hands-on' experience.

If learning languages has been a glaring omission in your education to date - it's not too late to rectify. And you can do it quicker, more easily than you expect. Through Linguaphone courses which let you teach yourself at your own pace, in privacy. By listening and repeating - until phrases and, later, conversations, come naturally.

The world famous Linguaphone method is renowned for rapid results. Whether you're a total beginner, want to brush up or polish your fluency - Linguaphone have a course to suit. In virtually every tongue spoken. Don't let another year go by without making the effort. Once you start with Linguaphone, you'll wonder why you waited so long.

For free sample cassette and brochure 'Phone:

LINGUAPHONE
732366 (24 hrs)
or call to our offices at
41 Upper Abbey St., Dublin 1.

Advertisements

SWIMMING IN HISTORY.

Ancient Hierapolis, the Holy City near Pamukkale was bequeathed to Rome in 133 B.C. by the last king of Pergamum. Today, you can still sit at the ancient theatre and imagine Romans acting a play by Seneca. Or take a plunge in the Magic Pool of History nearby. Thermal waters that Nature keeps warm at 35 °C will give you a crystal clear look at the Holy City. And a sun tan.

Our "Discover Turkey" program with 3 domestic stopovers for $119 and 5 stopovers for $189 is the best way to discover more of the wonders of Turkey. The only land where phrases like "swimming in history" can be taken literally.

TURKISH AIRLINES

Discover Turkey

Advertisements

WE'RE PREPARING FOR THE WORLD CUP IN 2002

At the 1990 World Cup Finals in Italy, Canon will be present as one of the official sponsors. However, we are already helping to prepare for football's future.

Through FIFA, Canon supports coaching and development courses throughout the world, encouraging the flow of information on developments in the sport and the notion of fair play. To give promising young players a far better chance in future years - wherever they may come from.

Canon

Official Camera, Copier, Facsimile, Calculator of the FIFA World Cup 1990

Advertisements

TRAVEL? BUSINESS?

Why be lost for words?

It has *never* been more vital to learn French, German, Spanish or Italian.

With Accelerated Learning you can be confident in another language in 3½ weeks, and genuinely enjoy it. Your new language is presented simultaneously in sound, vision and through physical involvement.

You *hear* your new language naturally on audio cassettes as a series of enjoyable radio plays. You follow the script of the plays and *see* the vocabulary pictorialised in unique Memory Maps. You get *involved* with the stories and create vivid mental images. When those images come back so do the words.

A new, and unique, feature is the Physical Learning Video. You watch action on the screen, follow the action, and repeat the words. The same way you learned English successfully as a child!

Another unique feature, the Name Game, unlocks the meaning of thousands of foreign words from the very first day.

Based on Nobel Prize winning research, and now used by thousands of major UK organisations, you need to try Accelerated Learning to appreciate how rapidly you can learn.

Consequently we offer a 15 day FREE TRIAL

" Makes learning as effective and effortless as possible " Brit. Assoc. for Comm. and Industrial Education.

☐ Yes, rush me Free Information

OB25/11/90

15 DAY FREE TRIAL

Name _____

Address _____

_____ Post Code _____

ACCELERATED LEARNING

Accelerated Learning Systems
FREEPOST Aylesbury
Bucks HP22 4BR

OR TEL: 0296 631177 (9-5 WEEKDAYS)

Advertisements
Killeen (Steel Wool) Advertisement (see page 370)

> **?** Questions and Assignments

1. What two products are being advertised?
2. Name the company advertising the products?
3. (a) When was the company founded?
   (b) Where is it located?
4. (a) What are the two main objectives or aims of the company?
   (b) Have these objectives been achieved?
5. How many types of 'pot scrubs' does the company manufacture?
6. Where can these products be bought? (Mention the types of retail outlet and the countries where the products are sold).
7. To what does the company attribute the success of its products?
8. Describe, in your own words, the process involved in manufacturing soap pads.
9. What new process and new product are specifically mentioned in the advertisement?
10. What does the phrase "the wheel has turned full circle" mean in the context of this advertisement?
11. Why are 4 packets shown in the illustration even though the company manufactures two products?
12. What type of person is this advertisement aimed at?
13. Do you think this advertisement is effective? In your answer refer to the **illustration** and the **copy**.

Advertisements

Killeen (Steel Wool) Ltd.

Killeen (Steel Wool) Ltd. was founded in Drogheda in 1987. The company was established to provide employment locally and to manufacture products which would provide import substitution. After a market research programme, steelwool soap pads were identified as a potential product. At that time all the soap pads sold in Ireland, both branded and private label, were imported. More research was undertaken to identify methods of manufacturing and suitable machinery suppliers. Finally, the whole exercise was costed out to ensure that it was commercially worthwhile. Everything fell into place, so the project was officially started.

Product : The plant, which is the only one in Ireland, manufactures steelwool and soap pads. Steel wire is drawn around a massive machine, which contains many blades. The wire is shaved each time it goes round, producing wisps of steel. These are accumulated into ribbons of steel wool. The ribbons of steel wool, in long continuous lengths, are then fed into separate machines which produce soap pads. These machines tear the ribbon into small rolls, make the "pouch" shape pad and inject liquid soap into the pad, all in one quick process. Pot scrubs, in both plastic and steel, are also produced on different machinery.

A new unique process has been developed for both the drying of the pad and the retail packaging. A lemon soap pad with lemon fragrance has been introduced. This is also a "first".

Customers : Killeen Soap Pads are available in every supermarket in Ireland. The success of the product has been because of the ongoing quality, together with the technical innovations in packaging. It has played a significant role, in its own field, in helping to fulfil its original objectives of local employment and import substitution. Soap Pads produced in Drogheda are now exported, under the brand name of some of the largest U.K. Supermarket groups. The wheel has turned full circle.

V - NOVELS

Novels
Goodnight Mister Tom
by Michelle Magorian

? Questions and Assignments

1. Imagine that Willie began keeping a diary when he arrived at Mister Tom's. As you read the book, write the entries that you imagine Willie would make in his diary. As a general guideline, each entry should be approximately 150 words in length and should cover the significant events of a single chapter.
2. What did Willie fear in the opening two chapters? At what stage does he overcome his fear?
3. What is your impression of Willie's life before he arrived at Little Weirwold? (Ch. 1 - 3)
4. (i) What details help to convey the fact that war was about to break out? (Chapter 4)
   (ii) How did the news that war had begun, reach the people of the village? (Chapter 5)
5. (i) How did Zach and Willie become friends?
   (ii) Describe the differences in character between Willie and Zach.
6. How did Willie surprise Tom in Chapter 8?
7. How did the characters of Willie and Tom change since Willie's arrival? (Chapters 1 - 14)
8. Was Willie's mother more to be pitied than despised? Explain your answer.
9. Sammy plays an important role in the story. Explain how. (Chapter 16)
10. Answer the following questions, referring to the book as a whole.
    (i) Describe, in your own words, the most (a) exciting (b) amusing (c) sad (d) happy event in the story.
    (ii) From the story select a minor character that you liked or disliked and explain your choice.
    (iii) How did the war affect the people of Little Weirwold?

The Silver Sword
by Ian Serraillier

? Questions and Assignments

1. Give an account of Joseph's escape from Zakyna and the time he spent in hiding with the old man and the old lady.
2. Describe how the children managed to survive after their mother was taken away and their home destroyed.
3. (a) How did Ruth become acquainted with Jan?
   (b) How did he change her life?
4. Describe the journey to Posan made by Ruth, Bronia and Jan. Tell how they found Edek.
5. Describe Edek's escape from the farm near Gubea.
6. Identify Jan's new pal and outline how they became acquainted.
7. (i) Why is Edek accused of stealing? (ii) Outline what actually happened.
8. Give an account of the children's stay at the home of the Bavarian farmer.
9. Describe the final part of their journey across Lake Constance.
10. After the war what happened to each of the children?

Novels
The Red Pony
by John Steinbeck

? Questions and Assignments

1. (a) Describe Jody's reaction when he was shown his gift.
   (b) How did Jody's friends react when they came to look at the pony?
2. Outline clearly how (i) Jody cared for the pony and (ii) how he broke him in.
3. (i) Why did the pony become ill? (ii) Describe the efforts made by Billy and Jody to restore the pony's health. (iii) Describe Jody's encounter with the buzzards.
4. Who was the stranger? Explain why he came to the ranch.
5. Describe the birth of the colt.
6. Imagine that Jody kept a diary. Write his diary entries, describing the significant events of the story and Jody's responses to them.

Going Solo
by Roald Dahl

? Questions and Assignments

1. Describe the author's cabin companion. (Chapter 1)
2. How were the blacks treated by the whites in *Dar es Salaam*?
3. Give an account of the author's encounter with the lion.
4. Write about the killings of the two Germans.
5. Describe the author's stay in hospital following the plane crash.
6. What kind of a person was David Coke?
7. Give an account of the first two "dog fights" in which the author was involved.
8. What was "The Argos Fiasco"?
9. Write an account of the author's homecoming.

The Hobbit
by J. R. R. Tolkien

? Questions and Assignments

1. Describe the encounter with the three trolls.
2. How did Bilbo manage to escape from Gollum and the goblins?
3. Describe the role Bilbo played in the dwarves' escape from the palace of Elvenking.
4. What was Smaug's weak spot and how did Bilbo discover this?
5. Outline the importance of the Arkenstone to the plot.
6. Describe the role Beorn played in the battle against the goblins.
7. Outline the differences between the elves and the dwarves.
8. Describe two episodes from the story where Bilbo acts on his own initiative and describe what each episode reveals of his character.
9. Write a brief note on each of the following: - Wargs, Roac, Rivendell.

Novels

Goodnight Mister Tom - Nine-year old Willie Beech is evacuated to the country as Britain stands on the brink of the Second World War. A deprived and frightened child, Willie gradually begins to flourish under the care of old Tom Oakley, a gruff widower who has lived an isolated life since the death of his wife and child. However, Willie's happiness is interrupted . . .

The Silver Sword - Although the silver sword was only a paper knife, it became the symbol of hope and courage which kept the four deserted and starving children alive through the years of occupation, and afterwards on the exhausting and dangerous journey from war-torn Poland to Switzerland, where they hoped to find their parents.

The Red Pony - A moving story of Jody, a young Californian farm boy who gets an unexpected gift. The day starts early for Jody on his parent's out-of-the-way ranch in California. He is used to the chores and discipline, so when his father returns from an auction with a pretty red pony he cannot believe his eyes.

Like most of his father's presents the colt has come with certain conditions, though Jody is proud and eager to work hard for his spirited new charge. But even Jody's stern upbringing fails to prepare him for the bitter and unexpected realities of life itself.

Novels

Going Solo - *Going Solo* is the second volume of Roald Dahl's autobiography, continuing the story he began in *Boy*. It tells of African safaris and deadly snakes; of fighter planes and incredible air battles with the enemy during World War Two.

The Hobbit - Whisked from his comfortable hobbit-hole by Gandalf the wizard and a band of dwarves, Bilbo Baggins finds himself caught up in a plot to raid the treasure hoard of Smaug the Magnificent, a large and very dangerous dragon . . .

The Machine Gunners - The story is set in Garmouth, a fictitious town on the north-east coast of England. It is the winter of 1940-41 and Nazi bombing raids are a nightly event. Chas McGill had the second-best collection of war souvenirs in Garmouth, and he desperately wanted it to be the best. His chance came when he found the crashed German Heinkel, with a machine-gun and all its ammunition intact. All he had to do was to remove it from the plane ...

The police, the Home Guard, in fact everybody in authority in Garmouth, knew the gun had been stolen. They were pretty sure the boys had it, but where? And did the boys realise that it could blow a hole through a wall at a quarter of a mile? It was essential to track it down before the boys killed themselves or anybody else.

375

Novels
The Machine-Gunners
by Robert Westall

? Questions and Assignments

1. Why did Chas run towards the wood?
2. Describe (i) what Chas discovered in the wood and (ii) what he did with his discovery.
3. What important details do we learn in Chapter 4?
4. *"By four o'clock Boddser was outside the Head's door sweating"*. (Chapter 5). Explain (i) why Boddser was outside the Headmaster's door and (ii) what happened to him.
5. Describe Granda's "old nightmare" and explain what caused it. (Chapter 6).
6. (a) "Sicky Nicky has something we need", said Chas. (Chapter 6). Explain (i) what the "something" was and (ii) how Chas set about getting it.
7. Give an account of the Fortress and how it was built.
8. (i) Trace Rudi Gerlath's movements from the moment he bales out from his plane.
   (ii) Describe his character.
9. Having read *The Machine-Gunners*, do you think that it added to your understanding of what life was like in war-time Britain? Refer to the book to support your answer.

Buddy's Song
by Nigel Hinton

? Questions and Assignments

1. Describe Buddy's feelings towards his imprisoned father.
2. Give an account of Buddy's visits to his father in prison.
3. Describe the attitudes of Buddy, Terry and Carol towards Des King.
4. Write an account of Terry's arrival home following his release from prison.
5. Write about the gigs Buddy did with The Hi Tone Four and The Reflections.
6. Describe the contrasting musical tastes of Buddy and his father.
7. What kind of things did Terry do to get the band going?
8. Did *Buddy's Song* give you any new insights into the rock music industry? Explain.

Carrie's War
by Nina Bawden

? Questions and Assignments

1. (a) Why did Carrie go to the valley in the first place?
   (b) What were the circumstances that caused her to return there?
2. What type of man was Mr. Evans? Base your answer on the evidence throughout the novel.
3. Describe the relationship Nick had with (a) Mr. Evans (b) Auntie Lou.
4. In Chapter 4 we are told that Nick and Carrie went alone to Druid's Bottom "on what was, perhaps, the most important journey they ever made together". Explain why the author makes this claim.

Novels

5. (a) How did Carrie view Hepzibah?
   (b) Would you agree with Carrie's view of her? Give reasons for your answer.
6. How did Mr. Evans react to Carrie's telling him Mrs. Gotobed's message?
7. Outline the importance of each of the following characters in the story.
   (a) Auntie Lou   (b) Albert Sandwich   (c) Mr. Johnny   (d) Major Cass Harper?
8. Why do you think Mr. Evans ended up alone?
9. Explain how the fire affected Carrie's life?
10. Imagine filming the three most important scenes of the book. Describe a series of "shots" you would take to create the feeling and the mood of these scenes.

Walkabout
by James Vance Marshall

? Questions and Assignments

1. Describe the difficulties that Mary and Peter faced before they met the bush-boy.

2. "The girl worked things out quietly, sensibly - she wasn't the sort to get into a panic." How true would you consider this view of Mary to be, in the light of the evidence in the entire novel.

3. "The children stood looking at each other in the middle of the Australian desert. Between them the distance was less than the spread of an outstretched arm, but more than a thousand years." Refer to details in the novel to explain this quotation.

4. How did the bush boy react to Mary and Peter?

5. Explain why "the barrier of twenty thousand years vanished in the twinkling of an eye".

6. How did Peter's attitude to the bush boy differ from Mary's?

7. What incidents in the story show that Peter was capable of making decisions and of asserting his independence?

8. Explain the significance of the title of this novel.

9. Discuss the bush boy's approaches to life and death.

10. Which character in the novel did you most identify with? Explain why.

11. What would you consider were the most important things that Mary and Peter learned from the the bush boy?

12. Is anyone to blame for the outcome of the story in the novel?

13. Write an eulogy in praise of the bush boy. Give him a name appropriate to his character.

Novels

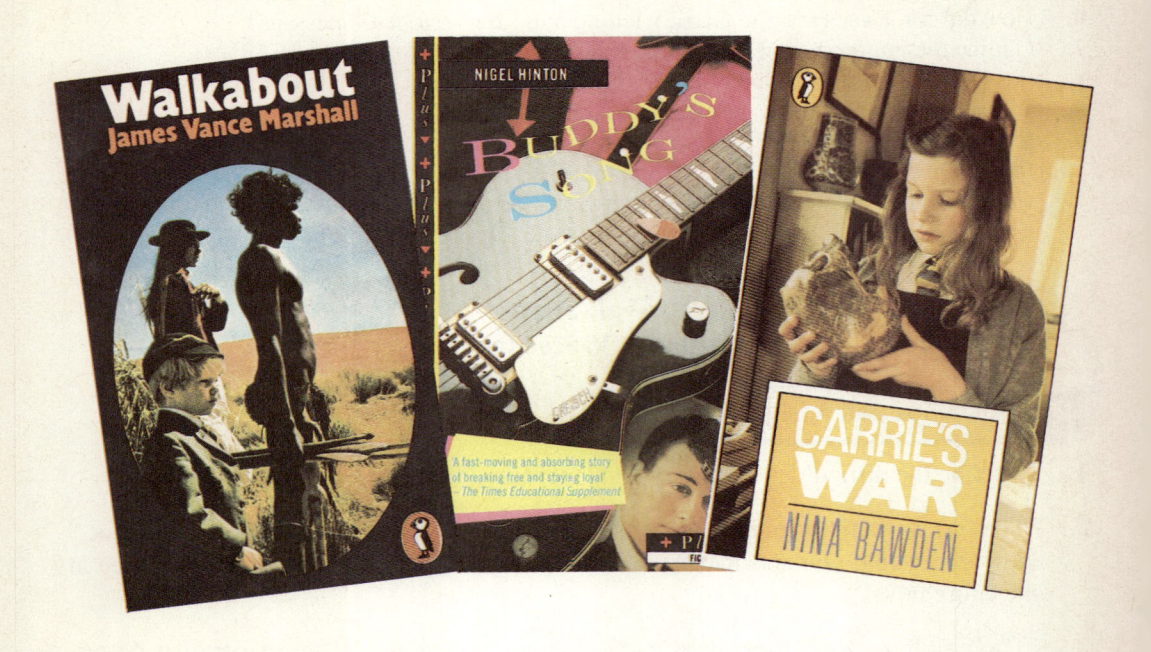

Buddy's Song - Buddy's in a bad way. His dad, Terry, is in prison and Buddy thinks it's his fault; people are being pretty nasty at school; and his mum is busy with her new job. He feels lonely and confused until one day he picks up a battered old guitar and decides to learn how to play it. He quickly discovers why his dad loves rock 'n' roll so much. There's excitement, happiness and a way of expressing feelings in music. Above all, there's the chance to dream - of girls, friends and a happy future. It's not long, though, before he finds out that his dad has even bigger and wilder dreams - dreams which could go out of control and threaten what Buddy wants most.

Carrie's War - Bombs were falling on London. Carrie and Nick were wartime evacuees billeted in Wales on old Mr Evans, who was a bit of an ogre, and his timid mouse of a sister. Their friend Albert was luckier, living in Druid's Bottom with Hepzibah Green and the strange Mister Johnny, and Carrie and Nick were happy to visit him there, until Carrie did a terrible thing, the worst thing she ever did in her life . . .

Walkabout - Mary and her young brother Peter are the only survivors of an air crash in the middle of the Australian desert. They are facing death from exhaustion and starvation when they meet an Aboriginal boy who helps them to survive, and guides them on their long journey; and then, because of a tragic misunderstanding, Mary causes his death . . .

Novels

The Ghost of Thomas Kempe - Strange messages, fearful noises and all kinds of jiggery-pokery . . . It began to dawn on James that there was probably a ghost in the house! But what kind of ghost was it that had come to plague the Harrison family in their lovely old cottage? Young James sets out to find the answer in this delightfully funny story.

Z for Zachariah - Lone survivor after a nuclear holocaust, Ann Burden sees her solitary peace threatened by an unknown intruder. She hides, he watches, they both wait. Is he a friend and ally, or the terrifying near-maniac she begins to suspect? Just as Adam was the first man on earth, so this man must be Zachariah, the last . . .

Rua, The Red Grouse - The story is about Rua, a Red Grouse who lives on Drumeen Bog in a remote part of Ireland. It describes Rua's home, a raised bog, in a magical but accurate way . . . slowly revealing the secret changes in the bog's wildlife over four seasons of the year. As the bog changes, so too do the attitudes of the humans who live around it . . . in such a dramatic way so as to put Rua's life in danger . . .

Novels
Z for Zachariah
by Robert O'Brien

? Questions and Assignments

1. What is revealed about the characters of Ann and Loomis in the first two chapters?
2. Outline the stages in Ann's discovery of what happened to Edward.
3. (a) Describe Ann's nursing of Loomis.   (b) Trace the steps in Ann's growing unease.
4. Write, in the form of a reference, Professor Kylmer's assessment of Loomis.
5. Describe the role of Faro, the dog, and comment on its significance in the novel.
6. (a) In what ways were the backgrounds of Ann and Loomis (i) alike and (ii) different?   (b) How did their backgrounds determine their behaviour?
7. Would you consider that Loomis is sane? Give reasons for your answer.
8. How important are - Edward, David, the Burdens, Professor Kylmer, in the novel?
9. How do dreams and nightmares affect the characters' behaviour and decision-making?
10. Would you consider this to be a depressing novel? Give reasons for your answer.
11. Select quotations from the novel which illustrate the two main themes of
    (i) survival   (ii) the role of men and women in a changed world.

The Ghost of Thomas Kempe
by Penelope Lively

? Questions and Assignments

1. What aspects of his new home and its surroundings appealed to James Harrison?
2. What early evidence of the ghost's presence did James notice?
3. James' first attempt to communicate with the ghost ended in disaster. Describe the happenings and their consequences for James.
4. Why did James feel isolated at times? (Chapters 5 and 6)
5. (a) Discuss the role of Mrs Verity in the story.   (b) Describe the vicar's visit.
6. How did Fanny Spence's diary help James?
7. What had Arnold Luckett and James in common?
8. "People have layers like onions" said James (Chapter 11) and Simon thought he was daft. What did he mean and of whom was he thinking?
9. Bert Ellison played an important part in the story. Discuss.

Rua, The Red Grouse
by Patrick Devaney

? Questions and Assignments

1. Describe the retired bank manager's role in the story.
2. A number of young grouse meet their deaths over the course of the story. Describe the circumstances surrounding the death of each.

Novels

3. Outline the case made by (i) the Drumeen Committee and (ii) the Co-op – on the future of the bog.
4. Describe the developments in the battle between the Drumeen Committee and the Co-op.
5. Write a note on the character of the cattle-dealer.
6. Read carefully the descriptions of (a) the arrival of Spring (Ch. 4) (b) the fire (Ch. 4) (c) the storm (Ch. 18) and say what features of these descriptions impressed you.
7. "A wonderful example of nature writing at its best" - this is an extract from a review of this book in "The Irish Press'. Would you agree with this assessment? Give reasons for your answer.
8. What did you learn about grouse from this book?

The Twelfth Day of July
by Joan Lingard

? Questions and Assignments

1. Give an account of Kevin and Brian's expedition into the Protestant area.
2. Give an account of Tommy and Sadie's expedition into the Catholic area.
3. (a) Explain why Sadie was making chips. (b) What trouble did the red-haired boy cause?
4. What happened when: - (i) Kevin went into the Protestant area on a second occasion (ii) Sadie went into the Catholic area on a second occasion?
5. Give an account of the night Sadie spent in Kevin's street.
6. Describe the street battle between the Catholic and Protestant crowds.
7. Why did it seem unfair that Brede was injured?
8. Describe how Tommy, Sadie and Kevin spend "The Glorious Twelfth".

To Kill a Mockingbird*
by Harper Lee

? Questions and Assignments

1. What flaws of Maycomb society are highlighted in the novel?
2. Outline how the following topics are presented in the story:- family life, snobbery, race relations.
3. Write a character study of Atticus Finch, outlining the aspects of his character that you particularly admire.
4. Outline how the characters of Jem and Scout develop over the course of the novel.
5. Discuss the importance of the following episodes in the novel:- the shooting of the dog, the visit to Cal's church, the children's meeting with Mr. Dubose.
6. Explain the significance of the title of the novel to the plot.

* *To Kill a Mockingbird* is recommended for Higher Course only.

Novels

To Kill a Mockingbird - ... a black man charged with assaulting a white girl. Through the young eyes of Scout and Jem Finch, Harper Lee explores, with exuberant humour, the irrationality of adult attitudes to race and class in the Deep South of the Thirties.

The Twelfth Day of July - It all started with a trip into Protestant territory by Kevin and his Catholic friends to daub slogans on a wall. But feelings run high in Belfast and in the end paint-splashing turned into something far more dangerous. The only good thing to come out of the reckless trip was that it brought Kevin into contact with Sadie Jackson - and that was to change his life.

Novels
General Questions on a Novel or Novels you have read

1. Many novels show us people who are under pressure, or facing a challenge, or undergoing a new experience.
   (a) Write down the title and author of a novel you have studied in which *one* of these things happens.
   (b) Choose a character from the novel and in a paragraph, explain how he or she was under pressure or facing a challenge or undergoing a new experience.
   (c) In another paragraph, explain the effect of the pressure, challenge or new experience upon the character you chose.

2. Novels may be

   | Moving | Disturbing | Exciting | Amusing |
   | Entertaining | Depressing | Inspiring | Satisfying |

   (a) Apply two of these words to a novel you have read. Give the title and author of the novel.
   (b) Write two paragraphs, one for each word, explaining why the words suit the novels. Head each paragraph with the word you have chosen.

3. In Column A are some common topics for novels. In Column B are some common responses to novels.

A	B
families	sympathy
facing a challenge	shock
a human problem	excitement
meeting prejudice	admiration
success/failure	satisfaction

   Head your answer with the title and author of your novel.
   (i) From Column A choose **one** topic and write at least a paragraph explaining how it was important in a novel you have studied this year.
   (ii) From Column B choose **one** response which you felt when reading this novel. Write at least a paragraph explaining why you felt as you did.

4. Imagine that you are writing a letter to your English teacher suggesting one or two novels that should be studied by next year's First and Second year classes. Use two of the starters below to write two parts of your letter. Do not use the same material in both answers.
   Write at least two paragraphs for each.
   Give the title(s) and author(s)
   (i) I think the ideas in this novel are important because . . .
   (ii) I liked the character . . . . because . . .
   (iii) I really enjoyed this novel because . . .
   (iv) I think the most important event in the story is . . . . because . . .
   (v) Something very clever about this novel is . . .

INDEX

	Page		Page
Allegory	224	Narrator	56, 114
Alliteration	229, 268, 270, 307	Noun	302
Ballad	215	O'Casey Seán	146
Book Reviews	344	Onomatopoeia	216, 244, 272
Changing moods	234	Paradox	166, 280
Characters	76, 83	Paragraphs	320
Character Development	30	Parody	246
Choosing Verbs	83	Personification	248, 280
Clauses	312, 313	Plot	83, 92
Cliches	307	Point of View	20, 218
Climax	30	Phrases	312
Colloquialism	322	Predicate	312
Conflict	30	Prejudice	317
Consonance	239	Puns	307
Contrast	37, 183, 282	Realism in Literature	37
Crosswords (1-5)	348 - 352	Reviews (T.V. and Radio)	342
Different Styles	316	Rhetoric	165
Editorials	324	Rhetorical Question	222
Essay Writing	339	Rhyme	226, 248, 276, 286, 297, 299, 307
		Rhythm	214, 280
Features	334	Run-on-Lines	239, 244, 255
Form	222	Satire	250
Formal Style	316	Sentence Structure in Grammar	314
H. G. Wells	114	Setting	76, 83, 129, 142, 274
Haiku	290	Simile	229, 272, 280, 294
Hardy Thomas	225	Slang	322, 330
Headlines	301	Sonnet	218, 219, 294
Hyperbole	268, 272, 292	Sound Effects	266
Idioms	322, 330	Style	122
Images	237	Subject	312
Irony	68, 92, 145, 183, 184, 250	Subordinate Clauses	313
		Suspense & Tension	103
Joyce James	81	Symbols	122, 129, 218
Kavanagh Patrick	251	Tenses of Verbs	305
Keeping a Diary	341	Themes	37, 76, 97, 122, 129, 253
Lament	234	Understanding Symbols	83
Language	142		
Malapropism	165	Verb	302
Metaphor	229, 270, 282, 286, 289, 293	Verbs in Headlines	305
Monologue	226, 260, 264	Writing Reviews	347
Mood & Tone in poetry	234, 242		
Music	246	Yeats W.B.	296